NASSER'S
BLESSED MOVEMENT

DR. AHMED H. IBRAHIM
BOX A3643
CHICAGO, IL 60690

STUDIES IN MIDDLE EASTERN HISTORY

Bernard Lewis, Itamar Rabinovich, and Roger Savory
GENERAL EDITORS

THE TURBAN FOR THE CROWN
The Islamic Revolution in Iran
Said Amir Arjomand

LANGUAGE AND CHANGE IN THE ARAB MIDDLE EAST
The Evolution of Modern Arabic Political Discourse
Ami Ayalon

IRAN'S FIRST REVOLUTION
Shi'ism and the Constitutional Revolution of 1905–1909
Mangol Bayat

ISLAMIC REFORM
Politics and Social Change in Late Ottoman Syria
David Dean Commins

KING HUSSEIN AND THE CHALLENGE OF ARAB RADICALISM
Jordan, 1955–1967
Uriel Dann

EGYPT, ISLAM, AND THE ARABS
The Search for Egyptian Nationhood, 1900–1930
Israel Gershoni and James Jankowski

EAST ENCOUNTERS WEST
France and the Ottoman Empire in the Eighteenth Century
Fatma Müge Göçek

NASSER'S BLESSED MOVEMENT
Egypt's Free Officers and the July Revolution
Joel Gordon

THE FERTILE CRESCENT, 1800–1914
A Documentary Economic History
Edited by Charles Issawi

ESTRANGED BEDFELLOWS
Britain and France in the Middle East during the Second World War
Aviel Roshwald

OTHER VOLUMES ARE IN PREPARATION

NASSER'S
BLESSED MOVEMENT

*Egypt's Free Officers
and the July Revolution*

———

JOEL GORDON

New York   Oxford
OXFORD UNIVERSITY PRESS
1992

Oxford University Press

Oxford   New York   Toronto
Delhi   Bombay   Calcutta   Madras   Karachi
Petaling Jaya   Singapore   Hong Kong   Tokyo
Nairobi   Dar es Salaam   Cape Town
Melbourne   Auckland

and associated companies in
Berlin   Ibadan

Copyright © 1992 by Oxford University Press, Inc.

Published by Oxford University Press, Inc.,
200 Madison Avenue, New York, New York 10016

Library of Congress Cataloging-in-Publication Data
Gordon, Joel.
Nasser's Blessed Movement: Egypt's Free Officers and
the July revolution / Joel Gordon.
p.   cm. — (Studies in Middle Eastern history)
Includes bibliographical references and index.
ISBN 0-19-506935-8
1. Egypt—Politics and government—1952   I. Title.
II. Series: Studies in Middle Eastern history (New York, N.Y.)
DT107.83.G67   1991
962—dc20   91-16836   CIP

2 4 6 8 9 7 5 3 1

Printed in the United States of America
on acid-free paper

Acknowledgments

I conceptualized this book as a study of the historical revisionism of a foundational revolutionary period in Egypt's national history. Anwar al-Sadat had dominated Arab politics throughout the period of my university education. In 1979 I saw his larger-than-life-sized portraits all over Cairo. When I returned in 1982, eight months after his death, most billboards had come down, some, but not nearly all, replaced by more sedate portraits of Hosni Mubarak. Egypt seemed changed in many ways. I sensed something larger than one leader seeking to establish his own identity. Egyptians appeared to be looking backward as much as ahead, some to Nasser but many to figures and symbols of the prerevolutionary *ancien régime*. When I returned to Egypt to commence this study in 1984, I no sooner alighted in central Cairo than a picture of Muhammad Nagib jumped out at me from a curbside book display, with a title proclaiming "I was President of Egypt!" Closer examination revealed scores of books and magazine articles on the origins of the revolution by other participants, winners and losers. On building walls I saw posters of Nahhas Pasha; across from my apartment an old villa was being whitewashed and converted into Wafd headquarters. As I describe in the prologue, not one but a variety of revisions of Egypt's recent revolutionary past were being proffered—and debunked—simultaneously.

This book originated as a doctoral dissertation in a not-too-distant past. My understanding of Egypt has been shaped in large part by my graduate mentor, Richard Mitchell. To Dick I brought my initial, confused impressions of what I had seen in 1982–1983. Old-regime Cairo enchanted me, and having grown up in Cook County, Illinois, I found the politics of the pashas familiar, so I thought to look at the fall of the parliamentary regime. Dick urged me to explore the early years of the revolution in detail. He had been in Egypt in the early 1950s and insisted the officers' consolidation looked, in retrospect, so crafted that the the possibilities, the hopes and fears, the spontaneity of the revolutionary moment had been forgotten. I set out to explore that spontaneity, and in so doing to analyze both the fall of an old order and rise of the new. Dick died in Cairo a year later; he did not live to read, question, or challenge my perspective on events that had so influenced his own understanding of Egypt. But his formative influence, as on so many fellow students, remains indelible, and I hope he would approve.

Many others, in many ways, deserve thanks for their assistance, criticism, and inspiration. The final interpretations are mine, as are most translations and transliterations, but the stamp of others is present, and I think my work better for it. Very special thanks are due C. Ernest Dawn, who introduced me to Middle Eastern history as an undergraduate and has remained a constant supporter and friendly critic, and whose recognition of me as a colleague has meant the most to me. Wilfrid Rollman, who read this in roughest form and helped me find a few diamonds in it, taught me to "wait until the buckets are at eye level" and convinced me that the pashas were, after a fashion, ward bosses in fezzes. One line borrowed from Mayor Daley is for him. Juan Cole pushed me to ask broader questions, to look beyond specific time and place, beyond the level of politics and politicians. Nathan Brown and Robert Vitalis, my *shilla* in Dar al-Kutub, read this in its most primitive scratches, filled the margins with commentary and a few well pointed barbs, and rooted for me during early conference presentations. Charles C. Stewart, James Jankowski, Donald Reid, Marvin Weinbaum, Andrew Ehrenkreutz, and Bradford Perkins all asked tought questions, and lent expertise, encouragement, and advice at one step or another. Ralph Coury and Carl Petry made the old regime come alive. Paul Woodward shared in exploring the back alleys of the Gamaliya, the good and bad times of roughly a decade, and ceaselessly corrected my *fusha*.

A Fulbright-Hays fellowship funded my research in Egypt and England. The American Research Center in Egypt helped facilitate that research and offered a base of operations. The Center for Near Eastern and North African Studies and Department of History at the University of Michigan funded preliminary research and writing. Gary Porton and Tadahisa Kuroda each did their utmost to encourage and enhance my writing when I held visiting teaching positions under their direction at the University of Illinois and Skidmore College. Staff members of Dar al-Kutub in Cairo, the Public Records Office in Kew Gardens, and the National Archives in Washington, D.C., and John Eilts, then Near Eastern librarian at the University of Michigan, and Elizabeth Barlow of the Near East Center deserve thanks for countless instances of assistance. At Oxford University Press, Nancy Lane, Paul Schlotthauer, and David Roll have guided this to print with what seems to me remarkable ease.

I am in great debt to the many informants who welcomed me into their homes and offices and who were willing to share with me some of their time, memories, and insights into Egypt's recent past. It is their thoughts and descriptions of events that allowed me to write with greater confidence about a period which they, not I, experienced. Several are no longer living, and I feel fortunate to have met and shared some time with them. No doubt some of my informants will disagree with at least some of my conclusions. I only ask their trust that I tried to listen to each with an open mind and weigh their words with care before writing any of my own.

I have also learned much from Egyptian scholars. During my stays in Egypt I attended a weekly seminar on modern Egyptian history at ʿAyn Shams University, and in one session, memorable at least to me, was able to present some of my ideas before Egypt's most eminent professors. I am grateful to them for encouraging a *khawaga* to study their history.

Away from the strict bounds of academia: Thanks to ʿAmm Salih for killing the rat, and to ʿAmm Ibrahim for that most Egyptian gesture of hospitality: handing me a glass of water to drink on my departure, *"ʿashan tigi tani."* Soon, God willing. I hope I can climb the pyramids at age seventy with the same zest as my cousin, Bernie Sevin. My parents, Aaron and Ellie Gordon, have been constant in their support, and model teachers. I have much to thank them for, not least the love of books and travel, a sense of compassion and humor, and learning to appreciate the muezzin's call at daybreak. I have been most fortunate to share a bit of the Middle East with my sister Becky, and with my brother David under the big top, a part of this country I otherwise would never have seen.

JoAnn D'Alisera told me early on she was the best thing that ever happened to me. I'm still not sure how she knew so soon. She has given me more than she'll ever know, or I can ever express. This book is for her. *Ana lik ʿala tul.*

Lancaster, Pennsylvania   J. G.
August 1991

A Note on Transliteration

Transliteration is according to the Library of Congress system, but, after Lawrence, I have taken some liberties. The symbol ' represents an *ayan*, and ' an *alif* in middle or final position. I have chosen to avoid cumbersome diacritical marks. Several names (Nasser, Farouk) are rendered as in common usage. Personal names of people and places in which the letter *jim* occurs are rendered to reflect Cairene Egyptian dialect by *g* in the text, including any text in end notes, and the index. This is purely a personal decision. For two years I lived as "Goel," and to my ears and eyes Nasser can only be Gamel, his rival Nagib. For reference citations in the notes and bibliography, however, I have resorted to *j;* Nagib in the text becomes Najib. Journal and book titles retain the *j* throughout.

Contents

PROLOGUE: Rewriting the Revolution   3

1. "A Country of Failure"   14

2. "The People's Army"   39

3. "Revolutionary Jurisprudence"   58

4. "Lift up Your Head"   79

5. "The Great Deception"   92

6. "The Secret of the Nine"   109

7. "A Revolutionary, Not a Politician"   127

8. "Stability, in Whatever Guise"   144

9. "Fondest Hope's of the West"   157

10. "Each of You Shall Be Gamal"   175

CONCLUSION: "A Pragmatic March Toward Democracy"?   191

Notes   201

Bibliography   233

Index   243

NASSER'S
BLESSED MOVEMENT

Rewriting the Revolution

In December 1953, sixteen months after they had seized power, nearly a full year after they had outlawed all political parties, members of Egypt's ruling junta marched in the funeral procession of one Hifni Mahmud. A former pasha—the officers had abolished the honorific title within days of their takeover—Mahmud had been a leader of the Liberal Constitutionalist party. A minority faction comprising primarily large landowners, it seemed an old-regime party the officers would hardly care to honor. Hifni Mahmud, to his credit, had been a bit of a freethinker. The pasha had often played foil to leftist intellectuals at nightly gatherings in the office of the editor of *Al-Misri*, Egypt's largest daily, that Gamal Abdel Nasser and other members of the military junta often attended. There they came to respect the "mocking philosopher's" satirical wit.[1]

A photograph of the funeral procession published in *Al-Misri* projects an interesting set of contrasts. Off to one side is Ahmad 'Abd al-Ghaffar, another Liberal leader. Walkingstick in hand, a tarbush (fez) atop his head, he personifies the old-regime pasha. At his side march four young officers, Egypt's new rulers, founders of a "new age." Two, Abdel Nasser and 'Abd al-Hakim 'Amr, are in uniform; two, 'Abd al-Latif al-Baghdadi and Salah Salim, wear suits. Salim, always one to play to crowd and cameras, still a more familiar face to the average Egyptian than Nasser, sports a tarbush, mocking not the deceased so much as his social class and milieu. Soon to pass from existence, the tarbush remained proper attire for the old generation, costume for the new.[2]

The picture captures with striking poignancy a period of transition in a country that, having seen its old political order overthrown, was treading an uncertain path in the name of "revolution." The presence of 'Abd al-Ghaffar, marching alongside the officers provides a stark reminder that treason trials of old-regime politicians are continuing. A month earlier he had faced the Revolutionary Tribunal and escaped with a steep fine. On this day he marches with his accusers, including the presiding judge of the tribunal, Baghdadi. However, if hopes for coexistence with the officers, perhaps even restoration of a reformed liberal order remained alive, the civilian attire of two junta members, both new cabinet ministers, pointed to a far different future.

In the following year the officers would shed all inhibitions about ruling Egypt, ruthlessly suppress their political opponents, and consolidate their authority over the coercive arms of the state. A military coup organized by junior officers with unfocused goals and limited ambitions became, over the course of the following decade, a revolution from above that transformed Egyptian society and reoriented the way Egyptians looked at themselves and the world.

From Coup d'État to Revolution

This study examines the formative period of the Nasserist revolution. The Free Officers seized power in the early morning hours of July 23, 1952. Declaring that they had acted in the name of the 1923 Constitution, they demanded King Farouk appoint a prime minister of their choice and purge the military high command. Four days later they forced Farouk to abdicate, allowing him to sail to exile in Italy. A military junta oversaw affairs of state in uneasy cooperation with a civilian government until early September, when the officers decreed a land reform program, appointed as prime minister their figurehead leader, General Muhammad Nagib, and ordered all political parties to apply for recertification. In December the junta abrogated the Constitution. Then in January 1953 the officers outlawed all political parties and announced the onset of a three-year "transition period" of martial rule. Almost in passing, they proclaimed their movement a revolution.

The officers spent the following two years trying to define the aims of that revolution. They did so primarily in the context of suppressing alternative political movements. In June 1953 the ruling junta, known since January as the Command Council of the Revolution (CCR), proclaimed Egypt a republic and appointed Nagib its first president. In January 1954 the government outlawed the Muslim Brotherhood. On February 28, 1954, the CCR denounced Nagib as a tyrant and ousted him. Over the course of the following month, known in Egyptian historiography as the "March crisis," the officers defused a mass movement calling for their dismissal. The crisis marked the crucial turning point in their determination to assert absolute authority and bring to heel all independent bastions of opposition to their rule: the army, press, professional associations, labor unions, and universities. On October 26, two days after Egypt and Great Britain initialed an accord providing for the evacuation of British troops from Egyptian soil, a Muslim Brother tried to kill Nasser at a rally in Alexandria. The regime moved quickly to destroy the movement; on December 9 the gunman and five Brotherhood leaders went to the gallows. In 1955, with internal opposition suppressed, foreign affairs began to dominate the regime's attention, and a new phase ensued in which the officers defined their revolution in terms of nonalignment and Arabism.

Because Nasserism provided a model for political mobilization and national development to other emerging nations, and because of Egypt's role in international affairs, much has been written on Nasser's Egypt. Studies of the "new middle class," the "integrative revolution," the "praetorian state," and the "stalled society" have generally focused on the state structure that emerged in the aftermath of Nasser's political triumph at Suez.[3] Lacking, and impossible until recently, has been a close examination of how the regime solidified its hold over the state and the effect that process, the political revolution, had on a nascent social revolution.

It is too often taken for granted that Egypt stood on the brink of a social revolution, and that if the Free Officers' takeover was not inevitable, their assumption of absolute power was. In retrospect, a certain logic seemed to guide events. It is difficult to imagine the officers sharing power, or even coexisting, with other political forces in the country: the political parties, the Muslim Brotherhood, or, at that stage, the Left. The regime's official history certainly propagated the notion of inevitability. Foreign scholars repeated uncritically much of the official history but often refused to accept the officers' declarations that they had seized power with limited ambitions, that the crisis of Egyptian politics had compelled them to expand their vision. Most foreign scholars too hastily perceived the coup d'état as the inevitable harbinger of revolution. Many saw a strategy for dictatorship behind every move the officers made; as one contended, "the swift abolition of the monarchy, the order to political parties to purge and reorganize their ranks, and the promulgation of the agrarian reform law were all frank indications of the Free Officers' aspirations to political leadership and control."[4] Never mind that the chronology is backward, that nine months elapsed between land reform and the declaration of a republic, or that the officers sat on the latter decision for three months. The Machiavellian outlook obscures the uncertainties that gripped the officers as they struggled to define their role in the political process.

To understand how the coup d'état of July 23, undertaken in the name of political and social reform, became the "July Revolution," questions about the decay of liberalism and the roots of Nasserism warrant reevaluation. What options did Egypt's political leaders promote as the old regime tottered? What alternative visions did antiestablishment forces proffer? Did the Free Officers have a preconceived political agenda? Having seized power, what options did the officers face at different points in time? To what extent did they control events and to what extent did events force their hand? What forces assisted or competed with them to influence the course of political development? How far did ideology and the considerations of politics and power guide these forces?

Too often inquiry has centered on the officers themselves. The period between 1952 and 1955 was one in which Egyptians looked, at once, backward, to define causes of the old regime's decline, and forward, to the creation of a stable democratic order. The failure to achieve the latter aim was the result of both internal and external factors. The officers did hold center stage but were acted upon as much as they acted. Political party members, communists, and Muslim Brothers all had to square ideology with realpolitik. Foreign powers played significant background roles. The aims and strategies of these myriad forces are no less important in determining what options the country faced, what factors determined the lines of conflict, and why the officers won in the end.

A wealth of materials relative to those available in most developing nations permits a rare, detailed glimpse into the process by which a military regime constructed a revolutionary ideology in the postindependence period. A confluence of factors made this study particularly timely. Under the rule of Anwar al-Sadat, Egypt went through a period of political liberalization that, although halting, inspired and even encouraged a large and literate elite of all political factions—old regime, Nasserist, and oppositional—to debate the merits and demerits of the Nasserist state in relative freedom. This has continued to an even greater extent since 1981 under the rule of Hosni Mubarak. The result has been a proliferation of memoirs, published interviews, commentaries, and personal accounts, many of which treat in great detail the early years of military rule. Egypt's willingness to tolerate a constant influx of foreign scholars intent on exploring its past, present, and future (even Egyptians who decry foreign intrusion in general often prove gracious hosts) should not be taken for granted. It allowed me the opportunity to delve beneath the written word; to speak personally to actors and observers of the events described herein; and to analyze and describe the period of military consolidation, I hope, in a more vivid, believable sense. Finally, a very lively Egyptian debate coincided with the thirtieth anniversary of the revolution and the opening, pursuant to U.S. and British "thirty-year rules," of government archives for the period.[5]

Legacies

Almost four decades after the July coup, nearly two decades after Nasser's death, the legacy of the man and the regime he founded spark controversy. Many of the same questions Egyptians posed in 1952 about the failure of liberal institutions and the constraints on nation-building remain unanswered. Old-regime forces, outlawed since 1953–1954, have been allowed to resume political activity. Men who had been imprisoned, exiled, and banned from political life now defend a legacy that for nearly three decades suffered excoriation at the hands of the Nasserist state, a political tradition that they claim as the true legacy of modern Egypt's struggle for national independence.

The political structure of the state is a focal point of debate. After their consolidation of power, the officers formulated six aims for their revolution (which they projected back to their secret organization in the army): battling imperialism and its Egyptian fifth column; abolition of feudalism; breaking up monopolies and the domination of foreign capital; application of social justice; strengthening the military; and founding a "sound" democratic system. Of these, the last is commonly held by all political factions to have remained unrealized. Despite several attempts to found a mass populist party, Nasserist Egypt remained under the rule of a praetorian elite, rooted in the officer corps, that dominated party and state bureaucracy, and that remained unwilling to open the political process.

Shortly after assuming power in 1970, Sadat purged leading Nasserists from the government, army, and party, then dissolved the party—the Arab Socialist Union—outright. He founded his own ruling party and embarked upon hesitant steps toward a multiparty system. Having distanced himself from Nasserist allies, seeking to construct his own power base, he turned to former opponents of the regime, many of whom he released from prison, or who returned from exile.

Sadat, who ruled uneasily in Nasser's shadow, tacitly promoted a revision of the Nasserist legacy, a demythologizing of the man and debunking of his associates. The primary documents are well known to students of Egypt. The author Tawfiq al-Hakim, confessing his own submission to Nasserist rhetoric, likened the country's reawakening under Sadat to a "return of consciousness" from a state of dreamy intoxication. The window of opportunity afforded eminent writers like Hakim sparked publication of a spate of prison memoirs in the mid-1970s. Harsh condemnations of life in Nasser's political prisons, these accounts focused more on a system gone awry, a regime obsessed with power, than on fundamental issues of political legitimacy. Nasser did not escape attack; rumors of personal corruption were leveled. Yet many felt the brunt of the blame for Egypt's predicament lay with those who surrounded the president, those who occupied what Egyptians called the "centers of power" (marakiz al-quwa), most of whom now sat in prison.[6]

Another type of memoir, potentially more dangerous, soon began to proliferate. Former political activists, academics, and a growing number of former officers trained their sights on the origins of the Nasserist state, the coup d'état and early years of military rule. Their accounts filled the pages of Egyptian periodicals, reopening old wounds and prompting lively debate. Leading members of the Nasser regime joined in, to a great extent defending conventional Nasserist wisdom, but revealing previously unknown details, and often expressing their own unease with much that occurred.

The thrust of the debate changed dramatically in 1977 when Sadat granted the Wafd, Egypt's majority party from 1919 to 1953, permission to resume political activity. The Wafd changed the terms of the debate from a divisive, but relatively safe, discourse on how Nasserism had gone wrong into a frontal attack on the legitimacy of the July revolution. When Fu'ad Sirag al-Din, the Wafd leader, denounced the Free Officers' rising as a mere "coup d'état" (inqilab) that had subverted Egypt's true "revolution" (thaw-rah), the nationalist uprising of 1919, he carried the debate onto unaccept-able turf. Sadat quickly drafted legislation to reimpose a political ban on old-regime politicians. The New Wafd party disbanded in protest.[7] But the jinn, having been released, would not vanish. With the formation of opposition platforms within Sadat's ruling National Democratic party (NDP), then their licensing as opposition parties, and the resurgence of the Muslim Brother-hood, the public reevaluation of modern Egyptian history continued.

Upon Sadat's death a new generation assumed power, one that had no direct links to the Free Officers and few to institutions of the Nasserist state. The struggle for a more open political process is the one issue that unites diverse opposition forces today. Discussion of the errors, crimes, or sins of the Free Officers carries no direct personal challenge to the legitimacy of Hosni Mubarak, his ministers, or leaders of his party, the NDP. In 1982 Mubarak licensed the Wafd, lifted the ban on its former leaders, and allowed it to publish a weekly paper. He permitted the Muslim Brotherhood, still officially illegal, to contest elections within recognized opposition coalitions. That year a Wafdist-Brotherhood alliance won 12 percent of the vote and fifty-eight seats in parliament. In 1987 the Wafd polled 10.9 percent, winning thirty-five seats, and the Brotherhood, allied with two smaller parties, won 17 percent of the vote, good for fifty-six seats. Since 1982 the opposition press has operated with relative freedom, although the Brotherhood has yet to receive permission to print its own paper.

As a consequence of the freer political atmosphere, the debate over the Nasserist political legacy resumed in full force, now with no limits imposed on the content of discourse. The ongoing discussion of Egypt's political future reprises many themes from a similar discussion in the early 1950s. Because so many of those active in politics today took part in political battles of the earlier period, a fundamental component of the debate concerns interpretations of historical events of that period.

Political forces and individuals who collaborated with the Free Officers prior to their takeover, participated in the coup, and supported the onset of military rule have been outspoken in defending, apologizing for, and renouncing their roles. Those who resisted military rule, either from the start or by 1954, portray themselves as righteous defenders of democracy. The 1954 March crisis, when the regime survived a widespread call for its downfall, has remained a particular issue of contention, almost an acid test of political acumen and idealism. At the time few could avoid taking sides. Wherever one stood in following years, those who stood against the regime in March, in the name of democracy, as well as those who supported the officers, against what they believed to be the precipitate restoration of Egypt's ailing liberal system, still assert that they were on the right side of the barricades at that particular moment.

This discourse within a nation rediscovering its "prerevolutionary" past centers on the guardians of two distinct and competing political traditions: liberal parliamentarianism and Nasserism. The Wafd, which dominated the parliamentary era, stakes sole claim to the liberal tradition. Leading independent politicians and technocrats, and many younger minority party members, due to their long-standing enmity to the Wafd collaborated with the military regime. They represent a crossover from the old-regime elite to the new. Some remained steadfastly loyal to Nasserism; others made a successful transition and worked for Sadat.

Against these two political traditions stand forces that constituted popular antiestablishment movements. The Muslim Brotherhood, the largest such force under parliamentary and Nasserist regimes, suffered at the hands of both. Brotherhood elders, nurtured in a liberal milieu, and a younger generation that developed a radical critique of the state while in Nasser's prisons, reject the Nasserist legacy entirely. The Egyptian Left, an antiestablishment force prior to the Free Officers' coup, supported the officers, then broke with them, only to make their peace in the late 1950s. In the 1960s communists collaborated with the regime, albeit uneasily, in an effort to steer the state down a path to socialism. The Left thus remains attached to basic social and economic provisos of Nasserism, while joining forces with its critics in promoting further steps toward democracy.

Interpretations

To understand the political dynamics of the transition period, therefore, requires assessing and synthesizing a variety of interpretations of events, interpretations that reflect on the Egypt of today as much as on the Egypt of four decades ago. These recent revisionist traditions pose dramatic challenges to the official history propagated by the regime, the version of events that dominated Egyptian historiography for two decades.

The officers undertook construction of an official history almost from the moment they seized power. They learned quickly to manipulate the press, where they published glorified accounts of their backgrounds and their takeover, and fabricated the role of troublesome opponents. A sociopolitical analysis of their movement, written by a civilian associate, appeared in late 1952. Nasser's manifesto, *Philosophy of the Revolution*, published in late 1954, along with a series of articles penned by Sadat in early 1955, later published as books and reissued in several editions, became definitive accounts of the Free Officers' roots. [8]

The official history changed little over the course of the next decade and a half; the junior officers who founded the movement came early to the idea of a political role for the military. They initiated contacts with other political forces but determined to go it alone. The officers seized power with the intent of restoring "sound parliamentary life." The political parties resisted calls to reform themselves. The Muslim Brothers and opportunistic fellow officers, notably Muhammad Nagib, all sought to assert "tutelage" over their movement. Confronted with such implacable resistance, the officers could either suspend parliamentary procedure and consolidate their power or allow the country to slip back into the grip of "feudalists" and "reactionaries" (Wafdists), or "merchants of religion" (Brothers).

The Wafd has yet to come to terms with its own role in the failure of liberalism. Wafdist historiography of the parliamentary era is one of constant struggle against "antidemocratic" foes. As a rule, Wafdists show little willingness to treat seriously the factionalism that undid their own party, particularly during its final term of office from 1950 to 1952, and hampered their efforts to combat the officers in late 1952. Party loyalists point an accusing finger, not without justification, at longtime minority rivals who attached themselves to the new regime and pressed the officers to subvert parliamentary rule. They boast, also not without some justification, of their early opposition to the regime's attempt to dictate the ouster of party leaders. Many Wafdists, however, welcomed the officers' purge call and looked upon the officers as a vehicle for social reform, as well as personal advancement. The political force that had the most to lose failed to see the danger of the military takeover and to unite until it was too late.[9]

Muslim Brothers regard the Free Officers as renegade Brothers, and Nasser as a wayward son who usurped their movement within the army. The Brothers assert that Nasser and his comrades led them to believe they acted, if not on the Brothers' behalf, then for common aims, and that they then brutally repressed the Brothers when the latter offered a covert alliance to help them formulate their program. The Brothers portray the officers as deceitful and themselves as duped, almost naively so. Although their thesis is rarely convincing, the Brothers' reexamination of the period has forced them to confront internecine rifts between supporters and foes of the regime, and even more elemental, between the Brotherhood's official leadership and the paramilitary secret organization, divisions that the military regime manipulated with devastating success.[10]

The Egyptian Left also claims the Free Officers as ideological kin, but with a clearer perception of factors that precluded political collaboration after the coup. Although wary of a purely military movement, and aware that the officers were not committed Marxists, many communists supported their takeover and looked to them to promote a democratic, reformist program. To this end, they were willing to tolerate a short interim period of martial law. Some in the Left fooled themselves into thinking they could collaborate with, even guide, the new regime. Soon after the coup, however, communists became the target of police repression and broke with the officers. Communists place the onus on "imperialist" powers, the United States in particular, and the undue influence of "antidemocratic" forces, primarily key minority party members who advised the junta.[11]

What of those "antidemocratic" forces that supported the regime in its early years? Minority party members, renegade Wafdists, and independents composed the real vanguard of the revolution. Young technocrats and disaffected politicians signed on with the regime, lending the officers their technical and political expertise, giving them the moral support necessary to proceed. Their culpability for the entrenchment of the military regime cannot be denied. When they perceived that the old political order stood in the way of social reform, they acquiesced in the extension and consolidation of military rule. Many later broke with the regime; the picture they paint is therefore ambivalent. Their stories vary, but one common theme emerges. They all argue that their motives were not rooted in hostility to democracy but, rather, to the forces that controlled Egyptian democracy, the Wafd in particular.[12]

The same thread running through revisionist accounts by those who considered the Free Officers ideological kin—leftists, including left Wafdists, and Muslim Brothers—is the officers' betrayal of trust and compromising of ideals. These accounts prompt queries about the extent to which the officers deceived friends and allies with whom they collaborated prior to and after July 23, 1952. More specifically, they raise questions as to what degree, if any, the officers as a group professed loyalties to young Wafdist, Muslim Brother, and Communist associates. From this follow questions of why alliances were broken and of the extent to which the officers' repression of alternative political forces was predetermined or guided by events. Such questions strike at the heart of the matter: the extent to which the officers did or did not set an ideological agenda prior to their takeover, and the extent to which they saw themselves as the sole legitimate rulers of Egypt.

Opinions have vacillated between extremes. The Free Officers have been portrayed by communists, left Wafdists, and left-wing independents as well-intentioned innocents, corrupted and led astray by "antidemocratic" or "imperialist" forces, captives of their own class affinities and military predilections. From the perspective of Muslim Brothers and old-guard Wafdists, the Free Officers emerge as masterly manipulators who, having determined to rule alone, slowly usurped legitimate civilian and, in the case of the Brotherhood, moral authority as well.

Scholarly treatments of Nasser's Egypt have done little to challenge such broad generalizations. Contemporary accounts of the officers' rise relied heavily on official sources and personal contacts with Egypt's new leaders. A generation of foreign scholars accepted the regime's official history of the Free Officers' consolidation of power. Studies written in the late 1950s, based in large part on the officers' version, became standard references for both popular biographers of Nasser and the first wave of social scientists who analyzed the Nasserist state that emerged after the mid-1950s.[13] Few scholars since have concerned themselves with the transition period in any detail. Despite the fact that it is only after 1954 that the old order can be said to have passed, historians of the old regime have traditionally set July 1952 as its terminating point. Some who wrote monographs on various political movements have looked beyond July, but often only as an epilogue.[14]

Two Egyptian scholars, Ahmad Hamrush and 'Abd al-'Azim Ramadan, influenced by the revisionist debate in the mid-1970s, have contributed greatly to rewriting the history of Nasserist Egypt, the early years in particular. Their work reflects the excitement of a more open political climate and the political discourse in which they themselves took part. Both reflect leftist interpretations of events. Hamrush writes as an insider, a leader of a communist movement in the army and an early collaborator with the Free Officers. Ramadan, an academic, shares Hamrush's perspective. Both helped return the Left to a position of prominence with other political forces and influences on the officers.[15] In the decade and a half since they wrote, the output of memoirs and personal accounts has accelerated. The sheer quantity and diversity of voices from all political factions allow for a far more nuanced evaluation of events and trends than was before possible.

In addition to the florescence of revisionist accounts, recently declassified

U.S. and British diplomatic records shed much new light on the period. Certain files remain under wraps and may remain so for some time, but what is available is of considerable value. Intelligence briefings, notes of closed-door discussions with officers and politicians, and reports of events censored from the press constitute a contemporary perspective, albeit foreign, frozen in time and untainted by the experience of the three decades that followed.

Confronting Power, Defining a Revolution

From the day they seized power, the Free Officers confronted the quandary of the extent and style of their rule. They had no clear vision of what they hoped to achieve except in the most abstract sense. The officers were not convinced the system needed leveling so much as reforming by force and, if necessary, a partial suspension of democratic procedure. In this regard they represented a main current of Egyptian public opinion.

The Free Officers were not ideologues. Their ideology, to the extent they had one, reflected general views of nationalism and social reformism that crossed all political lines, views shared by a generation that had grown disaffected from the country's political elders. Despite organizational links to Muslim Brotherhood and communist cells in the military, their movement, since its founding in late 1949, remained fiercely independent. This fact friends and allies either failed to note or chose to ignore. Passionate voices attracted the young officers, Nasser in particular. But Nasser and the others disliked the dogmas of the Left and of the Brothers, feared the extent of their political—and military—organization, and at the same time remained wary of internal rifts within these movements.

The transition period was thus one of experimentation, groping, shifting alliances, and, increasingly, the cynical use of power. At the outset Nasser and his comrades hesitated to exercise direct control. The officers turned instead to their civilian contemporaries, younger establishment politicians and intellectuals, with whom they felt they could cooperate. With no specific ideological agenda, the officers picked and chose allies and advisors freely. To draft their land reform, for example, they selected a young leftist economics professor; to administer it, a progressive young minority-party member from a landowning family. Increasingly, the officers turned away from old accomplices to those less bound by theory, men equally unsure of the future, and more willing to transfer former loyalties to new patrons. Such men lent the regime a vital degree of stability and even legitimacy.

Ultimately, the officers and the country confronted the issue of direct military rule. From the outset the junta faced countervailing pressures within the army, from the civilian intelligentsia, and foreign powers to extend or to limit their authority. Initially, *revolution* meant to them, as to many Egyptians who used the word, the ouster of a debauched king, the suspension of parliament, and a transitory phase of martial rule. With time the officers grew more self-confident of their ability to govern. The rallying of their political foes against them in early 1954 provided the spark that fused two strands—defensive retrenchment and a growing sense of mission—which led the officers to posit their revolution as the only alternative to a restored, unrepentant old regime.

The early 1950s marked another period of important transition. The U.S. embassy replaced the British embassy as the most influential foreign outpost in Cairo. The relationship between the United States and the Nasser regime in the years prior to Suez has been the subject of great deal of speculation. The Left, in particular, and the Muslim Brothers as well see an American bogey looming large behind the officers' consolidation of authority. Charges of direct U.S. complicity in the coup d'état cannot be established with any certainty. More important, is the role the Americans—and the British—played in advising the officers, fostering their self-confidence during a period in which they struggled for survival.

The personal role of Gamal Abdel Nasser also must be put in perspective. Traditional historiography has detailed—often with little accuracy—Nasser's personal odyssey to power, as if he were destined to lead Egypt and, further-more, as if he knew it. Regime-inspired hagiography is one thing, but myth became fact all too often for the outside observer. Nasser was the recognized, if not always undisputed, leader of the Free Officers before the coup, and of the CCR afterward. He exerted considerable personal influence over the course of events. But his emergence as a national and regional hero in the mid-1950s, which happened so suddenly and with such drama, overshad-owed an earlier period in which many Egyptians disliked, even feared him, and in which he himself hesitated to assume the role he soon came to personify.

By early 1955 the officers no longer viewed their revolution as the transi-tion to a restored liberal order but, rather, as a vital, ongoing process commit-ted to changing the face of Egypt. In the mid-1950s their focus shifted suddenly from internal to foreign affairs. By his obstreperous and bold chal-lenge to the West, Nasser emerged as the dominant figure in the Arab world. The origins of his personal power, rooted in the period of consolidation, thus have implications that reach beyond the scope of Egyptian history. As a prototype for military rule in the Third World, the officers' consolidation of their revolution makes interesting study. Their original assertion, that they had risen in order to purge the political establishment and hand power back to civilian leaders, seems today a well-worn cliché, a smoke screen to cover more dubious ambitions. For Nasser and his colleagues, this was not the case. Yet, six months after seizing power, they set about building a base of support and tightening their grip over the coercive powers of the state. Why this happened says much about the failure of liberalism in Egypt. How it happened reveals much about the roots of Nasserism. How two concurrent processes, the fall of an old regime and rise of a new order, are interpreted will bear directly on Egypt's future in a post-Nasserist, postrevolutionary era.

1

"A Country of Failure"

When Egypt awoke on July 23, 1952, the country greeted news of a military coup with nervous anticipation. Politicians and their colleagues, those not vacationing abroad, scurried to contact one another, to share news and trade rumors. Many gathered at the San Stefano Hotel in Alexandria, summer haunt for the political establishment. As it became apparent over the course of the following week that the army would change little and little blood would be shed (only two soldiers died, as a result of scattered gunfire outside the Ras al-Tin Palace on July 26), Egyptians heaved a sigh of relief. Few rued the army's action. Rather, a nation disillusioned by the instability and inefficacy of a parliamentary system gone wild considered the electric shock administered the body politic, as well as the deposition of a disgraced king, a blessing.

This initial response to the Free Officers' rising, cautious but hopeful, was rooted in twenty-eight uneasy years of parliamentary rule, years that had undermined faith in liberalism and left a large segment of the Egyptian intelligentsia amenable to the notion of military intervention in the political process. Chroniclers of Egypt's old regime revel in accounts of the decadence of king and courtiers, pashas and politicians. The system was discredited, its practitioners disgraced. By the mid-1930s "party politics" (al-hizbiyyah) had become synonymous with personal corruption and patronage. Antiestablishment movements with alternative sociopolitical visions captured widespread public sympathy and fought for control of the streets. By the late 1940s Egyptians spoke more and more of "revolution," some with relish, many with apprehension. By July 1952 the parliamentary order had virtually ceased to function.

The ease with which the army seized power reinforced a vision of a decadent monarch and scurrilous political elite. When the Cinema Metro, a Cairo movie palace and target of arsonists during antiforeign riots in January 1952, reopened after the coup, it screened *Quo Vadis* as its first feature. Few could miss the parallels between the Emperor Nero and the ill-fated Farouk, or the Roman patricians and Egypt's pashas. A media barrage of exposes and a series of show trials reinforced images of the "nights of Farouk." But Egyptians needed little reminder. Stories of governments ransomed, cotton hoarded, drugs and arms trafficked through palace offices, fiancées abducted, and coffins raided for royal treasures had long since become part of the political culture of the old regime.[1]

The liberal order collapsed because of its inability to overcome structural flaws and the self-destructive political ethos that those flaws engendered. In a very real sense the "liberal experiment" was doomed from the outset. The parliamentary order never recovered from the ouster, under British guns in November 1924, of Egypt's first elected government. Yet the system plodded along for thirty years, ruled by the same actors reading a tired script with few variations. Nevertheless, while generally regarded as chronically ill, the system was still believed by many to be curable, even after the Free Officers' coup. To understand more clearly the background to their coup and the political wrangling that followed, it is instructive to observe the parliamentary regime in its last years, between January 1950 and July 23, 1952. During this period in particular, reform-minded members of the political establishment struggled against those who, either ignoring vested personal interests or having surrendered to nihilism, continued to play politics as usual. Their failures spelled the end of liberalism in Egypt, most decisively because they turned their backs on the liberal order. When the Free Officers thrust themselves into the center of political life in July 1952, many of Egypt's political elites failed to note the threat posed to their hegemony. Rather, they embraced the officers, some more honestly than others, as saviors, reformers rather than levelers.

The Politics of Disillusion

Egypt's parliamentary order had been born in the wake of an earlier "revolution," the 1919 uprising against the British. On the pretext of restoring order and safeguarding Egypt's foreign population, the British occupied Egypt in 1882. Egypt's strategic importance persuaded them to prolong what they had intended to be a short stay. British policymakers soon accustomed themselves to the idea of a long-term occupation. In 1914, after the outbreak of the First World War, Britain declared a protectorate over Egypt.[2]

Hopes that the postwar settlement might bring Egypt its independence reinvigorated a fledgling nationalist movement. In November 1918, when the victors made plans to gather in France to reorder the world, a committee of fourteen nationalist leaders, members of a self-appointed "Egyptian Delegation" (al-Wafd al-Misri, hereafter referred to as the Wafd), approached the British high commissioner seeking visas so they might present their case before the peacemakers. The British refused. In March 1919, when authorities arrested the Wafd leaders, Egypt erupted in rebellion.[3]

The uprising set the terms of political debate and the ideals to which Egyptians aspired in the years that followed. Throughout Egypt workers struck and peasants destroyed telegraph and railroad lines, and attacked police stations and other symbols of the occupation. Religious leaders delivered nationalist sermons before mixed assemblies. Egyptian women took to the streets for the first time, defying British troops to express their solidarity with the nationalist leadership. These images of national unity inspired several generations of Egyptians, those who took part in and those bred on stories of the uprising, to continue the struggle for "total independence."

The 1919 uprising forced the British to strike a modus vivendi with Egyptian national aspirations but failed to free Egypt of the occupation. In 1922 Britain declared Egypt an independent nation but reserved the right to intervene in its internal affairs in four areas: the rights of foreign interests and minorities; the defense of Egypt against foreign aggression or interference; the Suez Canal; and the Sudan. Pursuant to these "four reserved points," Britain retained control of the Egyptian army and maintained its own standing force in the country. Egypt became a constitutional monarchy, Sultan Fu'ad its first king. A constitution, approved in 1923, provided for a bicameral parliament. Elections were held in January 1924 and Saʿd Zaghlul, leader of the Wafd, now an official political party, formed Egypt's first parliamentary government in the liberal era.[4]

Independent Egypt's first elected government lasted less than eleven months. Zaghlul quickly set about testing the power of his office in relation to the palace and the British residency. In November 1924, prompted by palace meddling in governmental affairs, Zaghlul threatened to resign. King Fu'ad, intimidated by crowds shouting "Saʿd or revolution," backed down. Later that month, when the British decided Zaghlul should go, a list of insulting demands, backed up by a gunboat in Alexandria harbor, forced his resignation. The king appointed a new prime minister, who dissolved parliament the following month, setting a precedent from which the liberal order never recovered.

Competing interests, foreign and national, doomed the parliamentary order from the outset. Power rested on a delicate balance between the British, the palace, the Wafd, and rival minority parties. These forces held each other in check. When one moved to bolster its position, the others, individually or as a group, reacted with countervailing pressures to defend their interests. Constitutional power rested with the monarch, who could dissolve parliament at will. Fu'ad (1921–1936) owed his throne to popular agitation but recognized that British fiat had handed him the scepter. By tying his fate to the British, Fu'ad fixed the palace as an adversary of the national movement; by abusing his considerable constitutional powers, he set himself in opposition to the aspirations of a new liberal intelligentsia. The British, who policed Egypt and controlled the coercive arms of state power, thought nothing of bringing down any Egyptian government that proved too vociferous in challenging their presence. The Wafd marshaled the power of mass popular support through which it made long-term rule by any rival party or coalition impossible.

The stalemate that resulted promoted chronic instability. The British, concerned with keeping order, ultimately would impress the king with the need to hold new elections, which, if free (and they informed him when they insisted this be the case) would result in another Wafd victory. A futile stab at renegotiating terms of Britain's occupation usually ensued, after which Wafdist intransigence moved the British either to order directly a change in government or to turn their backs, allowing the king to depose the majority party whenever he so chose. With only slight variation, the scenario endlessly repeated itself. Between 1924 and 1952 the Wafd held power for just under seven years.

Under the lead of Zaghlul (d. 1927) and his successor, Mustafa al-Nahhas, the Wafd fought ceaselessly against the autocratic aspirations of king and palace. This despite a series of defections from its ranks, which led to the formation of minority parties (the Liberal Constitutionalist party, founded in 1922; the Sa'dist party, in 1938; the Independent Wafdist Bloc, in 1942) that competed unsuccessfully for electoral support. Resentful of the Wafd's overwhelming electoral dominance, the minority parties worked in league with the palace as their sole means of attaining power. Collaboration entailed accepting power by royal fiat, proroguing parliament, and often administering rigged elections. Repeatedly banished from power, the bitterness of political exile produced in the Wafd an aggressive, self-righteous posture that its rivals as well as those holding dissenting views within the party found intolerable.

The animosity between the Wafd and its rivals poisoned the political climate and played into the hands of British and palace interests. The pattern of parliamentary politics fostered a cynical attitude among those who vied for power as well as those asked to place trust in elected officials. Political corruption, personal aggrandizement, and party patronage flourished in an atmosphere so inherently volatile. Major overhauls in the state bureaucracy and in provincial and local administrations quickly followed changes in government.

The year 1936 brought two important changes: a revision of treaty relations with Britain and a new king. In August the British established normal diplomatic relations with Egypt, pledged to support the abolition of capitulatory privileges for foreigners and Egyptians who held foreign passports, and agreed to withdraw its troops to the Suez Canal Zone. The capitulations were abolished a year later. But the treaty, described aptly by Berque as "too eagerly sought by one partner, too readily accepted by the other," had little long-term effect on Anglo-Egyptian relations due to the outbreak of the Second World War.[5]

Farouk (1936–1952), who assumed the throne at the age of sixteen to much popular acclaim, unlike his father fancied himself a nationalist, and adopted a confrontational stand against the British. When not escaping to enjoy the pleasure domes of Cairo or the Riviera, Farouk ruled Egypt with an unsteady but not unskilled hand. His compulsive personality reflected in a ballooning waist and scandalous antics, he increasingly withdrew into a world of constant excess in the late 1940s. Ralph Stevenson, Britain's ambassador to Egypt from 1950 to 1955, described an inner struggle between the king's sense of duty to his people and his insatiable personal appetites. "I would feel happier about it," Sir Ralph lamented in May 1951, "had I not a sneaking suspicion that where his own amusement and distraction are concerned the king in him is fighting a losing battle against the man."[6]

Farouk's inner circle of advisors reflected this struggle. The king took lessons in statecraft from some of the keenest political minds in the country. Men like Isma'il Sidqi, 'Ali Mahir, Ahmad Hasanayn, and Hafiz 'Afifi were not democrats, but neither were they mere opportunists, as they are depicted in traditional nationalist historiography. However, their visions of a modern, industrial, independent Egypt will forever be tarnished by their support for the monarchy. On the other side stood the sycophants: Antoun Pulli, court electrician and royal pimp; Karim Thabit, press attaché and hagiographer; Elias Andraos, special economic advisor to the Royal Treasury; and others even less qualified to advise the monarch. Against the wiser counsel of the former lot they corrupted the impressionable Farouk and in the end came to dominate him.

The rallying cry during the 1920s had been "total independence" (al-istiqlal al-tamm), Egypt's right to proclaim its own sovereignty and elimination of the four "reserved points" mandated by the British. During the 1930s the scope of political discourse began to widen, engendered by an antiestablishment that propounded alternative social and political ideals, and organized protests in the streets to denounce Egypt's political establishment. The Muslim Brotherhood, founded in 1928 in Ismailia by Hasan al-Banna, had spread throughout Egypt by the mid-1930s. Banna's advocacy of a moral political order rooted in Islamic principles and precepts, mixed with an appeal to Egyptian nationalism, struck a responsive chord in peoples of middle-class and rural backgrounds. By the 1940s the Brotherhood had founded clinics and schools, and begun organizing industrial workers and recruiting in the police and military. Young Egypt, founded in 1933 by two young law graduates, Ahmad Husayn and Fathi Radwan, espoused a populist credo modeled after fascist youth movements in Europe. Aping form more than ideology, Young Egypt attracted university and high school students, dressed them in green shirts, and sent them into the streets to demonstrate against the British and the Wafd. The streets had always been a political forum against the British and the palace, but the advent of paramilitary youth movements by Young Egypt, the Wafd, and the Muslim Brotherhood turned the nationalist movement in on itself, fostering "a common disdain for law and order" that would explode in the late 1940s.[7]

Egypt's experience during the Second World War escalated existing tensions between Egypt and Britain, as well as within the political establishment and between establishment and antiestablishment. The outbreak of war, in particular the threat of Italian troops in Libya and Farouk's ties to Italian advisors, caused Britain to reimpose martial law and reoccupy the country. In June 1940, when Prime Minister 'Ali Mahir balked at declaring war on the Axis, the British obtained his dismissal. On February 4, 1942, in an incident seared in every Egyptian nationalist's memory, British authorities led a procession of armored vehicles to Abdin Palace, where the authorities threatened to depose the king if he refused to appoint a Wafdist government. Salvaging a bad situation, Farouk cleverly posed as national hero, leaving the Wafd to bear the onus of collaboration. Two years later, the threat of war having passed, the British again turned their backs when he ousted the majority party.[8]

The palace also manipulated internal power struggles within the Wafd to create havoc. With palace backing, Makram 'Ubayd, the number-two man in the Wafd and widely recognized as the party's conscience, but increasingly on the outs, published a "Black Book" detailing corruption within the Wafd. When the party ousted him, 'Ubayd formed his own party, the Independent Wafdist Bloc. His subsequent willingness to serve in a series of minority coalitions tarnished his image and further destroyed hopes for a reform agenda emerging from within the parliamentary establishment.[9]

In the postwar period opposition movements changed the nature of political debate in the country. The street battles in the 1930s reflected popular cynicism about corruption and the inability to attain a British withdrawal. After the Second World War a succession of governments attempted to persuade Britain to retreat to the Canal Zone under terms of the 1936 treaty, then to renegotiate the treaty terms themselves. At the same time rising prices, population growth, and a general downturn in the economy sparked a call for social reform that went hand in hand with and at times surpassed the national question. In the 1920s and 1930s leading industrialists advocated protective tariffs and encouraged landed wealth to invest in the industrial sector as a patriotic duty. By the 1940s economic reform came to encompass plans for ameliorating the social ills from which the working and peasant classes suffered. Reformers offered plans for compulsory education, public housing, health projects, social insurance, and workers' compensation. Bureaucratic reform posed no less a challenge.[10]

Land reform came to dominate the reformist agenda. In 1940 large landowners, those owning fifty feddans or more (one feddan = approximately one acre) constituted .5 percent of all property holders and owned 37 percent of Egypt's arable land. On the other hand, three-quarters of the four million peasants actively engaged in farming owned less than one feddan or no land at all. Reformers proposed a variety of solutions. Some suggested that a heavy tax on landholding over a certain threshold would encourage large landowners to divest themselves of a significant portion of their property and invest in industry. Others wished to fix a legal limit on the amount of property a given individual or family could own. Talk of land reform aroused considerable passions; when, in 1945, a Sa'dist senator offered a modest proposal limiting the amount of future acquisitions, excepting inheritances, his Sa'dist colleagues wanted none of it. They drummed him out of the Senate and he left the party.[11]

The call for reform crossed political and, to an extent, generational lines. The radicalization of the working class fueled the spread of communist movements but also bolstered the ranks of the Muslim Brotherhood, which organized its own labor unions to compete with the Left.[12] Reform blocs emerged in most political parties, generally centered around younger members. The youth wing of the Wafd openly voiced disenchantment at the hesitancy of party elders to adopt a social reform agenda. A young guard breathed new life into the moribund Nationalist party. Independent technocrats and academics formed small parties or political coalitions, such as the Egyptian Front, the Socialist Peasant party, the Peasants League, or the Daughter of the Nile, committed to "social justice" (al-'adil al-ijtima'i). Those with political ambition found the system impervious; many forswore electoral politics altogether and remained outside the political process they still hoped to salvage.[13]

The call for social justice reflected a drift to the left, one that produced a spurt in communist activity, until then confined largely to intellectual circles. Communism never commanded the street power of either the Muslim Brotherhood or Young Egypt. Communist movements remained splintered as a result of ideological quarrels, police infiltration, and the state repression. The governments of Sidqi (February–December 1946), Nuqrashi (December 1946–December 1948), and 'Abd al-Hadi (December 1948–July 1949) succeeded in disrupting the workings of the larger organizations and destroyed many of the smaller groups. By 1950 most had either dissolved or merged to form new organizations. Despite these travails, the Marxist critique of Egyptian society, propounded primarily through journals and pamphlets, played a major role in shaping the reformist agenda of the postwar period.[14]

During the postwar years violence and disorder rent the country. Eight minority governments ruled, or tried to, between October 1944, when the king turned out the Wafd, and January 1950, when elections returned the majority party to power. The minority governments enacted stern measures but failed to repress the extraparliamentary opposition. Two prime ministers, Ahmad Mahir and Mustafa al-Nuqrashi, both Sa'dists, fell victim to assassins' bullets.

The Muslim Brotherhood stood at the center of the fray. In the early 1940s Hasan al-Banna sanctioned the formation of a secret paramilitary organization. Apologists for Banna contend he founded the special section in order to carry out armed struggle against the British, an argument that is disingenuous because the great majority of its acts were perpetrated against Egyptian foes. More telling, Banna's followers admit he lost control of the secret organization, which acted without his consent and against his express wishes.[15] The cycle of violence reached an apex in December 1948 when Prime Minister Nuqrashi outlawed the Brotherhood and was slain. Hasan al-Banna was killed, in return, in February 1949. In the months that followed, the new Sa'dist prime minister, Ibrahim 'Abd al-Hadi, ruling by martial law, oversaw the arrest of scores of Brothers and communists, and drove the remnants of the nonparliamentary opposition underground.

The False Hopes of 1950

In January 1950 Egyptians went to the polls for the last time in the parliamentary era and elected a Wafdist government. The circle had come full turn. In

July 1949, with upcoming elections promised, the Wafd joined a national unity government led by Husayn Sirri, a palace loyalist. Reluctant to resist renewed Wafdist calls for elections, the king charged Sirri to form a caretaker government to administer the voting. Overestimating the erosion of electoral support for the Wafd, the palace predicted the Wafd would be forced to join a coalition cabinet.[16] Instead, the Wafd captured 228 of 319 seats, attaining an absolute majority. The victors celebrated their triumph with a passion bred by five years of banishment from power. For ten days Wafd supporters paraded the streets between Mustafa al-Nahhas's Garden City villa and parliament. When the new prime minister opened parliament on January 16, he and other ministers were forced to abandon their vehicles and wade through the throngs. Echoing palace apprehension at the prospects of dealing with a Wafd majority, Husayn Sirri, newly appointed chief of the Royal Cabinet, described the Wafd's mood as "pretty cock a hoop."[17]

At the same time Nahhas and his colleagues recognized the immensity of the task they faced. In his "Speech from the Throne" opening parliament, Nahhas promised to spare no effort to achieve a British withdrawal and unify Egypt and the Sudan. The bulk of his address spoke to domestic issues. Nahhas promised to take immediate steps to end martial law, to lower the cost of living, to provide free primary and secondary education, legislate social security, and reorganize the government bureaucracy around merit rather than patronage.[18]

The new Nahhas government reflected a compromise between traditional party interests and a recognized need for new faces and younger blood. Leading Wafdists retained their grip on important cabinet posts: Fu'ad Sirag al-Din (interior), 'Uthman Muharram (public works), Zaki al-'Urabi (communications), and others. Nearly one-third of his nominees had no previous cabinet experience. Some, like Muhammad Salah al-Din (foreign affairs) and Ibrahim Farag (municipal and rural affairs), had climbed through party ranks. Most were more technically qualified to hold their assigned portfolios than was usually the case in a system where political weight within the party traditionally counted for more than professional ability.[19] In an unprecedented move, Nahhas entrusted four key portfolios to relative newcomers to the party. Collectively known as the "four professors"—Zaki 'Abd al-Mut'al (finance), Hamid Zaki (state), Ahmad Husayn (social affairs), and Taha Husayn (education)—each held a Ph.D. and could boast, if not governmental experience, expertise in his field.

The honeymoon, however, proved all too short. The public quickly perceived the primary goal of the new government to be the retention of power at all cost. Immediately upon taking power the Wafd undertook the traditional purge of political opponents from the state bureaucracy. It first targeted 'Abd al-Razzaq al-Sanhuri, the president of the State Council, a Sa'dist, but failed to dislodge him in the face of tremendous opposition. In May, overcoming stubborn resistance, the government passed "exceptional-promotions" legislation that reinstated, with back pay, patronage appointees who had been dismissed following the Wafd's fall in October 1944. To no one's great surprise, the measure was applied solely to Wafd loyalists.

The Wafd's intent to hold power at all cost was reflected most vividly in its policy of rapprochement with the palace. A series of concessions intended to court the king's favor underscored this assessment. Nahhas raised eyebrows when he kissed Farouk's hand at their first official encounter. "They have put a little water in their wine," Husayn Sirri noted, with evident satisfaction.[20] In February, in what one British observer described as a "remarkable manifestation of the Wafd's present obsequiousness to the palace," the government earmarked £E 1,320,000 to refit the royal yacht.[21] On April 28, the fourteenth anniversary of King Fu'ad's death, Nahhas delivered a eulogy, the first time any prime minister had so marked the occasion. Jefferson Caffery, the U.S. ambassador, noted its "interesting and amusing" historical revisionism.[22]

In June the government resisted appeals for a parliamentary inquiry into alleged government improprieties during the previous two years. The charges, which included arms profiteering during the Palestine War, implicated aides close to Farouk. The Wafd's tacit defense of palace interests created an uproar among the parliamentary opposition. In the ultimate comic opera of the liberal era, the minority parties condemned the palace for illicit acts they had tolerated while in power. The Wafd, which might have seized the opportunity to further the breach between its old rivals and lead the charge against corruption, opted instead to tie itself to the most crooked elements of Egyptian political life.

Then, in July, after being forced to open a parliamentary inquiry into scandals touching the palace, the government nullified all appointments to the Senate made during its absence from power. Twenty-nine senators lost their seats; Wafdist loyalists replaced most, giving the Wafd a majority. In enacting such measures the Wafd acted perfectly within its right as the parliamentary majority and did nothing out of the ordinary. Wafdist senators had suffered similar treatment in 1941 and 1945. Yet the blatant promotion of party loyalists and relatives of party bigwigs deflated popular expectations and hopes that this time, particularly after the violence of the late 1940s, things might be different.[23]

Furious at his aides for not taking greater measures to prevent a Wafd majority, Farouk quickly turned the party's courtship to advantage. He pampered Nahhas with petty gifts and allowed the prime minister minor breaches of protocol.[24] If each man thought he used the other, Farouk more often emerged the victor. Yet when trouble loomed greatest, the king surrendered to the man. In the summer of 1951, despite mounting pressures for abrogation of the 1936 Anglo-Egyptian treaty, Farouk sailed for Europe. He returned too late to halt abrogation in October. Afterward he resolved to dump the Wafd at the first opportune moment but then hesitated, afraid to attack the government during a crisis.[25]

Internal disarray contributed most to the Wafd's failure in power. Squabbles behind closed doors, in the press, and on the floor of parliament disrupted policy-making, led to the dismissal or resignation of the government's most promising ministers, sapped the party's strength, and further undercut

public confidence. The Wafd was polarized ideologically and torn by personal rivalry. These divisions warrant closer examination, for in addition to
undermining the hopes of 1950, they prevented the Wafd from confronting
the Free Officers as a united party after July 1952.

The rift between left- and right-wing factions has dominated traditional
accounts of the Wafd's last years.[26] To focus on this rift, however, is to lose
sight of a more fundamental dynamic, one that exacerbated both personal
and ideological differences. Party structure, which many considered undemocratic, lay at the center of the problem. The president ruled for life. He
appointed the executive committee, which according to party bylaws effectively ruled the party. Advancement up the hierarchy was painfully slow,
dissent from the party line looked at askance. Because of the executive
committee's stranglehold on the offices of party command, younger party
members had no real say in the determination of policy.[27] As a result, conflicts within the Wafd were fought to a great extent along generational lines.
By the late 1940s three generations vied for influence within the party, each
with its own style, its own vision, and its own set of political wounds.

The old guard, Nahhas and his colleagues, composed the first generation.
All in their late sixties or early seventies, they monopolized the executive
committee by virtue of their age more than their wits. Many had been
present at the Wafd's creation and stood with Zaghlul in 1919. The tribula-
tions of Egyptian politics, including the defections of so many comrades,
bred in them a bitter temper, a mixture of self-righteousness and cynicism,
which steeled an unwillingness to surrender power as well as a disposition to
abuse it. Fathers of the modern nationalist movement, they were medium to
large landowners and well-to-do professionals.[28] Most were pashas, the highest mark of social status. They did not lack sympathy for society's underprivi-
leged, but most failed to appreciate the danger of the growing disparity
between haves and have-nots.

The old guard's heirs, the second generation, had their power base in the
parliamentary organization. Muhammad Salah al-Din, Ibrahim Farag, and
others, men in their late forties, held their first cabinet posts 1950 and began
to distribute their own patronage. Their perspective differed little from that
of party elders. They came from a similar social class and professional background, although few had yet attained the rank of pasha. Groomed in a
political climate similar to that of the old guard's they shared the political
vision of their elders but were anxious to enter the higher echelons of the
party.

The great exception to the rule was Fu'ad Sirag al-Din, the party secretary and power broker. He was the Wafd's boy wonder, having held his first
cabinet post in 1942 at the age of thirty-two.[29] Six years later Nahhas appointed him party secretary; by 1950 he had established himself as the
leading candidate to succeed to the party presidency. His rise to prominence
in the late 1940s was rooted not only in his political acumen but also in an
energy that party elders could neither match nor tame. His success aroused
the resentment of older colleagues on the Wafd executive committee who

became relegated to the role of auxiliary elder statesmen, as well as of his contemporaries, only just beginning to come into their own.

Under Sirag al-Din's lead the party's right wing steadfastly checked reformist tendencies within the party. The scion of one of Egypt's richest families, Sirag al-Din had little appetite for social change, especially land reform. "I own 8000 feddans," he told the U.S. ambassador in late 1951. "Do you think I want Egypt to go communist?"[30] He referred to foreign policy, but as interior minister after 1950 he battled forces that sought to redistribute wealth, not least those within his own party.

By the late 1940s a third generation of Wafdists agitated persistently for a greater role in shaping party policy. Young professionals and students radicalized in the years after the Second World War organized themselves into a self-styled Wafdist Vanguard. They proposed changes in party bylaws to limit the power of the executive committee, which refused to recognize them. In league with young communists, some of whom had been Wafdists (some surreptitiously asserted they still were), they founded a series of campus coalitions and joint student-worker committees.[31]

The Wafdist Vanguard openly opposed, not without some success, "reactionary" measures initiated by the Nahhas government and publicly denounced the Wafd's servility to the palace. But the left wing was locked out of power because, with only rare exceptions, its representatives came from the youth ranks of the party. The most visible and in many ways most influential members of this generation were a group of slightly older, respected intellectuals that included 'Aziz Fahmi, Muhammad Mandur, and Ahmad Abu al-Fath, the editor in chief of *Al-Misri*. This latter group heralded the Vanguard position in the press and the Wafd's parliamentary organization.

Although the struggle between the Vanguard and party leaders certainly weakened the government, internal cabinet politics proved more decisive. Here the second-generation Wafdists exerted far greater influence on the course of events. The heirs apparent waged a simultaneous two-front battle. Those with ambition to succeed Nahhas as party boss sniped at rivals, a battle that, because fought among the most powerful, proved crippling. Concurrently, veteran second-generation Wafdists competed with the reform-minded newcomers for influence. The latter, men of similar age and social status, also strove for a greater say in party affairs. They differed in that they felt much less loyalty to the idea of the Wafd. As the political party most likely to achieve their social and national aims, the Wafd attracted them; when the attraction faded, they left the party and became some of its bitterest opponents.

A leadership crisis exacerbated the generational problem within the Wafd. Seventy-one years old in 1950, Nahhas was a party leader whose time appeared about up. According to the rumor mill, he worked only several hours a day, concerned himself primarily with attending to his toilet, and allowed himself to be manipulated by his wife, Zaynab al-Wakil, and Fu'ad Sirag al-Din. British and U.S. officials described him as "almost senile."[32]

Under such conditions, political ambition could not but be an issue in the

Wafd. Yet the old man did not have to run the Wafd in order to rule. As Zaghlul's sole successor, he served a symbolic purpose that allowed him to stand above the fray. So long as Nahhas chose to preside over the party, none challenged his position. Those waiting in the wings maneuvered against one another, not Nahhas. He could not be exonerated from the corruption that flourished around him, but most judged him to be merely an accessory to those considered utterly unscrupulous. Young Wafdists who decried the Wafd's rightward shift in the 1940s directed their attack against Sirag al-Din and his allies rather than Nahhas.

In the end, the promise of 1950 went unfulfilled. Corruption, internecine feuding, heavy-handed treatment of parliamentary opponents, and the policy of conciliation toward the palace overshadowed whatever achievements the government could claim and undermined the Wafd's popular base. Party elders continued to practice politics as usual, and one scandal followed another. The presence of reformers in the cabinet proved to be merely a facade. Of the four "professors," only Taha Husayn survived in office, and he just barely. 'Abd al-Mut'al and Ahmad Husayn collided head on with party patronage: the former was fired in November 1950; the latter quit nine months later. Hamid Zaki, considered a contender for the presidency, ran afoul of higher-placed rivals. He resigned in October 1951. When the reformers left the cabinet, old-line party loyalists filled their shoes.

In July 1951 a disgruntled Ihsan 'Abd al-Quddus, editor in chief of the influential independent weekly *Ruz al-Yusuf*, described Egypt as a "country of failure." "We in Egypt believe in failure and worship those who fail," he wrote, pointing specifically to Nahhas and his ministers. "Woe to the man of talent who looks at matters with a serious eye and works with determination to succeed. . . . Woe to him, for the doors are shut in front and behind him, oppressive power pursues him wherever he settles and false charges follow him every day."[33]

The Wafd's failure to meet the challenge it faced shattered public confidence in its ability to lead the nation and the ability of the liberal order to right itself. The tragedy of the Wafd, particularly Nahhas's generation, is that banishment from power that it rightfully should have held fostered an intolerance for dissent within party ranks, a tolerance for corruption, and, most damning in 1950, a willingness to compromise ideals in order to rule. The policy of appeasing the palace, a cynical pose adopted to cool royal tempers, succeeded in the short run. However, by defending palace interests, the Wafd cheapened its own image even as it prolonged its tenure. Nahhas and his colleagues may have considered the price a small one to pay, but their timing was bad.

The disillusion caused by the Wafd's failure to arrest the corruption of Egyptian politics and the direct attacks upon opposition movements by the government incited the movements to assume a more aggressive stand against the establishment. When the government sought to impose conditions on the Muslim Brotherhood's right to resurface as a legal political force, the movement proclaimed itself legal. Communists remained underground but quickly set about reorganizing. If the Wafd proved somewhat less ruthless than previous governments, the left wing of the party deserved some thanks for championing civil liberties.[34] Martial law was lifted in May 1951. Nonetheless, the government confiscated newspapers and clandestine publications, and raided communist cells. Ahmad Husayn, president of the Socialist party (not the Wafdist minister), was arrested in the summer of 1951; so was his vice-president, Ibrahim Shukri, even though he sat in parliament.

Only two months into the government's term the British ambassador worried that "unable to produce bread the Wafd may well produce, for popular applause, a nationalist circus."[35] In a series of talks over the course of 1951 and 1952, British and Egyptian negotiators achieved nothing. The Wafd demanded British recognition of Egypt's sovereign rights over the Sudan as a precondition to discussing the future of the Suez Canal base, a proposition the British rejected. With both sides stalled, the Egyptian government fell into a trap of escalating rhetoric. Finally, in October 1951, a year after promising to do so, Nahhas unilaterally abrogated the 1936 treaty.[36]

What is known as the "popular struggle" followed. Violence erupted in the Suez Canal Zone. Nearly 100,000 Egyptian workers walked off their jobs. The government ordered all who did business with the British base to desist. Guerrilla bands, popularly known as "liberation battalions," sabotaged British installations, stole vehicles, and sniped at British patrols. Squads organized by the Muslim Brotherhood acted in cooperation with sympathetic junior army officers.[37] British and Egyptian military authorities endeavored to avoid a major confrontation. However, as hostilities escalated, the British War Office proposed the implementation of martial law and readied plans to occupy Cairo.[38]

By its handling of the crisis, the Wafd demonstrated that it was more a prisoner than a leader of events. Compelled to support the armed struggle publicly, but fearing the consequences of unleashing the forces that bore arms, the government walked a tightrope. Interior Minister Sirag al-Din ordered that demonstrations be orderly, forbade all mention of the "liberation battalions" in the press, and kept channels open to the palace and to the U.S. and British embassies.[39] Unable to restrain the irregulars, the government tried in early December to co-opt them, encouraging the organization of student battalions. Untrained and ill equipped, the students received only cursory instructions before being sent into enemy territory, where most were captured and sent home. Responding to public outcry, in late December the government recalled its ambassador to London, dismissed all British state employees, forbade all cooperation with the British in the Canal Zone, and eased restrictions on civilians' rights to bear arms.[40]

The dramatic climax came on January 25, 1952. When British troops surrounded the headquarters of the Ismailia gendarmerie and ordered the police to surrender their weapons, Sirag al-Din instructed the Egyptian commander to resist. In the ensuing battle fifty policemen died and approximately one hundred were wounded (British casualties were three dead and thirteen wounded).[41] The following day angry crowds gathered in central Cairo. A raucous demonstration turned into a riot, during which the greater part of the city's business district was set aflame. The crowd vented its rage against foreign businesses, airline offices, hotels, cinemas, bars, and clubs. The army was not ordered into the streets until early evening. Twenty-six people, foreigners and Egyptians, died. That night, after pressing Nahhas to declare martial law, the king dismissed the government.[42]

It appeared certain that provocateurs exploited the crowd's wrath and directed its focus toward specific targets. The British, as well as the palace, blamed the Socialists. Socialist party president Ahmad Husayn was arrested and charged with inciting the mob to riot. Others, pointing to the damage directed at bars, nightclubs, and cinemas, accused the Muslim Brotherhood. Egyptian government reports, which the British accepted, exonerated the Brotherhood as an organization while conceding that individual Brothers most likely exploited the situation as it developed.[43]

Ardent nationalists accused the British of plotting the entire affair as an excuse to occupy the city. Fu'ad Sirag al-Din declared the palace had conspired to overthrow the Wafd. Farouk may certainly be charged with appalling negligence; while the city burned, he entertained guests with a lavish party honoring the birth of his son the previous week. Once apprised of the situation, perhaps unaware of its gravity, he resolved to exploit the disturbances in order to dump the Wafd and shift responsibility off his own shoulders. Enemies of the Wafd said the government had fanned the flames, a particular less easily dismissed. 'Abd al-Fattah Hasan, Sirag al-Din's closest associate, named minister of social affairs after Ahmad Husayn's resignation in July 1951, egged on those assembled outside his ministry earlier in the morning. Sirag al-Din at the time was concluding the purchase of some property on the city outskirts. Like the palace, the Wafd gambled on its ability to exploit public outrage, and lost.[44]

The Coming Revolution?

For many, the riots of January 26, 1952, confirmed fears that Egypt stood on the brink of upheaval, even revolution. Five months earlier the U.S. ambassador had surmised that "the factors of instability in Egypt outbalance by far the factors of stability." With his usual flair for the dramatic, Jefferson Caffery described the Egyptian mood as "somewhere between foul and very foul."[45] Talk of revolution floated through the tearooms and clubs where the elite gathered and was blazoned in the pamphlets and newspapers of the antiparliamentary opposition.

A cursory glance at the opposition press of the period supports the fears of those who saw the system heading pell-mell toward disaster. In June Socialist leader Ahmad Husayn warned, "There is no stopping the coming revolution if the situation continues in this manner."[46] Fu'ad Sirag al-Din served as a model for the pasha class:

He sleeps on ostrich feathers, immersed in silk. If the Egyptian people could visit the Sirag al-Din palace they would immediately realize what an enormous lie proclaims Sirag al-Din leader of the people. The man who lives in the likes of this palace can be nothing other than the enemy of the people. Gold on the walls, gold on the staircases, gold in the ceiling, gold on the tables and desks, gold, gold everywhere. Sirag al-Din lives in a world of gold.[47]

A leaflet distributed upon the pasha's return from abroad in September 1951 denounced him as the enemy of bread and the free press, the hero of high prices, high taxes, and fraud, and urged Egyptians: "Raise your voice loud and revolt—a real revolution to beat traitors and robbers of the money which you collected by blood and tears."[48]

As hard as he tried, Sirag al-Din could not destroy the opposition press. Tariq al-Bishri estimates that between 1950 and 1951 the circulation of Socialist party papers rose from several hundred copies to 50,000–100,000. U.S. embassy officers reported that the circulation of *Al-Da'wah,* the Brotherhood journal, jumped from 50,000 to 80,000 copies in its second week of publication in early 1951. By late summer, the British estimated the total circulation for all opposition papers at 150,000.[49]

But was revolution imminent? A leftist critique of Nasserism, formulated in the 1960s, argues that in fact the military coup precluded a true social revolution, an uprising of Egypt's native sons and daughters, tillers of the soil, spinners and weavers in the Delta textile mills. The seeds of this revolution are seen to have been sown in the labor strikes and peasant unruliness of the late 1940s. The "popular struggle" against the British in the Canal Zone is portrayed as a dress rehearsal for a mass movement against foreign occupier and collaborationist upper class. By seizing power when they did, the Free Officers preempted and usurped true revolutionary momentum. That momentum could be halted only by forceful repression of the working class.[50]

This reading of events is grounded more in sentiment, romantic pictures of social banditry and popular struggle, than in hard evidence. Lower and middle classes were discontented and becoming radicalized, but their loyalties remained divided. Disturbances at factory and farm threatened to escalate—in September 1951 a pillar of the British expatriate community informed the ambassador that an associate of his, a large landowner, "has not dared to leave with his family for Switzerland for the reason that he could not trust his peasants to pick instead of destroying the cotton crop if he were not present"—but to what end remained uncertain.[51]

Moreover, closer examination suggests the antiestablishment was not gearing itself for a popular uprising. Rather, while the liberal establishment, groping to find a way out of its chronic crises, increasingly came to accept the need for restrictions on political freedoms, popular opposition movements struggled to defend civil liberties and to define their place in the existing order. Although they had found their popular base in the streets, among Egyptians alienated from the political parties, Muslim Brothers, Socialists, and communists adopted a peculiarly ambivalent stand toward the parliamentary order. The opposition decried the "party politics" that crippled the political order, but it never came to terms with the basic question of the inherent evil of that order.

The Muslim Brotherhood, which prepared to resurface in 1950, lacked the spirit of cohesiveness imparted by its martyred founder. Following Hasan al-Banna's death, divisions rent the movement's upper echelons, which were played out in a struggle for leadership. Banna's brother, 'Abd al-Rahman al-Banna, and his brother-in-law, 'Abd al-Hakim 'Abdin, both sought to fill his seat. Salih 'Ashmawi, Banna's deputy since 1947 and editor of *Al-Da'wah*, and Sheikh Ahmad Hasan al-Baquri, a former leader of the Brotherhood's student movement whom many believed Banna had chosen as his successor, were considered the leading candidates. In the end the four contestants agreed upon selection of a compromise candidate from outside the Guidance Council, Hasan al-Hudaybi.[52]

The appointment of Hudaybi failed to restore harmony to the movement. The new general guide had not been elected by the Guidance Council under provisions set forth in movement bylaws; rather, a select few agreed to his appointment behind closed doors. A relative outsider, Hudaybi found himself confronted with a wall of resentment, even from those who accepted his nomination, some of whom forever challenged his legitimacy as Banna's successor. Hudaybi made his acceptance conditional on bringing his own men into the Guidance Council. Those who had been closest to the martyred leader suddenly found themselves distanced from the inner circle. By appointing his own men and replacing elected members, he alienated those whose support he needed most.[53]

Hudaybi's personal efforts to rehabilitate the Brotherhood's political image also met with bitter opposition. As a magistrate, Hudaybi's aura of establishment respectability attracted certain leading Brothers eager to dispel the movement's reputation as a terrorist organization. Hudaybi, however, overplayed the role in the eyes of many. His antagonists never forgave him for a visit he paid Farouk in November 1951, nor for his contacts with other political figures, especially Ibrahim 'Abd al-Hadi, the Sa'dist president and former prime minister, whom the Brothers held personally responsible for Banna's death.[54]

Hasan al-Banna's position on the question of participation in the political system had been ambivalent. After the Wafd's assumption of power in 1942, Banna considered running for parliament, but Nahhas dissuaded him with political promises. In the January 1945 election, which the Wafd boycotted and the Sa'dists rigged, Banna and five colleagues did run, only to be defeated. In January 1950 British embassy analysts suspected that as many as thirty Brothers, concealing their affiliation, filed for candidacy as independents.[55]

In early 1952 the British ambassador predicted Hudaybi might lead the Brotherhood toward "respectability." The day the Wafd fell, Ralph Stevenson speculated that Hudaybi would agree to serve in a coalition government if approached, that the king might one day even ask Hudaybi to form a government. A Brotherhood-led government, he predicted, would be qualified and, at least at the outset, less corrupt than the Wafd. Treaty negotiations would be tough, but if the government lasted, a Canal base accord might be reached.[56]

Hudaybi was, however, less a man of the political establishment than the British thought. He spoke the language of the system more easily than Banna, but in his disdain for the existing political order, he was truly his predecessor's disciple. Under his guidance the Muslim Brotherhood would remain outside and above the squabbles of parties and politicians. In March 1952, when a group of leading Brothers proposed they openly contest the elections announced by Prime Minister Hilali (see below), Hudaybi rejected the idea, and the movement followed his lead. On March 28 the Brotherhood announced a policy of "non-participation in the electoral contest, either in the name of the organization or as individuals, because elections since 1924 have been based on methods which contradict the standards of the Brotherhood and the nature of its call."[57]

Since its declared transformation from a youth movement into a political party in 1936, Young Egypt had assumed a variety of identities. In the early 1940s, trying to compete with the Muslim Brotherhood for support, the movement assumed an Islamic slant; when Young Egypt emerged in 1949 from a period of eclipse it did so as the Egyptian Socialist party. The movement retained its Islamic character, but its rhetoric, reflecting as well as leading the broadening of Egyptian political discourse, increasingly took on a reformist tone. In 1950 the Socialists sent their first representative, Ibrahim Shukri, the party vice-president, to parliament. Shukri established a reputation as a parliamentary gadfly (a reputation he retains today as leader of the opposition in parliament).

The Socialists, however, failed to transform themselves from a loosely organized popular movement into a political party with a cogent reform program. Much of the fault lay with their leader. More a rabble-rouser than an ideologue, Ahmad Husayn's inconsistent policy shifts drove away those with more serious political ambitions. (Fathi Radwan and Nur al-Din Tarraf, the most influential of these, joined the moribund Nationalist party, where they maneuvered to wrest power from party elders.) In the summer of 1951 Husayn proposed the formation of a popular front of all popular opposition movements. A brief period of cooperation with the Wafd followed, during which, according to British reports, Husayn landed a spot on the payroll of Fu'ad Sirag al-Din's Interior Ministry.[58] However in late January, several days before the battle in Ismailia and Cairo riots, Husayn suddenly called for the downfall of the Nahhas government. The extent to which Husayn's presence dominated the movement became readily apparent in the aftermath of Black Saturday when he was arrested. While he remained in prison Socialist party activities ground to a standstill.[59]

Although communist prisoners regained their freedom in early 1950 and pursued activities more openly, doctrinal and strategic differences continued to preclude unity of the Left. The largest group, the Democratic Movement for National Liberation (al-Harakah al-Dimuqratiyah lil-Tahrir al-Watani;

hereafter DMNL), opted for a visible political role. Advocating unity among all communist movements, DMNL members participated in coalitions like the Peace Movement and student organizations. From approximately five hundred members in 1950, the movement grew to about five thousand by 1952. As a consequence of its size and ideological flexibility, the DMNL suffered repeated schisms and proved a relatively easy target for infiltration by the security police. Rif'at al-Sa'id, at the time an organizer in the Delta, considers that "in this period of sudden growth [the DMNL] dropped its guard, perhaps forgetting that it was a secret organization." The central committee, constantly changing members and deprived of its driving force, Henri Curiel, who was deported in August 1950, provided little leadership to its cadres.[60]

The DMNL insisted on the Wafd's right, as the majority party, to govern. From prison in 1949, DMNL leaders issued a manifesto instructing members to vote Wafdist if known communists or working-class candidates did not contest a given seat in the 1950 poll. Throughout the two years of Wafdist rule the DMNL, while ever pressing for formation of a popular front, reiterated its support for the Wafd. A manifesto printed in February 1951 explained that the DMNL "has always drawn a distinction between the Wafd and all other bourgeois political parties." Unlike its rivals, the Wafd, "because of its makeup and history never rested in the least bit on reaction or imperialism." Endorsement for the majority party evolved over the course of the year to public denunciation of the government and support for the Wafdist Vanguard.[61]

The second-largest communist movement, the Egyptian Communist party (al-Hizb al-Shuyu'i al-Misri; ECP), founded by a small group of Marxist economists studying in France, maintained close links to the French Communist party. Unlike the larger DMNL, the ECP adopted a rigid, doctrinaire line, refusing official contacts with any other forces and denouncing leftist rivals as ideologically bankrupt. A tightly knit organization, according to its leader, Fu'ad Mursi, the ECP numbered some fifteen hundred members by 1952. Only the five to seven members of the secretariat knew his identity. Even as the party doubled its size in the years immediately after the coup, Mursi protected his anonymity.[62]

Much smaller, numbering about one hundred members in 1949, the Workers Vanguard (Tali'at al-'Ummal), preferred the secrecy of the ECP. The schisms suffered by the DMNL impressed upon Workers Vanguard leaders the need to maintain a small, more tightly organized and ideologically uniform movement. They undertook an open propaganda campaign, printing and circulating leaflets for public consumption. However in doing so, they carefully guarded the movement's identity, camouflaging its activities by constantly changing its name.[63] Like the DMNL, the Workers Vanguard backed Wafdist candidates in 1950. Most of the movement's founders traced their political roots to the left wing of the Wafdist student movement. Many continued to collaborate with Wafdist comrades, some concealing the fact that they had become Marxists.[64]

The ambivalence of the antiestablishment toward the ideals, if not the practices, of liberalism provides an ironic footnote to the twilight of the old regime. Factions in the Muslim Brotherhood pressed for participation in the political process. The Socialist party elected its vice-president to parliament. Of the three largest communist organizations, two advocated electoral support for the Wafd. The presence of these tendencies toward establishment politics, even as the liberal order disintegrated, raises important questions about the fears and hopes of those who saw—and afterward continued to see—Egypt on the verge of revolution.

That the mood, as Jefferson Caffery reported, was foul cannot be denied. Black Saturday underscored the anger beneath the surface of the Egyptian populace. The fury of the mob shook the political establishment. Yet Hudaybi, no doubt, looked upon the charred ruins of downtown Cairo with no less horror than Nahhas or other old-guard politicians. If agents provocateurs helped direct the mob, none of the antiestablishment movements actively prepared to mobilize that mob to overthrow the system. Ideology, organizational deficiency, and a mind-set that remained reformist precluded serious thought of revolution.

"In Temporary Need of a Dictator"

What, if anything, did the ruling class do to save itself in the aftermath of Black Saturday? The recipe for stability as Egypt emerged from the violence of the late 1940s had been a national unity coalition, when that failed, Wafdist rule. Between January 27 and July 23, 1952, the palace entrusted three independents with the task of restoring order and holding the political system in check. In the short run this entailed imposing emergency measures; ultimately, it meant bringing the economy under control, instituting social reforms, cleaning up government, and, not least, securing the evacuation of British forces from Egyptian soil.

Reflecting the prevailing sense of urgency, Egyptians referred to the postfire governments as "salvation ministries" (wizarat al-inqadh). The failures of each ministry reveal much about the ills of Egyptian liberalism in the waning days of the old regime. Each of the three prime ministers—'Ali Mahir (January 27–March 1), Ahmad Nagib al-Hilali (March 2–June 29; July 22–23), and Husayn Sirri (July 2–20)—isolated symptoms of the disease, but political constraints dictated their strategies, causing them to shorten their sights. By their actions and ignominious falls, each reinforced a growing disillusion within Egypt with parliamentary rule and its practitioners.[65]

The rhetoric of the period after January 26 reflects a growing despair among those committed to reforming the political order. Even as the "popular struggle" raged in the Canal Zone, a cause few dared criticize openly, some political leaders and members of the intelligentsia argued that Egypt should postpone the liberation struggle and direct its energies toward setting its own house in order. As a precondition to independence, they advocated a campaign of "purification" (al-tathir), a major overhaul of the political system and a purge of its leadership. Some argued that the situation called for a "just tyrant" (al-musta'bid al-'adil), a strongman who could stabilize and reform the political order without facing the constraints of party politics and parliamentary democracy.[66]

The reform-minded focused their sights upon the governmental process. Some asserted that the 1923 Constitution needed to be scrapped and rewritten in toto. Most agreed, at a minimum, that the election law needed revision. Proposed ethics legislation to mandate "purification" aimed at two primary targets. Reformers sought to eliminate immunity provisions that protected former ministers from prosecution and sought legal means to overhaul a government bureaucracy overweight with patronage workers. No such ethics legislation, reformers argued, could be enacted so long as partisan politics dominated the legislature.

The hopes of such reformers rested largely with the two men Farouk called upon to lead the country in the aftermath of the Cairo fire. 'Ali Mahir and Nagib al-Hilali had established reputations as reformers. Both had held cabinet posts, and Mahir had been prime minister twice, for a little over three months in 1936 and in 1939–1940. At one time one of Farouk's most influential teachers, Mahir had grown disillusioned with student and palace. Confined to the sidelines by the British since 1940, Mahir sought to curry favor with his antagonists in the postwar period. In the late 1940s he gathered around him a group of technocrats, collectively known as the Egyptian Bloc (Jabhat Misr), who advocated a program of bureaucratic reform.[67]

Hilali, an academic, joined the Wafd in the late 1930s. Close to Makram 'Ubayd, he inherited the latter's mantle as conscience of the party after 'Ubayd's ouster. Himself disillusioned, Hilali had rejected offers to join the 1950 cabinet, then finally lost his faith in the party. His opposition to the government's abrogation of the Anglo-Egyptian treaty led to his expulsion from the Wafd in November 1951. Thereafter, Hilali cultivated ties with the respectable faction of palace advisors, and a group of independent reformers with a decidedly anti-Wafdist orientation, including former protégés from the 1950 government.[68]

Mahir, who took office the day after Black Saturday—Hilali refused the king's offer—assembled a cabinet of technocrats and moved quickly to restore order and rein in prices. He initiated a series of measures to promote social welfare, creating a ministry of rural affairs and charging it to study proposals for land reform. By early February, curfew restrictions were lifted, and shops and schools functioned normally.[69] To some, Mahir appeared the ideal candidate for benevolent strongman. "Egypt is in temporary need of a dictator," Ihsan 'Abd al-Quddus wrote in early February. One who will act "for the people, not against them, for and not against freedom; a dictator who will push Egypt forward and not hold her back." The cartoon on the cover of *Ruz al-Yusuf* that week depicted 'Ali Mahir standing over a boiling pot exhorting party leaders, still at one another's throats, to stop their personal quarrels. A week later, a cartoon on the inside was less symbolic: the same politicians engaged in fisticuffs while Cairo burned in the background.[70]

Caught between the volatile forces of Egyptian politics, Mahir shunned his reputation as an unscrupulous strongman and assumed the role of mediator. Recognizing the hostility he faced from the palace, he turned to the Wafd, seeking détente. The majority party declined his offer of several cabinet seats but pledged cautious support. Disdaining the current vocabulary of "purification," a phrase heavy with partisan implications, Mahir instead proposed establishment of a national unity shadow cabinet. The prime minister staked his future on reaching an agreement with the British, pledging to do so within three months' time.[71]

Traditional party politics and British hostility killed Mahir's hopes. His treating with the Wafd alienated the minority parties and strengthened Farouk's resolve to finish with him as soon as possible. The parties scorned his invitations to join a unity front that included the Wafd. They and the palace pressed him to dissolve parliament and release an Interior Ministry report that implicated the Wafd for negligence in handling the Black Saturday disturbances. Mahir steadfastly refused.[72]

Although he approached the treaty question without the defiant tone of the Wafd, Mahir was distrusted by the British. Faced with Mahir's inability to coexist with the king, the British ambassador acquiesced in, and even played a role in, Farouk's scheme to force the prime minister's resignation. On March 1, without Mahir's authorization, the press announced a government decision to adjourn parliament for one month. That day two palace loyalists, Murtada al-Maraghi (interior) and Zaki 'Abd al-Mut'al (finance), quit the cabinet. The same day, at the request of Hafiz 'Afifi, chief of the Royal Cabinet, the British ambassador, citing a bad cold, postponed a meeting scheduled with Mahir in which the two were to discuss the resumption of Anglo-Egyptian treaty negotiations. Citing "obstacles placed in the way of my duty," the prime minister resigned.[73] Mahir, who had proven to be "by temperament a negotiator, not a dictator," left office bitter, but in the eyes of many a rare hero of Egyptian political life.[74]

Nagib al-Hilali succeeded Mahir and immediately embarked on a policy diametrically opposed to that of his predecessor. Postponing treaty negotiations, he decreed tough new "illegal-gains" legislation and created "purge committees" to supervise an overhauling of the bureaucracy. Hilali proved to be more of a tyrant than 'Ali Mahir, but a decidedly unjust one. The selective manner in which he pursued his purge reflected Hilali's bitterness against his former Wafdist colleagues. In mid-March, under martial law provisions that remained in force from the previous January, he placed Fu'ad Sirag al-Din and 'Abd al-Fattah Hasan under house arrest. A week later he dissolved parliament, something Mahir had refused to countenance. He set elections for May; in April he postponed them indefinitely. The Wafd, which had looked forward to an electoral victory, initiated a campaign of agitation against the regime.[75]

Hilali's policies also drew a flurry of criticism from circles that could hardly be considered sympathetic to Wafdist leadership. Ihsan 'Abd al-Quddus called on the prime minister to abandon his vendetta and enact a program of true reform. "Corruption does not mean corruption of the Wafd government alone," 'Abd al-Quddus protested in early March. Echoing the policy recently adopted by 'Ali Mahir, his candidate, he pointed to the British presence as the primary cause of corruption. "How," he asked, "can government be clean in an occupied land?"[76] Three weeks later he called upon Hilali to lift martial law. The just tyrant, he argued, does not need to rule by emergency decrees. While he does, he will never be a popular hero, and "the man who cannot be a popular hero does not deserve to be prime minister."[77]

As it had with Mahir, the palace engineered Hilali's downfall. However fierce his vendetta against the Wafd, the reformer's eyes eventually turned toward the palace. The talk over tea in Cairo was that Ahmad 'Abbud, the pro-Wafdist industrialist, paid Farouk £E 1,000,000 to unseat the prime minister. 'Abbud supposedly arranged the transaction with Karim Thabit and Elias Andraos, prime targets for any purge. Jefferson Caffery accepted the spirit, if not the letter of the charges. Both Thabit and Andraos had approached the U.S. ambassador seeking his blessing for Hilali's ouster. Word had it that Hilali planned to break 'Abbud's sugar monopoly and collect £E 5,000,000 in back taxes. Caffery credited Hilali with sensing that his position was untenable and seizing the opportunity to resign, which he did on June 29, while his honor remained intact.[78] Whether the story of money exchanging hands was true or not hardly mattered; the simple fact that so many believed it to be so is commentary enough on the political climate of the country on the eve of the Free Officers' takeover.

On July 2, after a four-day search for a replacement, Farouk appointed Husayn Sirri, the man who had supervised the 1950 elections too fairly, to head the government. Sirri boasted to the U.S. ambassador that, unlike his previous two tenures, this time his would not be merely a caretaker government. He informed Fu'ad Sirag al-Din, whom he released from house arrest at court order—and on promise of good behavior—that he did not intend to lift martial law or call elections in the near future.[79] Sirri's aspirations to be a just tyrant were, however, doomed from the start. As a palace man, an Anglophile, and a close associate of 'Abbud, the man believed responsible for Hilali's downfall, Sirri found himself entangled in an impossible web of intrigue and competing interests. Despite the untainted reputations of most of his ministers, without strong support from the palace, Sirri's government could not and did not last.

For the moment, the Wafd declared a truce with the new government. Several weeks after Sirri assumed office, Sirag al-Din and Nahhas both left for Europe, ostensibly for reasons of health. Sirag al-Din chose a vacation abroad rather than a return to house arrest; upon his release, Sirri had warned him to act judiciously, but he had failed to do so. Before his departure, on July 14, Sirag al-Din reminded the prime minister that the Wafd opposed negotiations with Britain, but wished Sirri well if he should choose to try. Nahhas spoke somewhat more firmly on the Wafd's desire for elections in the near future. He sailed for Europe one day before Sirri resigned. [80]

Prophetically, stirrings of dissent in the officer corps precipitated Sirri's downfall. In January, in a dramatic election, an opposition slate sponsored by the Free Officers had seized control of the Officers Club governing board. In mid-July Farouk responded by annulling the election and appointing his own men to the board. With a crisis brewing, Sirri offered the War Ministry to Brigadier General Muhammad Nagib, whom the dissidents had elected club president. Nagib refused and on July 20, after failing to persuade Farouk to adopt a more conciliatory pose toward the army, Sirri resigned. [81]

Farouk turned again to Hilali. He did so, said Jefferson Caffery, to silence allegations that he had deposed Hilali for bounty three weeks earlier. [82] The stubborn reformer approached his second summons with a greater resolve to confront the palace. As his conditions for accepting the job he demanded total freedom to select a cabinet and a promise that Farouk's inner circle would be purged. Yet, when at the last minute Farouk nominated his own brother-in-law as war minister, Hilali acquiesced. The dispute was irrelevant. Six days before Hilali's appointment the Free Officers had determined to move. The new cabinet took the oath of office on July 22. The next morning the king, under orders from the army, asked Hilali to submit his resignation.

Hilali's dilemma, the passion for reform and the willingness to compromise with the palace, highlights the crisis of Egyptian liberalism in its waning hours. Hilali believed that without fundamental restructuring of the political system, parliamentary rule could no longer work. It could neither free Egypt from foreign occupation, nor build a strong national economy, nor promulgate social reforms needed to stave off disorder in the streets.

The real crisis of liberalism in Egypt was that the structure of the political system and the dynamics of politics effectively undermined any substantive political reform. The electoral gulf between the Wafd and minority parties fostered an enmity that precluded cooperation. The constitutional prerogative of the throne allowed the palace to deny power to the former and coopt the latter. Egypt's political elites talked reform, but too many refused to sacrifice partisan and personal interests. The most able men in the country remained on the fringes of power.

Neither Hilali nor Mahir, men with no political bases but with rare reputations for integrity, would have become prime minister had not confidence in the system been so shaken. Their failures underline the bankruptcy of the just-tyranny idea. Of the two, Mahir was more the political animal, shrewd and unscrupulous. However, he assumed the role of mediator and guarantor of parliamentary life. Hilali, despite his oft-stated aversion to martial law, proved the more eager tyrant. The minority parties shattered Mahir's plans for a unity coalition; the Wafd, reinvigorated by Hilali's policies, drove him on the defensive. Farouk's cronies ultimately brought both down. The British and U.S. embassies, at best, turned a blind eye toward palace intrigue, at worst cooperated or allowed themselves to be used.

Myth of the Savior

"From Montazeh to Ras el Tin the Egyptian caravan of Pashas, procurers, politicians and eavesdroppers wandered aimlessly. It was obviously the end, a golden death agony on the beach."[83] The image became seared into the Egyptian consciousness. Farouk dining and Sirag al-Din purchasing property while Cairo burned, Nahhas and Sirag al-Din gracelessly departing Egypt, Hilali bowing shamelessly to Farouk's whims, Sirri dreaming of rising above his calling as caretaker.

How could Egypt's political establishment depart for European spas and Alexandrian casinos in the summer of 1952? For those who remained loyal to the liberal ethos, a myth of the savior prevailed. One more candidate always stood in the wings awaiting the call. The list grew shorter, but it always remained longer than the sight of those who refused to come to terms with the system's failure.

Despite his grandiose plans, no one gave Sirri much time, the summer at most. It had taken him four days to form a government. Three weeks later Farouk hesitated to accept his resignation. The leading candidate at the time seemed to be Murtada al-Maraghi, minister of interior in the Mahir and Hilali postfire cabinets. Passed over in early July, Maraghi represented, in Jefferson Caffery's estimate, Farouk's "last card." That the king instead turned back to Hilali pointed to Farouk's realization, in a moment of sober judgment, that somehow he needed to restore his credibility. He would save Maraghi for the last resort, for a crisis that required the imposition of an iron grip. "If Maraghi fails," Caffery predicted, "the fireworks will begin."[84]

Implicit in the savior myth was a steadfast belief that the army posed no threat to the political establishment. Stirrings of rebellion within the military had been noted, filed, and dismissed with relative nonchalance until mid-July, when the king had moved to regain control of the Officers Club. Even then, Farouk acted without fully comprehending the degree of opposition he faced. Sirri deserves some credit for his intuition, but after a feeble attempt to force the issue with Farouk he chose to walk away. Murtada al-Marahgi, like so many others, declares that he saw the handwriting on the wall, but they were all caught off guard when the army moved.[85] The Free Officers' rising, in the early morning hours of July 23, added an entirely new contingent to the political battlefield, one not entirely unexpected, but one for which no establishment force had made any plans.

Myths often die hard, but they may be adapted to changing circumstances. The Free Officers aimed to inject new life into the political order, not topple it. If many greeted the officers as conquering heroes, it was because all previous heroes, including those whose reputations remained somewhat intact, had failed. Similarly, many who cheered the army's rising did so not in the name of revolution but of stability. Disaffected liberals, progressives, communists, and Muslim Brothers constructed a new savior myth, one that would exert a profound influence on the future: that a military junta would, after imposing constitutional reform, restore parliamentary life and then return to the barracks. At long last, thought many, Egypt had found its "just tyrant."

2

"The People's Army"

The junior officers who seized power on July 23, 1952, acted out of a conviction that only the army could arrest the decay of the political order and, in so doing, save the nation. The pashas had misruled Egypt, accrued fantastic personal gain, but ignored the woes of the common man and failed to end the occupation. Rather than building a strong national military and mobilizing against the occupier, politicians had sent a ragtag army, ill equipped and poorly led, to defeat in Palestine. The Free Officers, ashamed and bitter soldiers, rose in rebellion to oust "Egyptian traitors" who, by their corruption and self-interest, stood in league with the "imperialists."

By July 1952 a Rubicon had been crossed, a readiness to carry out a coup d'état in the name of corps and country. The Free Officers' movement was the culmination of a dramatic political reorientation that took place in the officer corps between 1936 and 1952. Little more than a local constabulary, an appendage of the British occupation force, in 1936 the army became the domain of the Egyptian government. The officer corps, so long dominated by families with a tradition of military service, opened its ranks to a broader pool of ambitious recruits. The young men who entered the military academy in the years after 1936, schooled in the streets against British rule, brought nationalist politics into the military. The Free Officers represented the generation that turned away from the political establishment and rejected the leadership of its elders. They went through the same paroxysms, joined the same political movements, and shared the same disappointments as their civilian contemporaries. After the Second World War Egyptian officers joined secret cells organized by the Muslim Brothers and communist organizations. As soldiers, they developed a network of links and a spirit of camaraderie; the specific, even parochial concerns of the soldier reinforced natural bonds formed in the ranks. The relationship of the soldier to his country, to his people, to his commanding officers and king gave the young officers a particular perspective on the decay of the liberal order.

To what extent did the Free Officers form, during the conspiratorial stage, a political ethos that inclined them toward intervention in civilian politics? The Free Officers' movement, founded in late 1949, differed from others in the military in one important respect: the Free Officers remained steadfastly independent of any particular political ideology, party, or leader. Most of the founders of the movement were at one time members or associ- ates of the Brotherhood; some were communists. These ties raise natural questions about the ideological influence of these movements upon the Free Officers, as well as questions of political affinity, collaboration and, finally, betrayal.

"Soldiers of the Free Army"

Once before, the military had risen to intervene in national politics. The movement associated with Colonel Ahmad 'Urabi in 1881–1882 brought together a coalition of discontented Egyptian officers, provincial notables, and a proconstitutionalist urban intelligentsia. The officers' grievances stemmed from their rivalry with a Turco-Circassian ruling elite that domi- nated the higher ranks of the corps. Egyptian officers who filled the ranks of an expanding army during the reign of Sa'id (1854–1863) found promotion difficult under his successor, Isma'il (1863–1879). The highest ranks re- mained completely inaccessible. Under Tawfiq (1879–1892) matters came to a head. Pressed by the army and its allies, the khedive granted Egypt a parliament and, in February 1882, named 'Urabi's comrade, Mahmud Sami al-Barudi, prime minister. 'Urabi, appointed war minister, acted swiftly to address the grievances of the Egyptian officers. He sacked 40 Turco- Circassian officers, promoted 400 Egyptians, and elevated 150 sergeants into the officer corps. In addition, he ordered major salary raises for all ranks, with the largest increases decreed for junior officers.[1]

The British occupation, commenced in July 1882, ended 'Urabi's rule and brought the Egyptian army under foreign control. The British ordered Egyp- tian troops out of the Sudan and reduced their numbers, which had sur- passed eighty thousand by the late 1870s, to six thousand. In subsequent years the army grew, reaching sixteen thousand men by the early 1900s and falling slightly thereafter. A British officer, the sirdar, served as commander in chief. In 1905 British officers made up one-ninth of the officer corps; until 1922 they commanded down to battalion level. The Egyptian army remained little more than a constabulary, capable of quelling internal disorder and relieving British troops from their more tedious duties.[2]

Throughout the first decades of the occupation Egyptian nationalists con- sistently demanded sovereignty over the armed forces. The Wafd govern- ment elected in 1924 pressed legislation to reduce the number of British officers supervising the army. In November the assassination by Wafdists of the sirdar precipitated the government's downfall. The series of minority leaders who followed adopted a more moderate line, trying to coax the British to downgrade the status of its forces to a military mission. The Brit- ish, who had already cut back the extent of their command, changed the title of sirdar to inspector general. After 1924 only one British officer commanded a fighting unit.[3]

The 1936 Anglo-Egyptian treaty granted Egypt sovereignty over the military, but the British would remain. The treaty, which provided for an occupation force of 10,000 men in the Suez Canal Zone, granted Britain the right to reoccupy the country in the event of an international crisis. The Egyptian army still relied on the British for training and supplies. In January 1937 Britain sent a military mission comprising 32 officers and noncommissioned officers to Egypt. By 1939 the mission reached 51 officers and 98 noncoms. In exchange, Egyptian officers went to study at British military academies. In 1937, with British assistance, the army established training schools for officers in artillery, armor, light armaments, and military engineering, and founded a staff college. The first class entered the staff college in October 1938 and graduated the following June. By 1944 seven classes, each numbering approximately 20 students, had passed through the college. By 1947 the army had 188 staff officers. [4]

Free from the constraints previously imposed by the British, successive Egyptian governments increased the military budget and bolstered the ranks at all levels. In 1936 the armed forces consisted of 398 officers and 11,991 noncoms and enlisted men. The numbers soon reached 982 and 20,783, respectively. To bolster the officer corps, the high command doubled the size of the yearly entering class in the military academy from 150 to 300 cadets and shortened the course of study from nearly two years to twelve months. [5]

With the outbreak of the Second World War the army again became a source of diplomatic strife between Egypt and Britain. 'Ali Mahir's reluctance to declare war on the Axis led to his dismissal, at British behest, in June 1940. In October the British pressed Farouk to retire the popular nationalist general 'Aziz al-Misri, and ordered Egyptian troops to withdraw from key positions along the Libyan border and Mediterranean coast west of Alexandria, and to surrender arms and equipment to the British army. After taking power in February 1942, the Wafd, bowing to further British pressure, removed another popular officer, 'Abd al-Rahman 'Azzam, from command of the Territorial Army, put 'Ali Mahir under house arrest, and arrested Mahir's former war minister, Salih Harb.

After the war British troops withdrew to the Canal Zone, while successive Egyptian governments acted to expand and modernize the military. In 1947 the Nuqrashi government outlawed the "badal," a deferment fee by which those eligible for conscription could legally avoid serving in the army. The fee had promoted a system in which those most qualified to serve bought their way out of military duty. During the war years 40 percent of those eligible purchased exemptions, 90 percent of all conscripts were illiterate, and crime within the ranks flourished. In addition, Nuqrashi moved to phase out the British mission, a policy that the British reluctantly admitted they had no legal grounds to contest. In April 1947 Nuqrashi sent a delegation to the United States to explore possibilities of purchasing arms and arranging for a U.S. military mission. In 1951 the Wafd government, initially without British knowledge, sent another mission to Europe in search of arms. [6]

The founders of the Free Officers' movement and most of those who composed its inner circle all entered the academy between 1937 and 1939. The second rank of the movement, the bulk of membership, followed them in the early 1940s. These officers, the first products of the expanded military academy, stood apart from their predecessors in background, aptitude, and commitment. The latter mostly came from families with a tradition of military service. Those who made a career of the army advanced slowly until they had reached a comfortable niche. Those who did not advance had little incentive to remain in uniform longer than the mandatory five years of service.[7] Of junior officers who entered the academy prior to 1936, few became involved in political activity. Two who collaborated with the Free Officers, Rashad Mahanna and Yusuf Siddiq, were rare exceptions.

To solidify their populist base, the Nasserist officers in power portrayed themselves as representatives of the lower middle class, stressing ties to the countryside, however long ago they had left it. Anwar al-Sadat's pilgrimages, while president, to his ancestral village, Mit Abu al-Kum, are perhaps most familiar, but his were not the first. The image could be propagated in part because Nasser himself, the son of a petty bureaucrat in the postal administration, Sadat, and some others did come from a lower rung of the middle class. Many of their closest colleagues, however, came from richer backgrounds, and some were considerably more well-off. 'Abd al-Latif al-Baghdadi and 'Abd al-Hakim 'Amr were sons of village notables. Husayn al-Shafi'i's father was an architect; his father-in-law, the mayor of the Delta city Tanta. Tharwat 'Ukashah's father was an officer. Zakariya and Khalid Muhyi al-Din, cousins, came from a family with sizeable landholdings in the Delta.

The officers represented Egypt's middle class only in the broadest sense, the intermediate stratum between peasant (and worker) and aristocrat. To enter the military academy a cadet had to pay £E 60 in tuition, a heavy burden on a middle-income recipient (the average monthly income of a university graduate was £E 8 at the time).[8] They came, as Eliezar Be'eri indicates,

> for the most part from well-to-do families, some from the wealthy and upper classes, some from the middle and lower-middle classes. Most came from families whose income was their salaries; many came from families whose revenues derived from rents, particularly from land; many others from families whose members engaged in the free professions; while only a few came from families of capitalists, industrialists and businessmen. There were no officers who were members of Egypt's top social "aristocracy"; neither were there any from the great rural and urban masses.[9]

Be'eri bases his assessment on a list of eighty-seven officers killed in the Palestine campaign. The backgrounds of leaders of the Free Officers' movement support his thesis. Ahmad Hamrush presents fathers' occupations for thirty-five officers. The list includes nine government officials (inspectors, counsellors, and so on), eight landowners, three officers, three village notables, three engineers, two judges, two lawyers, two businessmen, and one teacher, journalist, and politician.[10]

Because of their background, attitudes, and political activism, the officers have been called an "intelligentsia in khaki." Born in the years just prior to and following the 1919 uprising, they were raised on stories of Zaghlul and the Wafd. They attended secondary school in the mid-1930s, when a national front restored the 1923 Constitution, Young Egypt's Green Shirts fought Wafdist Blue Shirts in the streets, and the Muslim Brotherhood spread rapidly throughout the country. They came from the same broad social stratum as their contemporaries who went to university and graduated into the professions. Nasser studied law for one term. 'Amr enrolled in the agriculture faculty before entering the army. If study bored them, if they found themselves too easily distracted, that is more a reflection of the times than a lack of personal motivation. [11]

Handicapped by inadequate training and equipment, the overall quality of the Egyptian army remained poor. In 1945 British military experts noted a lack of morale among junior officers, a lack of solidarity between officer and foot soldier, and a general slothfulness in the officer corps. [12] By the early 1950s little had changed. British analysts judged the Egyptian army capable of mounting a spirited defense but unable to sustain an offensive campaign. Maneuvers monitored by the British in late 1954 "did not suggest in any way that the capabilities of the Egyptian Army are higher than our present low estimation."[13]

All this considered, within the limits of their training the new junior officers were as a group certainly more skilled than their superiors. Five members of the Free Officers' inner circle—Nasser, Salah Salim, Zakariya Muhyi al-Din, 'Abd al-Hakim 'Amr, and Tharwat 'Ukashah—attended the staff college, indicating they stood at the top of their classes, the top 10 percent by 1947. Some went on to become instructors in the military academy. At the same time, because the pool of officers was small, promotions were accelerated. An average officer of the previous generation became a colonel at age forty-seven, after twenty-six years of service; those of the 1936 generation attained the same rank in their mid-thirties, after little over ten years service. [14]

The foundations of a political ethos, a belief in a role that the army could and must play, grew out of the influx of politicized young cadets into the military academy and the tremendous pressures they faced both as officers and Egyptians during their years of training and apprenticeship. The army provided them a unique focus for their patriotism and political dissent. Like-minded officers sought out one another and widened their circles. The élan of the ranks would be their base, the mess and the bivouac their rostrum. These initial contacts fostered a network that would withstand the disruptions of transfer, war, and, in some cases, arrest. That network would expand over the years as the officers rose in the ranks, commanded those who followed them into the academy, and those who studied under them when they became instructors in the staff college and field schools. [15]

The experience of the Egyptian army during the Second World War fostered nascent political activity in the ranks. When the British ordered

Egyptian troops in the Western Desert to turn over arms and equipment, some officers refused. Rommel's advance to the outskirts of Alexandria by June 1941 generated hopes of a German victory, and inspired endeavors to assist in defeating the British. The exploits of Anwar al-Sadat and comrades are well known, primarily due to Sadat's own accounts. Their ill-starred efforts to smuggle 'Aziz al-Misri out of Egypt and their subsequent liaison with the German spy Eppler landed the conspirators in jail. The British imposition of the Wafd at gunpoint in February 1942 left many officers ashamed of their uniform, and another flurry of scattered activity began. Politicized junior officers rallied around the king, decrying the Wafd's "treachery" and pondering ways to demonstrate loyalty to the throne.[16]

In the postwar period small-scale activity escalated. Cliques of officers attempted a series of political assassinations, most of which failed, and carried out acts of sabotage. Pamphleteering within the ranks provided another outlet for nationalist activity. Dissident officers directed their leaflets primarily against unpopular senior officers. Others targeted the British military mission, which they accused of providing Egypt with low-quality armaments and minimal training in a deliberate attempt to dominate the Egyptian armed forces. Military authorities arrested known troublemakers, but often sent them off with a hand slap. Several spent time in prison, including Sadat, who served two terms.[17]

The recurrence of the same names among those groups known by the authorities suggests that a small clique of officers, perhaps not more than twenty-five, participated in such activities. These officers constructed no secret society in any meaningful or lasting sense. They came from a variety of corps and never intended to give any organizational structure to their activism. Nor did they reflect any specific ideological direction. A group of eighteen junior officers arrested in July 1947, charged with planning to kill the chief of staff and install 'Aziz al-Misri by coup d'état, has been described as communist.[18] The group's ringleader, Colonel Mustafa Kamal Sidqi, an adventurer and philanderer, may be considered at best a pseudo-Marxist. His circle in 1947 did include Ahmad Fu'ad, a young reserve officer who later became a DMNL leader. But the group also included officers hostile to communism, such as 'Abd al-Mun'im 'Abd al-Ra'uf, a Muslim Brother, and Rashad Mahanna, whose sympathies lay with the Brotherhood. The broader social ideas contained in leaflets spread by the Kamal Sidqi circle expressed the general reformist outlook prevalent at the time. As such, Marxists, Muslim Brothers, and their sympathizers could easily support the expressed goals of the clique.

While these circles of dissident officers continued to attract the attention of the high command, beneath the surface more serious and far-reaching developments passed largely unnoticed or ignored. In the early 1940s the Muslim Brotherhood began recruiting junior officers into its secret organization. The Brotherhood's success at recruiting within the officer corps reflected its domination of popular opposition in the country at large, particularly after February 1942. A series of leaflets in the name of "Soldiers of the

Free Army" (Junud al-Jaysh al-Ahrar) that circulated in 1941 and early 1942 contained clear religious references but stressed national issues and called upon the nation to arm its soldiers for the battle against the occupier.[19] Nasser, 'Amr, Khalid Muhyi al-Din, Hasan Ibrahim, and others joined the secret organization in 1943–1944. In 1944 the Guidance Council authorized the creation of cells in the army and police autonomous from the secret organization. Hasan al-Banna charged Salah Shadi, a young police officer, with supervising the police cells. The army he delegated to Mahmud Labib, a retired major and old warrior from the Ottoman army.[20]

Under Labib's lead the Brotherhood spread widely through the officer corps. With the general guide's approval, Labib did not require membership in the Brotherhood as prerequisite to joining his organization. He deemed it more important to attract politicized officers, hoping that with time he might enlist them in the movement.[21] In one of these cells Nasser, Khalid Muhyi al-Din, Kamal al-Din Husayn, 'Abd al-Mun'im 'Abd al-Ra'uf, and several other officers met in one another's homes on a weekly basis from 1945 to 1948. They discussed politics and their role in the national liberation struggle far more than religion. They also circulated pamphlets, some in the name of the "Free Officers" (Al-Dubat al-Ahrar), in which they asserted the solidarity of the army with other nationalist forces.[22]

By 1948 much of this activity lapsed. The successful crackdown on the Kamal Sidqi circle in 1947 led to a general abeyance of pamphleteering. With the onset of the Palestine campaign and the government's proscription of the Brotherhood, its secret cells in the army disbanded. Those officers who stayed in contact did so on a purely personal basis. Many, such as Baghdadi, Hasan Ibrahim, Kamal Husayn, and 'Abd al-Ra'uf joined irregular units formed by the Brotherhood to fight on the Syrian and Jordanian fronts. The high command permitted these officers to resign their commissions temporarily; when Egypt entered the war, they returned to their units. Others, including Nasser, secretly helped train irregulars.

The Egyptian army saw its first real combat in the 1948 war, a conflict for which it was ill prepared. This baptism under fire steeled a growing feeling among those in the middle levels of command that they had been sacrificed for devious ends, sent off to battle as a result of internal political wrangling and abandoned to defeat with faulty equipment while those in high places turned a handsome profit on the arms market. The experience profoundly affected those who commanded units in Palestine. The admonition of Nasser's dying comrade, Ahmad 'Abd al-'Aziz, that the "biggest battlefield is in Egypt," perhaps apocryphal, captures succinctly the officers' sense of betrayal.[23] Many returned home committed to pursuing fundamental changes in the military.

For those not committed ideologically to its program, the Muslim Brotherhood had lost much of its appeal in the aftermath of Palestine. Power struggles within the movement, the reckless adventurism of the secret organization, the cycle of violence preceding and following the Brotherhood's abolition in December 1948, and the leadership vacuum that resulted from

Banna's death the following February all contributed to a sense of disillusion. Security also posed a serious problem. Police crackdowns indicated that little of the secret organization, military or civilian, remained secret. Some, like Khalid Muhyi al-Din had converted to Marxism. Finally, Mahmud Labib had fallen ill (he died in 1951.) Without his strong, personal stamp of leadership, many officers drifted away.[24]

The Brotherhood's organization in the army by no means collapsed. Those officers who remained dedicated to its credo regrouped under new leaders. Like the Free Officers, they aided and abetted irregular units carrying out guerilla activities against the British in the Canal Zone during the "popular struggle" in 1951–1952.[25] The number of officers linked to Brotherhood cells far outnumbered both Free Officers and communists.[26] Yet, tied as they were to the central civilian leadership, the Brothers' military cells, like the movement as a whole, drifted without clear direction.

Communism, which spread slowly in the army in the early 1940s, began to achieve a significant inroad following the Second World War. Communism first took hold not within the officer corps but among noncommissioned officers and technical personnel. A group of approximately forty air force mechanics, aligned with the Egyptian Movement for National Liberation (Al-Harakah al-Misriyah lil-Tahrir al-Watani; the EMNL), the ideological precursor of the DMNL, formed the first noteworthy organization.[27] After its formation in 1947, the DMNL organized more widespread and centralized communist activity in the army. In 1950, after the release from prison of its civilian leadership, the DMNL central committee delegated as liaison a reserve officer and member of the civilian leadership council, Ahmad Fu'ad (previously cited for links to the Kamal Sidqi circle). He coordinated the activities of the military wing in coordination with Ahmad Hamrush, an artillery officer, and Shawqi Fahmi Husayn, a sergeant and founder of the original air force mechanics group. At the time of the Free Officers' coup, the DMNL military wing numbered sixty to seventy officers.[28]

As with the Muslim Brotherhood, the DMNL central committee supervised the movement's military wing. Civilian leaders, who rejected the notion that the army had a special vanguard role to play by itself, did not aim toward an eventual coup d'état. Nonetheless, unlike the ECP and other groups that viewed the army as an arm of the state and thus an inherently repressive force, the DMNL deemed the army as potentially a positive force in the nationalist struggle. For this reason, DMNL leaders encouraged cooperation between its military wing and the Free Officers, and collaborated in the printing and dissemination of leaflets.[29]

"Rally Around the Free Officers"

The Free Officers' resolve to retain autonomy from all other forces in the country defined the difference between their organization and others in the military, and shaped their vision of a political role for the army. They shared with their civilian contemporaries disillusion with the existing political order. Beyond that, as soldiers they harbored specific grievances. They had joined the military to defend their country and been unable to do so, held back, they believed, by their own leaders. Their experiences under fire in Palestine sharpened their focus on the army, their duties as soldiers, and their unique potential for action. Notions of a political role remained vague, but now the army stood at the center of their thinking.

The Free Officers' resolution to remain independent from other political forces has commonly been perceived as a tacit agreement to minimize the potentially divisive effects of conflicting political loyalties. This view accentuates differences in political and religious temperament that, while always present, emerged as problems after the coup but never really caused trouble in the conspiratorial stage. The overemphasis on personal differences and the unfortunate tendency to divide the movement's leaders into political factions betray a misunderstanding of the group's dynamics and fail to capture the movement's true spirit, the camaraderie that bonded the officers to one another and to their leader, Gamal Abdel Nasser.

The nucleus of the Free movement coalesced in late 1949. The founders all credit Nasser with bringing them together and instigating formation of a new movement. It is noteworthy that Nasser turned first to four comrades from his cell in the Muslim Brotherhood: 'Abd al-Mun'im 'Abd al-Ra'uf, Hasan Ibrahim, Khalid Muhyi al-Din, and Kamal al-Din Husayn. The core group quickly expanded to include Baghdadi, 'Amr, and Salah Salim by October 1949. These eight appointed themselves the executive committee, determined that all policy decisions would be put to a vote, and elected Nasser president. They resolved to undertake a propaganda campaign and vaguely discussed the eventuality of a coup d'état, a step that none anticipated taking for at least five or six years.[30]

The movement's organization reflected its specific military orientation. Unlike the Muslim Brothers or DMNL, whose cells cut across military branches, the Free Officers founded their strength on a sense of camaraderie within each corps. As it grew, the executive committee also tried to maintain a parity between members of different corps. With the addition of Gamal Salim and Anwar al-Sadat in the latter half of 1951, the committee expanded to ten members: Nasser, 'Amr, and 'Abd al-Ra'uf (infantry); Ibrahim, Baghdadi, and Gamal Salim (air force); Husayn and Salah Salim (artillery); Khalid Muhyi al-Din (armor); and Sadat (signal corps). Each committee member was responsible for fixing a chain of command to form autonomous cells within his corps.

This pyramidal structure fostered an esprit de corps within each branch. As battlefield commanders in Palestine, the movement's founders had come into contact with younger officers whom they now recruited. As instructors in the staff college after the war, they found themselves separated from their units. Therefore, finding close colleagues who had direct contact with the troops became a top priority. Gradually, the inner circle of the movement expanded. An operational command evolved parallel to the executive committee. These officers maintained contact with the second-line officers who constituted the operational command within each corps but played no role in political discussions of the executive committee before the coup.

In fact, few Free Officers knew who stood atop the pyramid and directed the movement's activities. Tharwat 'Ukashah says he knew Nasser led the movement but knew nothing of its organization. Husayn al-Shafi'i first realized Nasser headed the movement in September 1951. He recalls a long political conversation in his office at general headquarters initiated by Nasser, whom he first met in 1945–1946. What Shafi'i assumed was a chance encounter may well have been a recruiting mission, for that afternoon 'Ukashah and another officer informed Shafi'i that he had been selected to command Free Officers in the armor corps. Zakariya Muhyi al-Din, an architect of the plan to seize power and who was intimately involved with events in the days prior to the coup, declares he knew nothing of the existence of an executive committee separate from the operational command until after the takeover.[31]

By the time of the coup the movement numbered ninety to one hundred officers recruited in every branch of the services except the navy.[32] The movement apparently managed to avoid infiltration by the secret police. Friends recruited who chose not to join, as well as Muslim Brother or DMNL allies kept silent. Rashad Mahanna, a popular artillery colonel, an older officer with strong nationalist credentials, declined membership and a role in the operational command. Nonetheless, he attended the meeting, in late 1951, in which the Free Officers and allies decided to run an opposition slate for the Officers Club board. Because of his falling out with the officers shortly after the coup, he became a prime culprit in the regime's official history. Yet, for all his later faults the officers could not deny that Mahanna never betrayed them, and that when called upon to act the night of July 23 he responded promptly. Free Officers' leaders approached another older colonel, 'Abd al-Mun'im Amin, the commander of key antiaircraft units, for the first time on July 21. Apprised of the situation, Amin accepted an offer to join the operational command.[33]

By examining the rhetoric espoused in Free Officers' leaflets and by charting the political and military activities of the Officers from 1950 through July 1952, one can trace the ideological development within the executive committee. The picture that emerges is of a highly politicized group with vague notions of a coup d'état at some future date but concerned more immediately with politics in the military. This then raises important questions about the influence of other political movements, to which the officers belonged or with which they collaborated, on their ideological development. As adolescents, the officers had had loyalties, to the extent they can be called such, that reflected the myriad forces of Egyptian politics. Some came from Wafdist families; some had siblings in the Muslim Brotherhood; others attended rallies staged by Young Egypt. In the army, most joined cells sponsored by the Brothers or communist groups; some maintained contact with Axis agents.

Too much may be made of such affiliations. To a great extent these young men followed the flow of the crowd in a turbulent period. In particular, the role of Young Egypt as a major factor in the ideological formation of Nasser and, through him, the Free Officers has been exaggerated. Because of its activist spirit and paramilitary regimentation, Young Egypt attracted many students their age. However, to a large degree that following was passive. Throngs turned out for rallies and swelled the ranks in the streets, but official membership remained minimal. Ahmad Husayn may deserve some credit for encouraging young Egyptians to enter the military, but in terms of ideological content the movement offered little in the 1930s beyond a profound sense of patriotism and hostility to parliamentary parties and institutions. His rhetoric in the late 1940s undoubtedly contributed to the growing disillusion among the officers and furthered ideas of social reform. However, by then many of those who would form the Free Officers had moved on to the Brotherhood or communism.[34]

That the core group came from Brotherhood cells suggests that the ideological ties of most Free Officers leaders to the Brothers had been superficial. Those who had joined the secret organization did so not from deep commitment to an Islamic order; they joined because the Brotherhood provided a structured framework, the best organized at the time, for political expression in the army. The ideals Nasser and his comrades shared with the Brothers, nationalism and a generic sense of social justice that entailed narrowing the gap between social classes, differed little from other reformist forces, whether affiliated with political parties or the antiestablishment. Furthermore, by recruiting sympathizers who did not swear fealty to the movement and directing their focus to national liberation, Mahmud Labib unwittingly nurtured the development of a tightly knit core of officers who would eventually desert the Brotherhood. Whatever the extent of their ties to Labib and the Brothers, those Free Officers founders considered the most sympathetic to Brotherhood aims, with the exception of 'Abd al-Mun'im 'Abd al-Ra'uf (of whom more later), swore ultimate loyalty to a movement in which religion would play no role.[35]

Throughout 1950–1951 the officers remained ambivalent about the political establishment. In a leaflet printed in mid-1950 the Free Officers proclaimed, "The army is the people's army, not the army of any particular individual," and warned the high command that one day those who now followed their orders might cease to do so. They greeted the abrogation of the 1936 treaty with enthusiasm and pledged support for the Nahhas government. Under the guidance of the executive committee, Free Officers trained and fought alongside irregulars. The Wafd's failure to declare all-out war against the British frustrated the officers, who responded with charges of treason in high places. Their rhetoric from late 1951 echoes sentiments from the Palestine War: "Men of the Free Army! The army will never be able to take the lead in its national duty in the struggle against imperialism until it has purged its ranks of traitors, the enemies of the nation!"[36]

Despite their hostility to Wafdist leadership, the Free Officers offered to support the government against common enemies. In early December 1951 emissaries from the executive committee proposed to Fu'ad Sirag al-Din that the Free Officers join the "popular struggle" against the British, and suggested a demonstration of military force should the king turn the Wafd out of office. These discussions never moved beyond the exploratory stage because the interior minister balked at the officers' proposals.[37] But contacts with the Wafd did continue on an operational level. Sirag al-Din aided the officers in the initial phase of a scheme to transport a sea mine to the Canal Zone, where it was buried. The story became a favorite of the officers, but Sirag al-Din's complicity remained veiled. At his trial in late 1953, he tried without success to take credit for the adventure. Baghdadi admitted to the connection for the first time in his memoirs, published in the late 1970s.[38]

In December 1951 the Free Officers executive, in conjunction with other nationalist officers, resolved to run a slate in annual elections to the Officers Club governing board, traditionally controlled by senior officers loyal to the palace. To head the ticket, the officers selected Brigadier Muhammad Nagib. Wounded three times in Palestine and decorated, Nagib was the only senior commander considered a bona fide hero of the war. Nagib, who shared the younger officers' outrage at its conduct, had written a series of anonymous columns for *Ruz al-Yusuf* in which he implicated superior officers for corruption and incompetence. The precipitate decision taken earlier that year by the high command to transfer him from command of the Frontier Corps to make way for General Husayn Sirri 'Amr, the primary target of investigations into arms racketeering during the Palestine War, made Nagib a particularly willing candidate.

The opposition candidates revealed themselves at a tumultuous meeting at the Officers Club in late December, called ostensibly for the purpose of amending club bylaws. Officers entering the hall were handed flyers promoting the alternative slate. The meeting turned chaotic; Rashad Mahanna, an opposition candidate but not a Free Officer, commandeered the microphone and restored order. In the election, held January 3, the dissidents scored a near sweep of the board. Nagib, pitted against three opponents, including the detested Sirri 'Amr, won 75 percent of the vote. On his coattails, five Free Officers captured seats—Zakariya Muhyi al-Din, Hasan Ibrahim, Gamal Himmad, Amin Shakir, and Hamdi 'Ubayd—as did three friends of the movement: Rashad Mahanna, who won the highest percentage of votes, Ibrahim 'Atif, and Galal Nida'. One member of the Free Officers executive, Gamal Salim, failed in his bid.[39]

The Free Officers executive gathered two days later to consider its next move. At the meeting Nasser revealed that in the interim, on January 8, he, along with Hasan Ibrahim, Kamal Rif'at, and Hasan al-Tuhami, staged an unsuccessful attempt on General Sirri 'Amr's life. When his colleagues censured him, he offered to resign, and the matter ended. The executive renounced political assassination as a tactic but apparently took no major decisions with regard to further action.[40]

After Black Saturday, the executive began to consider seriously its political aims in a broader sphere. The committee met the night of the riots. In a leaflet distributed several days later the movement declared:

> The presence of the army in the streets of Cairo is for the purpose of foiling the conspiracies of traitors who seek destruction and devastation. We will not accept a blow against the people. We will not fire one bullet against the people or arrest sincere nationalists. . . . Everyone must understand that we are with the people now and forever, and will answer only the call of the nation. . . . The nation is in danger. Take note of the conspiracies which surround it. Rally around the Free Officers! Victory will come to you and to the people, of which you are an indivisible part![41]

Baghdadi, who argued that the opportunity for an immediate demonstration of force should not be missed, withdrew from the committee when the others rejected his call. He absented himself until July 16, when his colleagues summoned him back. The majority did not expect to take action for at least a year. In the turbulent months that followed, when the political process appeared to grind to a halt, the officers shortened their sights. When Prime Minister Hilali dissolved parliament in March, they resolved that if he did not hold elections by the second week of November, the date on which the Constitution required a new parliament to take its oath, they would organize a show of force.[42]

Even as they contemplated political action, the Free Officers' immediate focus remained fixed on the liberation struggle and the role of the army. In a leaflet critical of Hilali's purges, entitled "A New Coup dÉtat," they accused the prime minister of deflecting attention from the crucial struggle with the British. They proclaimed the Black Saturday riots an imperialist coup. They praised 'Ali Mahir's failed efforts to seek a negotiated settlement and his resistance to pressure from "imperialists and Egyptian traitors" to "utilize martial law to severely punish the people." Hilali they chastised for complicity in a "new coup" against the people. By turning the national movement in on itself, Hilali had "forgotten that the source of the greatest corruption is imperialism, and that the struggle against internal corruption is impossible without rooting out its source."[43]

By the spring of 1952 the Free Officers began to consider seriously a coup d'état. The executive committee created a formal operational command, a separate body charged with responsibility for tactical matters relating to an uprising. They divided the command into two sectors: Cairo, under the direction of Nasser and Zakariya Muhyi al-Din (infantry), Khalid Muhyi al-Din and Shafi'i (armor), Magdi Hasanayn (supply), and Amin Shakir (signal corps); and al-'Arish, directed by Salah Salim (artillery), Gamal Salim (air force), 'Amr, and Yusuf Siddiq (infantry).[44]

The call to arms, when it came, was premature. The Free Officers were still in the process of defining a strategy for long-term action when events forced their hand. On July 16 Farouk ordered the governing board of the Officers Club dissolved. He replaced Muhammad Nagib with his brother, General 'Ali Nagib, a senior officer more of the traditional mold, and appointed a new board to assist him. Fearing arrest, Free Officers leaders acted quickly. On July 18 or 19, after briefly considering killing a group of hostile senior officers, they resolved to stage a coup. They set August 5 as the tentative date, time enough to organize, allow several units that had been ordered home from al-'Arish to arrive, and enable them to collect their paychecks. On July 18 an emissary from Husayn Sirri, offered Muhammad Nagib the war ministry. On July 19 Nagib informed the officers that the high command had a list of their names. On July 20 Ahmad Abu al-Fath informed Tharwat 'Ukashah, his brother-in-law, that the king planned to appoint General Sirri 'Amr war minister with a mandate to root out dissidents within the ranks. Apprised of the situation, the Free Officers executive advanced the date of the coup to the evening of July 21–22, then postponed the operation twenty-four hours in order to allow time to inform colleagues in the 'Arish sector.[45]

Zakariya Muhyi al-Din, 'Amr, and Nasser drew up the plan of attack. Motorized infantry columns under the command of Yusuf Siddiq and Colonel Ahmad Shawqi seized general headquarters. Armor and artillery units secured their own headquarters, sealed off central Cairo, and deployed detachments on roads leading out of the city to head off potential British attempts to intervene. The operation was scheduled to begin at midnight, but Siddiq moved his units out an hour early. This miscue perhaps saved the day and prevented the necessity of a gun battle because when Siddiq's units seized general headquarters, they captured key members of the high command who had gathered to assess reports of trouble.

The story of the coup is one of good fortune and near disaster, and not a small amount of clever extemporaneous acting. Nasser and 'Amr nearly sat out the crucial hour, being detained briefly by Siddiq's men until their commander arrived and explained that the two prisoners were in fact friends. Sadat's untimely visit to the cinema, a story that soon became well known, thanks primarily to his own wonderful penchant for self-mockery, caused him to miss zero hour. After arresting his commanding officer, Muhammad Abu al-Fadl al-Gizawi answered several calls from the commander in chief of the army. Pretending to be his superior, Gizawi assured the inquisitor that he knew of no extraordinary troop movements. Muhammad Nagib sat at home throughout the operation, the details of which he knew little if anything. When he received several phone calls from Interior Minister Maraghi, inquiring from Alexandria about reports of trouble, Nagib assured him all was calm.[46]

By 3:00 A.M. the officers had secured Cairo, summoned Muhammad Nagib to headquarters, and contacted loyal troops in Alexandria and al-'Arish. Colleagues in al-'Arish had not been forewarned of the operation; in Alexandria, where Farouk and his retinue summered, Free Officers commanders had been directed not to move until assured of success in Cairo. At 7:00 A.M., Anwar al-Sadat, broadcast the Free Officers' first message to the nation. Few shots had been fired.[47]

Despite their organizational autonomy, the Free Officers did not carry out their coup d'état unassisted. The relationship between the Free Officers and their allies remains controversial, clouded in charges and counter-charges of deception and bad faith, as adherents of both the Brotherhood and DMNL reexamine their respective roles in the formation of the movement and its ideology. The Free Officers' relationship with these movements differed in key ways; however, both movements collaborated with the Free Officers and had contacts at the highest levels. Presented with plans for a military takeover, both agreed to cooperate in subsidiary roles. As cooperators, their claims to some part in determining Egypt's course after the coup could not be dismissed, as the claims eventually were, without creating a sense of betrayal and, ultimately, open opposition.

Charges leveled by the Muslim Brothers betray a serious misunderstanding of, or failure to come to terms with, the Free Officers' independent streak. In spite of clear signs to the contrary, Brotherhood leaders continued to view the Free Officers as a wayward faction of their movement. According to Salah Shadi, Nasser resumed contact with Muslim Brotherhood leaders in early 1950, saying that he had rebuilt Mahmud Labib's disbanded organization. Nasser apparently asserted his loyalty to the Brotherhood but, citing infiltration by the secret police, stressed the need to maintain an organization independent of official Brotherhood ties. In fact, Shadi contends, Nasser usurped the organization from Labib's right-hand man and rightful successor, 'Abd al-Mun'im 'Abd al-Ra'uf, and redirected the officers' loyalties toward himself. Another Brotherhood officer, Husayn Hamudah, asserts that in a bedside visit to the ailing Labib Nasser persuaded the latter to give him a list of all officers enrolled in Brotherhood cells. [48]

If Nasser expressly declared loyalty to the Brotherhood, he may justifiably be accused of deceit. Even so, it seems unlikely that Brotherhood leaders failed to suspect him of steering his own course. By late 1950 many of the factors that Nasser had supposedly cited for keeping his distance were no longer compelling. The Brotherhood had reorganized and prepared to declare itself legal. A new general guide had been selected, a man supported by those in the movement to whom Nasser and the others were closest.

The expulsion of 'Abd al-Mun'im 'Abd al-Ra'uf from the Free Officers executive in early 1952 certainly should have prompted a reevaluation of the relationship. 'Abd al-Ra'uf's insistence that the movement follow dictates from the Brotherhood's Guidance Council provoked the ouster. Accounts differ as to how bitter the break in fact was. Most of those on record portray the decision more as an agreement to disagree. Kamal al-Din Husayn, the executive committee member with the strongest emotional ties to the Brotherhood, even states that the others offered 'Abd al-Ra'uf the option of rejoining the committee at any time he should so choose. [49]

Whatever ill will resulted from the ouster of so close a colleague, collaboration between the two movements continued. On Black Saturday highly placed Brothers allowed the Free Officers to store arms on the estate belonging to the family of Hasan al-'Ashmawi. [50] (In January 1954, when the regime ordered the Brotherhood dissolved, it conveniently rediscovered this cache

and heralded its existence as proof of the Brothers' plans to seize power.)
After the fall of the Wafd and cessation of hostilities in the Canal Zone, the
Free Officers maintained contact with the Guidance Council through Hasan
al-'Ashmawi and others. Several nights before the coup Nasser informed
Brotherhood contacts of the Free Officers' plans, and asked that they dis-
patch irregulars to check potential British troop movements along the Suez
road, and to safeguard foreign embassies in Cairo. Notified of the request,
General Guide Hudaybi consented.[51]

A different set of factors guided Free Officers' ties to the DMNL. In late
1949 or early 1950, Khalid Muhyi al-Din, by then a DMNL member, introduced Nasser to Ahmad Fu'ad, the civilian liaison between the DMNL central committee and military wing. Fu'ad was an old schoolmate of Khalid's to
whom the latter gives credit for his introduction to Marxism. The DMNL
central committee delegated Fu'ad liaison to the Free Officers; he and Nasser maintained direct contact with each other. A small circle of DMNL and
Free Officers collaborated to draft Free Officers' leaflets, which they printed
on DMNL presses. The group included Nasser, Muhyi al-Din, Ahmad
Fu'ad, and Ahmad Hamrush. After January 1952 the DMNL agreed to distribute Free Officers' propaganda through its own channels.[52]

A general ideological compatibility between the two movements made
such cooperation natural. DMNL rhetoric, if not its social theory, conformed
closely to the thinking of a majority of Free Officers leaders. Nasser and his
comrades, Khalid excepted, did not accept a Marxist analysis of society. In
general, they had only scant knowledge of communism and tended to view it
as monolithic. Many remained hostile. Yet, they implicitly accepted much of
the social critique espoused by the Left.[53] This general commonality of views
about the political situation in Egypt and the role of the army—unlike other
communist movements the DMNL recognized the potential for the army to
act as a popular nationalist force—caused DMNL leaders to hope they might
ultimately bring the Free Officers under their influence.

Nevertheless, a constant tension, rooted partly in ideology and partly in
organizational competition, pervaded the relationship. The anti-U.S. rhetoric of the DMNL disturbed Nasser and most of his colleagues, who viewed
the United States as a potential friend and, more immediately, a source of
leverage against the British. When traces of that rhetoric appeared in leaflets
coauthored by DMNL members—the leaflet criticizing Hilali cited above,
for example, denounced "Anglo-American imperialism"—Nasser issued instructions that all further negative references to the United States cease.[54]

Competition between the two movements for recruits could be only
thinly veiled. Nasser and Khalid Muhyi al-Din were close, and Nasser
trusted that Khalid put his loyalty to the Free Officers before his DMNL
ties. Khalid would warrant this trust after July 23, but until then he appears
to have been somewhat ambivalent. Ahmad Hamrush, a leader of the
DMNL military wing, refrained from joining the Free Officers in order to
avoid such a conflict of interest. Yet he and others worked quietly to infiltrate
the Free Officers with DMNL members, and Nasser played a similar game.[55]

Skeptical of the ideological validity of a coup d'état, DMNL leaders lent wary support when the Free Officers confronted them with the plans. On the evening of July 22 Nasser informed Hamrush and charged him with mobilizing loyal units in Alexandria. Before departing, Hamrush informed Ahmad Fu'ad, who has said the news shocked him. They contacted Khalid Muhyi al-Din, with whom they made contingency plans to go into hiding should the coup fail, then informed Sayyid Rifa'i of the DMNL secretariat, which issued a statement the morning of July 23 supporting the uprising.[56]

"Another 'Urabi"?

Any discussion of the Free Officers' organization, political alliances, and developing ideology must consider the personal influence of Gamal Abdel Nasser. Nasser was the driving force and uncontested leader of the movement. He had sought out his closest colleagues in late 1949, formed the nucleus of an organization, and set the movement on an independent course. He involved himself in every aspect of organization and took personal charge of the most important outside contacts. Like his colleagues, Nasser was not an ideologue. But to the extent that the Free Officers developed a political agenda, he, more than any of the others, influenced the movement's slant.

However, the movement should not be considered his personal vehicle. He did not dictate policy, nor did he surround himself with sycophants. His closest colleagues were men of charisma and conviction, men who, like him, inspired devotion in fellow officers. The executive committee, later the junta, functioned as a democratic body with all major decisions put to a vote. Within that council Nasser stood first among equals, a status he recognized, and on occasion abused. He knew that a dissenting vote on his part would force reconsideration of any given issue and that a threat to resign would always facilitate compromise. His style reflected a shrewd sense of leadership and an ability to command loyalty. At the same time Nasser shared his comrades' sense of allegiance to the group. As yet uncertain about the goals he hoped to achieve with his movement, he routinely sought their counsel and support.

Still, Nasser demonstrated early on a tendency to shun democratic process. On more than a few occasions he acted unilaterally, alone or in league with several others. The attempt on the life of General Sirri 'Amr was a dramatic example. He concealed the extent of his collaboration with the DMNL from those colleagues who would not approve, and minimized differences between the Free Officers and the Muslim Brothers to those who supported the broad political goals, if not the leadership, of that movement. After July 19, with the date of the coup set by committee, the executive did not meet again until the evening of July 21, when it decided, in conjunction with the operational command, to postpone the operation twenty-four hours. During that time Nasser, who maintained contact with all his colleagues individually, made unilateral decisions based on their advice, much as he would do during later crises when in power.[57]

Ultimately, the palace and the political establishment must bear responsibility for the ease with which the military thrust itself into the center of the political arena. Indifference to increasing manifestations of dissent within the officer corps at a time when the political system hung by a thread proved disastrous. The persistent view that trouble could be contained by manipulating the high command blinded the palace to the real trouble spots in the ranks. In November 1950, amid widespread public discontent, the king sacked his commander in chief, Muhammad Haydar, and chief of staff, 'Uthman Mahdi, both popularly perceived to have been guilty of negligence during the Palestine War. Haydar had been the chief target of leaflets circulating in the ranks throughout the summer of 1950, when rumors of a coup abounded.[58] In this case Farouk buckled under to civilian rather than military pressure, and when public outcry diminished, he reappointed Haydar, who commanded the armed forces until the coup. The Free Officers' victory in the Officers Club elections challenged palace hegemony over the military and furnished the palace a list of dissidents, but Farouk and his advisors continued to see the problem as rooted in the senior ranks. In mid-July, when Prime Minister Sirri tried to appease Muhammad Nagib by offering him the war ministry, Farouk blocked the appointment, fearful of creating "another 'Urabi" in the ranks.[59]

Coupled with this misplaced focus on the senior ranks was a complete lack of respect for the abilities of junior commanders. King's men and government officials believed that young hotheads could be easily controlled by transfers and hand slaps. Success in uncovering several secret cliques in the late 1940s inspired overconfidence and distracted the attention of those who should have paid closer attention to the Free Officers. A month after the Officers Club fiasco Farouk assured the British ambassador that the army remained loyal. In the king's view the only potential source of trouble might be pro-Wafdist sympathy in the ranks. "There were," he informed Sir Ralph, "about twelve unsatisfactory officers and these would be got rid of." That said, Farouk promptly dropped the matter until mid-July.[60]

By dissolving the Officers Club board and appointing his own men, Farouk set in motion the process that led to his downfall. Prime Minister Sirri resigned over the matter. When the new nominee, Hilali, refused to accept Farouk's candidate for war minister, Sirri 'Amr, the king insisted upon the appointment of his own brother-in-law. Colonel Shirin, "a decent, presentable sort of chap" to the thinking of one highly placed British official in the African Department, had no credible rank or qualifications for the position.[61] Under normal circumstances his appointment probably would have provoked a sharp outcry in the officer corps. Instead it passed largely unnoticed by those hurriedly concluding plans for their uprising.

The officers did not seize power convinced that it should be theirs to wield. The role of the army, they felt, was to fight forces of the occupation. Soldiers belonged in the barracks or on the battlefield, not in the seats of power. But power had been abused. The army had been sent to Palestine unprepared to face defeat; in 1952, rather than having been used to fight the occupier, it had been used to restore order in the streets when nationalist sentiment erupted into an inferno. The officers had warned the high command that one day they would cease to follow orders. Now, rushed by anticipation of their arrest, they again took their troops into the streets, this time to chase the "traitors" from the seats of power.

Because they acted long before they had deemed it feasible or even possible, the Free Officers' encounter with power proved crucial in forming the direction their movement would follow. In the early morning hours of July 23, before Egypt awoke to news of their coup, the officers pondered their next steps. They had little time to reflect on political considerations or the long-run implications of their action. They solved problems as they arose. They decided to turn power over to a civilian prime minister but had no candidate in line when they marched on general headquarters. Keenly aware of their political inexperience, the officers eagerly turned for advice to those with whom they shared a common sense of how Egypt might be put on a "sound" course. They looked with special interest to their contemporaries among the intelligentsia, men who proved willing to countenance a new base of popular leadership and threw in their lot with the young officers.

3

"Revolutionary Jurisprudence"

During the first six months of their rule the officers slowly came to see themselves not only as the vanguard of the struggle for national independence but as legitimate rulers of their country. Initially, they opted for an indirect role, intending less the construction of a new social and political order than a swift housecleaning, a purging of political ranks accompanied by constitutional reform. For them, as for disillusioned liberals, the specter of chaos hovered over a decaying social and political order. Revolution from below could be forestalled only by reform from above. In time they adopted a more aggressive posture toward political antagonists. Finally, frustrated by the resistance of the old political establishment, the unwillingness of the old guard to hand power to a new generation of leaders and, ultimately, of many young guard allies to burn bridges with their elders, the officers abolished the political parties and assumed direct authority over the country. In doing so, they declared their revolution.

From the events of this period there are lessons to be learned about the failure of the old political establishment to confront the challenge posed by military intervention into affairs of state. For example, in their revision of official Nasserist history, Wafdists argue that they welcomed the coup and supported social reform measures proposed by the junta. At the same time, they credit themselves with being the sole defenders of the liberal tradition, demanding the restoration of parliamentary life and, when new legislation threatened their existence as a party and the existence of the political system as a whole, challenging the government in the courts. To a great extent their case is solid. Yet, however valiant their stand, the Wafd, like all other parties, divided within and suspicious of rivals, fueled the officers' animosity toward the ruling order and reinforced their willingness to subvert legal institutions. The motivations and strategies of establishment leaders, too often posited in simplistic terms of democratic and antidemocratic tendencies, must be understood within the broad context of the breakdown of confidence in liberalism and its institutions.

"The Blessed Movement"

The Free Officers did not seek to demolish the liberal system, abolish the monarchy, or impose a military dictatorship over Egypt. At the outset they called their takeover a coup d'état. They referred to themselves simply as "the army movement" (harakat al-jaysh), "the movement" (al-harakah), or, with some embellishment, the "blessed movement" (al-harakah al-mubarakah). They had acted, they stressed, in the name of the Constitution, to preserve order and restore "sound" parliamentary life. They still spoke primarily of purging "traitors" from the military high command.[1] They adopted a moderate posture as much to soothe public anxiety as to allow themselves to catch their breath and take stock of the situation. Nonetheless, their promise was not insincere. The officers did not envision themselves as politicians, practitioners of a profession they viewed with mixed feelings of distrust and admiration.

A sincere desire not to involve themselves in the daily affairs of state did not preclude a political role. However ill defined their program, the Free Officers seized power with a clear sense of duty and purpose. They aimed above all to effect a turnover in the ranks of the political establishment, to clear the way for a new generation of leaders, to root out corruption in the bureaucracy, to narrow the gap between rich and poor, and to destroy the political power of the pasha class. They sought to lead the way but not to govern. Aware of their own inexperience, they turned to a civilian prime minister, to whom they entrusted the unenviable task of implementing decisions handed down from above.

Free Officers executive committee members made up the junta that assumed direct command of the armed forces and remained a secretive, anonymous partner in the political ruling structure. The committee re-elected Nasser president but agreed that Muhammad Nagib, appointed commander in chief of the army on July 24, would become its official spokesperson. The junta referred to itself as the "command" (al-qiyadah) or "general command" (al-qiyadah al-'ammah). Junta members instructed the press to make no mention of their names and print no photographs of any except Nagib. Until mid-August Nagib did not officially sit on the executive committee. Then the junta invited him and four other comrades who had shouldered major responsibilities during the planning and execution of the coup to join its ranks.

With the inclusion of Nagib, Zakariya Muhyi al-Din, Husayn al-Shafi'i, 'Abd al-Mun'im Amin, and Yusuf Siddiq, the junta numbered fourteen members. All were considered equal and all major decisions were put to a vote. These decisions represented a consensus hammered out behind closed doors. As a result, the junta exercised a hidden hand over policy-making. Those who dealt directly with the officers found that hand often clenched in a fist. But to the public, until the officers moved to exert direct control over the political process, the waving hand of a smiling Muhammad Nagib represented a paternalistic and protective army.

The choice of 'Ali Mahir to head a civilian government was hardly the mark of a movement with a radical vision for the future. The least tainted of Egypt's old-guard independent politicians, Mahir had reinforced a reputation for toughness and honesty during his last, ill-starred tenure of office after Black Saturday. Mahir's attraction at the outset, however troublesome it would later prove, was his establishment aura. He guaranteed the rule of law and the stability of the political process. Offered the prime ministry by the mutinous officers in the early morning hours of July 23, he made his acceptance conditional on the king's approval and insisted on taking a legal oath before him. The officers demurred. Mahir admittedly knew little of their intentions when he agreed to take office. He was, he told the British minister, "entirely sympathetic" with their expressed grievances and had no suspicions of their intentions to depose Farouk until charged with informing the king on July 26.[2]

The officers did not decide Farouk's fate until the night of July 24. The king's life hung in the balance between those who sought his head and the majority, who deemed it wisest simply to be rid of him.[3] On July 25 the junta ordered the ouster of Farouk's entourage from the palace, without exception. On the morning of July 26, a shaken 'Ali Mahir informed the king he was to abdicate and leave the country. The officers took care to assure that the abdication conformed, as much as possible, to the law. That afternoon Farouk signed an official statement handing power to his six-month-old son, Prince Ahmad Fu'ad. Failing to win passage to exile for his most trusted aides, the king, bargaining through Mahir, convinced the officers to grant him a generous baggage allowance. At 6:30 P.M. on July 26, Farouk I, former king of Egypt, sailed for Naples.[4]

The moment Farouk left Egyptian soil, a pressing constitutional question, selection of a regent for the six-month-old crown prince, forced the officers to assess the political role their movement would play. A constitution that granted ultimate authority to the monarch could not speak directly to his overthrow. The charter specified the process by which a regency was to be appointed in cases of the monarch's retirement or death. In either case it invested parliament with authority to deliver the oath of office to the regent. If not in session, parliament was to be recalled within ten days; if the chamber had been dissolved and a new body not yet elected, the previous assembly was to be summoned. A debate ensued between those who judged the situation analogous to the monarch's retirement or death and those who contended that the matter fell outside the purview of the Constitution. Inseparable from the constitutional debate lay a more pressing question: the officers' willingness to share power with the Wafd by recalling the 1950 parliament dissolved by Nagib al-Hilali the previous March.

Debate revolved primarily around traditional partisan lines. The Wafd adopted an unequivocal position in favor of recall. Mustafa al-Nahhas did not hesitate to raise the matter at his first meeting with the junta, an uneasy encounter that unsettled the officers and created instantly an atmosphere of tension between junta and majority party. Nahhas came away apprehensive, but in following days, in private meetings with Mahir and Nagib, as well as in the press, the Wafd boldly advocated summoning parliament.[5]

A ground swell of opposition quickly isolated the Wafd as old antagonists pressed the government to act without recourse to parliament. 'Ali Mahir, the defender of parliament six months earlier, now steadfastly opposed its recall. Minority parties advocated new elections and constitutional reform. Makram 'Ubayd, leader of the Independent Wafdist Bloc, proposed a popular vote to elect the regent. Sayyid Sabri, a distinguished professor of law at Cairo University, argued that the army takeover voided the entire charter. The issue was open to what he termed "revolutionary jurisprudence" (al-fiqh al-thawri).[6]

The government brought the issue before the State Council, the supreme legal body in the country. In a special session on July 31 the Council voted 9-1 to grant the government authority to appoint a regent. 'Ali Mahir admitted to British embassy contacts that the ruling may very well have subverted the spirit of the law.[7] The State Council was hardly free of partisan sentiments. Its president, 'Abd al-Razzaq al-Sanhuri, and his deputy, Sulayman Hafiz, both harbored deep antagonism toward the Wafd. Wahid Ra'fat, the sole dissenter, describes the atmosphere of the special session as charged. Sanhuri argued strenuously in favor of special judicial prerogative, and Hafiz sanctioned the use of force to suppress any attempt on the part of the dissolved chamber to reassemble.[8]

The issue was not, as it is often depicted, a simple case of democratic versus dictatorial rule, nor was the junta's acceptance of the ruling a resolution to overthrow the political order. Most junta members accepted 'Ali Mahir's argument, as reported by the British ambassador, that the "immediate return of constitutional procedure" would "leave the country saddled with a defective constitution, an unsuitable electoral system, and an inefficient, party-ridden administration."[9] A minority, Nasser among them, argued for recalling parliament. Nasser walked out of a meeting and threatened to resign, but did not push his colleagues to reverse their decision. He relented he told them, because he feared a split within the ranks. His withdrawal facilitated a compromise within the command, which tempered its decision with a commitment to call elections within six months.[10]

The selection of a three-man regency council to oversee palace affairs signaled the officers' conservative orientation as well as their inclination toward compromise. They selected a second counsin of the king, Prince 'Abd al-Mun'im; a respected lawyer with family ties to the Wafd, Baha' al-Din Barakat; and Colonel Rashad Mahanna. The prince's appointment signaled their intent to respect the monarchy. By naming Barakat, a nephew of Sa'd Zaghlul, the officers hoped to placate the Wafd and soften the blow of their transgressing an important parliamentary privilege.[11] They appointed Mahanna, a popular and more senior officer, in an effort to placate his ambition while distancing him from the centers of decision making.

During the first six weeks of its rule the new regime legislated a series of popular reform measures. Some were symbolic, such as the elimination of the government's summer recess to Alexandria, ending the subsidization of private automobiles for cabinet ministers, and the abolition of the honorific titles bey and pasha, all ordered within the first week after the coup. Other measures addressed financial inequities. The government decreed income, profit, and inheritance tax reforms, pay raises in the military, and 10 to 30 percent decreases in rent. It proclaimed the independence of the judiciary and formed judicial commissions in each ministry to oversee its individual affairs.[12]

The keystone of the officers' social program was land reform. Within two weeks of their coup the officers began to study the matter. For assistance in drafting a proposal they turned to a young Alexandria University economics professor, Rashad al-Barawi, a former teacher of Khalid Muhyi al-Din.[13] In an article published in *Al-Zaman* in early August that had caught the junta's attention, Barawi argued that an imposed ceiling on landholding would force down the price of land and result in lower agricultural rents. Stability of small owners would insure social stability. At the same time, he stressed the importance of land reform as a means of undercutting the political power of the landed aristocracy by stripping away its economic base.[14]

Barawi and the officers settled on a ceiling of two hundred feddans per family, far less restrictive than other plans proffered in recent years. *Al-Misri*, given an exclusive scoop, had published the first news of the junta's intent on August 12. For the next month the press reported progress toward a final plan. It soon became apparent to the officers that popular expectations far exceeded realistic appraisals of the amount of land that could conceivably be distributed. Reports of peasants refusing to till rented land until it became their own property fostered a sense of unease and reflected broader concerns about a breakdown of public order in the wake of the coup.[15]

In mid-August disturbances at the mill town Kafr al-Dawwar seemed to vindicate those concerns. On August 9, textile workers struck one of the town's three large plants. A demonstration on the night of August 12, held while worker and company officials met, turned violent. Troops were summoned to the scene in the early morning hours. In the ensuing clash four workers, two soldiers, and one policeman were killed. Authorities arrested 545 workers and charged 29 with arson and incitement to riot. On August 15 the junta delegated one of its members, 'Abd al-Mun'im Amin, to oversee a special military tribunal. A day later the court found two workers guilty. They were hanged on September 7.[16]

Rising expectations in the wake of the coup appear to have inspired the Kafr al-Dawwar workers to strike. Labor had been locked in bitter conflict with management over the right to organize. Workers now appealed to the new regime for justice, shouting slogans in praise of Muhammad Nagib. The U.S. labor attaché, who visited the plant the morning after the disturbances, noted that the workers had inflicted very little damage on the physical plant itself; rather, they had burned the homes of company police, destroyed employee files in company offices and medical facilities, and smashed equipment used to test productivity. The attaché described the outburst as an "explosive challenge to industrial discipline and authority." Furthermore, the commanding officer of troops dispatched to restore order admitted to him that because of exaggerated reports from the scene, more troops than needed had been mobilized.[17]

The officers took little solace in the workers' sympathies. Muhammad Nagib met with one of the condemned men, Mustafa al-Khamis, but the gesture was largely political. Convinced the two workers were guilty as charged, the junta hesitated to carry out the death sentences. Fear of the mob and the potential for the political parties to exploit disorder—despite sketchy links between Khamis and communist movements, several officers indicated to British and U.S. officials their suspicion of Wafdist involvement—led the junta to execute sentence posthaste.[18]

The junta's response to an ill-timed report of impending dismissals in the civil service bureaucracy underscores the tension at general headquarters in the wake of Kafr al-Dawwar. The morning edition of *Al-Misri* carried the story two days after the disturbances. Under normal circumstances a phone call to Ahmad Abu al-Fath would have sufficed to squelch the story and elicit a retraction. Instead, the junta opted for a public demonstration of force. Armored vehicles surrounded the newspaper offices. The regime accused the newspaper of rumor mongering and threatened to shut it down.[19]

Except in such rare cases the junta opted for a background role, relying upon the government to administer the country and institute the junta's reforms. In seeking guidance for policy-making, the officers solicited opinions from a wide variety of sources. A circle of civilian advisors quickly emerged that came to dominate the attention of the junta. Countervailing pressures within that circle, the basis of which has been called a conflict between proponents and foes of democracy, need to be reexamined in order to understand the pressures under which the junta operated and the decisions it took.

"Afraid of Details . . . and Politicians"

The failures of the parliamentary order, particularly in the two years preceding the Free Officers' coup, fostered a tolerance for antidemocratic measures among liberal intellectuals that led them to collaborate with the military junta after July 23. Wafdist leaders, eager to resume power as the parliamentary majority, perceived the coup as a mixed blessing. The military had perhaps served the nation by providing a positive shock to the body politic and deposing Farouk; in any case, what was done was done, and the officers belonged in the barracks. Most others, however—and this included many rank-and-file Wafdists—welcomed the officers' intrusion into the political realm and the opportunity for a period of military supervision, seeing the army as the interim power needed to purge the old regime and instill stability into the political order.

This proclivity toward, or, at best, acceptance of, military stewardship represented a majority of the Egyptian intelligentsia. Within this majority two factions may be discerned. These factions, which may be considered minimalist and maximalist, differed in one crucial respect: their assessments of the ability or willingness of the political establishment to undertake meaningful reform under pressure from the army. This difference produced a fundamental divergence in attitude toward the issue of direct military rule. As a result, the officers of the junta found themselves pushed in two directions by those they counted as their friends, and ultimately found themselves forced to choose between two camps.

Minimalists supported a short period of military trusteeship, which, they believed, would facilitate a transfer of power within the ranks of the political establishment. To this end, they backed the officers' demand that the parties purge corrupt leaders. Egypt did not oust the king, protested Ihsan 'Abd al-Quddus, a leading minimalist, so that power could be handed back to Sirag al-Din and 'Uthman Muharram.[20] At the same time, minimalists pressed the junta to restore political rights and declare a timetable for new parliamentary elections. In the interim, they urged the officers to define clearly the short-term nature of their political role and the extent of their authority. This, they argued, was a necessary prerequisite for true stability.

Those affiliated with *Al-Misri* and *Ruz al-Yusuf,* mouthpieces of the liberal Left, enunciated this position most clearly. Ihsan 'Abd al-Quddus viewed the junta in much the same way he had 'Ali Mahir six months earlier. Ahmad Abu al-Fath and his left Wafd associates saw in the officers the means by which they could assert greater authority within their party. Links forged by the Free Officers prior to the coup d'état to the Wafdist Vanguard and DMNL caused minimalists to feel confident that in the long run they and the officers shared similar aims.

Maximalists pressed the army to take a more active, long-term role not only in affecting a purge of the political establishment but in legislating reform. Hostility to the Wafd provided a common denominator for maximalists, many of whom came from the ranks of the minority parties or, as independents, had established anti-Wafdist reputations. As such, they campaigned vigorously against a precipitate return to parliamentary life, which, without major structural change in the political order, meant a return to Wafdist rule. Leading maximalists were the two jurists 'Abd al-Razzaq al-Sanhuri and Sulayman Hafiz, young guard members of the Nationalist party led by Fathi Radwan, and 'Ali Mahir. Mustafa and 'Ali Amin, owners of the *Al-Akhbar* presses, provided a counterweight in the media to Abu al-Fath and 'Abd al-Quddus.

Because they urged and later participated in the onset of direct military rule, the maximalists stand accused in Wafdist and communist revisionist accounts of pushing Egypt toward dictatorship. To the extent that they coaxed the officers to assume a more direct role in governmental affairs and provided legal justification for dismantling parliamentary institutions, the maximalists are guilty as charged. Sanhuri and Hafiz in particular became legal architects of the new order, lobbying for harsh measures against the political parties and drafting statutes allowing the government to prosecute their former rivals.

Maximalists may have intentionally subverted the rule of law, or bent it to accommodate their own political ends. Yet the issue is not that simple. A constitution so sorely in need of revision was more an impediment to be hurdled than a sacred writ. 'Ali Mahir, who had served on the committee that drafted the 1923 charter, knew "that reform must start with the first line of the constitution and end with the last."[21] To a certain extent everyone but senior Wafdists who had an immediate interest in the restoration of the status quo ante accepted the pressing need for what Sayyid Sabri called "revolutionary jurisprudence." Disillusioned intellectuals, despite the rhetoric they employed, did not perceive their turn from liberalism as a renunciation of its chief tenets. Rather, both minimalists and maximalists perceived military rule as a temporary but necessary evil. Forces committed to the restoration of parliamentary democracy thus proved willing to collaborate with a military junta, blinding themselves to the ultimate threat that their collaboration posed to the future of liberalism.

At the outset the common ground of minimalist and maximalist positions bolstered the officers' determination to effect some overhaul of the political establishment. Initially, the officers engaged in two primary contests: a wrestling match with 'Ali Mahir for real power and a shoving match with the political parties over the question of voluntary purges. Uneasy with Mahir's stubborn independent streak, the officers dismissed him in early September and appointed Muhammad Nagib to replace him. Displeased with the parties' reluctance to purge themselves, the junta adopted a harsh policy aimed at retiring old-guard leaders. The Wafd stood at the center of this struggle, a natural target of hostility and, concurrently, the promised wellspring of new national leadership. As a consequence of the junta's policy, however, minimalist Wafdists grew increasingly alienated from the regime. As the officers saw old allies desert them, they drew closer to newer, maximalist friends.

'Ali Mahir assumed office with the broad outlines of a reform program already in hand. Mahir's program included a major overhaul of the government bureaucracy. More than a purging of ranks, he sought to destroy the patronage system by taking the power of civil service appointments out of the hands of individual ministries. In addition, Mahir intended to extend the purview of "illegal-gains" legislation and to grant the "purge committees" established by Hilali the power of detention and the authority to subpoena financial information from banks. Amending election laws was another priority, and Mahir hinted that the Constitution needed significant, if not total, revision.[22]

Having been frustrated in his previous tenure as prime minister, Mahir was now ready to assume the role of "just tyrant." He rejected calls to reassemble parliament or to announce early elections, even though this meant suspending constitutional procedure. He favored the retention of martial law and the postponement of elections for at least six months. During the interval he planned to form his own political party. If the Wafd caused trouble, Mahir indicated privately he would arrest its leaders.[23]

As his first order of business, Mahir sought to establish his autonomy from the junta. He was confident—the British ambassador described it as "boundless confidence"—that he could coax the officers into retirement. But Mahir did not assume this would be easy. His first weeks had been extremely trying. Although the prime minister felt he had fared well, he expressed a wish to maintain close contact with British officials. Hoping to curry favor with the British, he offered to postpone all discussions of Anglo-Egyptian relations for at least two months, a policy that amounted to a total about-face from that of the previous January.[24]

However much they respected Mahir, the officers never fully trusted him. They were, Ihsan 'Abd al-Quddus told a British official, "afraid of details," and therefore inclined to rely on the prime minister. At the same time they were "afraid of politicians," which led them constantly to challenge Mahir's judgment.[25] Mahir and the officers became embroiled almost from the outset in a series of confrontations, tests of will that the prime minister invariably lost. On August 10, instead of announcing that elections would be held in early February, as the junta instructed, Mahir delivered a stinging rebuke to the parties for their failure to initiate voluntary purges. The junta retracted his statement the following day.[26] Later that month Mahir resisted pressure from the officers, who were eager to bring younger faces into the government, to shuffle his cabinet. He complained to his British contacts that the officers handed him an unsatisfactory list of nominees, unknowns with whom he refused to work. In the end Mahir compromised and instigated a minor shuffle on September 5. The following day the officers dismissed him.[27]

'Ali Mahir's open opposition to land reform convinced the officers that cooperation with him no longer remained possible. A wealthy landowner himself, Mahir contended that dividing the large estates and distributing small lots to the peasantry would sharply curtail productivity, sow economic disorder, and discourage foreign investment. His argument, as well as his alternate proposal—a revised tax structure that would place a progressively greater burden on landowners, encouraging them to dispense of excess holdings—were by then common to property owners threatened by talk of confiscation. When Mahir saw he could not forestall the imposition of a ceiling on ownership, he proposed a five-hundred-feddan limit, well over the junta's two-hundred-feddan proposal. Even then, Mahir rejected proposals to confiscate and redistribute surplus feddans. He suggested instead an 80 percent tax on all land over the ceiling.[28]

Mahir appears to have determined to make land reform the issue that would either cement or terminate his authority. When he realized the junta would not compromise, he took his campaign directly to the officer corps. On a holiday trip to the Western Desert he met with a group of junior officers, to whom he expressed disenchantment with the proposed legislation.[29] Back in Cairo, on September 4 he welcomed a delegation of twenty-two large landowners who made no secret of their reservations about the proposed bill. Incensed by Mahir's obstructionism, the junta informed the U.S. ambassador on September 5 that if Mahir did not take immediate steps to implement their plan, he was finished. Jefferson Caffery apprised Mahir of the situation, but the latter did not relent.[30] Instead, he lent his name to a statement drafted by the landowners with whom he had met that warned the proposed reform would "destroy the national economy. . . . It will make everyone poor for it will ruin the rich and the poor will not profit." The landowners, for their part, suggested a one-thousand-feddan ceiling with additional exemptions of one hundred feddans per wife and son and fifty feddans per daughter.[31]

By now the junta brooked no thoughts of compromise. Open opposition to land reform precipitated not only Mahir's ouster but a dramatic demonstration of force. The officers proceeded with the minor cabinet shuffle of September 5 largely as a smoke screen while they weighed Mahir's future and looked for a successor. That night they ordered the arrest of sixty-four prominent politicians and former palace men. The list, which comprised a virtual "who's who" of the old regime, included leading members of all political parties except the Nationalist and Socialist.[32] The following day the junta dismissed Mahir. Muhammad Nagib took the oath as prime minister and formed a new government on September 8. The following day the government decreed its land reform. The final plan set a two-hundred-feddan ceiling on landholding, with the possible exemption of an additional one hundred feddans for members of the immediate family.

By this show of force the junta reasserted its domination over the political arena. The midnight roundup of September 7–8 demonstrated the power of an angry military; at the same time it revealed an aura of confusion surrounding the change in government. Although the officers expected a decisive showdown with 'Ali Mahir as early as September 5, they had made no plans for the transition. At the last minute they failed to locate several prospective ministers and turned to alternate candidates. Some of those summoned that same night to fill cabinet posts assumed they had been arrested. Several nominees who had accepted cabinet posts only the day before, now distraught at the show of force, chose not to retain their portfolios.[33]

The decision to appoint an officer prime minister, the first since 1882, the junta took largely by default. The junta's leading candidate, 'Abd al-Razzaq al-Sanhuri, was willing to serve, but the officers yielded to U.S. pressure not to appoint him. Incontestably qualified to lead the government, Sanhuri, because he had signed the Stockholm appeal of 1951, drafted by the international peace movement, was deemed by the Americans an "extremist." Sulayman Hafiz, the officers' second nominee, preferred a background role. He accepted the twin positions of vice-prime minister and minister of interior. The two jurists nominated Muhammad Nagib and convinced the junta that it was perfectly proper in the aftermath of a military coup for an officer to lead a civilian government.[34]

The new cabinet reflected a strong maximalist orientation. Sulayman Hafiz handpicked most of the ministers. Except for 'Abd al-Galil al-'Imari (and, technically speaking, Nur al-Din Tarraf, who had joined the cabinet only two days before), the new body consisted entirely of first-time ministers. With few exceptions the group was young, a mixture of technocrats and members of the Nationalist party youth faction. Fathi Radwan, the leader of that faction, was appointed minister of state. Two associates of the Muslim Brotherhood also joined the government. Sheikh Ahmad al-Baquri, a former Brotherhood student leader and onetime candidate to succeed Hasan al-Banna, became minister of pious endowments. The officers named Ahmad Husni, a friend of the Brothers, minister of justice.[35]

The youthful look of the new cabinet and the ideological orientation of its key members indicate the direction in which the junta was turning. Mahir and his associates, deemed "too old and too cautious" by the officers, gave way to new men who saw the army movement as their vehicle to attain power and influence, their ticket to entry into a political order that had been out of their reach before July 23. The officers viewed them as a political and technical brain trust to which they could turn for ideas and expertise. They trusted the young ministers, who, as men of their own generation, had not been tainted by the corruption of their elders. The young ministers, in turn, learned to respect the officers when they realized that the junta would not act merely as a rubber stamp for their policies.

Fathi Radwan, Nur al-Din Tarraf, and Ahmad al-Baquri formed a circle to which the officers' increasingly turned for political advice. Of these three, Radwan's role in this period was most significant. Imprisoned following Black Saturday, Radwan was freed within days of the coup at the behest of Sulayman Hafiz, who suggested to 'Ali Mahir that he might serve as intermediary between junta and government. Radwan, who knew little if anything of the Free Officers, shrewdly played the part assigned him. He spoke their language, denouncing 'Ali Mahir and insisting that the times called for new, younger men to assume positions of power. Radwan has been called to task for portraying himself as the junta's chief counsel at the time. Yet he clearly played an advisory role in the formation of the Nagib cabinet. In November 1952 he established a new ministry of national guidance. As its chief until early December and then again as minister of state, he created in large part the propaganda of the regime.[36]

"Purification"

Under the new government the regime adopted a new policy designed to push old-guard leaders aside. "Purification" (tathir) had become a standard word in the vocabulary of Egyptian political reform by the end of 1951. Nagib al-Hilali, its most recent champion, had established "purge committees" in March 1952 to root out corruption in the government bureaucracy. After their takeover the officers went one step further. In public pronouncements and in a flurry of meetings with party leaders between July 24 and July 26, Muhammad Nagib and 'Ali Mahir admonished the parties to oust corrupt members tainted by affiliation with the old regime. The government provided neither guidelines nor a list of names, and indicated no willingness to assume any direct role in the process.

The junta's position reflects a seemingly incompatible combination of hope and cynicism. The officers hoped to clear the path for younger party members, their contemporaries, to take command of the political establishment. Nasser apparently wanted Ahmad Abu al-Fath and Ibrahim Til'at, a lawyer and leader of the youth faction, brought into the Wafd executive.[37]

The officers did not presume that the old guard would roll over and accept retirement without the threat of force. A minority within the junta recommended forthright action from the start: the imposition of new leaders by military decree or dissolution of the parties. At the outset the junta adopted a more moderate policy, a stern but open-ended call for the parties to "purify" themselves, with a promise that if the parties cooperated, elections would be held within six months' time.[38] If necessary, the officers were prepared to unsheathe their swords. According to 'Ali Mahir, even as they spoke of restoring constitutional rule within six months, they discussed the option of imprisoning party leaders for up to five years.[39]

The confrontation between the government and political parties evolved through several phases. After Nagib became prime minister, the junta hardened its position, even as the officers remained hopeful that the parties could be frightened into reform. While they demonstrated a willingness to exercise force against striking workers and communists, they hestitated to tackle the Wafd until they felt surer of themselves, and until they felt they had no alternative. The parties, divided within and suspicious of rivals, failed to confront the government as a united front. Had they done so, the officers might well have seized direct power earlier than January 1953.

Party leaders responded to the call for "purification" with varying degrees of caution, patronizing support, and self-righteous arrogance. Liberal Constitutionalist President Muhammad Husayn Haykal declared that if the government wished the parties purged, it should take the lead by setting guidelines for them to follow. Makram 'Ubayd, denying the need for housecleaning in his own party, proclaimed, "The Wafdist Bloc is the purified Wafd." The Sa'dist newspaper, *Al-Asas*, supported "purification" for others while describing Sa'dist rule as having been "responsible," "progressive," and "socialistic."[40]

The Sa'dists, however, came closest to undertaking a model housecleaning. Ibrahim 'Abd al-Hadi, the party leader, favored a policy of conciliation. He believed the officers would of necessity align with one party, and assumed somewhat presumptuously it would be his. Vice-president Hamid Gudah, to the contrary, feared the officers would read acquiescence to their demands as a sign of weakness. Deadlocked and confused, party leaders delegated a group of younger members to approach the junta to seek clarification of the purge order. Sayyid Mar'i, a member of the delegation, recalls that the officers were neither forthcoming nor polite. Impressed and intimidated by their stern demeanor, the Sa'dist young guard seized control of party machinery and formed a new secretariat under the leadership of an-

other senior party member, Mahmud Ghalib. Both 'Ali Mahir and Nagib
publicly praised the purge as an example to be followed.[41]

"Purification" Wafd-style, from above, satisfied neither the junta, the
prime minister, nor those Wafdists who, like their young Sa'dist counterparts, looked to the army for support in their struggle to reform the party.
Despite declarations of "ardent support" for the idea, the Wafd executive
feared the long-term implications of "purification." Fu'ad Sirag al-Din, like
Haykal of the Liberals, argued that the burden should be upon the government either to name names or to spell out criteria. A majority in the Wafd
executive deemed it best to maintain a facade of submission; at the same
time, senior Wafdists did not overlook the opportunity to settle old scores
within the party. They hastily formed a purge committee, which on August 4
summarily expelled fourteen members of the parliamentary organization,
charged with disloyalty to the party. Of the fourteen, only Hamid Zaki, the
ill-starred former minister in the 1950 government, had carried any weight
within the Wafd. No one was fooled. "I am not pleased," Muhammad Nagib
responded bluntly. "The corrupt elements are still present in the [Wafd's]
leadership."[42]

The expulsions also provoked open rebellion within the Wafd. Those
ousted took their case before the public. Their only crime, they proclaimed,
had been the promotion of party reform. "I have the honor of being named
amongst those expelled," wrote one. Hamid Zaki answered his expulsion
with a frontal attack against "the real leader of the Wafd, Fu'ad Sirag al-
Din."[43] On August 10, seventy representatives of the Wafdist Vanguard,
claiming to speak for a caucus of two thousand, met with Muhammad Nagib.
They handed him a manifesto calling for the expulsion of Sirag al-Din and
others, and demanded elections to determine party leadership.[44] In following days 'Abd al-Salam Gum'ah, Sirag al-Din's predecessor as secretary,
broke ranks with the executive and emerged as a spokesman for the dissidents. Renouncing the early August expulsions, he urged the executive not
to interfere with the purge committee.[45]

By late August a clear division had emerged between the executive and the
parliamentary organization. Having failed to appease the army with their
orchestrated purge, old-guard Wafdists decided to resist the regime's call for
"purification." 'Uthman Muharram, the first Wafdist leader targeted by the
new regime, faced impending corruption charges, stemming from his last
term as minister of public works in the 1950 government. Nahhas and the
executive adamantly refused to take any action until his guilt was confirmed.[46]

Second-generation Wafdists, members of the parliamentary organization,
however, were more willing to purge Wafd elders. For them, preservation of
the party and personal advancement became wedded in a policy of appeasement. This fracture between first- and second-generation Wafdists created
an ad hoc alliance between the disaffected youth vanguard and those in line
to succeed to party leadership. Second-generation leaders did not necessarily share the officers' ideas of who should run the Wafd, but they welcomed

the opportunity to do away with Sirag al-Din, Muharram, and others who stood in their way.

Wafdist allies of the Free Officers found themselves in an increasingly tenuous position. Ahmad Abu al-Fath and Ibrahim Til'at, who were closest to the junta, maintained a steadfast loyalty to their party, if not its leaders. They rejected the officers' proposition that they be named to the Wafd executive by fiat. At the same time neither betrayed the officers' confidence. They did not, as they might well have done, reveal the secret of who held true power within the junta. Rather, they endeavored to impress party leaders with the wisdom of adopting a flexible, compromising stance toward the young officers. In particular, they pressed party leaders to support land reform.[47]

The land question polarized forces within many parties and became a standard carried by those seeking the ouster of party elders. Muhammad al-Khattab, drummed out of the Sa'dist party in 1945 for proposing a modest reform, rejoined the party in late August after the shuffle in command. Land reform also became the primary issue of contention within the Liberal Constitutionalist party, which came asunder in late August, causing Husayn Haykal to cut short a European vacation upon which he had embarked somewhat brashly several weeks before.[48]

Those with real power in the Wafd opposed the idea. After participating in preliminary discussions with the junta and other civilian advisors, Abu al-Fath and Til'at urged the officers to approach Wafdist leaders. The officers invited Sirag al-Din to discuss the matter on August 14. Participants describe the meeting, which lasted four to six hours, as one of complete candor in which Sirag al-Din argued against an imposed limit on landholding. He proposed instead, much like 'Ali Mahir, a tax scheme that would place a greater burden on large holders.[49] He met subsequently with Rashad al-Barawi, who stressed the officers' commitment to the measure. This must have had some effect, for on September 6, three days before the bill became law, Sirag al-Din announced that the Wafd agreed with it in principle. The party, however, had a number of reservations that, he said, would be elucidated at a later date. This position did not satisfy the junta, particularly since it coincided with Nahhas's stubborn defense of 'Uthman Muharram.[50]

The mass arrests that preceded the change in government on September 8 stemmed as much from the officers' frustration with the uneven response to the government's call for voluntary purges as from perceived resistance to land reform. Their primary focus remained the Wafd. Zakariya Muhyi al-Din told the British military attaché in mid-August that "the army and the government were urgently trying to amass evidence against Sirag al-Din but they did not wish to move against him until they had a cast iron case. . . ."[51] By now jailing Sirag al-Din, Muharram, and others, the junta spoke directly to the arrogance of the Wafd executive. Several days after assuming the prime ministry, Muhammad Nagib explained to the British ambassador that it had been necessary to punish a defiant Wafd, but to have singled out the majority party would have been a political error. On his first day in office the new prime minister announced that the government had no intention of dissolving the parties, but by now many expected a major change in strategy.[52]

Indeed, on September 9, in conjunction with land reform, the regime unveiled an aggressive new party policy. The Party Reorganization Law defined guidelines for "purification" and gave the government legal authority to intervene in the process. Under the law's terms, all parties were dissolved pending recertification by the Interior Ministry. Prospective parties were required to file a platform, a list of founding members, and a financial statement by October 7. During the following month the government reserved the right to refuse certification to any party or membership to any individual. Anyone facing corruption charges was automatically ineligible for party membership. Appeals were to follow a normal course through the State Council.

The political establishment greeted the law with dutiful obedience. The parties formed founding committees to set about drafting platforms and reenlisting members. Whatever its other effects, the law forced party leaders to ponder their programs with a greater degree of seriousness than they had in the wake of the coup. Platforms published pursuant to the law were far more detailed than the cliché-filled statements many parties released immediately after July 23.[53]

As a consequence of this new policy, those civilians who had been closest to the Free Officers began to view events with a more critical, uneasy eye. In a series of front-page columns in *Al-Misri,* Ahmad Abu al-Fath criticized the parties, especially the Wafd, for not responding to the junta's call for "purification." In doing so, however, he placed part of the blame squarely on the officers for not revealing their specific wishes. Denouncing the arrests of September 7–8 in harsh terms, he called for charges to be leveled or for the detainees to be released. Abu al-Fath continued to support the army leaders, who he said were committed to democracy. Yet he admonished the military to stay above politics. The burden remained on the parties to help the army achieve its victory. "If not," he wrote, "God knows where we are headed."[54]

Internal strife continued to cripple the Wafd. Eligibility restrictions for party membership presented party leaders with a fait accompli in several instances, but Nahhas steadfastly pushed a hard line. He refused to meet with Prime Minister Nagib while Sirag al-Din and others remained incarcerated, and scolded party members who advocated appeasing the regime. But without his closest aide at his side, Nahhas could not withstand pressure from the internal opposition. The Wafd's parliamentary organization protested bitterly when the executive appointed a three-man committee to supervise party reorganization. Younger party leaders forced the acceptance of new bylaws that gave the parliamentary organization the power to elect the Wafd's president and executive committee. The names of Sirag al-Din and Muharram did not appear on the list of party founders. Finally, on September 16, Sirag al-Din tendered his "final, total, and unconditional" resignation from both the executive committee and the parliamentary organization.[55]

The Wafd's actions, however, failed to appease the government, which for the first time attacked Nahhas personally. Emboldened by the successful uprising in the party against Sirag al-Din, the officers had determined to punish the Wafd president for his belligerency. On September 22, Sulayman Hafiz informed the Wafd by letter that the government rejected Nahhas as party president and founding member. Reflecting the interior minister's disposition, the letter described Nahhas as a "tumor in the body politic."[56] The language was his own, but Hafiz would not have attacked Nahhas without a green light from the junta.

Had Nahhas given his blessing to party reform, a dramatic collision course might have been avoided, certainly postponed. The officers viewed the Wafd chief with ambivalence. Aware of his popularity, they were reluctant to attack him directly or imprison him. Influenced by the rhetoric of young Wafdist associates, some held out hope that unshackled from his dependence on Fu'ad Sirag al-Din, Nahhas might yet exert a positive influence in the Wafd. But the Wafd chief's view of politics was hopelessly rooted in the past. He had rushed home from Europe in late July to assume the mantle of national leadership only to find his beloved Wafd again besieged. His reaction, as it had been in 1951, was to circle his wagons and resort to the tired rhetoric of old battles. Now Mustafa al-Nahhas stood with those who represented, in the officers' eyes, the worst of the liberal establishment. In part to punish him, in part to clear the way for those more likely to pursue reform, and in part to demonstrate again they were not to be taken lightly, the officers added Nahhas to their blacklist.

In the short run the junta succeeded in driving a wedge between Nahhas and those Wafdists preaching appeasement. Trying to rally the party, the old guard proclaimed, "There will be no Wafd without Nahhas." On September 27 party leaders announced that the Wafd would not apply for recertification. Countervailing forces, however, bolstered by new defections from the executive, proved stronger. On October 6, one day before the deadline for filing, Nahhas relented. 'Abd al-Salam Gum'ah, on behalf of a new founding committee, submitted an application to the Interior Ministry. With the tacit acquiescence of Sulayman Hafiz, the application listed Nahhas as the party's honorary president.[57]

The junta's offensive against Nahhas further undermined confidence in the officers within minimalist circles. Nahhas found little support outside the party, but some independents accused Sulayman Hafiz of deliberately courting confrontation in an irresponsible manner.[58] Wafdist Vanguard adherents were divided. Ahmad Abu al-Fath, who now stood with Nahhas, waged a campaign in the pages of *Al-Misri* to arouse public indignation. With the aim of isolating Hafiz from the junta, Abu al-Fath scored the interior minister for taking the law into his own hands. Most young Wafdists, however, continued to denounce party leaders and appealed to Nahhas to step aside, for the "good of the nation."[59]

Sensing a waning in Wafd support, indicated in part by a fall in the circulation of *Al-Misri*, the junta broadened its offensive. At the end of September Muhammad Nagib went on a whistle-stop tour of the Delta, the Wafdist heartland, where for three days enthusiastic crowds greeted him at every step. In his brief speeches Nagib stressed the apolitical role of the army. "The army is the nation and every Egyptian a soldier," he repeated. "Patience, patience," he beseeched his audience. "It tood God six days to create the world," he told them, and asked for six months.[60] The tour, described as "triumphal" in the American press, exhilarated the officers. They had, a close colleague told the U.S. embassy's public relations officer, taken a calculated gamble to test their popularity. Nagib's itinerary had been kept secret and orders had been issued to local officials not to stage organized rallies.[61]

As a consequence of the Party Reorganization Law, after October 7 the junta found itself confronted with fifteen applications and a variety of interparty and intraparty squabbles. The number of parties seeking certification pointed to a fragmentation of the political establishment that few considered sound. Of the fifteen parties seeking certification, eight either were splinters of established parties (New Nationalists) or represented specific interest groups or issues. Of these latter parties, the simple overlap of names (Workers, Workers and Peasants, Socialist Peasant, Republican, Egyptian Republican, Democratic, Democratic Nile, Nationalist Women, Daughter of the Nile) underscored the sense of disarray. Most of these parties represented little more than small cliques with slim chance at best for any electoral success.

The squabbling between factions further undermined the officers' confidence in the viability of a reconstituted liberal order. Disputes like that between the Socialist Peasant party and the Workers and Peasants party— the former accused the latter of stealing its name—seemed absurdly trivial. Because of the Nationalist party's connections to the regime, the rift in its ranks attracted the most notice. Fathi Radwan and his colleagues filed for certification as a separate New Nationalist party. Nationalist party elders protested that the Radwan bloc aimed to usurp their party and took the case before the State Council.[62]

By November 8, the government's deadline for rejecting applications, seven parties had been licensed: the Saʿdist, Liberal Constitutionalist, Nationalist, New Nationalist, Wafdist Bloc, Workers, and Daughter of the Nile parties. The government persuaded the National Women's party to change its status to association. The Interior Ministry rejected the Republican, Egyptian Republican, and Democratic parties, each for promoting abolition of the monarchy. The Socialist party agreed to delete a similar plank from its platform. It, along with all other parties not rejected outright by the cutoff date, was legally entitled to certification.[63]

Three days prior to the deadline the government reneged on its agreement with the Wafd, refusing to accept Nahhas's status as "honorary president" and rejecting the inclusion of another founding member, ʿAbd al-Fattah al-Tawil, on grounds of corruption.[64] Based on their prior experience with the Wafd, the officers assumed that younger party members would press Nahhas to resign. This time the party drew together and held fast. On November 8 a constituent assembly voted to take the case before the State

Council. In a preliminary hearing later that month the Wafd challenged the legality of the party law and dared to speak for all parties. "The case before you," Ibrahim Farag, previously a key advocate of appeasement, told the court, "is not the case of Mustafa al-Nahhas or 'Abd al-Fattah al-Tawil, but of parliamentary life in Egypt!"[65]

"To Strike with All Ferocity"

To the junta in the fall of 1952 the maximalist agenda seemed more compelling. A series of legislative acts and subtle changes in rhetoric point to the officers' reassessment of their role. They moved cautiously, ever wary of the political support their primary antagonists, Nahhas and the Wafd, could command. They knew that popular support for the Wafd was waning, but they also feared popular impatience with their administration. The six-month timetable that the officers had promised—indeed, that had been a cause of contention between them and 'Ali Mahir—they still occasionally echoed in official statements. But in private the officers began talking of a transition period of at least three years before parliamentary elections would be held.

By late November the junta's star appeared to be in decline. The officers had made no positive steps toward negotiations with the British. Price controls imposed on basic foodstuffs had produced serious shortages. Retailers refused to purchase goods with fixed prices, and peasants hesitated to plant fruits and vegetables from which they could reap no profit. The Wafd, rallying around Nahhas, seemed poised to make a bid for power. Rumors of dissention within the junta promoted an image of weakness.[66]

A series of challenges in the courts and on university campuses fueled the officers' disenchantment. In addition to the Wafd case pending before the State Council, Sirag al-Din, Muharram, and other politicians interned since September initiated a lawsuit against the government protesting their detention without their having been formally charged. Rumors spread of a drawing together of old antagonists in prison. In response, the authorities placed the offenders in solitary confinement.[67] More disconcerting to the regime, unrest erupted at Cairo University, where student elections pitted traditional rivals, a communist-Wafdist coalition and the Muslim Brothers, against each other. With the junta openly supporting the Brothers, the elections became a tacit referendum on the regime. When the coalition won, the government arrested some one hundred students, dissolved the student union, and closed the university.[68]

While Sulayman Hafiz, as vice–prime minister, presided over the cabinet, the officers huddled in nightly meetings discussing their future.[69] Between November 24 and December 6 the government released the September prisoners. Because December 6 was the last day the prisoners could be legally held without charges being brought, many perceived the move as one of weakness. The day the last prisoners were released Nahhas, as he had promised, paid the prime minister a courtesy visit. Nagib returned the visit the following day. Outwardly congenial, the encounters sparked new rumors of a national unity government led by Nahhas.[70] On December 9, in an effort to restore confidence, the junta shuffled Nagib's cabinet, replacing several ministers holding economic portfolios. The new supply minister promptly announced plans to ease price restrictions.[71]

Then, just as the regime appeared to backpedal, it took a sudden leap forward. On December 10 the government annulled the Constitution and announced its intent to nominate a committee of fifty experts to draft a new charter that would be submitted to a popular referendum. Political leaders of all affiliation welcomed the move. The constitutional committee of fifty formed on January 13, 1953, represented a broad spectrum of the intelligentsia. In addition to some of Egypt's most respected jurists, the government appointed delegates from all the major parties, including the Wafd, which had five representatives, all friendly to the regime, and the Muslim Brotherhood, which had three delegates.[72]

Although the move was popular, the officers had ulterior motives. Sulayman Hafiz had from the outset decried the persistence of immunity provisions that hindered his authority to take legal action against former cabinet ministers.[73] By now scrapping the Constitution, the junta erased all legal obstacles to prosecuting old-guard politicians. On December 22 the government announced the creation of a special "Treason Court" (Mahkamat al-Ghadr) to try cases of corruption and abuse of power under the old regime. The first set of indictments was handed down on January 1. Six former ministers and seven former parliamentary deputies, all Wafdists, were charged. Fu'ad Sirag al-Din and 'Uthman Muharram headed the list.[74]

Despite the regime's aggressive stance, Wafdist leaders failed to read the writing on the wall. They continued to view the junta as a transient phase and never questioned their own ultimate return to power. This blind self-assuredness along with the party disunity that plagued the Wafd throughout the early years of the revolution precluded a forceful, united stand until it was too late. How much of a hand the junta had in fostering internecine conflicts at this time is difficult to glean in an atmosphere so poisoned with hostility. Those who supported the regime faced charges—and still do—of disloyalty and opportunism from fellow Wafdists.[75]

Mustafa al-Nahhas appears to have been genuinely deceived by Nagib's amiability and his own mistaken assessment of the Wafd's relative strength vis-à-vis the junta. In his meeting with Nagib in mid-December, the Wafdist chief warned the prime minister against banning the party. Shortly thereafter, he let it be known he would not cooperate with a constitutional committee appointed by the government. Sirag al-Din and perhaps others perceived more clearly the threat posed by the junta, but they failed to see that the old rules of political conflict were changing. In late December 1952 or early January 1953 Wafdist insiders contacted the British embassy, hoping to reingratiate themselves with the British. Their sights were totally blurred.[76]

Officials in both the British and U.S. embassies knew that the time for old tricks had passed, that the officers had no intention of handing power back to the Wafd. They recognized that by freeing the September prisoners and flattering Nahhas with an official visit the officers had engaged in a tactical retreat. The officers and their closest associates spoke openly with U.S. and British embassy officers. ʿAli Sabri, close to the junta and a primary contact to the U.S. embassy, outlined a minimum three-year schedule of constitutional reform and indicated that the army would in no way relinquish or diminish its hold on power. Nagib, in a slightly different tone, told Ralph Stevenson that he could not foresee elections before the end of 1953. He was quite willing, he said, to yield power to a statesman in whom the officers had confidence. But frankly, he could think of no candidates.[77]

The Wafd case came before the State Council on January 10, 1953. An *Al-Misri* correspondent captured vividly the drama of the opening session. "Never before," he wrote, "has the State Council witnessed such a tumultuous session, full of loud tempests, exciting surprises, legal, constitutional and juridical discussion, violent debate, and vicious quarrels. . . ."[78] The Wafdist defense counsel, twelve lawyers strong, challenged the Party Reorganization Law, attacked its author, and defended the integrity of the two rejected Wafdists, Nahhas and Tawil. As in November, Ibrahim Farag provided the spark. "The Wafd will never be dissolved," he told the court. "Only the people will dissolve the Wafd, not you and not Sulayman Hafiz!"[79] After four days, the latter three much quieter than the first, the court recessed promising a decision on February 19.

On January 17, four days after the State Council adjourned, the junta decreed the dissolution of all political parties. In conjunction with the decree the officers announced the onset of a three-year transition period, during which time Muhammad Nagib would rule. The "blessed movement" now began to fancy itself a "revolution." Nagib remained prime minister, but his authority rested on his responsibilities as "Leader of the Revolution." Although it never decreed a formal change in title, the junta soon became known as the Command Council of the Revolution (CCR/Majlis Qiyadat al-Thawrah).[80]

Ever concerned to work within a legal framework, even in the absence of a constitution, the CCR quickly promulgated a series of supplementary decrees to bolster its position. The government reasserted the legality of all measures enacted between July 23 and January 10, the date of the Constitution's abrogation. Several days later an administrative court rejected the claim of a landowner who challenged the state's right to confiscate his land under terms of the agrarian reform.[81] On February 10 the government unveiled a temporary constitution. The charter, which consisted of eleven articles, granted sovereign authority to the Leader of the Revolution in the name of the CCR.

Too late, the Wafd had summoned its resources to stage a gallant defense of liberalism. Wafdists, who today admit that the hearing was run fairly, assert that had the State Council been allowed to render a judgment, it would have ruled in favor of the Wafd's right to exist, and perhaps have overturned the Party Reorganization Law. They see the threat of a Wafdist legal victory as the primary impetus for the abolition of the parties.[82] In reality, the Wafd case merely marks a postscript to a decision taken by the junta over a month before and now implemented for a variety of reasons. The timing of the officers' declaration of their revolution had less to do with Wafdist opposition than with internal political problems within the military, which will be treated later.

Yet, in announcing the abolition of the old order, the officers focused blame upon the political parties. Their proclamation of abolition spoke directly to the controversies of the previous six months: the resistance to voluntary "purification" and party reorganization, and opposition to land reform. In it the officers also began to enunciate their own vision of the betrayal of liberalism and set the groundwork for their revolution. "It has become clear to us," reads their pronouncement, "that personal and party interests which corrupted the aims of 1919 seek to reassert themselves in these dangerous times in our nation's history. . . ." The officers indicted the parties' "old style, reactionary mentality" as the source of "dissension and discord" within Egypt. They promised to "strike with all ferocity the hand of any who stand in the way of our aims."[83]

Had the officers really expected the parliamentary establishment to welcome their reforms? They had not, but at the same time they had hoped that the parties could be prodded to purge their ranks and that landowners could be cowed into accepting a ceiling on their property holdings. The officers had underestimated the stubborness of the elders, their determination to maintain their hold on power, their blindness to the implications of a military junta's overseeing government affairs. More important, the officers had underestimated the loyalty of many young parliamentarians, particularly Wafdists, to party, process, and even certain progenitors. When Ahmad Abu al-Fath and others like him lined up with Mustafa al-Nahhas, they caused the officers to reevaluate the role that such friends would play in the future. The ambivalence of the minimalists pushed the officers into the arms of the maximalists.

These divisions within the liberal establishment would persist throughout the early years of the revolution. Minimalists, truly alarmed at the prospect of long-term military rule, drifted further from the officers and became more openly critical. Maximalists continued to collaborate, until the specter of military dictatorship loomed larger than that of Wafdist rule.

4

"Lift up Your Head"

Throughout 1953 and into the early months of 1954 the officers struggled to define the political agenda for the revolution and to create a base of popular support. They intended their revolution to be temporary. However, hoping to clear the path for a turnover in party leadership, they had instead overturned the liberal order, and in so doing had alienated many of those whom they had hoped to place in power. They still shared the goals of young liberal intellectuals: "sound" parliamentary rule, constitutional reform, and social justice. Their assertion of direct power reflected a sober realization that Egypt's political reform required a bolder, more long-term strategy.

The officers had maneuvered with great success through unfamiliar political waters, sowing discord already brewing within and among the political parties. Yet they remained painfully conscious of their failure to achieve any of their major goals. However secure in power, until they could rally popular support the officers remained on the defensive from the attacks of the parliamentary establishment they had displaced. Not used to the vicissitudes of politics, the officers remained extremely sensitive to public criticism and were tormented by rumors of internal discord. They tolerated no overt signs of dissent. When unrest broke out on university campuses in early January 1953, the authorities ordered mass arrests. Yet at the same time they endeavored to downplay the repressive aspects of the regime and to foster a more positive public face. Instead of prison, the students were detained in the military academy. There, Nagib said, they would remain as "guests" until they learned to behave."[1]

In retrospect, the first year of the revolution, January–December 1953, is seen as a period in which the CCR steadily consolidated its hold on the offices of power, civilian and military. But at the time the period seemed one of false starts and stalled initiatives. The officers failed to inspire confidence in their rule or enthusiasm for a political agenda that remained vague. Faced with the mounting opposition of its enemies, the unfulfilled expectations of the general public, and the failure to reach an agreement with the British, the CCR found itself groping for direction. The strains of ruling during the transition period often tested its patience. On several occasions it contemplated stepping back from direct rule and entrusting more power to civilians. Yet its momentum led toward greater involvement in governing.

The officers defined their rule less in terms of their achievements than in relation to the old regime. *Revolution,* the term they once shunned, now became the watchword of their movement. But *revolution* still meant, above all, emancipation from the corrupt rule of the parties and the monarchy. Their vision of the future political order contained a new lineup of faces—including their own—but very little new structurally. The Revolutionary Tribunal, formed in September 1953, hinted at their capacity for draconian rule. By taking the offensive against the old regime, the officers succeeded in undermining the base of the parliamentary establishment. These show trials, however, proved to be less than successful in demoralizing the liberal opposition and less a reign of terror than projected at their outset. More than anything the trials revealed the uncertain groping of the revolution.

"One United National Front"

The same intelligentsia that had cautiously welcomed the July coup responded to the abrogation of the political parties and the assumption of direct power by the CCR with mixed emotions. Few political figures or intellectuals had advocated such a drastic step. The reform-minded had welcomed the call for party purges and many had accepted the Party Reorganization Law as a necessary step. Some advocated a major restructuring of the political system based on two or three parties. Others pressed the officers to form their own party to work within the existing political order.[2] In late December 1952 and early January 1953, when rumors spread that the junta might dissolve the parties, most party leaders reasserted their commitment to an open multiparty system.

Now faced with a fait accompli, many liberals chose accommodation with the regime. Not one party figure appointed to the constitutional committee only four days before the parties' abrogation resigned his seat, including the Wafdists. The young guard of the minority parties continued to collaborate with the regime. The Socialists, once vanguard of the antiparliamentary establishment, had spoken in favor of pluralism in December. Now they adapted to changed circumstances. "We had no feelings of sadness or any sense that we had to resist [the regime]," recalls Ibrahim Shukri. "Why resist this revolution that was following the very course we had called for?"[3]

The CCR hoped to tap such sentiments and mobilize popular support through a new political movement, the Liberation Rally (Hai'at al-Tahrir), founded in January 1953. The Rally was the fruition of long hours of soul searching on the officers' part, dating back to the unsettling weeks in late 1952. In mid-November the officers considererd forming a nonpartisan Free Officers front that would not necessarily displace the political parties, at least immediately, but would stand above the political fray. Members of existing parties would be encouraged to join.[4] On December 6, the day the government released the last wave of September prisoners, the press first reported the impending formation of this organization, now called the Liberation Rally.[5]

The government published the Rally's charter on January 16, the day it decided to outlaw the parties. The document represents the extent of the officers' political agenda at the time. It calls for unconditional British evacuation from the Nile valley and the Sudan's right to self-determination. The regime reasserted Egypt's commitment to both the Arab League and the United Nations. On the domestic front, the officers placed primary emphasis on the promulgation of a new constitution to be based on "faith in God, country, and self-confidence." The basis of society and economy would be "social justice," defined as a fair distribution of wealth and the means of production, basic civil rights, freedom of thought and religious belief, and security for job, health, and old age.[6]

The rhetoric of the new front encouraged national unity. Its chief slogan, "Lift up your head, my brother," spoke to peasant and worker. Misri Effendi, the national caricature, dimunitive, pudgy, bespectacled, light skinned, sporting a tarbush and clutching a rosary, would not disappear, but he would hereafter split time with a swarthy, muscular, galabiyya-clad fellah.

The regime inaugurated the Liberation Rally on January 23, six months to the day after the coup. CCR members assumed ceremonial posts. Muhammad Nagib was named president and Nasser secretary, Baghdadi general supervisor and Sadat chair of the Cario committee. The real directors were second-rank Free Officers, Ibrahim al-Tahawi, appointed assistant secretary general, and 'Abd Allah Tu'aymah, chief of the labor bureau. The junta charged them with organizing chapters on campuses and in factories, and with recruiting sympathetic old-regime and Muslim Brotherhood leaders to serve as spokespersons.

The Rally proved quite effective at organizing mass rallies and public fetes, often on the occasion of new national holidays. The first of these, Liberation Day, marked the anniversary of the massacre in Ismailia the previous year. Foreign observers described the celebrations, four days of parades and speeches, as orderly and festive. The popular enthusiasm they felt to be genuine and a boost to the regime's morale.[7]

As a grass-roots political organization the Liberation Rally never succeeded in surpassing its rivals, the Wafd and the Muslim Brotherhood. It did attract a number of independents, several disgruntled Wafdists and other old-party figures, and some Muslim Brothers, but few proved willing to play leading roles.[8] Overt Wafdist hostility to the regime and the Brotherhood's unease with the formation of a rival political front effectively blocked efforts by the Rally's organizers to create a civilian power base for the CCR. The Rally remained an organization run by the military that fostered the military mold of the regime.

Nor did the officers' realize their vision of a political movement encompassing young progressive members of the intelligentsia. Initially, some found the prospects attractive. 'Ali Amin compared the Rally to the spirit of

1919, "one united national front."[9] Ihsan 'Abd al-Quddus saw the Rally as the fruition of his advice to the officers that they found a political party to challenge the Wafd. However, this initial excitement dampened with the dissolution of the political parties. "There will be no victory without a battle, and the battle will not be fought if there are none to struggle with." 'Abd al-Quddus wrote in early February. The Liberation Rally would win nothing unless it competed with "honest parties."[10]

Popular attitudes are difficult to trace, especially as the regime tightened its grip on the media. Most journals directly affiliated with political parties, and a spate of smaller papers, some palace affiliated, others independent, had ceased publication on a regular basis by late 1952. The few party papers that survived shut down upon the parties' abrogation. The surviving Egyptian press, dailies and weeklies with wide circulation, operated under increasing constraints of the censor. They covered public rallies, the burgeoning number of new national holidays, and meetings of the constitutional committee, and printed cursory accounts of cabinet meetings. Foreign correspondents submitted their cables to government censors and wrote very little on the national mood.

Foreign diplomatic reports provide a more comprehensive view, revealing a national mood of anything but overwhelming approbation for the new regime. "It has become apparent that considerable sections of the people are growing tired of the Army Revolution," British Ambassador Stevenson noted in May.[11] While the Egyptian press described triumphal tours through the countryside, British embassy officials in late April and May reported instances of workers' greeting the officers with disinterest and even catcalls when they toured factories in the Delta and Canal Zone, causing them to cancel several appearances on short notice. In late May students heckled Nasser when he visited Alexandria University.[12]

Campuses and factories remained key centers of discontent. Politicized university students split loyalties between the Muslim Brotherhood, Wafdist-communist coalitions, and to a small degree the Liberation Rally. So long as the Brothers remained allied to the regime, as they did uneasily until late 1953, a standoff prevailed.[13]

The general discontent of the working class made industrial laborers receptive to antiregime agitation, especially communist. The government had implemented some measures to improve working conditions, such as a contracts law, issued in December 1952, that provided higher benefits and compensation for dismissed workers. At the same time, by instituting and manipulating a trade union confederation, restricting the scope of labor organization, and mandating arbitration, the regime moved to dominate the labor movement.[14] In July 1953 the ministry of social affairs opened two employment offices in Cairo and another in Alexandria. New legislation required industrial employers to report vacancies and hire only those registered. The measure produced minimal effects. Unemployment was stabilized but not reduced. By the end of August eleven thousand workers, thought to represent one-third of the unemployed in Cairo, had registered.

Workers remained on edge. In one reported incident troops arrested five hundred workers who staged a sit-down at a textile plant in Giza when informed an entire shift faced dismissal.[15]

What did the average Egyptian want of the regime? In mid-July, Salah Salim (accompanied by an *Akhbar al-Yawm* reporter and photographer) held an impromptu press conference with patrons of a cafe in a middle-class district of Cairo. Pressed to voice their concerns, those present addressed a variety of issues. They inquired about the struggle to end the occupation, the U.S. role in Anglo-Egyptian relations, unemployment among the educated, rent, social security, and, perhaps the most telling response to the Liberation Rally, the extravagance of public celebrations.[16] The acid test for the CCR in the public mind remained its ability to rid the country of the British and improve the daily lot of the people. Basic foodstuffs were still in short supply. Rumors abounded of internal strife within the CCR—some not unfounded— but average Egyptians worried about more immediate matters.

Reluctant Republicans

Cloaked in the garb of transitional martial rule, the CCR implemented significant structural changes in the political order and gradually concentrated power in its own hands. On February 21, Muhammad Nagib convened the first session of the constitutional committee of fifty. Few failed to note the regent's absence, and the symbolism of a general sitting in the seat of the former monarch at the opening ceremony, held in the Chamber of Deputies. Setting about its business, the committee elected 'Ali Mahir president. Mahir then divided the body into five subcommittees and selected a five-man executive committee. In late March the executive committee approved a resolution favoring establishment of a republic.[17]

The officers viewed the committee's work with ambivalence. They had formed the committee to represent broad political and religious concerns. They certainly regarded its task seriously and paid close attention to discussions of electoral reform and, particularly, the debate over the respective merits of presidential and parliamentary republican systems. Increasingly, the committee's work became theatrical in their eyes, a salve to ease popular disquiet at their extended authority. When the committee concurred on fundamental principles of political organization quicker than perhaps envisioned, it threatened to become a nuisance, only furthering popular perceptions that the CCR remained uncertain of its ultimate goals and perhaps reluctant to surrender power to parliamentary authority.

On June 18, bypassing the constitutional committee, the CCR unilaterally abolished the monarchy, declared Egypt a republic, and named Muhammad Nagib president. Having allowed the momentum built by the committee of fifty in April and early May to abate, the CCR now backed into what should have been a momentous occasion. With the first anniversary of the coup only one month away, the timing for the decree seems particularly ill-conceived. The officers' feeling that their movement was foundering appears to have motivated them not to wait. They had hesitated in May, undecided over whether Nagib should be named president. They offered the presidency to Lutfi al-Sayyid, an éminence grise of political circles, and perhaps to 'Ali Mahir. In the end their declaration coincided with another cabinet shuffle, precipitated primarily by the failure of yet another supply minister, the fourth since September, to insure a steady stock of basic foodstuffs in the market.[18]

Long expected and poorly orchestrated, the move generated little excitement, even among friends. Ahmad Abu al-Fath, whose continued friendship rested on past experiences and a fading trust on both sides, pressed the CCR to hasten promulgation of a constitution and restore civil rights. Those who accepted or even championed the parties' demise increasingly came to suspect the style of rule emerging under the CCR. The Amin brothers, who still offered their journals as a platform for anti-Wafdist rhetoric, also urged the CCR to press on toward a new constitution and to bring more civilians into leadership positions. In a rare instance of reproach, two days after the regime declared Egypt a republic, Mustafa Amin warned against the ills of one-man rule.[19]

With declaration of the republic, CCR members assumed cabinet portfolios for the first time. Nagib served as both prime minister and president. Nasser became deputy prime minister and interior minister, Salah Salim, minister of national guidance and minister of state for Sudan affairs, and Baghdadi war minister. In October Zakariya Muhyi al-Din and Gamal Salim joined the cabinet as ministers of interior and communications respectively.

With these appointments the CCR assumed full control of the internal security apparatus and began to monopolize control of the media. Under Nasser, and then Zakariya Muhyi al-Din, the Interior Ministry joined military and civilian intelligence forces under one command.[20] In September Salah Salim warned the press against rumor mongering and threatened to suspend the license of any journal that deviated from the "upright path."[21] In October and November he and his brother presided over purges of the Communications Ministry and the Egyptian broadcasting administration.[22]

The year's end saw the demise of two daily newspapers with long traditions, and the birth of a new government-sponsored daily. *Al-Zaman*, although traditionally linked to the palace, had in recent years become an organ for reformers such as Rashad al-Barawi, whose columns on agrarian reform had influenced the Free Officers. *Al-Balagh*, often a mouthpiece for the Wafd, at times a bitter opponent, was also tainted with old-regime affiliations. Suffering from low circulation, both now succumbed to market pressures. Mustafa Amin, perhaps gratuitously, perhaps sensing that an era was ending, eulogized the passing of *Al-Balagh*, which he compared to "the fall of a prize horse or a great bank's collapse."[23]

Edgar Gallad, owner of *Al-Zaman*, sold his plant to the government. His managing editor, Husayn Fahmi, with financial backing from the CCR, founded a new daily. *Al-Jumhuriya* (The Republic), to serve as the regime's organ. The first issue appeared on December 7. Fahmi recruited young progressive writers and intellectuals for his staff. His first issues featured columns by Muhammad Mandur, Khalid Muhammad Khalid, and Louis Awad.

If many did not recognize clearly the extent of the changes taking place in Egypt or the long-term implications of the CCR's steady concentration of power, much of the reason lay in the officers' own indecisiveness and unwillingness to assert openly their authority in the streets, factories, campuses, or mosques. The officers still hesitated to bare their swords. They wanted to woo Egypt, not subdue it. The propaganda machine ran at full speed, creating new heroes and new occasions for revelry. The censor scrupulously, although not always efficiently, suppressed rumor and deleted criticism. If many Eypgtians still looked to a parliamentary order purged of the old guard, it was because the CCR, in rhetoric and action, left that door ajar. It had outlawed the parties but not yet replaced them with a viable political alternative.

Trials of the Old Order

The Wafd stood in the wings awaiting a comeback, and the officers' uncertain steps only encouraged hopes for a revival. The party's morale, which had rallied during the legal battle in defense of Nahhas, collapsed just as quickly when the regime outlawed the parties. The Wafd's funds were confiscated, its headquarters closed, its leaders watched, and its journals so rigidly controlled that they could express only the mildest political critique.

Demoralized by defections and arrests, Wafdist leaders watched events helplessly. Mustafa al-Nahhas virtually disappeared from public sight. The government insisted it had issued no orders confining him to his home, but the authorities undoubtedly monitored his moves. In late May the censor ordered *Al-Misri* to cease printing its daily calendar of the party president's doings. His number-two man, Fu'ad Sirag al-Din, had been arrested on January 19. Relatives trying to gain his release proposed that he be allowed to leave the country, but the CCR refused. Without his forceful leadership, the party stood no chance of confronting the regime. In late April Jefferson Caffery cabled an obituary for the Wafd to Washington:

> Whether Nahhas dies soon or not he is too old and senile ever to resume effective political leadership. With Serageddine, his principal lieutenant and the brains of the old Wafd organization in jail or political exile, the prospects for any resurgence of the Wafd as a cohesive political body appear slight indeed.[24]

The only tactic Wafdists could adopt to resist the regime was to refuse to recognize the legitimacy of the CCR and the Liberation Rally. Except for a few figures who openly supported the Rally and served on the constitutional committee—Muhammad Salah al-Din and 'Abd al-Salam Gum'ah most notably—Wafdists overwhelmingly spurned the regime's efforts to mobilize support. Toward the summer of 1953, however, the Wafd realized that the regime was losing its ground swell of goodwill in the country, and took heart.

Ironically, this revival was fueled by the government's decision in late May 1953 to prosecute old-regime figures for corruption and abuse of power. The trials fell under the auspices of the Treason Court founded the previous December. In early January 1953 the authorities had indicted thirteen former Wafdist ministers and deputies, but after the parties' abolition the CCR saw little to gain by bringing the cases to trial. Now, frustrated at the early failure of the Liberation Rally to capture public enthusiasm, the officers changed their minds.

These trials, which dragged on into the winter of 1953–1954, failed to fire public spirit and did little to bolster the regime. The Treason Court had no power to hand down prison terms. Its charge was restricted to stripping the guilty of political rights, levying fines, and confiscating property. Furthermore, the composition of the tribunal, four military and three civilian judges, and the lack of judicial precedent for such trials created confusion.[25]

Prosecution gained the regime little political capital. The first case, against palace cronies and partners in graft, Karim Thabit and Ahmad Naqib, ran one month. Both lost their political rights, for ten and five years, respectively. Next, Farouk's special secretary, Muhammad Sulaymani, lost his political rights for fifteen years. Of the thirteen senior Wafdists indicted in January 1953, only 'Uthman Muharram faced the court, charged with ten counts of corruption, two in conjunction with Madam Nahhas. The names of Sirag al-Din, two of his brothers, Madam Nahhas's brother, and others were reportedly brought before the court, but none were tried. Sirag al-Din's name reemerged from time to time throughout the summer, but the CCR dared not try him. He remained in prison until early August, when he was quietly released for health reasons.[26]

These were show trials but poorly orchestrated, and verdicts were not fixed in advance. Wahid Ra'fat, codefense counsel for 'Uthman Muharram in several cases, challenged the tribunal's legality. Nonetheless, he believed the trials were run fairly under the circumstances and credited the civilian jurists for insuring a degree of due process. His proof rested in part on his client's acquittal in two cases he argued.[27]

Rather than daunt the Wafd, the trials gave the party a public forum to challenge the regime, one in which Wafdist barristers excelled. The ten counts against Muharram consumed the most time, prolonging the hearings into the fall of 1953. The defense refused to be cowed. Wahid Ra'fat argued that the entire proceeding defied due process; Ibrahim Farag insisted the nation should thank Muharram, builder of roads, not indict him. Muharram himself, with a brash, assured demeanor, dominated the courtroom (much as Sirag al-Din would do eight months later before the Revolutionary Tribunal.) He played to a sympathetic visitors gallery, deriding his accusers as "jackasses" and "simpletons," drawing the admonishment of the bench.[28]

Other Wafdists used the courtroom as a political arena in another series of

trials. Ibrahim Farag and Mahmud Ghannam defended Wafdist and communist students brought to trial in July. Even with minimal media coverage they
managed to keep the image of the Wafd alive in the public mind. Their
particular roles point to a degree of reconciliation between Wafdist youth and
party leaders. Ghannam, the assistant party secretary, had been a bête noire
of the Wafdist Vanguard, which had succeeded in forcing his resignation from
the executive along with Sirag al-Din's in September 1952. Farag, who had
been an early proponent of appeasing the regime, subsequently emerged as
Nahhas's right hand in Sirag al-Din's absence. Neither, it can be assumed,
would have accepted these cases without Nahhas's knowledge or consent.[29]

Nahhas, himself, again defied those who were quick to dismiss him as a
spent political force. In late August he made several public appearances that
the British oriental counselor wrote, "have been the occasion of minor popular demonstrations."[30] On the anniversary of Saʿd Zaghlul's death, a Wafdist
holiday, Nahhas spoke to a crowd gathered at the founding father's tomb. In
his speech, copies of which soon found their way into the streets, the Wafd
chief accused the regime of undermining Egypt's national interests and
called for the restoration of political freedoms. Soon after, Nahhas visited the
main mosque in Alexandria, where, according to Ibrahim Tilʿat, a not so
spontaneous rally ensued. The police escorted Nahhas home.[31]

Such omens of a Wafdist revanche shook the officers' confidence. The
press, which reported neither incident, did print in full another speech
delivered in homage to Zaghlul. Makram ʿUbayd's address echoed Nahhas's
call for greater freedoms but without the latter's hostile tone. The officers
could not have been totally pleased with ʿUbayd's noticeable lack of references to the army movement or the revolution. But in order to steal the
Wafd's thunder, they encouraged the revival of old political squabbles.[32]

With the formation of the Revolutionary Tribunal (Mahkamat al-Thawrah)
in September 1953, the officers for the first time hinted at a willingness to
resort to naked force to establish their dominance over the political process.
Their intent in bringing old-guard political figures to trial for treason before a
court empowered to decree capital punishment was at once to shock unrepentant liberals and monarchists into submission and to unite the general
public around the revolution. The new tribunal tried defendants accused of
conspiring with foreign powers to sow discord, unsettle the revolutionary
regime, and bring about a return of royal or corrupt party rule. Unlike the
Treason Court, a mixed civilian-military tribunal, three members of the
CCR, Baghdadi, Sadat, and Hasan Ibrahim, sat as sole judges.

Salah Salim's speech in Republic Square on September 15, in which he
announced the tribunal's formation, provides insight into the officers' thinking at the time. The Free Officers, he proclaimed, had dedicated themselves
to "the struggle against imperialism and the Egyptian traitors who served its
cause." "Foreign imperialism did not rule in this country nor did it consolidate its foothold by the force of arms or soldiers. Rather, it ruled Egypt until
July 23, 1952, by means of Egyptian traitors." Salim spiced his speech with
well-known anecdotes of how the political parties stopped at nothing to gain

and keep power, most of which harked back to the 1950 Wafd government. He mentioned no names. But a stinging imitation of a party leader insisting he be allowed to kiss the monarch's hand unmistakably mocked Nahhas's mannerisms. The traitors' deceit, Saliim told his audience, was no longer so overt. It was manifest in "rumors and more rumors everywhere," intended to destabilize the economy, encourage foreign criticism, and foster disillusion and unease in the country and hate toward the army. He pointed to the universities as a particular trouble spot.[33]

Within a week of Salim's announcement the government arrested eleven leading old-regime figures, and placed Nahhas and his wife under house arrest.[34] The tribunal convened on September 24 to consider the case of former prime minister and Sa'dist chief Ibrahim 'Abd al-Hadi. The court charged the defendant with multiple offenses, ranging from corruption to personal responsibility for the murder of Hasan al-Banna. The flagrant abuse of judicial procedure followed by the death sentence meted out on October 2 stunned Egypt. Its commutation to life imprisonment three days later was greeted with uneasy sighs of relief.[35]

At the same time many Egyptians felt little sympathy for the former Sa'dist leader. The regime targeted 'Abd al-Hadi as its first victim precisely because he represented the primary old-regime figure with whom Egyptians, particularly those sympathetic to the Muslim Brotherhood, associated the violence and abuse of civil liberties of the late 1940s. The Brothers, with the significant exception of their leader, Hasan al-Hudaybi, greeted his trial with enthusiasm.

In the following seven weeks the court tried fourteen cases, concluding each in several sessions. It handed down progressively lighter sentences as it turned its attention to lesser figures. Ibrahim Farag of the Wafd and Karim Thabit, Farouk's press attaché, received life sentences that the court immediately reduced to fifteen years. Mahmud Ghannam, Prince 'Abbas Halim, and two palace men received fifteen-year suspended sentences. Another Farouk crony was stripped of rank and property. A defendant in the Palestine arms case and two officers in Farouk's political police were sentenced to fifteen years. Ahmad 'Abd al-Ghaffar, a Liberal party leader, was fined £E 63,000. Finally, an employee in the Social Affairs Ministry received ten years for rumor mongering.[36]

In addition to the trials of senior political figures, the Revolutionary Tribunal had a second face. The court tried thirteen common citizens accused as British agents and collaborators in the Suez Canal Zone. Their trials gave Egyptians a sober warning of the penalty for cooperation with the enemy. Of the thirteen tried, eleven were convicted. Four were hanged. One received a life sentence, the others sentences of ten or fifteen years. British diplomatic records validate the legitimacy of the charges against most of the accused, many of whom had been British army or RAF employees. Some had indeed provided information about guerrilla activities, and several most likely participated in the interrogation of captured partisans. Some were merely merchants or skilled laborers in British employ.[37]

In this initial phase the Revolutionary Tribunal failed to achieve a major propaganda success. It would be wrong to say that the trials quickly became commonplace events. They continued to command interest and provoked debate, but none of the defendants who followed 'Abd al-Hadi came close to matching his villainous image. Nor could the regime credibly demonstrate the existence of any royalist-party conspiracy. The public greeted the spurious charges, or at best highly circumstantial evidence presented the court, with cynicism.[38] As a result, most cases focused on corruption and abuse of influence prior to July 23, barely distinguishing them from cases heard simultaneously before the Treason Court. It soon became apparent to the CCR that if it wanted to reap a major success, it needed to tackle greater personalities.

With the trial of Fu'ad Sirag al-Din, the Revolutionary Tribunal entered an entirely different phase. When Sirag al-Din faced the court in December none pretended that it was not the Wafd, in the person of its most powerful and controversial leader, that stood accused. The case against the Wafd boss, the man described as the power behind the party's throne, consisted of five major counts: illegally benefiting from road paving as transport minister in 1945, accepting a £E 5000 bribe, conspiring to obstruct the investigation into arms racketeering during the Palestine War, allowing the king to transfer funds abroad illegally, and conspiring to corner the cotton bourse, the last four counts between 1950 and 1952. The trial, which lasted nearly eight weeks, far surpassed the bounds of the indictment as the prosecution focused on the defendant's rise to prominence in the party, his presumed control over Mustafa al-Nahhas, and personal responsibility for the failings of the 1950 government.

The court admitted any sort of damning testimony.[39] Sirag al-Din's bitterest rivals—Nagib al-Hilali, Zaki 'Abd al-Mut'al, Husayn Sirri, 'Ali Mahir, Muhammad Husayn Haykal, and Makram 'Ubayd were the most prominent—testified against him. Hilali recounted the falling-out between Nahhas and Makram prior to the latter's ouster, and revealed how the Wafd undermined Anglo-Egyptian negotiations carried out by the Sidqi government in 1946. The former prime minister also recounted his own falling-out and break with the Wafd in 1951, and accused the defendant of having conspired with the British and palace to secure his ouster in June 1952. 'Abd al-Mut'al detailed how the accused, along with Madame Nahhas, ran the Wafd behind Nahhas's back, and plotted to corner the cotton exchange in 1950. Makram 'Ubayd recalled Sirag al-Din's precipitate rise in the party and his own related fall. His testimony, which included a rather lengthy digression on Nahhas's romantic failures and the circumstances surrounding his marriage to Zaynab al-Wakil, revealed in a striking manner the extent to which animosity rent the ranks of the old establishment. Most of the others were no less sparing. If they recognized the self-destructive nature of their testimony, they were too consumed by malice to care or to control themselves. Some, like Haykal, tried to be circumspect and rebuffed efforts by the court to goad them into equating the system with the man on trial. Only 'Ali Mahir appeared genuinely offended by the process.[40]

Sirag al-Din fought staunchly in his own defense and often dominated the proceedings. He posited himself as a champion of the nationalist struggle. He played loose with the facts, taking credit for opening the investigation of the Palestine arms case, an investigation he had, in fact, tried to obstruct, and for organizing the "popular struggle" in the Canal Zone in 1951. He blasted Hilali for bowing to British pressure and ordering his arrest in April 1952. He vigorously denied accusations of corruption and decried charges he sought to corner the cotton market as a "tempest in a teacup." At the same time, the defendant responded lamely to questions about "exceptional promotions" of party loyalists within the government bureaucracy. "It is not a matter to agree or disagree with," he said. "It was a general policy since 1928."[41]

Throughout this circus the regime remained reluctant to bare its teeth. The officers thought they could bully Sirag al-Din, and at times his judges appeared amused by his bluster. They certainly underestimated the man's fighting spirit. In the end, the man set up to symbolize the evils of the old regime received a fifteen-year sentence.[42]

Their continued hesitance to bring Nahhas before the Revolutionary Tribunal and the relatively light sentences passed on Sirag al-Din and the others betray the officers' lingering doubts about their popularity and hold over the country. In an anticlimactic gesture, they next pressed charges against Zaynab al-Wakil, Madam Nahhas. Every bit as impudent as Sirag al-Din, she challenged the authority of the court. Citing ill health, she refused to appear for her trial. The court tried her in absentia and on March 7, 1954 fined her £E 10,000. Amid the power struggles of February–March 1954 the case passed largely unnoticed.[43]

The question that then must be asked is how successful was the Revolutionary Tribunal in demoralizing the opposition? The trials did suceed in impressing upon the old guard the repressive capabilities of the regime. The CCR demonstrated a will to survive that dampened expectations of its impending or inevitable fall. Moreover, by jailing the real power brokers and spearheads of Wafdist resistance—Sirag al-Din, Ghannam, and Farag—the regime ensured that no organized opposition would emerge from the top. But from the standpoint of demoralizing the opposition the trials clearly failed, for the attack was misdirected. Organized opposition to the regime increasingly came not from party elders but from younger Wafdists allied with communist counterparts who shed no tears for Sirag al-Din and his minions.

How successful were the trials in discrediting the old regime, in building credibility and legitimacy for the CCR? Public reaction is difficult to gauge. It may best be generalized as ambivalent. The manner in which the trials were run alienated the intelligentsia. Buy many young intellectuals continued to support the regime in the hope that when this phase, a relatively moderate and half-hearted reign of terror, passed, the officers would continue to support progressive reform and move to end the transitional period.

On balance, the trials succeeded in revealing the old regime for what it was and checking any tendencies to look back on the prerevolutionary period with nostalgia. When, in March 1954, the officers faced their consummate test of survival, confronted by revived forces of the old political establishment, they prevailed, in part, by positing their revolution as the only alternative to a return to the corrupt, opportunistic party politics of the old order. The parade of former ministers and party bosses indicting one another before the Revolutionary Tribunal undoubtedly played a major part in preserving that image in the public mind.

This is why the funeral procession of Hifni Mahmud, described at the outset of this study, seems so poignant. At the very moment in which the CCR grappled with Fu'ad Sirag al-Din for authority in the courtroom, CCR members marched alongside Ahmad 'Abd al-Ghaffar, a prior defendant, in what looked to be relative amity. Was reconciliation possible and democracy around the bend once the show trials had ended? Liberation Rally placards enjoined Egyptians to lift up their heads. But Egypt's young leaders looked back more than forward. Their rhetoric focused increasingly on excuses for failure—traitors in their midst, backsliders, and rumor mongerers—rather than pride in the "new age" they tried to inaugurate. By the year's end the officers had strengthened their hold over the country, but they faced other antagonists besides the political parties: communists, Muslim Brothers, and factionalism within the army and their own ranks within the CCR.

5

"The Great Deception"

In the rhetoric that emerged during 1953 and that culminated in the show trials that autumn, the CCR defined its revolution primarily in contradistinction to the old "reactionary" political establishment. In doing so, the CCR faced troubling questions about the role of antiestablishment movements that shared a common disdain for old-regime politics but that now constituted ideological challenges to the developing revolutionary agenda and comprised alternative bases of power in the country. The Muslim Brotherhood and DMNL, the largest and least doctrinaire communist movement, had collaborated with the Free Officers and played significant supporting roles in their coup. The officers thus faced twin questions: What debt, if any, did they owe their allies? And, What ideological influence would these movements exert on the course of social and political reform?

The answers to these questions became readily apparent within the first six months of junta rule. Having seized power, the officers drew back gradually from the Brothers and abruptly turned on the communists. At the same time the officers continued to seek the counsel of friends in both camps, particularly those on the Left. The junta drew closer to the Brothers in late 1952, but the friendship remained forever strained, and in the following year deteriorated.

The breakdown in relations between the junta and its allies is rooted in both the ideological orientations of the officers and the exigencies of their growing resolve to assert political authority. Prior to the July coup, allies of the Free Officers had failed to grasp the implications of the movement's resolve to remain independent. The response of the DMNL and the Muslim Brothers to the coup reflected their ambivalent feelings for the parliamentary order, as discussed earlier, as well as to the idea of military intervention in politics. Initially, each looked upon the coup with favor. The Brothers, more hostile to the party system, adopted a maximalist stand, pressing the officers to extend their authority and refrain from a precipitate restoration of parliamentary life. The DMNL proffered a minimalist position. Accepting the fait accompli of military intervention, it encouraged the officers to enact social and political reforms and make way for civilian rule. Neither sought to share power in any direct sense. Both, however, clearly expected a degree of influence in setting policy for the future.

Ideology and power politics are not easily separated. The officers' vision prior to and even after January 1953 was of a "purified" liberal parliamentary order, one that, to the Brothers' regret, was to be secular in nature and, to the dismay of the Left, refused to tolerate Marxism. At the same time, the officers feared precisely what these movements offered as political allies: powerful political machines. The Brotherhood could rally mass support second only to the Wafd, and with its paramilitary secret organization and cells in the army and police, indeed appeared to be, as the CCR would later label it, a state within a state. Although splintered and relatively small, communist movements were well organized on campuses and in factories, and had also infiltrated the officer corps. Both the Brothers and communists, like the Wafd, suffered greatly from factiousness and internal rivalries, a problem they would only begin to resolve at far too late a stage in the confrontation.

"Abandoning His Commmitment to the People"

Despite the cooperation between the Free Officers and DMNL, as well as the attraction Marxism held for certain members of the junta, the officers as a group never considered sharing power with or even tolerating the existence of an active communist movement. The leftist social critique had influenced the officers more than any other antiestablishment credo, and they would continue to share common goals and ideals, but most Free Officers rejected Marxist doctrine outright. Moreover, close collaboration with the DMNL bred a grudging respect for the communist underground network within the officer corps and outside the military. That, plus their uncertainty at the degree of communist infiltration in their own movement produced a great degree of anxiety after July 23.

The speed with which the junta turned on communist allies belies any notion of potential cooperation. Communists from all movements blamed the United States for pressing the junta to turn so suddenly against the Left. U.S. and British diplomatic records verify a strong foreign role, which will be discussed in a later chapter. However, while both governments pressured the regime to get tough on communism, the junta needed little convincing. From the outset the officers expressed clearly their desire to eradicate communist activism and asked the Americans and British for help.

The threat of working-class unrest posed by the disturbances at Kafr al-Dawwar, despite the strikers' projunta stand, heightened the officers' resolve to crush the Left. In the wake of the disturbances the junta approached both the U.S. and British embassies seeking assistance in battling communist cells.[1] Although they told U.S. embassy officers they suspected the Wafd of fomenting trouble, evidence pointed to a communist hand. Khamis, one of the two condemned workers, the one with whom Nagib met, was a communist, although his actual role in the events at Kafr al-Dawwar remains clouded.[2]

The multiplicity of mutually hostile movements, divided over strategy and dogma, and competing for cadres, precluded any real chances for the Left to challenge the consolidation of military rule. The three most important communist groups greeted the coup with varying degrees of caution. Within weeks of the coup two of them, the ECP and Workers Vanguard, denounced the junta as reactionary.

ECP Secretary General Fu'ad Mursi has spoken of a three-day grace period, July 24–26, before his movement began to denounce the junta. The decision to exile Farouk withou' ∟rial, the failure quickly to restore political rights or abolish the monarchy, and the close association, already apparent, with the U.S. embassy, asserts Mursi, verified ECP misgivings about the validity of a progressive role for the military in national affairs. Ties between the Free Officers and leading DMNL figures undoubtedly also alienated the ECP command, which soon dubbed the army movement the "great deception."[3]

Closely allied to the Wafdist Left, the Workers Vanguard looked primarily to the junta's policy toward the Wafd and restoration of parliamentary rule as acid tests of the officers' progressive credentials. Hilmi Yassin, a member of the secretariat, recalls learning of the coup in Huckstep prison, along with other communists who had been imprisoned either by the Wafd in 1950–1951 or the Mahir government after Black Saturday. He says communist prisoners greeted the news with unease. DMNL members, who soon received details from the outside, then turned jubilant, while others remained skeptical. When Yassin was released on July 28, part of a widespread amnesty for political prisoners, his comrades advised him to disappear until the army's intent became clear. The junta's decision not to recall parliament troubled Vanguard leaders. After Kafr al-Dawwar the movement denounced the junta as fascistic, Nagib as a dictator.[4]

The DMNL, with two members in the junta, Khalid Muhyi al-Din and Yusuf Siddiq, expected its collaboration with the Free Officers to continue. When the regime turned on the Left, and on the DMNL specifically, the movement rationalized its persecution. DMNL leaders adopted a minimalist position regarding military rule, hoping against hope that civil liberties would be restored and the arrests of cadres cease when the situation in the country stabilized. In fact, during the first year of the Free Officers' rule the DMNL suffered the brunt of the regime's anticommunist offensive. Sorry they had opened political prison doors so hastily in late July, and responding to British and U.S. complaints, the officers arrested DMNL members in the Delta city Al-Mansurah in early August.[5]

At the same time Nasser and other junta members maintained contact with DMNL leaders. They invited Ahmad Fu'ad to attend preliminary discussions on land reform, which Rashad al-Barawi and Ahmad Abu al-Fath also attended. They also delegated Ahmad Hamrush to found a monthly journal directed at the military. *Al-Tahrir* (Liberation), which premiered in early September, featured essays on social problems—land, housing, inflation—and specific military concerns—salaries, pensions, suffrage—by

Abu al-Fath, Barawi, and Yusuf Siddiq, as well as short stories by Yusuf Idris and Fathi Ghannam. Hamrush's editorials heralded the "army movement" a "revolution"—his opening piece did so seven times.[6] Nasser and several comrades attended Abu al-Fath's nightly discussion group in the *Al-Misri* building with some regularity, where they discussed current events with leftist intellectuals, including Fu'ad, Idris, and Lutfi al-Khuli. All this as arrests of cadres and seizure of printing presses continued.

The hangings of the two Kafr al-Dawwar workers, now canonized by all on the Left, did not provoke a change in thinking within the DMNL secretariat. Rather, the movement denounced the strikers as agents of "imperialism and reaction." The officers reportedly promised DMNL leaders they would overturn the capital sentences, a promise they may have initially intended to keep. Instead, in the immediate aftermath of the disturbances the authorities arrested thirty to forty DMNL cadres.[7]

Gradually, the DMNL found itself pushed into the opposition. In late October Ahmad Hamrush was dismissed as editor of *Al-Tahrir*. His replacement, Tharwat 'Ukashah, took over with instructions to watch the "red" tone of the journal. However, the journal changed little under its new editor, and Hamrush contributed a regular column signed with his initials.[8] The DMNL finally broke with the regime over the dissolution of the political parties and the arrest, the day before, of Hamrush and other dissident officers. In a decree dated January 25 the movement denounced the regime in the person of Muhammad Nagib, who, "abandoning his commitment to the people [had] lifted his veil to reveal a fascistic face." Citing a chain of arrests, DMNL leaders accused the junta of trying to turn Egypt into a vast prison.[9]

The war against communism continued throughout 1953, police raids netting for the first time members of groups other than the DMNL. Communist activity remained restricted to campus politics, trade union organization, and the clandestine dissemination of propaganda. On the campuses, cautiously reopened by the authorities in late January, dissident activity continued, occasionally marked by public demonstrations. A military decree of January 18 outlawed the publication of all newspapers and journals affiliated with communist movements. Still, pamphlets and makeshift journals found their way into factories and the streets, and sometimes the newsstands. One such publication, *Al Ghad* (Tomorrow), had an initial run of 100,000 copies.[10]

Published irregularly, communist literature was often timed to coincide with major events, such as the visit to Egypt of U.S. Secretary of State John Foster Dulles in May 1953 and declaration of the republic in June, or anniversaries, of Kafr al-Dawwar and of abrogation of the 1936 Anglo-Egyptian treaty. Communist literature, no matter who the author, contained several constants. Communists consistently denounced the CCR as the "fascist military dictatorship," the "fascist gang," and the "agent of imperialism." Some manifestoes were theoretical, directed at an audience schooled in Marxism, and some contained self-criticism. For example, in September DMNL ideologues conceded that their early support for the regime had disregarded sound class analysis. Spelled out in simpler terms, the communist critique continued to ring true for a growing number of workers, impatient for jobs and better working conditions, and disappointed at the lack of progress under CCR leadership.[11]

The attrition of arrests and confiscated printing equipment threatened to offset whatever inroads communists could make among workers and students. The majority of arrests came in two waves. In March–April 1953, prior to the Dulles visit, the authorities targeted the ECP, and for the first time seriously disrupted that movement, which, according to a U.S. embassy official, had "of late been the most active in its propaganda work." Nasser promised the Americans that the DMNL would be next, and kept his word. The second wave of arrests, which commenced in August and continued throughout the fall of 1953, netted some one hundred DMNL cadres, including the entire secretariat.[12]

Between July 1953 and September 1954 the government brought most of those arrested to trial. A special military court presided over closed proceedings. Because of the secrecy surrounding the proceedings, the regime gained little political capital from them. The press reported the commencement of major cases and revealed a limited amount of information about the accused. Sometimes the censor allowed names to be printed.

If the officers had considered orchestrating show trials, provocative defense tactics quickly made them reconsider. The first trial publicly noted, the case of twenty-five ECP members, commenced on July 27, 1953. Chief counsel for the defense, Mahmud Ghannam, the Wafd's assistant secretary, challenged the legality of the tribunal, and sought permission to subpoena Nagib, Nasser, and other CCR members in order to ask them why the defendants stood trial for distributing leaflets similar in content to Free Officers' literature printed prior to the coup. According to the press, the officers initially considered accepting the challenge. Instead, at the behest of the prosecution, the court heard the testimony of the Mufti of Egypt, the highest Islamic legal official in the country, who amid the defendants' heckling, denounced communism as subversive to state and religion.[13] Thereafter, defense counsels routinely protested that their clients and the regime shared common cause on issues of land reform, democracy, and republicanism, insuring that further proceedings remained closed to public scrutiny.

In response to the threat of long-term military rule, the DMNL endeavored to create a national front of opposition movements, including the Wafd. However, because of the Left's persistent inability to overcome doctrinal disputes, unity remained an elusive goal, even in the face of a greater foe. Fragmentation in fact worsened under the pressures of government repression. Rival communist movements rebuffed DMNL calls for solidarity, critical of the DMNL on ideological grounds and wary of its propensity to splinter. Such fears proved justified in late June when, rejecting the notion of a popular front, the DMNL secretary general and other influential comrades bolted the movement to found a separate organization, the DMNL Revolutionary Current (Al-Tayyar al-Thawri). [14]

Although a variety of ad hoc coalitions continued to operate on an informal basis, the idea of an official, organized coalition between communists and Wafdists remained illusory. The idea, however, remained alive, if unattainable. Each communist movement had contacts with leftist Wafdists with whom its members collaborated, often surreptitiously pretending to be Wafdists themselves. Several such coalitions took on the name. The DMNL and its Wafdist allies published a newsletter titled "The National Front" (Al-Jabhah al-Wataniyah); Workers Vanguard and Wafdist allies published one called "The Front" (Al-Jabhah). [15]

High-level Wafdist cooperation with the former has been asserted and appears to have been initiated. Zaki Murad of the DMNL secretariat declared before his death that his movement and the Wafd formed a joint committee in April 1953 to supervise antiregime activity. A government report used in the trial of forty-four DMNL cadres in September 1954, referred to by the regime as the "National Front case," implicates Ibrahim Farag as the Wafd's representative. Farag does not discuss the matter in his memoirs, and has denied that any high-level contacts with the DMNL occurred. [16] But the fact that he and Mahmud Ghannam defended communists before the military tribunal suggests that Wafd leaders began to view the Left with more kindness than in the past. Still, it seems doubtful that the higher echelons of the party would have offered or accepted overtures for any formal relationship with communist movements, clandestine or otherwise. Reports of a formalized national front appear to be exaggerated.

Cooperation between Wafdist Vanguard and communist students remained confined to rare campus demonstrations and the dissemination of propaganda. This collaboration produced an interesting revisionist rhetoric, almost reactionary in some respects, given the prior rhetoric of its authors. Leaflets coauthored by communists and left Wafdists resounded with communist slogans. At the same time, DMNL-Wafd allies advocated restoration of the 1923 Constitution. A leaflet printed to commemorate abrogation of the 1936 Anglo-Egyptian treaty lauded the Wafd's "heroic stand" and praised its leader, who "bowed to the will of the people and unleashed bullets and fire against the imperialist." [17] Ignored, despite the constant reminders before the Revolutionary Tribunal, was the Wafd's subservience to the palace, the nepotism that plagued the 1950 government, and the fire that ravaged Cairo less than two years before.

However successful the regime proved at infiltrating and smashing opposition cells, however confined those cells' activities were, their opposition posed a threat the CCR felt it could ill afford to ignore. As the officers felt themselves losing momentum, struggling to maintain a national consensus, and unsure on what to base it, even a whisper of dissent roared like thunder. At the same time, disunited and reeling from mass arrests, communist move-

ments and communist-Wafdist coalitions posed no serious threat to the regime, certainly not in comparison to the Wafd and Muslim Brotherhood.

"Those who Traffic in Religion"

The confrontation between the regime and the Brotherhood passed through
several distinct stages. During the first six months of their rule the officers
hoped to maintain friendly relations with the Brothers, albeit from a distance. To an extent, their strategy mirrored their policy toward the Wafd.
The officers regarded the Brothers with a mixture of fear and guarded optimism. They feared the Brothers' street power and capacity for violence, and
mistrusted senior Brotherhood leaders, particularly Hasan al-Hudaybi, pre-
ferring to consort with their contemporaries. As their conflict with the political parties intensified in the fall of 1952, they drew closer to the Brothers,
hoping to co-opt the movement by promoting a particular set of friends from
within. Internecine strife within the Brotherhood allowed the CCR to effect
a divide-and-rule strategy to great effect. However, when internal meddling
failed to bring allies to the fore, the CCR, nearly one year to the day after it
outlawed the political parties, ordered the Muslim Brotherhood dissolved
and arrested most of its leaders.

After July 23 Brotherhood leaders elected to assume a low profile. They
expressed public support for the takeover but denied the veracity of widespread rumors, not all unfounded, of Free Officers-Brotherhood ties. Hudaybi, like the party leaders, stood in line to meet with 'Ali Mahir and Muhammad Nagib. To each the general guide urged restoration of civil liberties, the
release of political prisoners, and major constitutional reform with greater
reliance on Islamic law.[18]

The Brothers no doubt looked to the regime with both favor and apprehension. Several days after Farouk's departure, Nasser met Hudaybi at the
home of another Brother. Each side later produced divergent accounts of this
encounter, both of which reflect more upon subsequent disappointments and
suspicions. The Brothers say that Nasser told Hudaybi in no uncertain terms
that the officers did not consider themselves beholden to the movement.
According to the officers, the Brothers proposed forming a secret joint committee to oversee policy formulation for the new government, a proposal that
the junta rejected. Given Hudaybi's cautious manner, such an outright proposal at this time seems unlikely, as does Nasser's purported message, which
would seem to be a final severance of ties.[19]

In fact, during the first months after the coup the officers made little
attempt to hide, and even heralded their former ties to Mahmud Labib and
the Brotherhood. Later, as the movements drifted apart, the officers minimized the connection, ultimately erasing the Brothers from any positive role
in the official history of the coup.[20]

However perturbed by this encounter, Hudaybi and his associates resolved to back the Free Officers. In a public statement released August 1, the

Guidance Council clarified its support for the army movement and proposed a political platform for the new government. The Brothers urged the junta to initiate a purge of political parties and the state bureaucracy. They advocated restoration of parliamentary democracy only after constitutional reform, without which all talk of representative government was senseless. Three necessary phases for political change were envisioned: (1) freeing the "oppressed," defined as all political prisoners; (2) banishing the "oppressors," the corrupt party bosses, from political life; and (3) ameliorating "conditions which produced the oppression," the British occupation. In addition, the Brothers prescribed measures to transform Egypt into a truly Islamic society. These ranged from specific religious reforms, such as instituting charitable foundations, outlawing usury, fixing the mosque as the cultural center of society, and teaching religion in the military, to general economic policies of salary increases, land reclamation, industrialization, and agrarian reform.[21]

The Brothers publicly applauded the call for voluntary party purges and the government's appointment of a regency without recourse to parliament. They also supported the harsh measures taken against striking workers at Kafr al-Dawwar, whom they denounced as "enemies of the revolution."[22] Reservations about land reform, however, set the Brothers at odds with the officers. In its August policy statement the Guidance Council had approved an imposed ceiling on the number of feddans a landowner might hold. Suddenly, in early September, just before the measure became law, Hudaybi publicly expressed reservations. The Brotherhood accepted the principle of setting a limit on property rights, he explained, but now, without explanation, he suggested the ceiling be raised from two hundred to five hundred feddans.[23] By arguing in this manner, Hudaybi appeared to the officers no different from 'Ali Mahir or his landowner friends, who, despairing at the imminent announcement of land reform, hoped to cut their losses by negotiating the limit upward.

Although the officers increasingly suspected Hudaybi of duplicity, the Brothers as a movement had not yet become a problem.[24] The officers felt much closer to younger Brothers, contemporaries of theirs such as Hasan al-'Ashmawi, Salah Shadi, and Sayyid Qutb. Matters were complicated by the fact that those younger Brothers with whom the officers maintained most intimate contact ranked among Hudaybi's closest loyalists. Because of this, the officers did not initially turn, as they later would, to rivals and enemies of the general guide. Rather, they hoped to undercut Hudaybi's authority by working through his allies.

Rather than foster good feelings, the junta's offer to include several Brothers in the first Nagib cabinet widened rifts within the movement and furthered the officers' unease. Due to the disparity of participants' accounts, details of the controversy remain difficult to piece together. The officers apparently informed the Brothers of their plans to dismiss 'Ali Mahir several days in advance. Hudaybi either nominated or accepted the officers' nomination to the new government of Hasan al-'Ashmawi and Munir al-Dilla, both Hudaybi men (Dilla has been cited as most influential in arranging the compromise that led to Hudaybi's selection as general guide) and friends of the junta. Under pressure from civilian aides, notably Sulayman Hafiz and Fathi Radwan, both of whom argued that neither 'Ashmawi or Dilla had requisite experience, the officers either withdrew their offer or rejected Hudaybi's nominees. Radwan then nominated Ahmad Hasan al-Baquri, an old comrade from campus politics in the 1930s and a leading contender for the post of general guide following Hasan al-Banna's murder. The officers approved Baquri as minister of pious endowments. For the second slot, justice minister, they selected Ahmad Husni, an associate but not a member of the Brotherhood.[25]

The question of participation in the government divided the Guidance Council. Under Hudaybi's lead the council voted against approving the two new nominees. None could be too displeased with the selection of Husni, but the nomination of Baquri, a powerful rival within the Guidance Council, displeased Hudaybi, who enforced his expulsion from the movement. Baquri, who did not attend the meeting, accepted his ouster and threw in his lot with the new regime. As a religious figure and close associate of Hasan al-Banna, Baquri's presence in the government lent the regime an important degree of legitimacy when it later made war on Hudaybi and the Brotherhood.[26]

Internal opposition to the general guide soon crystallized around the ongoing dispute over the Brotherhood's political status. In March 1951 Hudaybi had thwarted efforts of those who sought to contest elections planned (but postponed soon afterward) by Prime Minister Hilali. The controversy now revived as a consequence of the Party Reorganization Law decreed by the Nagib government on September 9. Hudaybi again insisted that the Brotherhood not declare itself a political party, arguing that to do so would subject the movement to govermental supervision. His opponents rallied their supporters at a special session of the Consultative Assembly called in late September to discuss the matter. A faction dubbing itself the Free Brothers (Al-Ikhwan al-Ahrar) called upon Hudaybi and his close associates to resign and proposed new bylaws restricting the general guide's term to three years.[27] On October 6 Hudaybi submitted his resignation and retired to Alexandria. Two days later, one day prior to the deadline for filing application with the Interior Ministry, the Muslim Brotherhood registered as a political party. Pressed by his supporters, the following week Hudaybi withdrew his resignation. Bypassing the Consultative Assembly as well as opponents within the Guidance Council, he and his allies submitted a new application with the government that redefined the Brotherhood as a religious association.[28]

Primarily because of the officers' escalating conflict with the parties, neither the Baquri ouster nor Hudaybi's reassertion of authority seriously affected ties between the junta and the Brotherhood. Instead, from mid-October on the junta moved closer to the Brothers, to the point of open association. On October 16 the government pardoned, with only several exceptions, all political prisoners arrested between August 26, 1936 (the date of the Anglo-Egyptian treaty), and July 23, 1952. The amnesty decree did not cover those convicted of arson, murder, or espionage. But in several cases—the killings of the Sa'dist prime minister, Nuqrashi; the Wafdist minister, Amin 'Uthman; and a prominent judge, Khazindar—all perpetrated by Muslim Brothers, the regime issued exceptional pardons.[29] The government next announced its intention to reopen the case of Hasan al-Banna's murder, for which no indictments had ever been handed down. In mid-November the regime openly supported Brotherhood candidates in elections to the Cairo University student union. Nasser, in an official capacity as representative of the prime minister, attended rallies in which he stood on the rostrum with Hasan Duh, the leader of the Brotherhood's student movement and its candidate for president.[30]

Growing opposition to the regime, demonstrated most vividly in the Brothers' defeat on campus, drew the allies even closer. Hudaybi applauded abrogation of the Constitution in December. In January the regime named three Brothers to the constitutional committee of fifty: two Hudaybi allies, Hasan al-'Ashmawi and Munir al-Dilla, and one antagonist, Salih 'Ashmawi. By being so recognized, the movement attained an unprecedented degree of political legitimacy. The regime underscored this status when it exempted the Brotherhood from the ban on political parties. Accepting the terms of the petition submitted by Hudaybi the previous October, the CCR defined the Brotherhood as a religious association. The Brothers responded with swift and unconditional support for the officers' assumption of direct power.[31]

Rather than enhance the Brotherhood-CCR alliance, the January decrees initiated a new phase in which relations quickly soured. Emboldened by the special status granted their movement, Brotherhood leaders sought to formalize their ties to the CCR. Upon hearing news of the parties' abolition, several Hudaybi deputies approached the junta. According to the official regime history, they again proposed a secret advisory committee to oversee the promulgation of all legislation, and the officers rebuffed what they considered a claim to trusteeship over their revolution. Brotherhood sources assert that the January decrees took them by surprise and that they approached the officers in good faith, to remind them that the Brotherhood represented the sole legal and moral popular force in Egypt and to impress upon them the benefits of closer collaboration, even if it remained veiled.[32]

When the CCR, in turn, tried to enlist Brotherhood leaders into the Liberation Rally, the relationship devolved into one of unspoken competition. Hudaybi and his deputies did not denounce the Liberation Rally but perceived it as a rival organization intent upon subsuming their movement within its ranks. The secular nationalist rhetoric of the Rally particularly irked the Brothers. Looking back on the period, shortly before his death, 'Umar al-Tilmissani, general guide after Hudaybi, explained the situation as such:

> The founding of the Liberation Rally was not itself the cause for the cooling of relations between the Abdel Nasser government [*sic*] and the Society of

Muslim Brothers. Rather, it was Abdel Nasser's repeated and open efforts to
dissolve the Muslim Brotherhood into the Liberation Rally. . . . The Brothers advised him that a fabricated organization [the Rally] would never attain
the popularity sought by the revolution. . . . The Muslim Brothers proposed
to Nasser that they assist him in reinforcing the Liberation Rally by helping it
formulate its concept and the conduct of its members, and to establish the
basis of its organization without disbanding the Society and dissolving it into
the Rally.[33]

In August 1953 the Guidance Council, with CCR approval, delegated one of
its members, al-Bahi al-Khuli, as religious advisor to the Rally. But neither
side took the appointment seriously. To the Brothers the Liberation Rally
remained a glaring symbol of the regime's autonomy and the emptiness of
the officers' professions of CCR-Brotherhood solidarity. The Brothers' cool
reception rankled the officers.[34]

Nevertheless, Hudaybi struggled to protect the fragile alliance and preserve his movement's privileged position. His response to British overtures
to discuss Anglo-Egyptian affairs in February 1953 exemplifies his efforts.
Approached by the British oriental counselor, Trefor Evans, Hudaybi contacted Nasser. With Nasser's approval and a promise to report back to the
CCR, Hudaybi met Evans in late February.[35]

The officers later used these contacts with the British against the Brothers when they moved to ban and, later, destroy the movement. They reported the incident completely out of context, concealing their own assent,
exaggerated its import, and fabricated the agenda. Hudaybi and Evans most
likely discussed Anglo-Egyptian relations. The officers' specific accusation
that Hudaybi agreed to diplomatic concessions they were not prepared to
accept are inconsistent with Brotherhood policy as stated publicly and privately by the general guide. After July 1954, facing public criticism themselves for having granted concessions they stood resolutely against in public,
the officers tried to turn the tables on the opposition, portraying the Brotherhood as even weaker bargainers.[36]

Hudaybi avoided scrupulously any public utterance that might be con-
strued as critical of the regime. In May, when the officers' frustrations at the
lack of progress in Anglo-Egyptian talks led them to initiate a new round of
guerrilla warfare, he rebuffed their efforts to draw Brotherhood irregulars
into a united command. However, when the hostilities erupted later that
month, he supported the campaign publicly and dispatched "liberation
squads" to the Canal Zone.[37]

While he refrained from public criticism of the regime, in private
Hudaybi scorned the CCR, the Liberation Rally, and the increasing intrusion
of the military into government affairs. In an internal memo distributed at
midyear, he called for an end to martial law and press censorship, and urged
the government to rely on popular support, by which he implied the Brotherhood, rather than the "force of laws."[38] In conversations with U.S. embassy
personnel Hudaybi expressed doubts about the wisdom of renewing the
armed struggle against the British. Nonetheless, he asserted that the Brother-

hood felt compelled to participate as a patriotic duty. Hudaybi considered the officers sincere nationalists and deemed Egypt better off than under Wafdist rule. But he also indicated that the Brothers would be glad to see several of them, in Caffery's words, "eliminated."[39]

The officers did not sever ties with their closest Brotherhood contacts, most of whom remained loyal to Hudaybi. Yet early in 1953 the officers began to cultivate ties to his rivals, encouraging them to resume their offensive against him. Salih 'Ashmawi, Hasan al-Banna's deputy and once a leading contender to succeed him, emerged as the most vocal leader of the opposition. He accused Hudaybi and his colleagues of failing to keep pace with the spirit of the army movement: reform and internal "purification." Hudaybi's rule over the movement, 'Ashmawi asserted, perpetuated a policy of "stagnation and meekness." As always, the opposition reminded the Brothers that Hudaybi had never been one of Banna's inner circle.[40] 'Ashmawi, Banna's brother, 'Abd al-Rahman al-Banna, and others agitated for revised bylaws to limit the powers of the general guide and impose conditions that would terminate Hudaybi's tenure. At an emergency meeting of the Consultative Assembly in early September Hudaybi critics ruled the floor. The meeting focused on CCR-Brotherhood relations, in particular the crises over participation in the government, the decision not to apply as a political party, and the discussions with the British oriental counselor.[41]

The CCR looked on with pleasure. Salah Salim told Trefor Evans that the CCR had Hudaybi on the defensive, and Nasser predicted that pro-CCR candidates would capture control of the Guidance Council.[42] In early October, during another special Consultative Assembly meeting, Hudaybi resisted a motion to limit his term to three years, the equivalent of a demand for his resignation, and won an oath of loyalty for life. Nasser was quick to point out that the general guide's victory was tarnished. The Consultative Assembly had given ultimate authority to the Guidance Council, and he counted five newly elected members as pro-CCR.[43]

By this time Nasser, who directed CCR-Brotherhood relations almost single-handedly, was playing a dangerous, duplicitous game. Among the Hudaybi foes he cultivated were those associated with 'Abd al-Rahman al-Sanadi, maverick leader of the secret organization. Nasser held no illusions that the CCR could coexist with Sanadi and his paramilitary force. On at least several occasions that spring he had insisted that the Guidance Council dissolve it.[44] Hudaybi had been receptive to this demand but took no steps to accede to it. Now Nasser, reckoning that he and his colleagues knew far more than Hudaybi about Sanadi's operation—Nasser told the British oriental counselor the general guide was ignorant of the secret organization's workings—acted to turn the movement's rifts to CCR advantage.[45]

How direct a role the CCR, or Nasser personally, played in provoking the showdown that ensued between Sanadi and Hudaybi is impossible to say. On November 19, Sayyid Fa'iz, the number-two man in the secret organization and a recent convert to Hudaybi's camp, was killed by a bomb hidden in a box of candy delivered to his home, presumably by Sanadi loyalists. Hudaybi responded five days later by ousting Sanadi and three others from the Brotherhood. During the following three weeks the general guide faced incipient revolt within his movement. In the end, with the support of the Consultative Assembly, Hudaybi ousted eight Brothers, including Salih 'Ashmawi.

For his part, Hudaybi still struggled to avoid a break. After withstanding votes of no confidence in September, the general guide made overtures to the CCR in an effort to improve relations.[46] In November, the night before he moved to expel key opponents, he played dinner host to Nasser and other CCR members.[47]

The officers were not interested in rapprochement with the general guide; nor were they particularly keen to see his antagonists prevail. For the time being they were content to see the Brothers in disarray. The crisis reached its climax on November 28 when anti-Hudaybi forces besieged the general guide in his home, demanding he resign. At this point Nasser intervened, summoning 'Ashmawi to warn him that the CCR would tolerate no disorder, particularly from the secret organization.[48]

Nasser now tried to mediate the conflict. He suggested the Brothers create a committee drawn from both factions to adjudicate the grievances of ousted members. This has led some to contend that he intervened on the side of 'Ashmawi and the expelled Brothers.[49] Had Hudaybi's resignation come quickly during the ensuing crisis, the CCR presumably would have accepted it with pleasure. But as the crisis escalated and the outcome grew less certain, the officers maintained their distance. They did not support the rebels when it counted, and instead ordered them to withdraw. In the aftermath of the most serious internal crisis the Brotherhood had ever faced, Hudaybi, having won a loyalty oath from the Consultative Assembly, remained in power, albeit on the defensive. Nasser maintained his ties with both factions.

In mid-December the CCR discussed for the first time the option of outlawing the Brotherhood. The officers still considered the move too risky. Instead, they sanctioned a policy of promoting discord within the movement, approving what had already been Nasser's policy for nearly a year.[50]

The decision to outlaw the Brotherhood, taken a month later, signaled an abrupt shift in CCR policy. The change in strategy can be traced to Hudaybi's success in securing his position as leader of the movement.. Although Salih 'Ashmawi continued to decry Hudaybi's leadership, others whom the officers considered supporters of the regime appeared to be closing ranks behind the general guide. Hudaybi's reassertion of authority occurred at a particularly inopportune time. The officers approached a new round of Anglo-Egyptian negotiations with pessimism. They anticipated no breakthrough, and harsh criticism from their opponents. To make matters worse, Fu'ad Sirag al-Din resolutely defended his party as the champion of the nationalist struggle before the Revolutionary Tribunal.

The CCR also undoubtedly knew of secret talks held in the aftermath of the power struggle between Hudaybi backers and Captain Muhammad Riyad on behalf of Muhammad Nagib, from whom the officers had grown estranged. Accounts vary as to which side initiated these discussions. Riyad claims that Munir al-Dilla and Hasan al-ʿAshmawi first contacted Nagib, who delegated him to meet them. A Brotherhood officer, Husayn Hamudah, testified before the People's Tribunal in November 1954 that Riyad first communicated Nagib's overtures to Hudaybi. In any event, Hudaybi and Nagib never met, and exploratory talks between their deputies produced no agreements. Nagib's hostile colleagues, wary of his private diplomacy, heightened their guard.[51]

Particularly troubling to the CCR, Hudaybi replaced the boss of the secret organization, Sanadi, with his own man, Yusuf Tilʿat. Hudaybi, it appears, no longer considered dissolving the special section. His recent scrape with defeat impressed upon him the value of a well-organized front of loyal cadres. Two Hudaybi loyalists, Salih Abu Ruqayq and Salah Shadi, already directed the secret cells in the army and police. He now delegated Tilʿat to purge Sanadi loyalists and give the organization a "proper orientation." The CCR could not tolerate the prospect of a reorganized secret civilian section. That its new chief was an unknown quantity compounded the officers' concerns.[52]

A scuffle between Brotherhood and Liberation Rally students at Cairo University on January 12 sparked the CCR to take steps is had considered but postponed a month earlier. By most accounts Rally students instigated the incident when they interrupted a rally organized by the Brothers to commemorate student martyrs of the nationalist struggle. Blows were exchanged, some vehicles were burned (including the sound trucks used by the Rally students to disrupt the gathering), and weapons were produced by both sides. The next day authorities arrested most Brotherhood leaders and some 450 members, many from the army and police. Writing in *Al-Jumhuriyah,* Anwar al-Sadat blasted those who "traffic in religion." It seems unlikely that the CCR planned the provocation. Evidence is the scant press coverage; besides Sadat's column, only a short article reported news of the melee. What the incident did was convince the officers of the need to act. Two days later the government outlawed the Muslim Brotherhood under terms of the decree banning all political parties.[53]

By design, the crackdown was more a propaganda campaign against Hudaybi and his allies than a concerted effort to destroy the Brotherhood. Official communiqués and personal statements by the officers criticized the general guide and his "deviate" rule, not the movement's aims as given life by Hasan al-Banna. Hudaybi's contacts with British officials highlighted the charge sheet. The decree dissolving the Brotherhood promised, "The revolution will never allow reactionary corruption to recur in the name of religion and will allow none to play with the fate of the country for personal desires, no matter what his call [daʿwah], nor to exploit religion in the service of selfish aims."[54] "Do not think that the decision to dissolve this society was intended to dissolve its idea, never!" Husayn al-Shafiʿi told workers at Mahallah al-Kubra one week later. "The idea of the Islamic call is not dying and will never die!"[55]

The regime left avenues for future cooperation open. By the end of January over one hundred Brothers recently arrested had been released. The CCR had ordered the arrest of many close contacts and former army comrades, including 'Abd al-Mun'im 'Abd al-Ra'uf and Salah Shadi. Yet only those Guidance Council members closest to Hudaybi were detained. This latter group included several whom the officers originally counted among their proxies. Leading Hudaybi opponents and those the CCR still hoped to woo remained free.

On February 12, the anniversary of Hasan al-Banna's murder, Nasser and other CCR members—but not Nagib—visited the martyr's grave. With them stood 'Abd al-Rahman al-Banna, the slain leader's brother; Salih 'Ashmawi; 'Abd al-Qadir 'Awdah, Hudaybi's deputy; and the ousted leader of the secret organization, Sanadi. Nasser eulogized the founder of the Brotherhood, who dedicated his life "to the cause of exalted principles for the benefit of all, not the temporal desires of individuals."[56]

To Brotherhood leaders not imprisoned, Nasser outlined three preconditions for restoration of the movement's legal status: dissolution of the secret organization, cessation of proselytizing within the army and police, and an internal purge of Hudaybi and his followers.[57] This time Brotherhood leaders did not swallow Nasser's bait. Those who remained free ignored CCR overtures and quickly set about rebuilding the movement. The government did not shut down *Al-Da'wah*, but after January 15 Salih 'Ashmawi abruptly ceased his attacks on the general guide. 'Abd al-Qadir 'Awdah, the ranking member of the Guidance Council left free, resolutely demanded restoration of the movement's legal status and freedom for jailed Brothers. Although the dissolution order and the mass arrests had caught the Brothers off guard, they had, according to American observers, recouped their losses and were effectively back in business by early February. British intelligence reports note rumors of clashes between Brothers and police in the Delta and covert meetings held in Ismailia.[58]

The distrust engendered between them and the regime now precluded efforts to seek anything but a precarious rapprochement in which each side would gird for a preemptive strike. Between July 1952 and January 1954 the dubious alliance between the two sides had deteriorated to the point of unveiled enmity. By their rhetoric the officers still tried to separate the Brotherhood from its official leadership. At one time their conflict had been with Hudaybi. Now, because of the general guide's repeated success in overcoming challenges by his rivals, such a distinction mattered little. In private, Nasser told American officials that the CCR would never retract the dissolution order during the transition period to constitutional rule.[59]

Allies to Antagonists

In determining the relationship between the CCR and the Muslim Brothers and communist movements, power politics assumed far greater importance than ideological affinities. It cannot be overemphasized that whatever goals the Free Officers shared with these movements, the officers in the aggregate never agreed with the ultimate ends sought by either communists or Muslim Brothers. Individual members of the junta, to be sure, felt closer links than other comrades. Kamal Husayn and, to an extent, Husayn al-Shafi'i felt strong ties to the Brotherhood, although not to its leader. Khalid Muhyi al-Din and Yusuf Siddiq both belonged to the DMNL. The latter always saw himself as a DMNL representative on the junta and broke with his comrades in January 1953, but Khalid did not. On the other hand, a majority of officers on the junta felt little attachment to, if not outright hostility toward, one or both of these movements. They viewed Egypt's political options in a very narrow framework. If the liberal establishment could not rule—and the first six months after July 23 decided this—they felt the army should govern the state.

The Brothers and the communists posed similar challenges. Both enunciated a critique of the old order that, by its very similarity to Free Officers' rhetoric, indicated that the country did have options other than military rule. The officers could claim no monopoly on condemning the sins of the old regime. The Brothers' call for a moral, Islamic order and the communists' call for an egalitarian social structure both threatened to dilute the message of their revolution. The Brothers' lack of enthusiasm for the revolution and the vocal opposition of the Left maintained pressure on the officers to prove that they, while they held power, could deliver where their antagonists could not. This meant, above all, a negotiated end to the British occupation, the transition to a stable, clean parliamentary system, and progress toward narrowing the gap between rich and poor in the country.

The officers resolved to deal with the political challenge of each antagonist in drastically different fashions. The Brotherhood, with strong support in the countryside, a secret paramilitary organization, and cells spread throughout the army and police, posed at once the greater threat and the greater promise as an ally. When the officers failed to bring the Brothers under their sway, they determined to sow discord, already rampant, within the movement. They succeeded but, unwilling to back their allies to the limit, saw their antagonists emerge even stronger. When the officers finally resolved to dissolve the Brotherhood, they not only failed to destroy its spirit but furthered a drawing together of enemies, much as they had in the Wafd.

Toward the communists, the junta mounted an immediate offensive. In the officers' eyes communism represented a truly subversive force. It mattered little that the largest communist movement had consistently supported the right of the Wafd to govern and adopted a position toward the junta identical to that of liberal minimalists. The officers saw a hidden agenda in communism and distrusted its proponents. The disturbances at Kafr al-Dawwar heightened their sense of the disruptive potential of the Left. They also knew they could gain American support by cracking down on communists, a factor that contributed to but did not underlie their anticommunism.

The battle against communism proved far more frustrating than the CCR probably expected. The nature of the movements, small, disparate, and much less centralized than the Brotherhood, made them difficult to crush, no matter how many cadres were arrested and printing presses captured. Nonetheless, the regime succeeded in snaring many communist leaders, leaving the DMNL, for one, in disarray by late 1953.

Indeed, by early 1954 the CCR could evaluate its handling of both communist and Muslim Brother antagonists with a degree of satisfaction. To their bitter denunciation of the "reactionary" parliamentary establishment, the officers had suddenly added, in January, the "merchants of religion." Communism remained largely an unspoken threat. For reasons probably rooted in anxieties about inciting workers and peasants, however exaggerated, as well as alienating key members of the junta and its inner circle, the regime did not embark upon a vigorous public campaign against communism. Only vague press reports of trials and occasional denunciations, like the testimony of the Mufti in August 1953, pointed to their assault on these former friends. With time, in the aftermath of the officers' brush with defeat in March 1954, the communists would join the Brothers and the old politicians in the rogues gallery of the CCR propaganda campaign. Until the CCR had decisively eradicated the lingering shadow of the old political parties, the Brothers were to be conciliated in public, communists crushed in private.

6

"The Secret of the Nine"

The officers' confrontations with forces of the political establishment and anti-establishment steeled their resolve to govern Egypt on their own. Resistance to land reform and party reorganization, the hesitance of young Wafdists to support the regime's purge of party elders, the concomitant support voiced by anti-Wafdist politicians, conflicting messages from a divided Muslim Brotherhood, and the indefatigable efforts of communist movements in the face of repression prompted the officers to reevaluate and expand their personal political ambitions. With the appointment of Muhammad Nagib prime minister in September 1952 and the assignment of junta members to supervise government ministries, the officers took initial steps—even if they did not see it at the time—toward defining a new role in the political process. Experience in government administration bred confidence that, coupled with their overriding suspicion of civilian politicians and bureaucrats, weakened their inclination to remain in the background. Gradually, the officers came to see themselves as most qualified to initiate and carry out their developing reform agenda.

What role did they envision for the army, the real breeding ground for their politicization and focus for many of the particular grievances that had stirred them to action? And what role did they envision for their own movement, the Free Officers, the secret society they had nurtured, then led into the streets on July 23? If the Free Officers executive committee, now the ruling junta, could not resist the temptations of power, how could the committee expect fellow officers to return to the barracks?

However ambivalent they felt about their own role, the leaders of the Free Officers' movement determined early on that the military as an institution would not participate in politics. Several immediate concerns strengthened that resolve. They knew well the extent to which the Muslim Brotherhood and DMNL had organized within the officer corps, even perhaps penetrated their own movement. They suspected other popular officers, some more senior then they, who might engage in free-lance politicking, covertly or overtly. And in the immediate aftermath of the coup, when Free Officers leaders endeavored to guide government policy behind a cloak of anonymity, to present themselves as benevolent guides, personified collectively by the gentle warrior, Nagib, they learned how difficult it would be to suddenly depoliticize their movement.

The process by which the junta isolated itself from the officer corps is one that is largely ignored in most accounts, official or revisionist. Relations between CCR members, in particular the growing strain between Muhammad Nagib and his younger colleagues, dominate the usual story. In light of the crisis of February–March 1954, when internecine rifts threatened to tear the CCR apart and bring its rule to an end, such a focus has been understandable. Nonetheless, the broader dynamic of relations between an increasingly isolated military junta and the officer corps from which it emerged must first by analyzed. This relationship bears directly on the officers' decision not only to depoliticize the military but to seize direct political authority themselves. The growing discord between the officers and Muhammad Nagib, too often posed in terms of preconstructed parameters—old regime versus new order by the official chroniclers, democrat versus tyrants by the revisionists—can then be discussed in a more nuanced context, that of a power struggle between the young officers, disheartened by failure to stir public support for their revolution, growing ever bolder in ambition and confidence, and a senior officer with similar aims but who, reaping the popularity that eluded them, resisted attempts to harden the edges of military rule.

"The Secret of the Nine"

On the last day of July 1952 Muhammad Nagib, newly appointed commander in chief of the Egyptian army, ordered his troops back to the barracks. By naming a civilian prime minister and resolving to remain faceless, save for Nagib, the ruling junta elected a background role for the army in Egyptian political life. In the immediate aftermath of the coup the junta addressed pressing grievances within the officer corps: promotion, pensions, and entry requirements into the military academy. In following months the new high command oversaw the retirement of some 450 officers, approximately 10 percent of the officer corps. To quell their resentment, most of those cashiered were assigned posts in the state bureaucracy, some filling vacancies, others new jobs created for them, at equivalent rank and pay.[1]

In mid-August the junta asked Muhammad Nagib and four other close colleagues to join its ranks. Prudent military politics, as well as a desire by most sitting on the Free Officers executive committee to widen its circle to include trusted comrades, prompted the decision. Several members who warned against spreading decision-making powers too thin were overruled. Nagib, who helped plot the Officers Club coup and now represented the Free Officers to the general public, was an obvious choice. Zakariya Muhyi al-Din, a fellow officer in Palestine who helped draft operational plans for the July 23 coup, and Husayn al-Shafi'i, ranking Free Officer in the armor corps, immediately fitted in with the others. 'Abd al-Mun'im Amin and Yusuf Siddiq, who had commanded key units on July 23 but had not been Free

Officers, were also invited to join the junta. For different reasons, both Siddiq and Amin remained peripheral members, and each ultimately severed relations with the junta within its first year of rule.

The junta kept a wary eye out for rivals, malcontents, and mavericks, within the officer corps. Between August and December 1952 military intelligence disclosed several groups of junior and noncommissioned officers that appeared to harbor delusions of grandeur. In late August some thirty warrant officers and senior noncoms were arrested and charged with plotting a coup on behalf of General Fu'ad Sadiq, commander of forces in the Palestine War, a man the Free Officers had briefly considered as a possible figurehead leader for their movement. The regime did not arrest Sadiq, who was believed to know nothing of the plot, but took the precaution of detaining three junior officers slated by the rebels to join a new high command under the general's lead. The same month the junta cashiered Colonel Mustafa Kamal Sidqi, an officer with leftist inclinations who had organized several not so secret cells in the late 1940s but was more renowned for his romance with the film starlet Shveikar. In December some twenty air force noncoms were arrested. In public, as well as in private conversation with foreign embassy officers, regime spokesmen and junta members dismissed these officers as reckless adventurers motivated primarily by personal ambition.[2]

The cloak of anonymity, a sincere effort by the officers to demonstrate their limited personal ambitions, posed unforseen problems for them during the first months of their rule. These were good times to be a junior officer in Cairo. In the flush of popular enthusiasm for the heroes of the "blessed movement" many officers put on airs, basking in public approbation and declaring themselves to be close to the centers of power.

The relationship between Free Officers leaders and their own movement became increasingly ambiguous. The movement had never operated as a democracy; the executive committee had handed down orders through a chain of command within each branch of the army. Free Officers leaders never totally abandoned the protocol of rank, but networks developed within the branches fostered an egalitarian spirit that strengthened morale. In the days immediately preceding the coup large ad hoc meetings of officers, including some who were neither members of the executive or the operational command, coordinated activities. After July 26 the executive committee reestablished its dominant position and put an abrupt end to such gatherings. Contacts with Free Officers cells did not cease, although some in the junta believed that they should.[3]

Because most of its members were staff officers and instructors, the junta lacked direct contact with the ranks. As a consequence, Free Officers leaders had often relied on their own students or men who had served under them in Palestine and who now commanded units to establish the bulwark of the movement. These second-rank officers, men about five years younger than the junta members and their inner circle, played critical command roles the night of the coup, leading their units into action only a day after learning of plans for the uprising. After the situation in Alexandria had stabilized and the king had sailed for Naples, they led their units back to the barracks. Having entered the political arena, if only briefly, many of the officers now proved reluctant to accept a normal chain of command and resentful of the elevated status of the junta members.

Complaints multiplied as rumors of indiscretions and unbecoming behavior proliferated in barracks and mess. According to the grapevine, junta members lived like pashas, and held themselves superior to fellow officers. Salah Salim supposedly was having an affair with Farouk's sister, Princess Faiza, and reputedly helped her smuggle jewelry out of the country. Anwar Sadat was reportedly courting the actress Nahad Rashad, wife of the king's personal doctor. 'Abd al-Mun'im Amin and his wife, wealthier and more comfortable in an old-regime milieu than many others, attracted untoward attention when they continued to frequent former retreats of the king and his coterie, such as the Auto Club. Amin's wife, in particular, was accused of flaunting her husband's influence and putting on royal airs.[4]

Remembering better days, second-rank Free Officers expressed their complaints openly before Nasser and other junta members. Faced with mounting criticism from fellow officers, the junta ceased all regular contact with Free Officers cells, which they ordered disbanded. Contact with second-rank officers did not cease entirely because to have severed relations with them would have been unwise. Disgruntled officers continued to petition junta members, demanding attention and ultimately incurring their wrath.

Anonymity also proved troublesome in the face of a perceived rival whom the officers had mistakenly allowed to bask in the limelight after the coup. Colonel Rashad Mahanna, older and more senior than Free Officers leaders, a man of great personal charm who inspired devotion in his men, had collaborated with the Free Officers in their successful bid to control the Officers Club governing board the previous January. Offered formal membership in their movement, Mahanna had refrained. In retrospective accounts the officers chastised him for unreliability and accused him of faintheartedness. Nevertheless, when unable to contact comrades in Al-'Arish on the night of July 22–23, they had informed Mahanna of their operation. He passed the word and rallied his troops, but when he arrived in Cairo on July 25 to a boisterous reception from artillery units the junta sounded the alert. 'Abd al-Mun'im Amin, a fellow artillery commander, has since admitted that he invited Mahanna to Cairo, assuming the latter was involved in the coup's planning. Fearful of Mahanna's motives, the junta named the charismatic colonel to the regency council, hoping at once to placate him with a figurehead post and isolate him from his units.[5]

Rashad Mahanna never accepted the ceremonial role assigned him. He took advantage of his public position, capturing the attention of the media and provoking the jealously of junta members. He maintained old political contacts, primarily with the Muslim Brotherhood and Socialist party, and attempted to sidestep the junta and influence policy. Other party leaders, viewing him as more favorably disposed to collaboration, and probably overestimating his influence, approached Mahanna, seeking to influence the junta on a variety of matters.[6] He voiced initial disapproval of land reform, supporting the graded tax option proposed by 'Ali Mahir and Fu'ad Sirag al-Din. Although he eventually seconded the two-hundred-feddan plan, the officers took his original stand as sincere. In mid-October 1952, in the wake of Nagib's triumphant tour through the Delta, the junta charged Mahanna with interfering in governmental affairs and asserting that he spoke on behalf of the army, and dismissed him.[7]

By acting against Mahanna, the officers also responded to growing pressure from sympathetic civilian circles to clarify the nature of their political role. In a two-part article published in conjunction with Mahanna's ouster, Ihsan 'Abd al-Quddus posed the question that troubled even those, like himself, who knew the answer: "Who is responsible for governing Egypt today?" The author did not reveal his own intimate ties to the junta. Rather, by posing the question openly, he hoped to prod junta members to go public. The Mahanna case, he wrote, highlighted the confusion within government circles about the role of the junta, and the army at large, in setting policy. The veil that hid the faces of Muhammad Nagib's companions allowed every army officer to claim membership in the junta. If the army had in fact returned to the barracks, it would be one thing, but because Nagib's associates remained political figures, 'Abd al-Quddus argued, the public had a right to know their identities.[8]

Partially in response to this call, partially further to undercut Mahanna's public image, the officers suddenly shed their veil. The day after the regime announced Mahanna's dismissal, an article written by Mustafa Amin and entitled "The Secret of the Nine Officers" appeared in *Al-Akhbar*. The piece, which narrated the junta's decisions to expel the king, revealed in an almost offhand manner the names of the original nine junta members. In doing so, Amin indicated explicitly that Rashad Mahanna neither belonged to the group that organized the coup nor played any role in the junta's fateful decisions.[9] Amin relates that Nasser solicited the article directly and approved its final text. When the piece provoked a storm of protest among a growing circle of vocal officers, the junta retreated. Nasser apologized and instructed Amin to pull his article from later editions.[10]

The treatment of Mahanna and new premonitions of elitism further widened the gulf between junta and junior officers, setting the stage for a dramatic and in many ways tragic confrontation between Free Officers and their leaders. For a group of artillery officers loyal to Mahanna, his summary dismissal by the junta represented all that was rotten in relations between the high command and its officer corps. Intensifying such sentiment, at least among a group of artillery officers, no doubt, was the fact that two of the three junta members most often accused of unseemly behavior, Salah Salim and 'Abd al-Mun'im Amin, came from their corps.

To a circle of officers close to Mahanna the junta's explanation for the ouster rang hollow. In late September, when Kamal al-Din Husayn visited the artillery mess and denounced Mahanna, many officers accepted his word. Hamzah Adham, one of the conspirators, recalls that "because I trusted Kamal al-Din Husayn totally, I believed every word he said about Rashad Mahanna. . . ." By mid-October his attitude had begun to change.[11] In late October, after Mahanna's dismissal, Adham, Muhsin 'Abd al-Khaliq, and Fath Allah Rif'at began sounding out comrades to whom they revealed their own disquiet at the course of events. A small group of artillery officers began meeting weekly.

At the outset these officers made no effort to conceal their activities. They openly approached the junta, seeking to mediate between Mahanna and his enemies. As the group expanded, thoughts turned to formalizing the relationship between the Free Officers' movement and the junta. The group proposed to the junta formation of a ten-man general command consisting of five permanent members—they suggested Nasser, 'Amr, Baghdadi, Kamal Husayn, and Salah Salim—and five elected Free Officers representatives. The junta rejected the proposal outright, but Nasser led the artillery group to believe that it would be considered.

Frustrated by unfulfilled promises, the group in late December began to talk of the use of force. Seeking allies, the artillery officers expanded their contacts outside the corps. Comrades in the armor corps counseled patience. Mushin 'Abd al-Khaliq, one of the ringleaders, approached two former Wafdist ministers, Muhammad Salah al-Din and 'Abd al-Fattah Hasan, to whom he offered cabinet posts in a proposed government. They were not convinced, but discussions with the Muslim Brothers, some with Hudaybi personally, seemed promising. But the Guidance Council refused to commit itself, and Muhsin 'Abd al-Khaliq charges that Hudaybi betrayed their confidence to Nasser.[12]

The artillery officers remained uncertain of their general aims and divided over acceptable tactics. Talk of violence—proposals to arrest junta members and impose a new command under Nagib—alienated some members of the group. In the end the officers agreed to postpone all such plans. They resolved instead to mount an opposition candidate for elections to the Officers Club in early January 1953. None missed the irony of this strategy, one year following the triumph of the Free Officers slate headed by Nagib. When the artillery candidate won a seat on the board, the junta decided to act. On January 15 it ordered the arrest of thirty-five officers charged with plotting to overthrow the regime. Although Rashad Mahanna had only indirect links to the movement, the junta took the precaution of placing him under house arrest.

The crackdown strengthened the junta's resolve to insure the army remain apolitical and prompted the decision to declare the revolution. Two days after moving against the artillery conspirators, the regime decreed the abolition of political parties and the onset of a three-year period of martial rule. While the official decree made no mention of troubles in the military, focusing entirely on the recalcitrance of the parties, a government spokesman did link the two.[13]

The prospect of mutiny in the armed forces had provided the spark for action. The Wafd had pushed the junta's back to the wall by contesting the Party Reorganization Law in court, but had they wished, the officers might have postponed decisive action until after the State Council ruling, expected in February. That would have allowed time for the Liberation Rally to be inaugurated and the constitutional committee to commence its work, and given the officers a bit of breathing room. Characteristically, they acted only after matters reached a boiling point.

Charges that the artillery group conspired to overthrow the government apparently were overdrawn, but the junta also had legitimate cause to fear the group. The British oriental counselor, Trefor Evans, reported several weeks later: "The High Military Command admit that there was no fully worked out plot. There seems no doubt, however, that real trouble was brewing, that the High Military Command was seriously worried (even from the point of view of their own personal safety) and that the 'conspiracy' was not merely a convenient excuse for liquidating the parties."[14] Twenty-three years later, junta member 'Abd al-Mun'im Amin recalled:

> There was no plot in the sense of preparing a conspiracy and agreeing on a coup. Some [officers] loudly declared their disapproval of what was happening and they thought that members of the CCR were officers just like them. But the council was extremely sensitive, and fearing developments arrested them.[15]

Leaders of the artillery movement still contend that they constituted an open lobby and hid nothing from the junta. But a growing sense that the junta, and Nasser personally, merely humored them, led some members of the group to discuss a turn to force. Ahmad Hamrush, no stranger to conspiracy and himself an accessory victim of the crackdown, admits, "When officers act to impose their opinion the matter cannot be kept within the bounds of democratic discussion, but always leads to the use of force."[16]

Detailed discussion of the dissident artillery movement remained absent from official histories of the regime. This was a painful moment, an incident best passed over. Former junta members Baghdadi, Kamal Husayn, Shafi'i, and both Muhyi al-Dins still dismiss the artillery officers as jealous and politically naive, and a genuine threat to their rule. In his otherwise detailed memoirs, Baghdadi sidesteps the issue. Nor has the artillery movement received detailed coverage in revisionist accounts. Mahanna first recounted his own version of events for the press in early 1976. Neither Hamrush nor Ramadan give more than brief mention, despite devoting substantial sections to relations between the junta and the army. In Hamrush's case this is particularly surprising, considering he was arrested in conjunction with the plot. In 1983 a young journalist, 'Adil Hamudah, published a series of interviews with several of the conspirators loosely strung together to form a narrative. His book, *Nihayat Thawrat Yulyu* (The end of the July Revolution), is the first to address the artillery movement directly.

Hamudah's treatment, although revisionist in spirit, reinforces the potential gravity of the threat. He himself gets caught in an ideological dilemma.

He portrays the conspirators as sincere proponents of greater democracy within the Free Officers' movement, unfortunate victims of the junta's absolutist rule. He also sees the seeds of military dictatorship in the junta's isolation from the movement. Yet he cannot and does not contend that the artillery conspirators served the cause of democracy in a broader political context, that their success in winning over or overthrowing the original junta would have spared Egypt military rule. His subjects are victims—perhaps noble—of emerging Nasserism, and therefore honored. But they are not real heroes to the revisionist camp.

Following the arrests of the artillery conspirators, the junta faced further challenges to its authority within the officer corps. When news of the arrests spread, four hundred artillery officers staged a sitdown in their mess hall. They agreed to disperse only after Nasser appeared and personally promised to undertake an internal investigation, a promise that he never kept.[17] Then on January 17 the regime ordered the arrest of Colonel Husni al-Damanhuri, a Free Officer and commander of armor units in the Western Desert. Damanhuri was charged with plotting to incite the armor corps to mutiny. For his part, Damanhuri has admitted he planned to stage a demonstration. He was tried in special session by junta members and sentenced to death.[18]

Nasser and his colleagues remained wary of further alienating the army. They postponed Damanhuri's execution, and ultimately commuted his sentence to life imprisonment (he remained in prison until 1958.) Fourteen other officers who stood trial before the CCR in the spring of 1953 received terms varying from one to fifteen years.[19] The leniency shown most would become characteristic of the regime's treatment of military dissidents. Those who made trouble would spend some time in prison or exile, after which they would be released and given civil service positions. The first test of this strategy—one that proved successful—came in March 1954, when the regime released the artillery officers jailed in January 1953 in order to boost morale in the wake of a strike in the armor corps.

In the wake of the incipient insurrection in the artillery, the regime extended its dragnet to head off other sources of dissent in the army. Ahmad Hamrush, leader of DMNL cells in the military, was detained for seven weeks without being charged. His arrest sealed the DMNL decision to break with the regime but also effectively disarmed the movement's military branch. When Hamrush later tried to contact his comrades in the army he found that the organization had totally collapsed. Shortly thereafter, the DMNL disbanded its military wing outright.[20]

The artillery crackdown also had repercussions within the junta, exacerbating ongoing conflicts and precipitating the departure of two members, Yusuf Siddiq and 'Abd al-Mun'im Amin. Siddiq, along with Nasser, 'Amr, and Khalid Muhyi al-Din, had been a steadfast proponent of a minimalist agenda within the junta. He had advocated the immediate recall of parliament and decried the trend toward greater exertion of martial authority, had recommended junta members stand for elections, and had criticized the regime's close American ties. Unwilling to subordinate ideology to group consensus—

as did his DMNL comrade on the junta, Khalid Muhyi al-Din—Siddiq's relationship with the others grew strained. He threatened to resign, or resigned and reconsidered, on several occasions. The artillery conspirators, who heard rumors of his impending ouster in December, contacted him to express their concern. The junta's crackdown on fellow officers for expressing grievances with which he sympathized, the arrest of his comrade Hamrush, and the usurpation of political power by the junta in January prompted the final break. Despite efforts by DMNL leaders to dissuade him, Siddiq quit the CCR and the army. He retired to Aswan and in March 1953 left the country.[21]

'Abd al-Mun'im Amin had found himself caught directly in the crossfire of the conflict brewing in the artillery corps. Amin had played a major role in establishing links between the new regime and the U.S. embassy. He tried the Kafr al-Dawwar workers and subsequently assumed responsibility for labor affairs in the Social Affairs Ministry. Amin's good relations with Rashad Mahanna alienated him from junta colleagues; at the same time he was one of the junta members most maligned by dissident officers for excessive bravado in power. In the face of steady criticism of his personal behavior, Amin agreed to take a leave of absence prior to the crackdown on the artillery circle. Upon the arrest of the conspirators, he offered to resign from the junta but resisted efforts to send him abroad. In October he finally accepted a diplomatic posting in Europe.[22]

In addition to supervising the machinery of government and suppressing the opposition, their scrape with the artillery corps impressed upon CCR members that ruling Egypt meant policing the armed forces. Farouk and his military chiefs had underestimated the threat posed by disgruntled junior officers. They believed that by manipulating commanders at the top they could prevent younger officers from rallying around a popular general, thus avoiding trouble in the army. Free Officers leaders knew from their own experience the difficulties an isolated high command faced trying to maintain loyalty in the barracks. As staff officers and instructors in the staff college, they had had little personal contact with the members of their movement prior to the coup. Now their leadership still rested on the loyalty of second-rank officers. If they lost that loyalty, as they nearly did in the artillery, they had only coercion on which to fall back. The CCR representatives from the artillery, Kamal Husayn, Salah Salim, and 'Abd al-Mun'im Amin had each lost credibility in the barracks. Artillery officers striking the mess hall after the arrest of their comrades would speak only to Nasser. Nasser's promises restored order, but unlike their own commanders a year before, he and his colleagues knew that they sat on a potential powder keg.[23]

Insistent that the army remain outside the political realm, Nasser and his colleagues were forced to dismantle the Free Officers' movement. Concurrently, they faced the need to staff unit commands with officers they could trust. This meant turning to old comrades, many of whom had been Free Officers; it also meant turning to individuals who were not best suited for command. In certain corps, as things turned out, efforts to depoliticize the army failed. The long-run effect of their strategy was the army's weakening as a fighting unit.

Discontent in the highest ranks and jealousy among certain junta members also resulted. The first republican decree issued by President Nagib in June named 'Abd al-Hakim 'Amr commander in chief of the armed forces. 'Amr was promoted from major to general with one pen stroke. A genial young officer too easily influenced by friends and acolytes, 'Amr won the position because he had Nasser's trust. His selection, as the selection of any individual CCR member would have, aroused a degree of resentment among the others. Most, accepting the need for one of them to assume command of the army, recognized 'Amr's status as Nasser's closest friend and confidant. Less easily, they agreed to cease all contacts with their units and cede full authority to the new commander in chief.[24]

'Amr's promotion caused a greater stir in the upper ranks. The high command had recently issued 144 promotions, the first since the coup.[25] However, professional officers resented the placement of a political commissar as their superior, and the air force commander resigned. Extremely conscious themselves of rank and military protocol, CCR members endeavored to soften the effect of 'Amr's extraordinary promotion by treating senior corps commanders with deference and granting them a degree of administrative autonomy.[26]

Above all the CCR relied on the vigilance of military intelligence, under the direction of Zakariya Muhyi al-Din, to head off future trouble in the ranks. Appointed minister of interior in October 1953, Zakariya efficiently coordinated military intelligence and internal security operations. The disarray of the Left by the year's end and the inability of the DMNL to reorganize its military branch point to Muhyi al-Din's success. But in another important respect military intelligence and the CCR were caught napping. The growing rift within the council between the officers and Muhammad Nagib increasingly distracted Nasser and his colleagues, but they remained blind to the implications of their struggle within the officer corps. The CCR kept tabs on key Nagib loyalists. Its own animosity for its figurehead leader, however, caused it to underestimate the sympathies Nagib had engendered among junior officers.

"A Small Parliament of Twelve"

The power struggle between Muhammad Nagib and his colleagues erupted at a time when the CCR first faced the consequences of its decision to assert direct authority over the country. The entreaties of Ihsan 'Abd al-Quddus and others that they emerge from the shadows now seemed compelling advice, and the officers set out to create a political identity for themselves. If they had nearly forfeited their popularity in the officer corps, they could perhaps still capture the countryside. The officers' coming out changed dramatically their perspective on power and politics. The intimate camaraderie of campfire and barracks could be preserved only so long as they huddled in general headquarters. Once in the spotlight, that intimacy vanished. The pressures of 1953 taught even the most self-confident of them the rigors of public service and the pressures of accountability.

In the late fall of 1952 Egyptians first witnessed the emergence of several junta members into public light. To the average Egyptian, Salah Salim, because of his role in directing Sudan affairs and a flair for publicity, became a personality well before Nasser. On a diplomatic mission to the southern Sudan in early 1953 Salim mugged for photographers in native garb and took part in a local ceremony, earning notoriety as the "dancing major." As spokesman for the regime following his appointment as minister of national guidance in June 1953, Salim remained a far more prominent figure than other colleagues, save Nasser. When *Al-Misri* ran a back-page feature at year's end on influential figures of 1953, caricatures of Salim and Nasser appeared with those of Eisenhower, Molotov, and Mossadegh.[27]

Nasser's name first appeared in print on October 15, the day after Rashad Mahanna's ouster. His name dominated Mustafa Amin's "Nine Officers" column, which, according to Amin, he solicited and helped edit. As the October 15 issue of *Al-Tahrir* went to press, Nasser requested that authorship of the second of a two-part account of the coup written by a staff writer be attributed to him. Mustafa Bahgat Badawi, managing editor and a Free Officer, composed a preface that revealed that the author, "the hero who performed a major role in the liberation movement . . . was Colonel Gamal Abdel Nasser."[28]

By November, Nasser's picture began to appear in the press, usually alongside Nagib, with his name mentioned in captions. He stumped for Muslim Brothers student union candidates as special deputy to the prime minister. His name was headlined for the first time in late December 1952, on the occasion of a harsh rebuke of British policy. Over the course of the following year, Nasser supplanted Salah Salim as the most visible member of the CCR after Nagib. His picture appeared with regularity. In political cartoons he joined Nagib as a symbol of the revolution. In late February his speeches were accorded prominent press coverage, and in early April Muhammad Hasanayn Haykal, a correspondent for the Amins, chronicled a tour he made of the Delta in glowing terms.[29]

In the early spring of 1953 the other CCR members became recognized public figures. In mid-March, under the auspices of the Liberation Rally, the officers were assigned as personal envoys to their home provinces. In early April they began making regular public appearances, in small groups or alone, speaking at rallies and in mosques, all chronicled by the media. The experience proved initially discomfiting for most. At home in a military milieu, the officers were reserved before public assemblies. Baghdadi recalls an early outing in the Delta where he appeared with Nasser:

After Nasser spoke, he said: "What did I say?" It wasn't rehearsed. "I don't know what I just said!" I told him it was fine. Three years later he was

practiced and could speak for hours, but at first it was like that. He spoke for
five minutes, said two words, was shy. "I don't know what I just said!" I told
him it was fine.[30]

As anonymity had bred one set of problems, so fame now brought its own
travails. The press heralded CCR members' rallies as triumphs, created
personas and contrived friendly satirical caricatures of the officers.[31] The
public, however, did not always receive them warmly. Rumors abounded
about strife and rivalries within the revolutionary command, rumors that the
officers could not suppress, and that ultimately proved to be all too true.

In an interview in late November 1953 Nasser described the CCR as "a
small parliament composed of twelve members who bear the army revolution
on their shoulders." He stressed that each member of the council had an equal
vote, including the president of the republic.[32] In reality, by sheer force of
personality and growing political acumen Nasser dominated his colleagues and
guided them in directions he deemed wisest. Those quick to point to factions
within the ruling junta failed to grasp the spirit, the common sense of mission
and trust in Nasser, that held the officers together. When faced with difficult,
potentially divisive decisions, the officers maintained their unity. Certainly, to
reveal differences would, they feared, only strengthen their enemies.

However strong their ties and strenuous their denials of internal strife,
the growing discord between Muhammad Nagib and his younger colleagues
did increasingly upset the internal stability of the CCR. In every sense a
struggle for power and influence, the conflict between Nagib and the others
has been described by partisans of both sides in predictably contradictory
manners.

To the officers, Nagib, the figurehead whom they endowed with leadership of their movement, became intoxicated by popularity and overcome by
a desire for self-rule. We made Nagib, the officers insisted (and continue to
insist), and he turned on us in an attempt to monopolize popular support.
The public denigration began on February 25, 1954, when the CCR told a
stunned nation that Nagib, who had played absolutely no role in the July
coup, now sought dictatorial powers over the ruling council. After Nagib's
final fall from grace the following November, the official history of the regime
minimized his role to the point where he became a virtual nonentity.[33]

In recent years Nagib's image has been rehabilitated with a natural
amount of hagiography and much blatant distortion. His partisans stress
ideological differences between Nagib and the other officers. They champion
the general as a constant opponent of Nasser's tyrannical tendencies and
make exaggerated claims for his influence on the Free Officers prior to the
coup. Two ghost-written versions of Nagib's memoirs have been published
since Nasser's death, *Kalimati lil-Tarikh* (My words to history), published in
the mid-1970s, and *Kuntu Ra'isan li-Misr* (I was president of Egypt), published in 1984 around the time of Nagib's death. The second book reads
much like the first but makes far greater claims on Nagib's behalf. Both
depict Nagib as a guileless victim of deceit, a lone battler for democracy and

civil liberties. Each has succeeded in rekindling public memory of a once-beloved leader. But on balance with other accounts, neither reflects accurately Nagib's true standing within the group, his position on a variety of vital issues that confronted the CCR, or the dynamics that led to his isolation and banishment.[34]

The officers' preoccupation with minimizing Nagib's role in their movement and the coup reflected their own insecurity more than any effort by Nagib to take undue credit for his actions. The officers had in fact approached Nagib, offered him leadership of their movement, and thrust him into the spotlight. But Nagib had not played an entirely passive role. He agreed to lead the slate of opposition candidates for election to the Officers Club in late 1951. He participated in at least one strategy session with Free Officers leaders in January 1952, after Black Saturday when they first discussed seriously plans for a coup d'état.[35] Although he took no part in organizing the uprising, the officers did contact him several days beforehand to inform him of their plans. When they called out their troops, Nagib was prepared and astutely dissembled when contacted by agitated government representatives in Alexandria.

At the outset Nagib's political views did not differ appreciably from those of his younger colleagues. Nagib was not, as some now claim, a constant defender of democracy. Sharing the younger officers' aversion for the political system, he distrusted establishment leaders no less than they. Within the junta he stood apart from those—Nasser, 'Amr, Yusuf Siddiq, and Khalid Muhyi al-Din—who supported the immediate recall of parliament. He accepted the army's role as temporary trustee of power until the political order reformed itself, and assumed leadership of a government committed to mandating party reorganization. He supported land reform, approved the hangings at Kafr al-Dawwar, and welcomed the ouster of Rashad Mahanna, a rival of his no less than the others, for whom he reputedly felt particular animosity. In January 1953, along with all his colleagues, he ordered the arrests of the artillery officers, the dissolution of the political parties, and decreed the death sentence for the dissident officer, Damanhuri.[36]

To label Nagib, as the Lacoutures did, "a man of the old regime, shocked by its abuses" minimizes the degree of his outrage and underestimates the steps he was willing to take as a conspirator and politician.[37] Rather than political views, fundamental differences in style, the natural outgrowth of two different generations of officers, precipitated the breach between Nagib and the other CCR members. From the outset, Nagib, at age fifty-three, stood apart, a father figure to the junior officers as well as to the nation as a whole.

Nagib's public demeanor—the indelible image of the gentle man puffing at his pipe—backed up by a firmness of purpose, pride in his uniform, and love of country made him an instant celebrity. He seemed at ease, if somewhat humble, in front of crowds. In private he was gracious and politic. When dealing with old-regime figures, even those he ordered jailed, he outwardly accorded them the proper respect due public statesmen. This in contrast to the gruff treatment described by Sayyid Mar'i and others who approached the officers after the takeover. Well aware of the contrast, Nagib endeavored to control his colleagues' headstrong tendencies. They were, he told the British ambassador three months after the coup, naive and inexperienced, but he was keeping an eye on them.[38]

By all accounts, Nagib accepted the role assigned him with humility. To be sure, he did not seem to have minded a degree of official fabrication to enhance his public position.[39] Still, he accepted the principle of majority rule within the junta. None have suggested that he resisted the others' emergence into the public spotlight. The officers' affection for him, still voiced by surviving members of the CCR, appears to have been quite genuine. They respected him as a model officer, a man of courage and moral conviction, traits rarely evident among their senior commanders. Yet their distrust for their elders, politicians and officers, soon carried over to include their chosen leader. In due course Muhammad Nagib fit too well, and himself cultivated the image with which he had been anointed, and that his younger colleagues soon came to resent.

The emerging ambitions of the younger officers, Nasser in particular, exacerbated their differences with Nagib. His great sin in their eyes was his ability to sustain his popularity while the political and economic situation in the country deteriorated. He did encounter his share of disgruntled workers and students on his trips throughout the country, but by virtue of his public image he was able to rise above events. When the man on the street complained of CCR rule, he directed his grievances more often than not at the stern-faced younger officers who surrounded the kindly general. Nagib, confronting public disapproval, played to the crowd and resisted giving his blessing to any decree that would tarnish his image. The struggle for power within the CCR emerged precisely at the time when the younger officers, frustrated at their failure to mobilize public support and construct an ideology for their revolution, resolved to adopt harsher measures toward the opposition.

Nagib never played a passive role in this struggle. He sensed the battle early on and began maneuvering for position. The issue of leadership had become an irritant by the early spring of 1953. The CCR began monitoring, and on occasion censoring, Nagib's public statements, which increasingly ran counter to its. He caused his colleagues to bristle when he told an American correspondent that although the CCR acted only when in unanimous agreement, final decisions rested with him. The CCR instructed the press to delete references to speeches Nagib delivered in a late March tour of upper Egypt that the officers deemed excessively anti-British. Nagib said nothing they had not said before, but the CCR, in consideration of upcoming negotiations had determined to soften its rhetoric. Nagib, playing to the crowd, had not followed suit.[40]

Trusting in his popularity, Nagib grew steadily bolder. Hesitant to name Nagib president, the officers postponed declaring Egypt a republic in May. When luminaries like Lutfi al-Sayyid demurred, the CCR had few options.

Reconciled to appointing Nagib, the officers tried without success to persuade him to relinquish the prime ministry. In what would become a characteristic tactic, Nagib walked out on his colleagues, refusing to leave his home until the CCR relented. Nagib also opposed the entry of other CCR members into the cabinet, as well as 'Amr's promotion, but acquiesced in these matters.[41]

In August Nagib made the pilgrimage to Mecca. While in the holy cities, he took part in several popular demonstrations staged on his behalf by loyal retainers. The British ambassador in Riyad reported that Egyptian pilgrims, "armed with pots of glue and portraits of the photogenic general," plastered the streets of Mecca with Nagib's picture, much to the displeasure of his Saudi hosts.[42] Upon his return, Nagib's colleagues on the CCR found him less inclined to bow to their will, even when outvoted. Nagib opposed the formation of the Revolutionary Tribunal and the order to place Nahhas under house arrest, objected to the death sentence decreed for Ibrahim 'Abd al-Hadi, and criticized the decision to prosecute Fu'ad Sirag al-Din. After the court passed sentence on 'Abd al-Hadi, Nagib left Cairo in protest. Nasser, 'Amr, and Zakariya Muhyi al-Din followed him to Alexandria and persuaded him to return. In his absence, the CCR appointed Salah Salim and Zakariya Muhyi al-Din to the cabinet. Neither took the oath of office before the president.[43]

In response to Nagib's grandstanding in Mecca and his newfound independence, the other CCR members acted to isolate him from officers loyal to him. Colonel Ahmad Shawqi, commander of the Cairo garrison, was the first of a number of officers against whom the CCR moved in subsequent months. Shawqi, who was close to Nagib, had accompanied the general on his pilgrimage, where he presumably took the lead in organizing the pro-Nagib demonstrations. In late September 'Amr cashiered him. In January 1954 Muhammad Riyad, commanding officer of the Presidential Guard and Nagib's contact to the Muslim Brothers, was pressed to take leave abroad.[44]

Nasser took the lead in rallying the CCR against Nagib. His personal antipathy for the general, according to witnesses, became apparent in the spring of 1953. During this period Nasser moved to formalize his own authority over the government and his comrades on the ruling council. In June he became deputy prime minister and for three months held the interior portfolio. Through 'Amr and Zakariya Muhyi al-Din, he exercised personal control over the army and the intelligence apparatus. While the CCR continued to function as a "small parliament," Nasser assumed greater control of policymaking and more frequently took unilateral decisions, much as he had for the Free Officers executive. He personally directed CCR-Muslim Brotherhood relations. In the first six months of rule he had delegated other junta members to maintain personal contacts with the U.S. and British embassies. By the time Anglo-Egyptian negotiations approached in May 1953, Nasser had established himself in American eyes as the prime mover of the regime.[45]

In a contest of wills between Nasser and Nagib, the sympathy of the other officers naturally rested with the former, and he convinced them that his jealousy was theirs. In December Nasser initiated two secret CCR resolutions that, in tandem, formalized his own position within the council and isolated Nagib. First, he proposed that the officers meet without Nagib prior to all scheduled council meetings so that they might confront the general as a united front. Soon after, Nasser won his comrades' assent to his making policy decisions without summoning the group. The officers understood that he would poll each member individually, and thus establish a consensus without the need for a formal session.[46]

Their trust in him, as much as antipathy to Nagib, led the officers to grant Nasser such power. Most of Nasser's colleagues at the time did not perceive his requests as a threat to their positions. According to Baghdadi, only he and Salah Salim voiced protest (but not support for Nagib.) Others, like Gamal Salim, who were more prone to resent Nasser's monopoly of authority, presumably accepted the move as a tactic to isolate Nagib, who represented a greater threat in their eyes.

Their willingness to accede to Nasser's leadership should also be viewed from a broader perspective. CCR meetings were often long-winded all-night affairs. As supervisors of ministries or ministers themselves, judges, editors, and staff officers, CCR members found themselves burdened with multiple duties. Even Nasser, who by this time was clearly grooming himself for the prime ministry, if not already looking ahead to the presidency, complained of his work load and contemplated naming a civilian to head the government.[47] Instead, more prudently, he hoped to streamline the decision-making process. The CCR would approve broad lines of policy rather than discuss minute details. This became all the more important as the officers found themselves increasingly preoccupied by their differences with Nagib.

By early 1954, Nasser, consumed by what witnesses describe as a vitriolic hatred for Muhammad Nagib, had managed to isolate his rival within the CCR and separate the general from his most loyal compatriots. The hostility between the officers and Nagib became less veiled. Nagib, already in contact with the Muslim Brothers, opposed their dissolution in January. In February, when the officers paid their respects at the grave of Hasan al-Banna, Nasser firmly told Nagib not to attend. On this occasion Nagib submitted, but he certainly knew that a showdown was imminent. Baghdadi describes February 1954 as emotionally exhausting, a period of disillusion and pessimism. On several occasions, he relates, Nasser proposed a tactical withdrawal, that he and his colleagues yield to Nagib and withdraw from politics until the people called them back. Most CCR members rejected such talk.[48]

The stakes of the power struggle had become all or nothing. In late February the officers discussed seriously easing Nagib from leadership.[49] On February 21 Nagib discovered the CCR was in session without him. Two days later he submitted his resignation, most likely at the prodding of close associates who presumed the CCR would call him back. Nagib did not play his cards unwisely. After the stormy encounter on February 21, the officers had resolved to strip him of the prime ministry. Nagib's resignation turned the tables on them, but rather than retreat the officers chose to take their case to the people. On February 25 the CCR denounced the president as a power-hungry tyrant and accepted his resignation.

"We Are Not Dictators"

The first year of the revolution had been a time of false starts, disillusion, and frustration for the CCR. Had the old regime been vanquished? The officers seemed as unsure as anyone. Fu'ad Sirag al-Din stood before the Revolutionary Tribunal, but it was difficult to tell prosecutor from defendant. The spectacle of old-guard politicians hurling barbs at one another reinforced the need for political reform but did nothing to breed confidence in the new order. Throughout 1953 the regime continued to promise a return to democracy. Nasser told *Al-Misri* in late November that the Revolutionary Tribunal had nearly completed its work, and dismissed rumors that the government would lower the ceiling on landholding to fifty feddans. "We are not dictators," he asserted. One month later he told workers at Shubra al-Khayma: "We did not undertake this revolution in order to rule, but to restore parliamentary life and return power to men of judgment who will rule for the benefit of Egypt."[50]

The regime's actions, however, pointed to the opposite. Throughout the year the CCR members had concentrated power in their hands. By year's end they were indeed a small parliament, but one isolated from civilian and military allies alike. The dispute with the popular general drew the CCR inward, increasing its hostility to outside influence, even as its members struggled to create a favorable impression with the public. Nagib's play for power in late February 1954, a move that caught the others off guard even as they planned to ease him aside, sparked the March crisis. They confronted opposition from—at least at the outset—every popular political force in the country, including units within the army. However splintered, their opposition united because of a common disbelief in the regime's stated commitment to the restoration of parliamentary rule, a mistrust of the officers' aims and ambitions. As patience with the CCR wore thin, and as rumors of discord within its ranks proliferated, the opposition crystallized around the figure of Nagib.

Nagib's image as father figure, benevolent strongman, and first president of the republic dominated the public consciousness. The officers stood off to the sides, stern reminders of the nation's difficult times, the hard edge of the revolutionary period. Nagib's smile blunted that hard edge. Astute observers of the CCR had come to recognize the reality of power in the ruling council. Wafdists, leftists, Muslim Brothers, and many army officers viewed Nagib as preferable to CCR rule and thought to work through him to depose Nasser and the others. In late February 1954 they rallied to Nagib's support in the face of the CCR's stinging denunciation. The support Nagib found in the streets revealed to Nasser and his colleagues the extent to which they had failed to rally the masses and managed to alienate former allies in the intelligentsia.

More distressing, Nasser and his colleagues came face to face with the fact that they had lost touch with their comrades in the officer corps and to a frightening degree sacrificed their trust. Large segments of the corps, particularly armor officers, stood with Nagib. Despite the precedent set by the artillery conspirators, the CCR was caught off guard. Those responsible for watching the army had spotted potential troublemakers among close associates of Nagib, and acted to distance them, but remained blind to political sentiment in the barracks. Second-rank Free Officers knew that Nagib had been ancillary to the movement that seized power on July 23. The "blessed movement" was theirs, not his. But to many officers who felt that their movement was being usurped by their leaders, Nagib remained, if not an alternative to the CCR, a necessary component, a crucial check against the isolationist tendencies of Egypt's military strongmen.

7

"A Revolutionary, Not a Politician"

In 1954 the CCR succeeded in consolidating its authority over the country and established itself as the only viable alternative to the old regime. The pivotal moment was the March crisis, when the CCR faced the combined opposition of the old political parties, the Muslim Brotherhood, the Left, much of the independent intelligentsia, and significant units within the armed forces. The extent and scope of this opposition underlined for the officers the immentsity of their failure to silence active antagonists, and impressed upon them their failure to capture public support for their revolution, either the reforms or the purges. The call of the March opposition, sparked by the dismissal of Muhammad Nagib, resounded loudly and clearly: power must return to civilian hands, the officers must return to the barracks, the revolution must end.

Above all, the March crisis represented a crucial test of the officers' political will. Decry as they might the specter of old-regime resurrection, distort as they would the agendas of those critics who sought to move Egypt forward not backward, the officers realized that rhetoric, censorship, manipulation of the media, even selected arrests could not save their rule. After two years of hesitant, often impulsive, decision making, the officers now stood with their backs to the wall.

The March crisis has been the focal point of virtually every account of the period. Official chroniclers described the crisis as a confrontation between progress and reaction. Nasser's biographers and early students of Nasserism largely accepted the regime's version of events. Some portrayed the officers as shrewd manipulators of public opinion, others noted that the chaos within CCR headquarters mirrored that in the streets. Virtually all presented the opposition in a negative light, as an obstacle to modernization, rationalization, and political serenity. In the mid-1970s revisionists looked back on the crisis from the perspective of Nasser's dictatorship. By forcing individuals and factions to declare who stood where and account for their actions, revisionists reopened old wounds and revived old controversies about representative democracy. The discussion subsided in the late 1970s when the aggressive rhetoric of the Wafd and other old-regime parties drew Sadat's wrath, then resumed in the early 1980s in the more open political atmosphere fostered by the Mubarak government.

The public record, complemented by recently declassified foreign documents, sheds much new light on the events of March 1954, particularly with regard to the role of the CCR. The dilemmas faced by the officers at various points throughout the crisis, the strategies proposed and actions taken, may now be reevaluated with a greater sense of what options the officers faced, as well as the lessons they learned and the implications of March for their consolidation of authority.

The crisis passed through three distinct phases. The first commenced on February 23, when Nagib resigned, and ended on March 1, with his triumphant return to office. In the second phase, played out largely behind closed doors from March 5 to 25, Nagib attempted without success to wrest greater powers from the officers and formalize a dominant position for himself in the CCR. During the third phase, March 25–31, the CCR mobilized loyal street forces to defeat Nagib supporters.

The street demonstrations on behalf of the CCR in late March are most often pointed to as the turning point in the crisis. In fact, the officers' most dangerous moment occurred during the first phase, when the armor corps threatened to mutiny on behalf of Nagib. But it was the second phase, when, after defusing the immediate threat of insurrection, the CCR secured the army's support, that proved to be the crucial period. This steeled the officers' will to reassert their authority. They had no real long-term strategy. They proved their mettle in willpower and improvisation far more than in Machiavellian ploys.

"Long Live the Revolution"

News of Nagib's ouster, announced on February 25, sparked street demonstrations that carried over into the following day. Despite widespread rumors of rifts within the CCR, the public was neither prepared for the abrupt ouster nor for the open animosity directed against Nagib. The demonstrations lasted three days. "The goal of the revolution . . . was not to place any individual or group in power," the first CCR decree proclaimed. Nagib resigned after failing to impose dictatorial terms on the CCR. His relationship to the Free Officers had been marginal; the officers had made him their figurehead, but he had sought greater personal authority. Nasser, now openly identified as the original leader of the Free Officers, was proclaimed Commander of the Revolution.[1]

While Nagib supporters took to the streets of Cairo, the army demanded the attention of the CCR. On February 26 some two hundred officers from the armor corps gathered at their barracks to protest Nagib's ouster. Husayn al-Shafi'i, the corps commander, went to hear their grievances. Armor officers denounced the unilateral decision taken by the CCR, demanded Nagib be reinstated, and threatened to refuse any orders to take their units into the streets to suppress public demonstrations. Word of similar protests among units in Alexandria added to the crisis atmosphere. When Shafi'i failed to dissuade them, Nasser went to the barracks. The scene recalled the stormy meeting in the artillery mess a year before. Nasser met with the officers for some six hours, into the early morning of February 27. Failing to appease them, Nasser accepted their demand that Nagib be reinstated as president. Beating a retreat, he promised to appoint Khalid Muhyi al-Din prime minister and dissolve the CCR. Khalid accepted and persuaded Nagib to withdraw his resignation.[2]

While armor corps commanders stood behind Nagib, other unit leaders acted to defend the CCR. Close Free Officers colleagues—Kamal Rif'at, Muhammad Abu al-Fadl al-Gizawi, Wagih Abazah, and 'Ali Sabri are most often mentioned—and their subordinates, about sixty strong, gathered at general headquarters. When they learned of the CCR decision to resign, they took matters into their own hands. Two officers abducted Nagib from his home and spirited him to a base on the outskirts of Cairo. Commanders of artillery units turned their guns on the armor barracks while air force planes circled above. Faced with impending civil war in the ranks, the CCR acceded to loyalist demands that it remain in power. With renewed confidence, Nasser summoned armor leaders to a meeting at headquarters, en route to which they were arrested. No shots were fired.[3]

That the armor corps stood alone allowed Nasser and his colleagues to act quickly to disarm the rebels. The infantry, air force, and artillery sided wholeheartedly with the CCR. The loyalty of these units probably had less to do with any ill-will toward Muhammad Nagib than with contentment with CCR rule. Influential commanders most inclined to protest CCR policy had been isolated or removed from command of these corps. The artillery conspirators remained in prison (although they would be released shortly thereafter and prove to be born-again loyalists). Several artillery officers who had not been involved with the dissidents—Muhammad al-Gizawi, Muhammad Fayiq, and others—took the lead in mobilizing on the CCR's behalf.[4] Nasser, 'Amr, and Zakariya Muhyi al-Din, the brain trust of military intelligence, all came from the infantry. Potential agitators within their corps—Yusuf Siddiq, Ahmad Shawqi, Muhammad Riyad—had also been removed from command.

The military intelligence dragnet had obviously failed to penetrate the armor corps, or to gauge the extent of disillusion with the CCR. In July 1953, when the CCR sacked Tharwat 'Ukashah as editor of *Al-Tahrir* and banished him to Europe for pursuing a line too close to that of the Left, his fellow officers took affront. The matter passed quietly, 'Ukashah says, because he rebuffed plans for a demonstration on his behalf.[5] Yet the corps continued to move toward a position at variance with the CCR. Here the outstanding influence on armor officers was Khalid Muhyi al-Din, the charismatic major and ever-more-alienated member of the CCR.

Khalid's ties to his CCR comrades trace back to a Muslim Brotherhood cell, which he joined in 1944 and where he met Nasser and Kamal al-Din Husayn. Separated for several years by the time he and Nasser reunited in late 1949, Khalid had become a committed, although he admits unsophisticated, Marxist, a member of EMNL (later DMNL). Even so, Khalid became a founding member of the Free Officers. He introduced Nasser to DMNL leaders and initiated collaboration between the movements. His own continued contacts with DMNL military leaders Ahmad Hamrush and Ahmad Fu'ad, with whom he made contingency plans to flee should the coup have failed, hint that Muhyi al-Din remained ambivalent about his ultimate loyalty to the Free Officers.

Following the coup, Khalid remained a loyal junta member, if often in dissent and always a bit on the outside. Like Yusuf Siddiq, he threatened to resign over policy disputes on a number of occasions in late 1952. Yet when Siddiq left the junta in January 1953, Khalid remained, opting to work within the CCR to influence policy. To what extent he remained a DMNL "agent" is uncertain. His CCR colleagues, who knew his political leanings, trusted him. If they tired of his frequent dissent, they also saw fit to keep him aboard.[6]

The extent of Khalid's role in the armor protest remains unclear. The others clearly believed, and continue to believe, he was in league with the rebels. He did maintain closer ties to his corps than did other CCR members, who became more isolated after the appointment of 'Amr as commander in chief. On a trip to upper Egypt in the autumn of 1953 he and Nagib discussed their shared misgivings about developments within the CCR, presumably the consolidation of power in the hands of Nasser and 'Amr, and the regime's uncompromising stand against popular movements (although Nagib's sympathies leaned toward the Wafd and, by then, the Brotherhood, Khalid's squarely toward the Left). There is little reason to presume Khalid alerted Nagib to the others' practice of meeting without him. Had he done so, Nagib might have forced the issue sooner. Khalid should not be viewed as a conspirator or active agitator prior to the outbreak of the March crisis. He says he supported the decision to accept Nagib's resignation on the condition he not be called upon to justify the action to his troops.[7]

When the crisis erupted, Khalid emerged as a popular leader of the armor corps and newfound ally of Nagib. That Khalid instigated or led the dissident armor officers' protest is not certain; that they looked to him as their champion is. He was not present at either CCR headquarters or the corps barracks when word reached the council of the armor protest. His alibi, that he was at the cinema, hints that he deemed it wisest to steal away for the moment. Nasser told U.S. embassy contacts that when he met with the disgruntled officers in their barracks, he identified the ringleaders and linked them to Khalid.[8]

Officers who mobilized against the armor corps on behalf of the CCR feel, with some justification, that they saved the regime on February 26–27. In their accounts of the episode they describe CCR members as overcome by emotion and exhaustion. Thirty years later, CCR members feel somewhat freer to admit the truth of this, but dismiss as exaggerations depictions of vacant stares and heads resting on tables. A week after the incident Nasser calmly told Jefferson Caffery that his promise to appoint Khalid prime minister was a stratagem designed to exploit divisions in the ranks. "I knew the army would never accept it, but from the time I talked with the cavalry officers I planned the whole maneuver to bring Khalid out in the open," he asserted. "I was only surprised at how quickly the officers reacted."[9] Nasser's self-assured tone fails to convey the prevailing sense of defeat and disarray that gripped the CCR that night. It is perhaps more indicative of his growing self-confidence as the crisis moved into a new, less pressing phase.

After surviving the night of February 26, the CCR faced the issue of what to do with Nagib and Khalid. Late in the afternoon on February 27, after having adjourned the CCR for several hours, Nasser decided to reinstate Nagib as president. He did so at the urging of Salah Salim, and the others learned of the decision when Salim announced it over the radio. The officers were divided on how to deal with Khalid. Nasser accepted the argument of Zakariya Muhyi al-Din and others that Khalid had never misled them about his position. He convinced his colleagues to focus instead on the problem of how to coexist with Nagib.[10]

Photographs of Nagib and Nasser embracing, smiling, and proclaiming the fuss merely a "summer storm" belied what all knew well. Upon news of Nagib's return, throngs of his supporters took to the streets in Cairo, Alexandria, and provincial centers. The revelers, described as "good natured" by the U.S. embassy, dissipated around midnight. The next morning, February 28, when university students found campuses closed, they set out toward the presidential palace (formerly Abdin), picking up numbers along the way. Police tried to prevent Cairo University students from crossing the Qasr al-Nil bridge in central Cairo, and in the melee an undetermined number were hurt, some wounded by gunfire. At the palace the crowd called for Nasser's head, urged the CCR to resign, decried the abolition of the Muslim Brotherhood, and denounced the force used against them on the bridge. In an impromptu balcony speech, Nagib promised sweeping changes and an investigation of police brutality against the demonstrators. He was joined by 'Abd al-Qadir 'Awdah, the Muslim Brothers' interim leader, who delivered a stinging rebuke of the CCR that Nagib, even in his euphoria, felt compelled to restrain. While the demonstration proceeded the CCR sat closeted inside, pondering the likelihood of a breakdown in civil order. The danger posed by the mob outside prompted talk of resignation. All agreed that a victorious Nagib with a popular mandate would prove intolerable.[11]

The CCR never reconciled the matter in council. In the confusion of events following Nagib's surprise offensive the officers discussed myriad options in endless, heated sessions, which resolved nothing. Various CCR members proposed collective resignation in favor of civilian rule; others called for direct action to restore their authority. Individual members often changed opinion from day to day. Nasser himself vacillated between tactical-retreat and forward-march camps. All council members agreed on one thing:

if they and Nagib were to coexist, even for the short run, Nagib would serve as figurehead president only, no longer prime minister or official CCR chief.

Unsure of how best to contain the momentum of public opposition, the CCR adopted contradictory strategies of assault and conciliation. On March 2 the CCR ordered the arrest of 118 "reactionaries," most of them Muslim Brothers and Socialists, charged with inciting the crowds on February 27–28. 'Abd al-Qadir 'Awdah and the Socialist party president, Ahmad Husayn, headed the list. 'Awdah paid for his balcony speech, Husayn for a letter he sent Nasser in which he made continued support for the regime contingent on the restoration of parliamentary life.[12] Then on March 5, in line with the course of reform promised unilaterally by Nagib, the CCR announced provisions for the election in July of a constituent assembly to finalize a constitution and pave the way for election of a new parliament. To insure that the election took place in a atmosphere of total freedom, the CCR announced an end to all restrictions on the press and the impending abrogation of martial law. From March 6 to 25 the regime released between two and three hundred political prisoners, the great majority Muslim Brothers.[13]

In the wake of what he considered victory, Nagib tried to secure greater authority over the CCR. On March 7 his three chief political allies, Sulayman Hafiz, 'Abd al-Razzaq al-Sanhuri, and 'Abd al-Galil al-'Imari, submitted his list of demands. Nagib sought veto power over all CCR and cabinet decisions, sole power to appoint military commanders down to battalion level, a public referendum on the republic, a general presidential election before ratification of a constitution, and the return of CCR and Liberation Rally officers to the ranks. In a combined meeting with the cabinet Nagib agreed to withdraw his demands on the condition he be reappointed prime minister. Reluctant to reopen hostilities, the officers accepted the compromise. Unnamed sources told the Americans "in strictest confidence" that had Nagib stood fast they were prepared to try him before a revolutionary court.[14]

Nagib and his backers, focusing on demonstrations in the streets, ignored hints of newfound harmony within the barracks that boded ill for his growing ambition. They believed the CCR faced no alternative but retreat. Until assured of the army's loyalty, his antagonists treated with him, while taking shrewd steps to insure the army stood with them. In early March the CCR released the artillery conspirators in exchange for a promise of support. The CCR refused clemency to Rashad Mahanna, but those released had seen enough of prison and believed enough of the CCR version of events to accept the deal.[15]

On the evening of March 9, the CCR staged a mass meeting at the Officers Club in an effort to rally support. Before an audience estimated at between fifteen hundred and two thousand, CCR members bade their comrades stand united against common enemies, imperialism and reaction. "The armed forces are one idea, one agent, with one goal in mind: working for the sake of Egypt and Egypt alone," 'Abd al-Hakim 'Amr declared in brief opening remarks. Nasser, who spoke next, mixed a call for solidarity with a personal pledge of steadfastness. He reminded the officers that they, the army, had made the revolution, and he swore it would continue. "I promise you here and now that I will never betray or deceive you." he proclaimed. "Nor will ever I beg you." Nagib, who spoke next, failed to move the audience. In contrast to Nasser he projected an image of weakness. He implored the army to put aside internecine quarrels. He spoke not of the revolution but of the "army movement," a throwback to earlier days. "As I stand among you on this occasion," he told the assembly, "tears of gratitude fill my eyes." After his remarks the audience called upon the others to speak. Each managed a few impromptu words. The meeting, which impressed the CCR officers with their hold over the army, marked the turning point in their battle with Nagib.[16]

However assured of the army's loyalty, however vigilant to exploit opponents' weaknesses, the CCR reeled from the onslaught of public criticism. The officers had unleashed the press on March 5 in part to gauge the extent of support for the regime and to identify friends and enemies. The abandon with which critics immediately set about denouncing them surprised and disappointed the officers, who continued to debate retreat versus the iron fist without resolving anything. Tough public statements belied private confusion. On March 18 the CCR reimposed censorship on the tabloid daily *Al-Qahirah* after it reported that Farouk, in cahoots with former British Ambassador Lampson (the same who had threatened the king with deposition in February 1942), planned to stage a comeback. Salah Salim warned the press against "irresponsible" reporting.[17] Midmonth, the officers again considered forming a political party to contest elections. The idea still garnered support among the intelligentsia, but when news of the plan appeared in the press, Nasser quickly doused any enthusiasm. Asked about his future political ambitions, he replied brusquely, "I am a revolutionary, not a politician."[18]

True to his word, Nasser decided to seize the initiative and force events. He collaborated with several, but not all, of his CCR colleagues, as well as others outside the council. The full council approved all strategies and resolutions, but for the remainder of the crisis a small brain trust—Nasser, Zakariya Muhyi al-Din, Salah Salim, and Sadat—worked to foster a crisis atmosphere, to create a situation analogous to that which held prior to July 1952, in which the army provided the only alternative to corruption and disorder. *Al-Jumhuriyah,* under Sadat's supervision, worked to promote confusion by running stories of old-regime figures poised to restore corruption and revoke land reform.[19] On March 20, a day six bombs exploded in different parts of Cairo, Baghdadi noted in his diary a greater resolve on Nasser's part that the CCR retain power. The bombings unnerved Baghdadi and other CCR officers who as yet had no inkling that they had been staged. Only Nagib resolutely resisted the call to implement emergency measures. Three days later Nasser told the U.S. State Department's Parker Hart that the country needed a lesson. He outlined no specific plan of action but hinted that he would allow the situation to deteriorate for a month or two.[20]

On March 25 the CCR again stunned the nation, announcing it would soon lift the ban on political parties and restore political rights to those convicted by the Treason and Revolutionary courts. The resolution provided for the election by popular vote of a constituent assembly, as promised on March 5, which now would exercise full parliamentary powers. Finally, the CCR declared it would not re-form as a political party but would dissolve itself on July 24 and declare the revolution ended.

Still thinking in terms of several months, plotters within the CCR braced for a new round of battle, never expecting the crisis would play itself out in the short time that followed. The full council approved the resolution, Nasser's brainchild, after a long meeting that left several members threatening resignation. Nasser and those with whom he conspired expected an outcry against their decision to withdraw from politics. The rally by loyal officers in February served as their model. Indeed, officers in the army and police, prompted in part by several CCR members who opposed the March 25 strategy, submitted petitions calling upon the CCR to retract its resolution.[21]

The March 25 resolution electrified Egypt. Old political parties quickly set about reorganizing, and, playing right into the officers' hands, old-style politics prevailed. After a series of joint meetings, former minority party leaders heralded the formation of a united front to combat the Wafd. Handicapped by the incapacity of its two most important leaders—Nahhas remained under house arrest, despite contrary claims by the government, and Sirag al-Din in the hospital—the Wafd moved more slowly. However, because the Wafd dominated professional associations, party members had other platforms available for political activism.[22]

The public onslaught against the CCR resounded from bastions of the intelligentsia. University students announced the formation of a "national union" coalition. The bar association and press syndicate drafted statements urging the officers to relinquish power at once. At a raucous meeting of the bar's general assembly, voices called for the arrest, expulsion, even execution of the officers. The bar's resolution denounced martial law as "an assault on human dignity and civil rights," and decried the reputed torture of three members jailed since early March: Muslim Brothers 'Awdah and Tilmissani and the Socialist party president, Ahmad Husayn. The assembly insisted upon civilian rule. The army deserved praise for its revolution, but

> the country wants to preserve the army for the defense of its borders. In order that no other duty preoccupy it, the assembly believes it is to the benefit of the country and the army itself that the officers return to their barracks, bearing with them the gratitude and esteem of their fellow citizens. For this reason the general assembly advocates the immediate dissolution of the CCR.[23]

For the opposition, for a day, the smell of victory was in the air.

Three days later the CCR turned the tables and reemerged as the undisputed authority in the country. Successful manipulation of the media, neutralization of the Muslim Brotherhood, intimidation of anti-CCR forces by orchestrated mob violence, and the ineffectual leadership of Muhammad Nagib sparked the officers' triumph.

The CCR depicted the stakes of the crisis as all or nothing: progress and reform with the CCR; without it, a full turn of the clock back to the old regime. Several days prior to March 25 *Al-Jumhuriyah* began reporting contacts between former party leaders. The paper dutifully revealed a visit paid Ibrahim 'Abd al-Hadi by government officials and Nagib allies, 'Imary and Sulayman Hafiz. Why the visit to this "man marked by terrorism"? "Perhaps Ibrahim 'Abd al-Hadi still dreams of the return of pashadom, the dress uniform, the political police, even the age of terror. . . ."[24] The Amin papers adopted a proregime line after March 25 no less vigorous than that of the government organ. On March 27 *Akhbar al-Yawm* printed verbatim the transcript of a telephone conversation between Nagib and Nahhas, provided the editors by the CCR. In the conversation, Nagib enquired about the Wafd leader's health and promised to lift the order confining him to his home. Journalists who were partisans of both factions recall this as a major public relations coup by the regime.[25]

A pact with the Muslim Brotherhood neutralized the regime's most troublesome and potentially dangerous foe. This was a daring gamble, coming in the wake of the Brothers' role in rallying forces on Nagib's behalf a month earlier. On March 2 'Abd al-Qadir 'Awdah and forty-four Brothers joined comrades imprisoned since January. On March 16 *Al-Misri* published an open letter from Hasan al-Hudaybi, also behind bars, to Nagib in which the general guide decried the dissolution of the Brotherhood. Soon after Nasser sent emissaries to negotiate with Hudaybi. On March 25 the CCR ordered the release of Hudaybi, all Guidance Council members, and some 220 Brothers. Nasser dined with Hudaybi that very evening. Hudaybi reportedly exacted from Nasser a promise to restore his movement's legal status and to clarify publicly the government's position. In return, Hudaybi adopted an ambivalent public stance toward legalization of the political parties. Another three hundred Brothers soon gained their freedom. During the battles of March 26–28 the Brothers remained conspicuously absent.[26]

The use of the mob marks a turning point in the CCR's consolidation of power. The Liberation Rally finally proved its worth. Its chief officers, Ibrahim al-Tahawi and 'Abd al-Allah Tu'aymah, proposed calling their forces into the streets and Nasser, sensing the ultimate opportunity to turn disorder to his advantage, assented.[27] For two days, March 26–27, a free-for-all ensued, with partisans of both sides holding simultaneous rallies. By March 28, because of superior organization, and mob and police violence, proregime forces succeeded in cowing the opposition and compelling the CCR to answer the louder cries for it to retain leadership of the country.

CCR representatives encouraged crowds that gathered outside CCR headquarters chanting, "No political parties and no democracy," "Long live the revolution," "Don't leave us, Gamal," and "Onward Gamal, to the Canal." The police stood by while a mob pelted the *Al-Misri* building with stones and bottles. Another mob organized by the military police stormed the chambers of the State Council and attacked the president, Sanhuri. The timely arrival of Salah Salim, pistol in hand, perhaps saved Sanhuri's life.[28]

The keystone of organized mob activity was a general strike declared by proregime trade union leaders on March 27. The leader of the transport workers, Al-Sawi Ahmad al-Sawi, planned and organized the strike in conjunction with the heads of major oil and tobacco unions. Al-Sawi apparently approached Ibrahim al-Tahawi, who took the idea to Nasser. Nasser gave his assent, with the caveat that the CCR would not officially recognize the strikers. On the evening of March 26 leaders of the transport union began a hunger strike. They raised the call for a general strike to force the CCR to "answer the peoples' call" to revoke its decision to restore the political parties and withdraw from public life.[29]

Nasser later boasted that he bought the working class for £E 4,000. In reality what he bought—and cost estimates vary—was the appearance of worker solidarity with the regime. Many unions, particularly those that were communist led, stood against the CCR. In Alexandria and in Delta factory towns the opposition was particularly marked. The vanguard of CCR support, however, came from unions that disrupted most effectively the daily operations of Cairo: transport workers primarily but also gas station attendants, and bank and cinema employees. If matters had not been resolved by March 29, electricity, gas, and water works were scheduled to shut down and truly paralyze the country. Nasser did not directly supervise the strikers' activities, but he monitored the situation closely. When dock workers in the Canal Zone joined the strike, threatening international transit, he issued an immediate order that their work stoppage cease.[30]

However spirited the resistance, opposition forces could not compete with state-sponsored coercion. Intimidated by the violence, the press syndicate canceled a scheduled meeting of its general assembly. Proregime forces in the bar association who dubbed themselves "Free Lawyers" fought for control of the assembly. A lawyers' strike scheduled for March 28 never materialized. On March 29 the officers announced their intent to assume "full responsibility" for restoring order and putting the revolution back on course. For all intents and purposes, the crisis had ended. Only university students, their numbers diminished significantly by the Muslim Brothers' noninvolvement, fought on until the police expelled them from the campuses in the first week of April.[31]

Overconfidence and a general lack of political savvy led to Muhammad Nagib's personal downfall. Allowing himself to be cast as a counterrevolutionary, he fell into the trap set for him by the CCR. Friends and advisors urged him to oppose the legalization of political parties, to enunciate instead a program that would guarantee the regime's reforms and facilitate parliamentary rule without resort to old-regime forces. Nagib, however, insisted publicly that no conditions be set for the parties' revival and proceeded to open contact with party leaders.[32] Nagib perhaps also inadvertently allowed the CCR to neutralize the Muslim Brotherhood. Whether realpolitik warranted their defection cannot be stated for certain, but Nagib blundered by failing to contact any Brotherhood leaders until after their release from prison, when it was already too late. When Nasser opened their prison doors, Nagib sensed trouble and hastened to contact Hudaybi. The general guide failed to return his call.[33]

When the crisis reached its climax, Nagib was paralyzed by indecision. He rejected proposals by officers loyal to him that they bring their units into the streets and arrest the CCR.[34] To them, as to the public at large, he pleaded for order and asked that the CCR be left to resolve its problems in private. When the CCR assembled at headquarters on March 28, Nagib entered unceremoniously through the back while his colleagues triumphantly rode the shoulders of those gathered outside. Overcome by mental and physical exhaustion, he collapsed the next day, and remained in hospital for several weeks afterward. His infirm condition, captured in photos allowed the press, served to highlight his political failings.[35]

"The Road to Stability"

The March crisis left a bitter aftertaste for winners and losers alike. Their experience taught the officers valuable lessons about the nature of power and how to keep it. Those who led the fight against the CCR in March would pay a steep price. In a sweeping offensive, the officers acted to dominate all centers of political opposition, in systematic fashion extending their control over the army and government bureaucracy, consolidating power in their own hands. For the first time, the state began to display a distinctly military look.

In speeches, interviews, and decrees the officers stressed the need for Egypt to put the crisis behind it and look ahead. Projects and plans filled the press: the CCR contemplated forming a national advisory council, ordered an investigation into royal family holdings, and studied blueprints for bringing drinking water to all villages, and building hospitals and housing for industrial workers, government employees, and students. But premonitions of other changes to come outweighed news of good works. In a reprise of the months following their takeover, the officers' rhetoric spoke with renewed vigor of "purification," with professional associations and unions the new targets. The officers did not hide their anger at those who had been so quick to denounce their rule or trumpet their mistakes. In a column entitled "The Revolution's Errors," Anwar Sadat wrote that the regime's primary mistake had been goodwill, toward the political parties and toward the press.[36]

Muhammad Nagib stayed on as president, but now with a much lower profile. As in late February, smiling photographs of reconciliation filled the press, but these would soon disappear. His photograph appeared infrequently, more often in picture magazines than the daily press. "Just enough publicity to remind people of his existence," quipped a British diplomat.[37] A series of political cartoons in a friendly paper chronicles the president's vanishing act. In late April Nagib stands prominent next to Nasser who drives a tram labeled "the revolution" (the caption: "This tram is express—it takes no detours). A month later Nasser is depicted as pyramid builder (the pyramid labeled "democracy"), Salah Salim studies the plans, while Nagib holds a plumb bob. In early June Nasser drives a steamroller paving "the road to stability." The others work with pickax and shovel, but Nagib is no longer among them.[38]

Khalid Muhyi al-Din paid for his part in the crisis as well. At the advice of Zakariya, Khalid had dropped out of sight for several days following the armor protest in late February. He returned to Cairo immediately after March 5, having taken no part in the decision to restore civil liberties, cautiously hopeful that he could help steer the CCR toward fulfilling its promises. He says several armor officers approached him shortly thereafter and asked him to lead a coup d'état, which he refused. In public he played down rifts within the CCR. On March 27, when all appeared lost, he left Cairo for an Alexandria hideaway. Before leaving, he says, he advised Nagib against rallying loyal units against the CCR. After rebuffing several attempts by Nasser and 'Amr to contact him, Khalid returned to Cairo on April 1 and agreed to go abroad as part of a trade mission to Europe. His parting with Nasser was sober, but not devoid of a shared sorrow.[39]

Hoping to defuse trouble in the ranks, the CCR treated the army with kid gloves. Soon after the crisis ended most of the armor officers arrested on February 27 were freed. In the first week of April Husayn al-Shafi'i, the corps commander, was replaced by a more senior officer, a move designed to placate disgruntled senior and junior officers. To temper reaction to Khalid Muhyi al-Din's departure, the regime officially designated him a representative of the CCR abroad, leaving the impression that his absence would be temporary.[40]

Few were fooled, or appeased. On April 28 the CCR arrested sixteen armor officers whom it accused of plotting to overthrow the government, the coup set for May 1. Many were former Free Officers; nine were said to have been among those arrested in February and then released. Nasser hinted in private at links between the officers and civilian elements. If he contemplated a major conspiracy trial, he quickly shelved such plans. The officers faced a court-martial in June. Nine received prison terms ranging from one to fifteen years.[41] The following week Colonel Ahmad Shawqi, a close associate of Muhammad Nagib, was sentenced to fifteen years.

Thereafter the CCR acted quickly to mold a loyal officer corps. In July, 'Abd al-Hakim 'Amr ordered widespread transfers and dismissals in the armor corps that, in the opinion of British military intelligence, were "severe enough to have impaired its value as a fighting arm."[42] In early October he ordered the promotion of approximately two hundred officers in all branches. Senior officers kicked upstairs were slated for early retirement, their promotions netting them higher pensions, a means to "take the sting out of dismissal." In the eyes of British analysts the promotions left the Egyptian army top-heavy with colonels and lieutenant colonels.[43] Placing loyalists in higher command positions achieved a political end but puts a premium on military inexperience even if it means that the CRC [CCR] have a tighter grip on the machine. The very fact of placing those whose loyalty could be relied on in key positions, the recently introduced system which encourages officer to spy on officer, and the use of security and guard battalions to segregate units shows that the CRC are well aware of the danger of disaffection. [44]

The CCR also moved to assert more direct control over the government. The culmination of the crisis saw the dismissal of cabinet members who had supported Nagib. Sulayman Hafiz, a legal architect of the early battle against the parties, and 'Abd al-Galil al-'Imari, finance minister from the beginning, resigned in late March. In mid-April Nasser officially assumed the joint positions of prime minister and military governor-general of Egypt. He appointed every CCR member to a cabinet post, with the exception of 'Amr and Sadat. On August 31 he shuffled his cabinet, bringing in the latter two, forming for the first time a government in which all CCR members held cabinet posts (the cabinet now comprised ten officers and ten civilians). [45]

In the immediate aftermath of March the officers resolved to silence independent political discourse in the media, professional organizations, and on campus. On April 14 the government announced a general decree stripping Wafdist, Liberal Constitutionalist, and Sa'dist party leaders of their political rights. The list, which numbered thirty-nine names, included Makram 'Ubayd and Nagib al-Hilali, both former Wafdists who had testified vehemently against Fu'ad Sirag al-Din before the Revolutionary Tribunal. Two leading Wafdists who had maintained cordial relations with the CCR until March, 'Abd al-Salam Gum'ah and Muhammad Salah al-Din—the latter Nasser denounced by name in a speech the same day—also lost their rights. 'Abd al-Razzaq al-Sanhuri, in addition to his beating by a proregime mob, paid further for his support of Muhammad Nagib. A member, but hardly a leader, of the Sa'dist party, he found his name among the thirty-nine. Then, ruled ineligible to serve on the State Council, he was expelled from office. Members of other parties would be banned, if so determined, by individual decree. The list included no independents. 'Ali Mahir, whom Nasser had also attacked by name, remained in the regime's good graces. [46]

The regime took similar steps against the press. Denouncing the media as "the weapon enlisted by the parties to deceive the masses," the CCR purged the press syndicate, placing a friendly editor, Fikri Abaza of *Al-Musawwar*, at its helm. As ostensible cause, the government revealed that seven of twelve syndicate officers had taken secret funds from the palace prior to July 1952. In total twenty-four publishers, editors, and reporters from fifteen journals were denounced for having at one time or another accepted money from a palace slush fund. The charge sheet, while legitimate, bore little relation to the present field of journalism in the country. Of the fifteen journals charged, all but *Ruz al-Yusuf* were by then defunct. The list of guilty individuals included old-regime stalwarts Edgar Gallad and Karim Thabit, as well as former friend Ihsan 'Abd al-Quddus, whom the CCR now jailed for his impassioned plea that the revolution end. Friends of the regime who presumably also took palace handouts escaped censure.[47]

The CCR singled out two journals for exemplary punishment. Ahmad Abu al-Fath had been warned to leave the country in mid-March. In late April the government indicted his brothers, Mahmud and Husayn, owners and publishers of *Al-Misri,* on treason charges. On May 4 a revolutionary court convicted both. It sentenced Mahmud, in absentia, to ten years in prison, and Husayn, who in addition had been president of the press syndicate, to a fifteen-year suspended sentence. The next day the CCR ordered their publishing license revoked. *Al-Misri,* until then Egypt's largest daily, shut down its presses. The following week the government pressed charges against Abu al-Khayr Nagib, editor of the much smaller *Al-Jumhur al-Misri,* who had published a series of articles, "The Revolution's Errors," that had particularly irritated the officers. The court sentenced Nagib to fifteen years and suspended his citizenship rights. Egypt, a country with a plethora of newspapers on the eve of July 23, now had only three major dailies: the friendly *Al-Akhbar,* the prudently independent *Al-Ahram,* and the government organ, *Al-Jumhuriyah.*[48]

The university campuses, recaptured by force in April, remained simmering centers of dissent. Cairo University, where students and police battled until April 2, reopened on April 10 for fourth-year classes only. On April 6 police finally cleared the campus in Alexandria; a week later the government announced the indefinite suspension of classes there for the law, engineering, science, and medicine schools, with exceptions made for final-year medical students. The CCR considered a major roundup of student and faculty activists but exercised moderation. The police arrested student ringleaders and ordered eight professors dismissed. The campuses remained relatively quiet as students prepared for examinations and summer vacation.[49]

Before the fall term commenced the government took steps to prevent a recurrence of trouble. In addition to national politics, student grievances concerned specific academic matters, increasing tuition and examinations. Student activists demanded that spring examinations, which an unusually high number had failed, be readministered. The government acted to appease them, declaring a 30 percent decrease in fees and offering scholarships to those who scored as low as 60 percent on their examinations. Still apprehensive, the government in mid-September decided to postpone the beginning of fall term. Later that month the Education Ministry ordered a similar delay for the opening of secondary schools. Education Minister—and CCR member—Kamal Husayn dismissed the steps as administrative, an effort to allow students to complete exams. In private, Foreign Minister Mahmud Fawzi told British contacts that schools would not reopen until after a new Anglo-Egyptian accord had been signed.[50]

In the interim the Education Ministry oversaw a major turnover in the administrative boards of the three main universities (Cairo, Ayn Shams, and Alexandria) and ordered the dismissal of forty professors who had participated in antiregime activities during March. The ministry assumed direct responsibility for university administration, thereafter appointing all directors, deans, and vice-deans, a right traditionally exercised by the faculty. In addition, the ministry nominated an under-secretary of state to sit on the council of each university. The decrees and dismissals aroused anger among students and faculty. When the universities finally opened their doors for the fall semester in early November, all who entered passed through a triple cordon of police.[51]

Toward labor, the bulwark of pro-CCR support in the crucial latter days of March, the regime made cautious overtures. In the wake of their victory the officers made triumphal appearances at union halls and entertained numerous labor delegations at CCR headquarters. On such occasions they proclaimed solidarity between army and working class, emphasizing the workers' role in preserving the revolution. The Egyptian Federation of Labor and the Cairo Chamber of Commerce asked employers to reimburse workers for pay lost during the strike.[52]

At the same time the officers endeavored to blunt the enthusiasm of the unions, hoping to discourage any thoughts of long-term political rewards. The CCR was aware that it had unleashed forces that could prove difficult to control. Because of crackdowns on communist movements, Liberation Rally organizers had gradually increased their influence over many trade unions, but trouble spots remained. The number of unions that stood with Nagib in March pointed to the persistent influence of the opposition. Labor legislation promulgated in 1953 had bolstered job security but in other regards strengthened management's hand. Even unions that supported the officers in March continued to demand the right to strike. Instead, the regime spoke of the need for the labor movement to purge itself of reactionary elements, insisting the regime stood as an impartial judge between the workers and the employers.[53]

The "masses" largely sat out the March crisis. They did not rally to the call of old-regime leaders; neither did they muster enthusiasm for the new guard. The ambivalence of the majority, reflected by passiveness, allowed the CCR to dominate the streets. Still, whatever the public perception of the struggle within the CCR, and to whichever side it leaned, most Egyptians seemed to regret Nagib's eclipse. The general had lent the regime an image with which most Egyptians felt comfortable. "The sentiment of the people," recalls Husayn al-Shafi'i, "was with the smiling face of Nagib, not the grim face of Abdel Nasser."[54]

Try as they might, the officers had little reason to smile in the months after March. Public opinion did not change appreciably, no matter how great the fears of "reaction," nor how substantial the promises for the future. Egyptians watched to see what direction the revolution would take, whether talk of political reform was real or whether the revolution entailed merely the replacement of one set of rulers for another. Ambivalent, cynical, afraid, and simply busy trying to cope with normal daily pressures, most recognized the authority of the CCR but felt no particular loyalty toward it and no great enthusiasm for the individual officers.

The tone of CCR rhetoric, what the officers stressed and what they downplayed, the rumors they felt compelled to deny and those they chose to float, reveals an overriding concern with this failure to win public support. The officers certainly tried to kindle enthusiasm for their rule. They made daily visits to the countryside. On two occasions in April they distributed land to peasants with much fanfare.[55] However, their rhetoric remained largely negative in tone. Echoing old themes, the officers emphasized the prevalence of "reactionary" forces and the need to "purify" the political system. The parties, they insisted, bore just as much responsibility for the corruption of political life as the king; even the Wafd had opposed land reform. The regime painted a picture of opposition forces as a broad conspiracy committed to sowing disorder and undermining social mores. In late April Nasser charged collusion between communists and Zionists, tied to the exiled DMNL leader Henri Curiel. He would repeat the charge throughout the summer. By late August he added the Muslim Brotherhood to the ranks of the conspirators.[56]

All indications are that the regime's rhetoric failed to sway the populace. Rumors dogged the officers, keeping them on the defensive: that Nasser had absconded with palace treasures, that Salah Salim had smuggled five million Egyptian pounds into a Swiss bank account. Public fetes in the spring and summer of 1954 provided opportunities to bring out the crowds, a risky barometer of public support except for the absence of celebration. The first anniversary of the republic passed with only scant notice, primarily because the officers balked at spotlighting Nagib. July 23 anniversary celebrations, according to foreign diplomatic observers, were "marked by improved organization, increased security measures, and decreased enthusiasm." Smatterings of catcalls and pro-Nagib and Muslim Brother exhortations greeted the officers. The police dispersed disorderly crowds when Nasser and several colleagues appeared in Alexandria on July 26.[57]

The signing of Heads of Agreement, the main points of a draft evacuation accord with the British, on July 27, changed little with regard to organized opposition to the regime or public apathy. After two years of wrangling with the British, the CCR achieved an agreement it hoped it could present to Egypt as a nationalist victory. The officers quickly learned how difficult it would be to sell the agreement to the public. Demonstrations organized on July 28 to celebrate the signing were described by British observers as "neither large nor enthusiastic." That night, proclaiming that the people had displayed sufficient joy, the Interior Ministry forbade all further public celebrations. Four months after the climax of the March crisis Jefferson Caffery observed that Nasser faced possibly the "toughest fight of his career."[58]

This time, however, the officers were better able to assess strengths and weaknesses, and to prepare for showdowns that they now anticipated. Their steady extension of authority throughout the army and government, infiltration of labor unions and professional organizations, and their muzzle on the press allowed the officers slowly to abandon their defensive posture and mount an open attack against their enemies, communists and Muslim Brothers. Here the officers moved with characteristic caution, awaiting the optimum moment to strike. When they did, however, they demonstrated a resolve to crush those foes that they had lacked prior to March 1954.

8

"Stability, in Whatever Guise"

Reeling from the shock of street demonstrations and the threat of mutiny in the armor barracks, the CCR on March 5, 1954, announced steps to end the period of transitional rule and facilitate the return of parliamentary life. Along with the decree, the CCR proclaimed an immediate end to all press censorship effective the following day. From March 6 to 28, when the officers reasserted full authority over the country, Egypt experienced a brief renaissance of open political discourse. During these three weeks, debate on the future of the country, constrained since the CCR's assumption of direct military rule in January 1953, flourished in an atmosphere of hope, expectation, and no small degree of reckless bravado.

The March crisis sounded a call to ideological battle stations that few could resist. For many, March was a brief, shining moment when raised voices decried the subversion of civil and political rights, and sounded the call for a return to parliamentary democracy. The perception of CCR weakness prompted a zealous opposition that now encompassed many former supporters of the regime who despaired of military rule and sensed an opportunity to hasten its end. For others, the specter of a resurgence by forces of the old regime, a return to the politics of the liberal era without the reforms so desperately sought prior to July 23, dominated concerns. Unsure of the direction in which the CCR led Egypt but wishing to press forward with the regime's reform program, and hoping—always hoping—that a revitalized, sound parliamentary system would emerge, they chose to stand with the officers and support the regime.

The rhetoric of March reveals much about how politically minded Egyptians, having lived through nearly two years of military rule, recalled the old regime and how they perceived the transition to a new political order. That many still spoke of transition underscores just how tenuous a hold the CCR or their "revolution" had on the minds of the intelligentsia. Political debate revolved around two major issues. The first was the structure of the future political system and the proper steps toward its constitution. The more mundane aspects of this question remained the domain not of political activists but of jurists, lawyers, and academics. The second major issue was the future of the revolution itself and the future political role of the CCR. Although few civilians favored the officers' long-term retention of power, few seriously believed the officers would renounce political activism. How to cajole the officers back to the barracks or, more realistically, persuade them to resign their commissions and rule as civilians was an issue none could ignore.

With regard to the question of military rule, the intelligentsia may still be divided into two camps, previously denoted as minimalist and maximalist. These factions did not differ in their ultimate desire to see martial law end, the jails emptied of at least some political detainees, and civilian rule restored. They disagreed only in their perceptions as to whether the time was propitious for a return to parliamentary rule or whether there remained aims best attained through a dictatorship that was ideally benign and just.

In many respects the particulars of the debate clouded more immediate issues of political power and camouflaged CCR maneuvers to reassert its authority. Given license to debate issues freely, intellectuals considered the comparative advantages of an appointed or elected constituent assembly, the proper number of political parties in a healthy parliamentary system, and the political rights of women. All the while the CCR worked behind the scenes to undermine the very forces it had set in motion. With no real strategy, the opposition front collapsed before the forces of state coercion and state-sponsored mob violence.

To a great extent the visions of March were totally out of touch with political realities of the day. Yet despite—even because of—that, the rhetoric of March, the ideals proffered and programs espoused, warrant closer consideration. The rhetoric highlights both the eloquence and impotence of the leaders of opposition. It raises serious questions about the ultimate wisdom of those who lent the regime their support. Above all, it provides the last clear insights into political currents in a country that would immediately thereafter suffer the repression and co-opting of its intelligentsia.

"I Write with Haste"

The CCR's March 5 promise to seat a constituent assembly nurtured hopes for progress toward a new constitution and electoral law. Throughout the turmoil of late 1953 and early 1954, the committee of fifty appointed by the regime in January 1953 continued work on the outline of a draft constitution. After some initial hoopla and press coverage the committee disappeared from public sight. Five subcommittees met on a semiregular basis. The committee's resolution in the spring of 1953 in favor of abolishing the monarchy and founding a republic heralded the regime's unilateral action decreed finally in June. Thereafter, the committee, which advocated a parliamentary republic, remained in reserve, proof of at least some progress toward ending the transition period.

On March 5, 1954, the committee chair, 'Ali Mahir, announced that the body had completed a first draft and would have a more polished text ready

to present a constituent assembly by July. Constitutional provisions for martial law remained a sticky point that needed further deliberation. Mahir
revealed the committee was deadlocked over whether to grant the president
authority to invoke emergency measures without parliament's approval.[1]

After March 5 the emphasis shifted to a discussion of the proper means
for writing and ratifying a new constitution. Few rejected the notion of a
constituent assembly. Those who did argued that the government had not
gone far enough. They pressed the government to grant the constituent
assembly full parliamentary powers. Ihsan 'Abd al-Quddus rejected the notion that the country needed a constitution before a parliament could sit. "I
write with haste," he asserted, "not as a legal expert, but as one of the
majority who want the situation settled quickly."[2] Legal experts echoed 'Abd
al-Quddus's impatience. Muhammad 'Ali 'Allubah, a member of the committee that had drafted the 1923 Constitution, and 'Umar 'Umar, Wafdist president of the bar association, argued that the existing committee of fifty, of
which both were members, should submit its draft directly to an elected
parliament for ratification. By doing so, Egypt could avoid the strain of two
elections in one year. A former Wafdist cabinet minister, 'Abd al-Magid 'Abd
al-Haqq, even suggested restoring the 1923 charter and electing a new
parliament to amend it according to provisions within that charter.[3]

Selection of the constituent assembly, specifically whether the body
should be appointed—as was the committee of fifty—or elected also generated debate. The government asserted it harbored no thoughts of an appointed body. The great majority of those who addressed the matter supported
that position. The list included ranking constitutional jurists 'Abd al-Razzaq al-
Sanhuri, 'Uthman Khalil 'Uthman, and Wahid Ra'fat, as well as 'Ali Mahir.
Arguing that the assembly should be nonpartisan and comprise experts, a
minority doubted the ability of the electorate to provide either. The jurist
Sayyid Sabri, the writer al-'Aqqad, and Ahmad Zaki, dean of Cairo University,
insisted upon an appointed body. Sabri argued that the existing constitutional
committee was just such a qualified body of experts. This, he stated, precluded any need for calling a constituent assembly at the present time. Others
expressed a willingness to accept an elected body, provided that a small percentage of the assembly's members was appointed.[4]

How to rebuild a multiparty system and yet avoid the pitfalls of Egypt's
parliamentary experience proved a more contentious question. The plethora
of parties that had filed applications for recertification in October 1952,
particularly small parties with overlapping constituencies (Workers, Socialist
Workers, Socialist Peasants, Workers and Peasants), had underscored for
many the system's weaknesses. Since January 1953 proregime spokesmen
had decried party politics as inherently corrupt, rooted in self-interest, even
un-Islamic. Nur al-Din Tarraf and Fathi Radwan, the most outspoken civilian
cabinet ministers, defended the one-party system as the guarantor of stability in the transition period. "If the one party system is not the Islamic
system," wrote Sheikh Baquri, minister of pious endowments, "it is closest to
the spirit of Islam."[5]

With rare exception defenders of the political parties had been shut out of the media, but champions of parliamentary democracy responded to the government line with outrage. They rejected the one-party state in any guise as a long-term proposition. Looking outward for examples, they denounced Soviet communism, proclaimed Ataturk's statism a failure, and condemned a lingering fascination with fascist Germany and Italy voiced by various members of the government and the CCR. The solution, they retorted, was to found parties based on principles rather than personalities. This was of course easier said than done, and had become a cliché long before the July coup. Some advocated imposing legal limits on the terms that party officers could serve. Many looked to England and the United States as models of stability and democracy. The crucial common denominator in these countries' political systems was that only two or three major parties contested elections.[6]

The idea of limiting the number of parties in Egypt roused considerable emotion. It was, its opponents charged, artificial and undemocratic. A plan proffered by 'Abd al-Razzaq al-Sanhuri in December 1953 focused the debate, which took on added importance during the March crisis. Sanhuri had proposed a three-party system to reflect the ideologies of a majority of Egyptians. A conservative party (hizb al-muhafizin) would "advocate a return to the country's glorious past and pledge to follow the steps of the venerable ancestors." A liberal party (hizb al-ahrar) would "advocate quiet progress" and promote individual and economic freedoms. Finally, a socialist republican party (al-hizb al-jumhuri al-ishtiraki)—the party Sanhuri unabashedly supported—would "stand vigilant guard over the legacy bequeathed the country by the revolution." That legacy included an activist social policy, exemplified by land reform.[7]

Sanhuri's most outspoken defender was Muhammad Mandur, once a leading figure in the Wafdist Left, now a disaffected intellectual writing for the government daily, *Al-Jumhuriyah*.[8] Mahmud 'Abd al-Mun'im Murad, a young *Al-Misri* columnist, denounced the plan as "naive, superficial, and arbitrary." Sanhuri's majority party was "plump, delectable, and comely," Murad complained. "They have taken the meat for themselves and left the others the bones and tripe."[9]

If Sanhuri's plan had its faults, the principle of legislating a set number of parties gained wide acceptance. Sayyid Sabri, arguing that capitalism and socialism constituted the major ideological cleavage in the world, offered his own three-party plan. Sabri proposed legislating conservative and socialist parties, balanced by a centrist liberal party that he likened to that in Britain. 'Abd al-Rahman al-Rafi'i, Nationalist party vice-president, echoed Sabri's plan. Muhammad Salah al-Din of the Wafd agreed that three or four parties would suffice. Wahid Ra'fat supported a legislated limit in principle and asserted his opposition to a legal communist party. Salih Harb, former leader of the Young Men's Muslim Association, believed that two parties were sufficient, a party of the revolution and the opposition.[10]

While the intelligentsia debated the shape of the future order, one issue—women's suffrage—leapt from the printed page to capture public attention. On March 10 the constitutional committee of fifty rejected the right of women to vote in elections to the constituent assembly. Two days later Dorya Shafiq and seven compatriots from her Daughter of the Nile movement entered the headquarters of the press syndicate and commenced a hunger strike. The strikers threatened to abstain from eating until Egyptian women were granted "full constitutional rights without exception or condition." They specifically demanded women's representation on the constituent assembly.[11]

The Daughters of the Nile, concerned primarily with issues related to the political, economic, and social status of women, had expressed support for the military takeover in July 1952, hoping that the officers' promises of political reform would include greater rights for women. The party was granted a license under the Party Reorganization Law that November. Shafiq, who applauded abrogation of the 1923 Constitution as the end of "the dark ages," requested that women be allowed representation on the constitutional committee. 'Ali Mahir and others expressed support for their aspirations, but nothing resulted. Now, frustrated in their efforts, Shafiq and her comrades chose to take advantage of the crisis atmosphere in the country.[12]

The strike lasted eight days. On the second day a group of women in Alexandria proclaimed a solidarity strike. The strikers in Cairo entertained a constant flow of sympathetic but skeptical public figures. 'Ali Mahir, Muhammad Salah al-Din, and Sulayman Hafiz, among others, endeavored to persuade them to abandon their protest. They also received delegations of female university students. On March 15, the fourth day of the strike, 130 female American University students rallied outside the presidential palace in Republic Square. On March 17 two of the hunger strikers were taken to a local Red Crescent clinic. The following day, amidst reports that four were seriously ill, all eight were transferred to a hospital. On March 19, after receiving a letter from Muhammad Nagib pledging to submit their grievance to a special committee, the women ended their strike.[13]

The hunger strike caused a considerable stir. The press carried daily photographs of the strikers, all middle-aged or older women, increasingly wan but with a steady, determined look in their eyes. These, as well as photographs of female university students demonstrating, inspired pride among women, mixed feelings of sympathy and horror among men. Passions polarized less around the issue raised by the women than the tactic they employed. *Al-Jil al-Jadid* (The New Generation), a new weekly published by the Amin brothers, described American University students who demonstrated in favor of the strikers as "the worst example to young women of the new generation."[14]

Except for the past and present rectors of al-Azhar and other religious figures, none spoke out categorically against women's rights. Closest to that extreme, 'Uthman Khalil 'Uthman, dean of the law faculty at Ibrahim University, asserted that in order to insure public confidence, the constituent assembly needed to be elected under existing electoral laws.[15] Expressing sympathy with their desires but outrage at their flagrant disregard for the law at a time when the government faced a major crisis, Taha Husayn chastised the strikers as "sinners." Dorya Shafiq and others answered him in the press and a lively exchange ensued.[16]

The final word naturally went to the CCR. Writing in the immediate aftermath of the March crisis, Anwar al-Sadat compared the two strikes that the officers had just confronted. The women's strike, regardless of the justness of their cause, he judged inappropriate. The women had exploited a crisis situation and not allowed the issue to be discussed in a rational manner. In contrast, the general strike of March 27–29, when crowds took to the street to denounce the return of political parties, reflected the will of the people.[17] Like all other constitutional issues, the question of women's suffrage would be shelved for the immediate future.

"Giving Poison to a Sick Man"

Communist movements prior to March 1954 remained in a state of constant upheaval. By late 1953 the regime had apprehended the entire DMNL governing body and begun to unravel the web of secrecy surrounding the ECP and Workers Vanguard. Internal schisms and mistrust between different communist movements continued to plague the Left. Because communism remained a political crime, the leftist critique of the regime appeared only in underground publications. However disseminated, the message remained powerful. After early efforts to capitalize on the trials of communist leaders for propaganda effect in the spring of 1953 failed, proceedings had been held in camera. The press reported the trials, sometimes listing names of the defendants, but provided no details of charges and certainly no account of defense statements.

The onset of the March crisis had little effect on traditional political positions within the communist movements. The ECP viewed the conflict between Nasser and Nagib as an "internecine power struggle, competition to serve imperialism and beat down the people."[18] The most dogmatic force on the Left, and by then the largest, remained adamantly opposed to collaboration on any scale with other forces. Yet when the crisis reached its climax in late March, ECP unions demonstrated against the CCR. Still small and organized primarily in the factories, the Workers Vanguard rallied its followers from the outset against the regime. A pamphlet dated March 8 called the workers to battle "to defeat the military gang in elections to the constituent assembly and in defense of independence, peace, and democracy." Its leaders asserted that if the people and the working class stood united, Egypt faced a great opportunity to overthrow the military dictatorship. The movement called for the CCR to dissolve itself and the Liberation Rally, and— little change from 1950—advocated formation of a coalition government under Wafdist leadership to oversee free parliamentary elections.[19]

Plagued more than any other movement by arrest, defection, and schism, the DMNL entered the March crisis lacking a united central command. Following the arrests in November 1953 of its entire central committee, leadership of the movement passed into the hands of younger members. Those in prison or exile viewed them as temporary leaders at best. Nonetheless, by mid-January 1954 the movement had regrouped, retooled its propaganda network, and resumed its assault against the regime.[20] If the DMNL lacked strong central leadership or ideological direction—the latter being the traditional charge of its leftist opponents—its members continued to play an important role on the university campuses and in the factories. The events of February–March evince this. The old leadership, however, stunned the movement by adopting a stance in favor of collaboration with the CCR.

A letter to the CCR signed by approximately twenty jailed DMNL leaders articulated this dramatic policy reversal. Praising what they saw as a new direction embarked upon by the CCR in the struggle against imperialism, the signatories of the "military prison manifesto" called for a reevaluation of relations between communists and the regime. A series of meetings initiated by Nasser in early March between officers and the jailed communists set the stage for the dramatic turnabout. According to several signatories, the officers who approached them hinted that the CCR was amenable to such a reevaluation. The emissaries told them that the junta had turned anticommunist from a desire to win U.S. support in the struggle against Britain. Now the CCR saw this as a lost hope. In addition, Nasser's envoys stressed progressive measures initiated by the regime, primarily land reform, and the officers' nationalist goals, which, so they argued, necessitated the retention of emergency measures. DMNL leaders, recently released from solitary confinement, discussed the matter among themselves. Agreeing that Nasser's overture was sincere, they concluded that despite its dictatorial nature, the regime was about to embark on a foreign policy that warranted communist support.[21]

That Nasser was dissembling seems clear. If his emissaries told the communists what the communists said they had, it was pure fancy intended to deceive them. Those who still see his overture as sincere mistakenly point to the rapprochement achieved between Nasser and the Left a year later, after Egyptian-U.S. relations had soured, making conditions for an alliance riper. As with the Muslim Brotherhood, Nasser hoped to divide and dilute the street power of antiregime forces. With the Brothers he succeeded, although their leadership held no illusions about his sincerity. In falling for his ploy, DMNL leaders exacerbated divisions within the upper ranks of their movement and failed to rally the legions. The active central committee suppressed the prison manifesto.[22] In the end Nasser elected not to release the jailed leaders. At best, they won an improvement in prison conditions. Most faced trial and were convicted later that year, sentenced to terms ranging from five to ten years.

If the DMNL had one bona fide hero, it was Yusuf Siddiq, the former member of the junta. Following his resignation in January 1953, Siddiq was posted to Aswan. In March of that year he left the country. Returning secretly several months later, he remained in hiding in his village. From there he contacted Muhammad Nagib, presumably to offer him his allegiance. Instead, he was placed under house arrest.[23] In late March 1954 he entered the poltiical fray. He wrote an open letter to Nagib that *Al-Misri* published one day before the CCR's decision to disband. In the bold statement Siddiq wrote:

> The continuation of the present government in power and of the organizations founded by it . . . after the people have rendered their judgment, means the continuation of a policy, the failure and danger of which has been proven. As long as the government has resolved to leave the people to manage their own affairs it has no right to impose or suggest anything. For we arose on July 23 to allow the people to manage their own affairs without any trusteeship imposed upon them. . . .

According to Siddiq, the government had two options. It could either recall the parliament dissolved in January 1952 or form a coalition government to oversee elections for a new chamber. That coalition government should include all popular factions in the country: the Wafd, Muslim Brothers, Socialists, and communists. He proposed Wahid Ra'fat be named interim prime minister. Any other solution he likened to "giving poison to a sick man."[24]

Siddiq's open advocacy of communist participation in a ruling coalition shook the basis of martial law. That Siddiq was not immediately arrested and muzzled probably reflects a shrewd decision on Nasser's part to gauge the sympathy his proposal would engender, as well as to exploit its relative extremism, particularly the call for Brotherhood and communist participation in government. Asked about Siddiq's proposal, Khalid Muhyi al-Din felt compelled to dismiss it as "meaningless."[25] Ra'fat, Siddiq's nominee to head the coalition government, had earlier in the month rejected calls for communist participation in the political process.

More than his proposal, Siddiq's acknowledged role as a former member of the revolutionary council threatened the integrity of the regime. Initially reluctant to discuss his participation in either the coup or the junta, Siddiq wrote openly of his dissent after the CCR announced its intention to resign. In articles published by *Al-Misri* and *Ruz al-Yusuf* he accused the junta of forsaking the goals of its revolution. He pointed in particular to his support of the artillery officers arrested in January 1953 and his advocacy of a national front. He had not ceased political activity while under house arrest, he said, and would continue to be active until the CCR restored civil liberties and the army returned to the barracks.[26] Shortly thereafter the CCR ordered Siddiq's arrest.

"The Revolution Will Continue"

The fate of the CCR stood at the heart of debate about just how civilian rule could be restored. The promise of a constituent assembly delivered in the

March 5 decree prompted speculation on the future role of the officers. Until Nasser dashed their hopes, many looked to the officers to form a new political party. Zuhayr Garanah, former minister in 'Ali Mahir's last cabinet, suggested that the CCR continue to play an advisory role from afar.[27] Few who approached the matter with any degree of sobriety—and there were many who did not—failed to note the unreality of expectations that the officers would return to the barracks. Ihsan 'Abd al-Quddus stood somewhere in the middle. How, he asked, in a column entitled "The Secret Society That Rules Egypt," published on March 22, can Nasser ever again stand before a general and salute him? He traced the development of the revolution, the emergence of the officers into the public light, and his own efforts to convince them to form a political party. Instead, he complained, they continued to act as a secret cabal, withdrawn and suspicious of the populace. Consequently, the people had lost faith in their leadership. 'Abd al-Quddus concluded that no nation can survive a prolonged revolution. It was time, he insisted, that Egypt's came to an end. He called upon the CCR to dissolve itself.[28]

The rhetoric of the opposition in March reflected reckless bravado. Oblivious to the greater political forces at play, many proclaimed victory long before the final vote had been tallied. The pace of events in February, when popular pressure compelled the CCR to recall Nagib, fostered within the opposition unrealistic expectations of a hurried return to power. The turn away from the Liberation Rally by those previously willing to collaborate points to the degree of newfound optimism among some of the most cynical old-guard politicians. Elements within the Wafd, although not the traditional leadership, went so far as to invite CCR members to join the party and reportedly offered party leadership to Nasser.[29]

In the euphoria spawned by the March 25 decrees, opponents of the regime issued a series of resolutions calling upon the officers to relinquish power immediately and return to the barracks. For a brief moment it did appear to many that the CCR was finished. Yet few expected the officers to vanish without a fight. Those with some sense of how close the army came to civil war in February predicted Nagib loyalists would fight pro-Nasser units in climactic combat. The battle, Ihsan 'Abd al-Quddus told a U.S. embassy officer, would make Black Saturday, the burning of Cairo in January 1952, look like "child's play."[30]

That many like 'Abd al-Quddus went ahead and openly attacked the CCR speaks to both their courage and naivete. When, in the final days of March, opponents of the regime realized they had miscalculated, it was too late to turn back. Committed to a strict win-or-lose proposition, they gallantly saw the crisis to its end. The final phase of the crisis sowed panic in opposition ranks. Many greeted with applause the CCR's March 26 proclamation that the revolution had ended. "The important decisions taken by the command council yesterday," wrote Mahmud 'Abd al-Mun'im Murad, "made the most favorable impression on the people." A day later that impression had changed. As reports of organized unrest multiplied, Murad warned that the situation was volatile.[31]

By March 28 panic reigned among the liberal opposition. Ahmad Abu al-Fath, already writing from abroad, decried "conspiracies against the people" perpetrated by proregime mobs. The people, he wrote, could not possibly want martial law to continue and fellow citizens to remain imprisoned without rights. In three separate appeals to workers, one specifically addressed to the striking transport union, *Al-Misri* editors blasted the "irresponsibility" of those who thought only of personal gain and mistakenly believed they acted in the name of the CCR. That day, while the police stood watching, a mob attacked the paper's offices. Ihsan 'Abd al-Quddus, in a follow-up column, tempered his critique somewhat, stressing the future role the officers might play within a restored liberal order. Yet by the time the column appeared on March 29 he was in hiding.[32]

While opponents of the regime jumped to take the offensive, others adopted a conciliatory posture. Some with foresight doubted that the officers would ever return to the barracks. They read CCR pronouncements as, if not deliberate feints, statements of political expediency. Fearing the antagonistic tone of the opposition and its emphasis on the regime's "errors," they praised the officers and celebrated their achievements. "Today we do not congratulate the people," the Amins wrote on March 6, the first day of renewed press freedom. "Rather, we congratulate the leaders who returned power to the people." Two weeks later they reported, "We have learned that the revolution will continue" and that any who talked of a return to the old regime misunderstood the decisions taken by the CCR. The same day Mustafa Amin wrote a column that makes an interesting companion to 'Abd al-Quddus' "Secret Society" piece, published two days later. Amin, too, criticized the secretive, conspiratorial nature of the CCR. Yet, while 'Abd al-Quddus, couching his argument in condemnatory terms, called upon the officers to end their revolution, Amin pressed them to step forward, to assume a more proper role as statesmen in leading Egypt toward independence and progress.[33]

Those who supported the regime viewed the crisis as a struggle between progress and retreat. They adovcated the restoration of civil liberties and a return to democratic rule no less vocally than did opponents of the CCR. They did not necessarily accept the tone of CCR rhetoric that portrayed monarchists and feudalists lurking in the background, dedicated to undoing all the revolution had achieved. However, they did fear that the only alternative to the status quo was a return to the discredited liberalism of the old regime, an alternative they rejected. Their own rhetoric, in the case of those who did not simply serve as mouthpieces for the CCR, advanced two main theses. Praise for the reform measures undertaken since July 23 carried a second message, implicitly or otherwise: if the revolution toppled, "it will not fall alone, but will take with it all that the people have won, and what is yet possible to attain."[34] Muhammad Mandur urged the CCR to declare republicanism and land reform inalienable principles of the new political order, opposition to these tenets a crime. With these bases of the revolution secured, the officers should then proceed with their intended plans to seat a constituent assembly and move to open up the political process.[35]

Mandur represented a minority among proregime voices, most of whom rejected the call for parliamentary elections (or political parties) at that time. The ultimate goal, the Amins wrote, remained restoration of parliamentary rule and "natural freedoms." But Egypt needed time to overcome "the self-ish mentality, the feelings of fear and impotence which remain from past ages."[36] If the revolution ends now, wrote columnist Galal al-Din al-Hamamsi, Egypt will revert to past practices, having gained nothing from the revolution. Addressing opponents of the regime, Hamamsi declared:

> I want to start from where past experiments concluded, in order to spare the people from the violent convulsions of our parliamentary life which shook the public's confidence in its ability to rule itself. You consider drowning the people in a torrential sea, so they might tempt and hasten death; then you seek to rescue them, if saving them is at all possible.[37]

"What is the value of parliamentary life now," queried Mustafa al-Shurbagi, a former minister of justice and member of the constitutional committee of fifty, "if it will cause the nation to be divided into factions, encourage zeal-otry, dilute our revolution and break our ranks?"[38] Hafiz Ramadan, the aged Nationalist party president, insisted that an occupied land could support only one party and one opinion. He deemed the selection of a constituent assembly an unnecessary and disruptive step. When the proper time arrived, parties should be formed and a parliament freely elected. He preferred to postpone such steps until the British had evacuated Egypt.[39] Above all, wrote Fikri Abaza, editor of the weekly *Al-Musawwar,* "Egyptians seek stability, in whatever guise, whoever their lord and master, and whatever his solution and means to achieve it." "We are not concerned in the least whether the council of the revolution remains or delegates parliamentary or 'partial parliamentary' rule," he continued, "as long as the bases of justice are observed, and as long as the regime is upright and righteous.[40]

For his loyalty, the CCR appointed Abaza president of the press syndicate after purging the board in mid-April. Like many others, he had spoken out in early March on behalf of greater freedoms and praised the officers for their plans to hasten the end of the transition. Then, when he saw who the real lords were and what were their means, he quickly did an about-face. Those who did not were swept aside. Ahmad Baha' al-Din, a junior editor at *Ruz al-Yusuf,* was no less critical of the CCR than Ihsan 'Abd al-Quddus. Yet he urged his editor not to publish the "Secret Society" column, sensing that its tone was too provocative. Instead, Baha' al-Din advocated a policy of appeasement, hoping to encourage the officers to take steps toward democracy. But as he recalls, "Ihsan was sure they were finished."[41]

Others watched attentively but silently from the sidelines. Conspicuously absent from the fray were leading independent old-guard politicians—'Ali Mahir, Nagib al-Hilali, Hafiz 'Afifi, Husayn Sirri—bitter, disillusioned, and above all, cautious. Mahir was thought to be behind Nagib. If so, he remained sufficiently discreet. He caused a brief stir in mid-March when the foreign press reported he favored ties to the West, but he denied this in an official statement.[42] Most important of the fence sitters were the Muslim Brothers. By withdrawing their forces from the streets and spurning the public debate, the Brothers allowed the officers to neutralize the best-organized force of popular opposition in the country. After his release from prison Hasan Al-Hudaybi sidestepped questions concerning the Brothers' attitude toward political parties or their inclination to contest elections.

Big business also sat on the fence, observing events from a safe distance. Ahmad 'Abbud for one, had worked quickly to ingratiate himself with the new regime. Initially, the regime saluted him as a patriot leading Egypt into the industrial age. Shortly after the coup 'Abbud had offered at least some officers in the higher echelons salaried positions in his financial empire. In March, when it looked as if the CCR would dissolve itself, 'Abbud, reiterated his earlier overtures.[43] The Amins' papers, *Al-Akhbar* and *Akhbar al-Yawm,* more than any of their competitors' consistently espoused the need for economic development and addressed the interests of big business. Their support for the CCR and arguments in favor of continuing the transition period reflected the thinking of capitalists who sought political stability and a favorable economic climate. Their reports that the revolution would continue, no matter what the appearance, along with similar notices in *Al-Jumhuriyah,* carried the weight of official contacts. Those whose economic future was at stake undoubtedly weighed these reports more heavily than the parade of calls for the officers to abdicate printed in the pages of *Al-Misri* or *Ruz al-Yusuf.*

"Crisis of the Intellectuals"

Shortly after the crisis ended Ahmad Baha' al-Din recalled the story of Abu Hurayra, a companion of the Prophet and transmitter of large numbers of hadith. Known for a humorous streak, and accused of engaging in idle talk, Abu Hurayra was portrayed by Baha' al-Din as a wily survivor of the early wars of Islam. As the columnist told it, Abu Hurayra prayed at the camp of 'Ali "because prayer with 'Ali is more upright," ate at the camp of Mu'awiyah where the food was "more plentiful," and disappeared the day of battle because "being far from battle is safer." "How many Abu Hurayra's have we in Egypt?" Baha' al-Din queried.[44]

Whether the one side was more courageous and the other more politically astute, the one foolishly zealous and the other cynically opportunistic has been judged differently by successive generations of Egyptians. Because of the political vicissitudes of the Nasser period, retrospective assessments of political stands taken by opponents, loyalists, and fence sitters tended to be either harsh or apologetic. Many who had stood with the CCR in uneasy détente declared their final break in March and paid the price with imprisonment, exile, or loss of carrer. Some, like Ihsan 'Abd al-Quddus, later made their peace with the regime, albeit uneasily; others, like Ahmad Abu al-Fath chose exile until Nasser's passing. Many, like the Amins, who kept the faith beyond March later lost it, broke ranks with the revolution, and suffered fates similar to their March rivals.

In 1961 Muhammad Hasanayn Haykal wrote of March 1954 as a "crisis of the intellectuals."[45] The "crisis," as Haykal defined the term, referred to the failure of the liberal intelligentsia, rooted in the mind-set of the old regime, to support the revolution. As a consequence, the intelligentsia had grown alienated from the masses (a situation that he asserted had not changed appreciably in intervening years). His polemic echoed the official history propagated by the regime, to which he was a major contributor. In two respects his analysis was sound. Those intellectuals who became engrossed in discussions about an elected constituent assembly and the proper number of parties—discussions that proved irrelevant in the end—had indeed lost touch with political realities. Likewise, those who represented what may be called a progressive opposition failed to impress the public that they advocated not a return to the old politics but a new reformed liberal order.

As Fikri Abaza wrote in the aftermath of March, Egyptians wanted stability above all else. Khalid Muhyi al-Din has echoed this assessment over the years. In late February the country preferred Nagib's leadership to Nasser's. When, a month later, the choice appeared to be between the CCR and unrepentant political parties, enough support shifted to the officers to allow them to overwhelm their opponents.

If March 1954 indeed reflected a "crisis of the intellectuals," that crisis should encompass both those who opposed and those who supported the regime. Both factions had at times nurtured the officers' ambitions to rule. Those who moved into the opposition stand rightly accused of overestimating their own political strength and failing to perceive the machinations of the CCR, even to fathom the officers' determination to prevail in the long, if not the short, term. By turning on the CCR when its back was against the wall, the opposition forced the pace of events, hastening not the return of parliamentary life but the officers' consolidation of power. Those who stood with the regime survived March, but the events of April and following months, when the regime acted to bring all sources of independent opinion to heel, quickly revealed that hopes of cajoling the officers toward restoration of what the Amins called "natural freedoms" glowed far dimmer in the aftermath of the officers' victory.

9

"Fondest Hopes of the West"

In the aftermath of the March crisis the search for an evacuation agreement with Britain headed the CCR agenda. With an accord signed, the officers hoped to proceed with political reforms, to bring the transition period, if no longer the revolution, to an end. The ultimate test of the new regime's political legitimacy remained resolution of the national question. They did not look toward negotiations with optimism. Throughout the first two years of their rule, discussions went nowhere as Egyptian and British negotiators haggled over a variety of issues, fundamental and symbolic. Despite attempts by the United States to broker a settlement, both sides remained deadlocked until the spring of 1954. Finally, that July Egypt and England signed a draft accord, that they then initialed the following October.

Underlying this halting but steady progress toward a Suez accord was a strong feeling in Washington, and a growing sense in London, that the officers shared common aims, strategic and domestic, with the West. From the outset Egypt's new leaders expressed privately a clear intent to promote social reform and to suppress communism at home. Most important, they expressed a strong to commitment to Western strategic interests, even participation, once British troops had left Egyptian soil, in a regional defense pact. Early on, U.S. and British diplomats in Egypt recognized that the officers offered greater promise for attaining a settlement than any previous negotiating partners. Aware of their inexperience and the political constraints under which they operated, the officers looked to the United States and to Britain, the latter always with a greater degree of suspicion, for support.

The extent and nature of the U.S. and British roles in nurturing and furthering the consolidation of military rule has remained a controversial issue in discussions of Nasserism and its origins. The most common questions (and charges) revolve around the question of whether the two powers, especially the Americans, knew of the Free Officers' movement and encouraged its political aspirations prior to July 1952. Egyptian leftists in particular see an American hand behind the officers' takeover and consolidation of power.

U.S. and British diplomatic correspondence indicates that foreign officials in Washington, London, and Cairo knew little, if anything, of the officers' plans. More important, these records do substantiate charges of close links between the U.S. embassy in Cairo and the new regime, and an early resolve by British diplomats in Egypt to follow the U.S. lead. Through political and technical advice, and more than a modicum of moral support, U.S. and British diplomats in Cairo helped instill confidence in the young officers at a crucial phase in their rule, implicitly acquiescing in their extending of their authority and at times explicitly encouraging them to do so.

The record also underscores the extent to which this period marks a significant transition in United States Middle East policy: the reluctant assumption of Britain's sphere of influence in the Arab world. U.S. and Anglo-Egyptian relations cannot be examined outside the context of Anglo-American alliance politics. The transition to United States dominance, however desired by London, produced strains between the allies. Initial American hesitancy bred British frustrations, then resentment when the United States embraced the new military regime and pressed Britain to abdicate its authority in the Canal Zone. To British policymakers the Americans, taken in by the young officers, undermined Western regional interests; to the Americans, the British, stubbornly clinging to empire, were the West's own worst enemy.[1]

The "Jugular of the Empire"

To many in British policy-making circles the Suez Canal remained the "jugular of the Empire." If no longer a lifeline of trade or passage to India, the Suez base remained central to allied strategic thinking, a staging ground for mobilization in the event of war with the Soviet Union. In 1951, 38,000 British soldiers, pilots, and technicians were stationed in the Canal Zone. The 1936 Anglo-Egyptian treaty allowed a force of 10,000, but during the Second World War Egypt had served as a major British base of operations. After the war Egypt had formally demanded renegotiation of the 1936 treaty, then abrogated it unilaterally in October 1951. Two stumbling blocks had doomed all talks to failure: Egypt's claim to sovereignty over the Sudan— British recognition of which Egypt demanded as a precondition to discuss the Canal base—and Egypt's demand for the withdrawal of British forces from Egypt.[2]

Until British policymakers—in the Foreign Office, War Office, and Cairo embassy—decided that the political and military costs of maintaining the base no longer justified retention, few countenanced compromise with Egyptian nationalist aspirations. The British tried without success to impress successive Egyptian governments that Egypt's national security depended upon the presence of foreign troops in the Canal Zone. Many in London and Cairo perceived Egyptian nationalism as merely a ploy by the pashas to distract attention from their own failings.[3]

British policy-making, William Roger Louis has argued, was characterized by an "intellectual paralysis." Old-line imperialists, personified by Winston Churchill and represented most vocally by the Suez Group, a powerful lobby within the Conservative party, who accused Labor of "scuttling" the empire, refused to countenance any compromise with Egyptian nationalist aspirations. To others, the Canal base remained simply a given, the most convenient base of operations in the region and therefore irreplaceable. The British chiefs of staff, who held Egyptian military capabilities in low regard, supported retention of the base with or without Egypt's consent. When a break with Egypt appeared inevitable, the chiefs and their allies in the Foreign Office pursued negotiations as a tactic to play for time.[4]

Under the direction of three foreign secretaries between 1950 and 1951, the Foreign Office lacked a consistent policy. By late 1950 Ernest Bevin concluded that Britain had no choice but to evacuate Egypt. Hoping to preserve Egyptian friendship, attain a reasonable transition period (he felt one year would be sufficient; the chiefs of staff, when finally reconciled to evacuation, argued for two years), and win the right to reoccupy the Canal Zone in case of war, Bevin proposed that Britain offer to train Egyptian replacements. Herbert Morrison, who replaced Bevin in March 1951, favored a position closer to that held by military hard-liners. Proposals drawn up by the cabinet in April read like an ultimatum, and the Egyptians rejected them outright. Anthony Eden, Conservative foreign secretary after October 1951, vacillated under party pressure between accepting British withdrawal and drawing the line in Egypt. His lack of clear leadership dismayed some of his closest colleagues, who urged him to challenge party leaders.[5]

Relations between embassy and home office are rarely devoid of tension. Roger Louis places British Ambassador Stevenson squarely in the camp of those who refused to recognize the sincerity of Egyptian nationalists. By early 1951, however, Stevenson was increasingly at odds with his superiors in London. Sir Ralph, who supervised Anglo-Egyptian talks in Cairo during the summer of 1951, began urging British policymakers to accept the eventuality of evacuation. Thus began a conversion that would evolve throughout the tortuous early months of 1952.[6]

The Nahhas government's abrogation of the 1936 treaty and the "popular struggle" that followed intensified British animosity toward the Egyptian political establishment, the Wafd in particular, and underscored for many the belief that Britain was a scapegoat for the pashas' political corruption. U.S. pressure on Britain to adopt a more flexible position, in particular to yield sovereignty of the Sudan to Farouk, further antagonized London. The British, who protested vociferously, warned the United States against allowing Egypt to exploit differences between friends.[7] British frustration is best reflected in the intensity of reprisals in the Canal Zone that ultimately produced the showdown in Ismailia on January 25, 1952, and a day later, Black Saturday, the burning of foreign establishments by outraged Cairenes.

In the wake of Black Saturday British policy was marked by retrenchment. London welcomed Nahhas's dismissal and pressed the new Mahir government to officially condemn the Wafd government for negligence in preventing the riots. "However the policies of the new [Mahir] government may develop," Anthony Eden cabled his ambassador, "it must be a gain to get rid of the Wafd."[8] Mahir, who assumed the prime ministry with a pledge to reach an Anglo-Egyptian accord within three months, sought to mend relations with London. At the same time he proposed formation of a national front including the Wafd, an unforgivable sin in British eyes, and to that end resisted pressures from the palace and the British to condemn the Nahhas government for its failings on January 26.

The British urged the palace to sabotage Mahir's efforts, then participated in a plot to unseat him. On February 29 the king asked Ralph Stevenson to cancel a meeting with the prime minister in which the two were to discuss resumption of treaty negotiations. Knowing full well the king sought to spur Mahir's resignation, Stevenson informed the prime minister he was "home with a chill." "It is not as though we had very much to offer him," he admitted in a cable to London.[9] "Ali Mahir did much to achieve public confidence and security and did produce an atmosphere conducive to negotiations," Stevenson later wrote Eden, "but since he wasn't willing to tackle Wafd or corruption King is probably right in turning to others more likely to do so."[10]

The British much preferred Hilali's policy of putting negotiations on hold while he directed purges against the Wafd. His resignation in late June threatened "the elimination of the only sound elements in Egyptian political life." Rather than back a new candidate for prime minister, the British, hoping to impress Farouk with some "home truths," urged leading candidates not to form or join a new government. Running out of options, the Foreign Office asked Washington to instruct its ambassador, Caffery, to speak to the king "without mincing words" about the situation in Egypt and to urge him to purge his coterie.[11]

Despite their awareness of discontentment within the officer corps, the Free Officers' coup caught the British by surprise. British intelligence analysts knew junior officers had trained and outfitted irregulars to fight in Palestine in 1947 and in the Canal Zone in the fall of 1951. Nonetheless, they apparently failed to perceive either the extent to which antiestablishment movements had infiltrated the officer corps or the significance of the challenge to royalist officers posed by those who pamphleteered in the barracks and mess. A War Office report of December 1951 described the army as apolitical, loyal to the king. Ambassador Stevenson did express concern about morale in the Egyptian army, but like so many others did not perceive the army as a direct political threat. Stevenson worried that a disaffected army would not, contrary to War Office predictions, take appropriate action should disorder erupt. Rather than military intervention, he projected a power vacuum, in which case the country might fall into the hands of "either an Egyptian Mussadeq or the Communists."[12]

Initial British embassy reports on the coup illuminate the poor state of British intelligence. Relying on information from Murtada al-Maraghi, just appointed interior minister in the new Hilali government, the British chargé d'affaires, Michael Creswell, cabled London that dissident officers were led by Mustafa Kamal Sidqi, the flamboyant colonel, who had mingled in pseudoleftist politics since the late 1940s, never very covertly. The movement was reportedly linked to both communists and the Muslim Brothers. A day later, still citing Maraghi as source, Creswell reported that Muhammad Nagib was a Muslim Brother. On July 25 the embassy revised its assessment of Maraghi's credibility, but Creswell reported, based on a conversation with 'Ali Mahir, that Sadat was the Free Officers leader. [13]

At the same time, fearing that the "insurgents" might embark on a "revolutionary programme," Creswell urged London to put forces in the Canal Zone on twenty-four-hour alert and dispatch the Mediterranean fleet to Alexandria. The Foreign Office agreed to put Canal units on notice—forty-eight hours toward Cairo (Rodeo Bernard) and ninety-six hours toward Alexandria (Rodeo Flail)—but declined to take any steps to rescue Farouk. [14] Ralph Stevenson returned to meet with Nagib, Sadat, and Gamal Salim on July 29. Stevenson assured the officers his government harbored no thoughts of intervening. [15]

"Walk a Tightrope"

Guided by a rather clear understanding of how British policy had gone wrong, American policymakers tried to reconcile an appreciation of postcolonial realities with Western strategic interests. In the wake of the Truman Doctrine the United States accepted financial responsibility for aid to the "Northern Tier" nations: Greece, Turkey, and Iran. In the Tripartite Agreement of May 1950 the U.S., British, and French governments pledged to limit military aid to the Arab states and Israel. Beyond that the United States envisioned Britain's maintaining its sphere of influence in the central Arab lands. However, by the end of the year that appreciation began to change. In January 1951 Secretary of State Dean Acheson proposed the theretofore unthinkable in a letter to his counterpart in the Pentagon. Recognizing that Britain "lacks the capability of successfully defending the area," Acheson proposed U.S. financial aid to the Arab states and Israel, even if that meant shifting funds earmarked for "Northern Tier" states. [16]

Reluctant to become entangled in Egyptian affairs, the Americans struggled to avoid direct participation in Anglo-Egyptian negotiations. While promising to maintain friendly relations with both sides, the United States increasingly pressured Britain to compromise on the treaty question. When talks collapsed in mid-1951, the United States, in a major policy shift, agreed to participate in a projected joint Middle East Command. Allied commanders considered transferring their forces to the Gaza Strip and Cyrenaica, their command post to Cyprus. [17]

When guerrilla warfare erupted in the Canal Zone in October 1951, the United States endeavored to "walk a tightrope" between the antagonists. Ambassador Caffery counseled moderation to all sides. While the Americans shared Britain's disdain for the Wafd, American policymakers saw no viable alternative. "Although eventually we may have to get rid of Wafd Government it would be folly to ask King to do it now," Caffery cabled in late October 1951. If the Wafd fell from power, Farouk "could not find at this juncture a government to take its place."[18] Caffery urged the Wafd to preserve order, not to break relations with Britain, and to reconsider again conditions for joining a defensive alliance.[19] As the crisis deepened, American policymakers considered encouraging the Wafd faction led by Fu'ad Sirag al-Din, regarded as friendly to Western interests, to oust the "rabble-rousers," the primary culprit being the foreign minister, Salah al-Din.[20]

Farouk urged the Americans to mediate, a role that Washington rejected. Even so, the United States floated with increasing regularity the notion of granting Sudanese sovereignty to the Egyptian monarchy. American officials in general perceived British retaliatory tactics in the Canal Zone as counterproductive, and Caffery did intervene on several occasions to restrain what he termed British "trigger happiness."[21] In the end the United States failed in this regard, and the frustration was evident. After the battle in Ismailia Dean Acheson lectured the British ambassador in Washington, according to an aide's notes, "that it did not impress him that the operation of Ismailia had been carried out with 'unusual skill.' He said the 'splutter of musketry' apparently does not stop things as we had been told time to time that it would."[22]

Still reluctant to exert direct pressure on either Britain or Egypt, American policymakers after Black Saturday observed the final crises of the old regime with a growing sense of gloom. No Egyptian government could survive, Ambassador Caffery repeated, without progress toward British evacuation. "This is not one the British can win by stalling," he wrote in February 1952. "Reoccupation, revolt, revolution may sound like overemphasis but they are all visible on the cards in Egypt today."[23]

Implicit now in many of Caffery's remarks was the understanding that the United States could, if it wished, assume the prerogative once exercised by Britain of making and unmaking Egyptian governments at will. Caffery and his superiors in the State Department resisted the urge, as well as offers from various palace factions that sought U.S. intervention against Prime Ministers Mahir and Hilali.

However, charges of covert activity persist. Such charges were raised most forthrightly by former Central Intelligence Agency operative Miles Copeland in his exposé, *The Game of Nations,* published in 1969, and widely cited ever since. Copeland asserts that the CIA dispatched Kermit Roosevelt to Egypt in February 1952 to foment a "revolution from above," specifically to bring about the downfall of 'Ali Mahir and his replacement by Nagib al-Hilali. He writes that Roosevelt conspired with two government ministers, Maraghi and 'Abd al-Mut'al, both of whom did quit the government, sparking a cabinet crisis, and both of whom did go on to serve under Hilali.[24]

No records, however, hint at any desire to finish with Mahir; rather, they speak to frustration at Britain's unwillingness to treat with him. Caffery, who thought Hilali's government "excellent," nonetheless bemoaned the new prime minister's lack of a political base, and the damage done his reputation by attaining office as a result of obvious palace intrigue.[25]

Moreover, if the United States sought Hilali's appointment to the extent of toppling Mahir, the Americans quickly retreated to a more familiar position of passivity. When palace minions maneuvered to dump Hilali, the U.S. ambassador, despite British requests, did not signal his government's disapproval. When Hilali quit, Caffery merely praised him for leaving with his honor intact. Assistant Secretary of State Henry Byroade reported Hilali's fall as unexpected.[26] In early July 1952, when the British asked Caffery to press the king to purge his coterie, the State Department advised its ambassador not to become invovled in Egypt's "domestic crisis."[27] The Americans continued to pressure London to take the first step toward breaking the diplomatic stalemate. Only in late July, a day before the Free Officers' coup, did Washington consider embarking on a major policy initiative. Noting that "the time has come when we ought to make greater use of our position in Egypt," Byroade suggested that if the United States recognized Farouk's sovereignty over the Sudan, the Egyptians might be willing to drop their insistence on British recognition as a precondition for negotiations on the Canal base.[28]

Did the Americans know a coup d'état was imminent in July 1952? Byroade's suggestion one day before the coup indicates that he and State Department colleagues did not. Like the British, the palace, and nearly anyone who followed political developments closely, the Americans certainly knew that trouble brewed in the ranks. Yet like the other threats, the immediate threat appears to have been judged minimal, even inconsequential. In August 1951, when Caffery assessed factors of political stability in Egypt, he included the army. Seven months later, after Black Saturday, he questioned whether the army would carry out action against the Wafd if so ordered.[29] Otherwise there is little to indicate the U.S. embassy paid the army much notice until late July, when Prime Minister Sirri resigned over palace efforts to disband the Officers Club board, captured by dissidents in January. Caffery and his colleagues looked to a dwindling list of palace politicians to maintain order; the ambassador's dire predictions of "fireworks" make no mention of the army.

Here again Miles Copeland has provided "proof" to those who decried an American conspiracy. Copeland contends that Kermit Roosevelt met with the Free Officers three times in March 1952. The fact of the meetings has been widely accepted, as has Copeland's statement that Roosevelt met with a "most trusted lieutenant" of Nasser's but not Nasser himself. Hamrush, who cites Copeland almost verbatim, concludes only, "There is no indication that Gamal Abdel Nasser made personal contact with Kermit Roosevelt prior to the coup." Members of the Free Officers executive committee deny any contacts between their movement and U.S. officials prior to July 23. Of course, it is highly likely that Nasser answered Roosevelt's overtures without the knowledge of the others.[30]

Copeland's more controversial assertion, that the CIA had targeted the

Free Officers as the answer to Egypt's political instability, and come to an "explicit understanding" with the officers that they would seize power and rule Egypt as strongmen is far more difficult to substantiate. That Roosevelt discussed the likelihood of revolution in Egypt with the officers and probed their own political inclinations would seem natural. Hamrush accepts that as a gesture of goodwill Nasser agreed to drop all references to U.S. imperialism from Free Officers' leaflets. Beyond this, little appears to have been gained aside from a degree of familiarity with basic aims of the movement. Roosevelt's report, as revealed by Copeland, however prescient in retrospect, did not appear to influence leading policymakers. Despite his assertion that a "popular revolution . . . was not in the cards" (Copeland's wording), Caffery continued to stress the threat in his diplomatic correspondence. Although Roosevelt argued that Farouk had to go and the army could not be kept from seizing power, some in the State Department still talked of extending the king's sovereign authority, and Caffery and others in Cairo looked to a dwindling list of respectable palace politicians to stave off disorder.

The record here does not tell the complete story, for other Americans, embassy officials and military officers, had contacts with Egyptian officers, some of whom were Free Officers. These contacts undoubtedly produced favorable impressions on both sides and laid the groundwork for cooperation after the coup. But obvious questions remain about whether these Americans knew they were in contact with members of a secret organization or merely discontented individuals, and if the former, how highly placed they might be.[31]

The Americans were the first to learn of the revolt. In the early morning hours of July 23 the Free Officers executive committee delegated two air force officers, 'Ali Sabri and 'Abd al-Mun'im al-Naggar, neither of whom knew of plans for the coup until the evening of July 21, to inform the U.S. embassy that the Free Officers had seized general headquarters. Their contact was the assistant air force attaché, Colonel David Evans, whom both knew from official business. Evans, the first foreigner to be officially informed of the coup, became the primary conduit of information from the junta to the U.S. embassy in the weeks following the takeover.[32]

Nevertheless, the coup seems to have caught the United States not only unaware and unprepared but largely ignorant of the perpetrators and their aims. "The self-styled 'Egyptian armed forces underground' headed by Naguib is actually an amorphous group of middle grade army officers bound together by common disgust with their superiors," Caffery reported on July 24. Nagib did not appear "particularly strong or intelligent."[33] U.S. diplomats were slow to learn the identities of those who had seized power. In late August when the embassy reported for the first time that a nine-man junta oversaw affairs, Sadat's was the only name cited. A month later, Colonel Evans reported all but three (however one was listed only as Major Khalid).[34] Although U.S. officials quickly judged Nagib a front man for the younger officers, Nasser did not emerge as the recognized leader until the fall, when Caffery first described him as the original organizer of the coup, the group's strongest member, "and probably the most moderate in his views."[35]

"Down with the Pashas"

Long before junta members became recognized as individual personalities, British and U.S. officials in Egypt rapidly discerned that the officers represented the only political force with which the British could negotiate an evacuation that would preserve Western strategic interests in the region. The British greeted the officers' takeover with cautious optimism; the Americans, with unveiled enthusiasm. Each of the allies, in its own way, provided moral support that bolstered the military junta during its formative period of rule.

From the outset the junta made no secret of its political inclinations. When Caffery met with the officers on July 25, they assured him they had no political ambitions, would leave governing to Prime Minister Mahir, would suppress communism, and would consider bringing Egypt into the Middle East Command.[36] During their first six weeks of rule, preoccupied with formulating a policy toward the poltiical parties, land reform, and their inability to work with 'Ali Mahir, the officers refrained from any diplomatic initiatives. In September, shortly after Muhammad Nagib assumed leadership of government, the junta informed the U.S. embassy it was ready to discuss foreign affairs. The officers proved no less stubborn on some issues than previous Egyptian regimes, insisting on British evacuation as a precondition for discussing any future defense arrangements, and expecting Britain to demonstrate good faith by making initial concessions.

Positive British support for the officers developed slowly, in part due to the adversarial nature of the Anglo-Egyptian relationship but also to divisions between the Foreign Office and the Cairo embassy. While his American counterpart quickly gained the officers' confidence, the British ambassador found his contacts limited to 'Ali Mahir.[37] Seeking to court favor with the British, Mahir complained that close ties between the Americans and the officers encouraged "the latter to think that they had United States support for all their ideas and their activities."[38] Rather than embrace Mahir, the British ambassador resolved to foster stronger ties to the junta. Ralph Stevenson rejected the persistent view in London that U.S. support for the regime encouraged the officers to take a bolder anti-British stand. The Americans "have much better opportunities of judging these men than I have," he cabled the Foreign Office. "They [the officers] are unsure and growing confidence will sober them."[39] "Stevenson seems completely won over to our line of thinking," Caffery cabled home a week later.[40]

In mid-September Stevenson cabled his and Caffery's "Joint Appreciation of the Egyptian Situation" to London. The report described the officers as sincere nationalists without personal ambitions. Despite the unfortunate presence of several "extreme nationalists" (Fathi Radwan and Nur al-Din Tarraf in particular), the Nagib government showed no signs of "extremism." While noting the officers' inexperience, the pressures they faced to maintain their popularity, and their lack of a clear foreign policy, the report concluded that the junta "may be inclined to face both the Canal Zone question and that of the Sudan in a more practical manner." The two ambassadors proposed "timely Western aid" to bolster the officers' standing. Thereafter, Stevenson consistently pressed London to be more forthcoming with military assistance.[41]

The responses of Foreign Office analysts to the joint assessment highlight the difference in thinking between Whitehall and the British embassy. The analysts describe the report as superficial, concerned more with shoring Nagib's power than securing an acceptable defense arrangement. Britain's, not Egypt's, national interests should dominate British policy, the policymakers repeated. Rather than shower the military regime with arms and money, the British government should present the junta with specific proposals regarding evacuation. The officers' response would dictate the future course of British policy. In the meantime, all judgment (not to mention aid) should be suspended.[42]

While British policymakers counseled caution, the Americans moved quickly to establish relations with the junta. The officers' political aims impressed the U.S. ambassador, who described Egypt's new rulers in glowing terms. The junta, he declared,

> aims at a peaceful social revolution designed to undercut and forestall all the chaos and perhaps outright communist takeover toward which the country seemed hypnotically drifting. If the movement succeeds in this aim the fondest hopes of the West for stability in Egypt and the Middle East will have been given a new possibility of realization.[43]

Stability in Caffery's eyes entailed reform and the suppression of anti-establishment movements. Both the U.S. and British governments greeted plans for land reform with favor—"Down with the Pashas, Up with the Fellahin," Churchill scrawled on a note to Anthony Eden—and dispatched advisors to work with the Egyptians. Amid reports of taxes withheld by those expecting to become landowners, Ambassadors Stevenson and Caffery warned the officers against letting peasant expectations run too high.[44] Both protested the officers' release of political prisoners in late July, and urged the junta to strike out against communists. Caffery claimed credit for the roundup of cadres in early August. When the junta excluded communists from a general amnesty for politicals decreed in October, the U.S. ambassador reported that the officers "have not released 14 hardcore Commies because I asked them not to do so."[45]

In general, U.S. and British diplomats applied the labels "extremist," "hardcore," and "commie" with little discrimination. Such categorizing narrowed the officers' options when they sought out civilian collaborators, and indirectly helped pave the way for military rule. This raises serious questions about the extent to which British, and especially U.S., policymakers were willing to tolerate a friendly, reformist, anticommunist dictatorship.

Ultimately, extended military rule was judged the best possible option for Egypt. Caffery's early postcoup cables spoke to a continuation of the status quo, with the military as ruling partner. The ambassador initially judged the partnership between 'Ali Mahir and the junta sound. Yet by mid-August, based in part on conversations with the officers, he predicted that "the military may find the direct assumption of power inescapable."[46] By the month's end, when Mahir's opposition to land reform pushed the officers to consider his dismissal, Caffery cabled, "Although my relations with Military are excellent and their leaders show many fine qualities I do not want them to 'run the show.' "[47] Caffery tried without success to mediate. The officers promised him twenty-four hours' notice of Mahir's dismissal, a promise that they kept. When it finally became apparent that Mahir could not be saved, Caffery advised the junta to "exercise the greatest care in selecting his successor and bear world opinion in mind."[48]

Then, informed that the junta planned to appoint State Council President 'Abd al-Razzaq al-Sanhuri prime minister, Caffery communicated his "personal objection." Sanhuri had signed the international peace movement's Stockholm decree in 1951—one of twelve thousand Egyptians to do so—thus earning American excoriation. Caffery also vetoed the appointment to the cabinet of Rashad al-Barawi, the architect of land reform, whom Caffery dismissed as a "commie."[49] Acceding to Caffery's advice, the junta rejected the jurist and economist, naming Muhammad Nagib prime minister. The Americans knew the junta considered naming a military man prime minister. Caffery, who saw the appointment injecting stability into the system, cabled: "The pattern of military supremacy is apt to exist at least until election and probably longer."[50]

Convinced of the officers' pro-Western orientation and presuming they would retain power for the immediate future, Caffery urged his government to honor Egyptian requests for economic aid at a "controlled pace," and to expect the officers to request military aid.[51] On September 18 the junta offered to trade secret commitments for military and economic assistance. The regime sought clarification on what sort of commitments the United States would want, and whether or not Nagib would be an acceptable signatory. Caffery cabled Washington:

> Eight weeks after original military coup it is more clear that new regime in Egypt is going to be around for a while. It is faced with tremendous problems and strong opposition groups but it has determined program and guns on its side and will not be easily upset or diverted from its objectives. It is equally obvious that it is only a question of time—and not much time at that—before West will be faced with necessity choosing to support, ignore, or oppose regime. Arguments in favor of support multiply as objectives of regime become clearer.[52]

Washington responded with guarded optimism. Secret commitments, even made orally, were acceptable with the expectation that more formal, open arrangements would follow.[53]

The U.S. ambassador consistently counseled Washington that the United States should not force the issue of Egyptian participation in a regional defense pact. He denounced British presumptions that Egypt could be threatened or bludgeoned as "medieval thinking."[54] In October 1952 Caffery cabled, "We have before us a basic job in diplomatic education, if proposals submitted in all seriousness by Western governments are to be understood and properly evaluated by these military officers turned apprentice statesmen who have not thought through problems for which they demand a solution."[55]

The special Egyptian-U.S. relationship evolved steadily in the months that followed. In the autumn of 1952 Kermit Roosevelt arrived in Egypt; shortly afterward the CIA provided instructors to train Egyptian intelligence officers. The junta kept the U.S. embassy abreast of developments, informing Caffery beforehand of the abrogation of the Constitution, the dismissal of Yusuf Siddiq, and formation of the Liberation Rally. "We believe it is absolutely essential to our interests that General Naguib remain in power and be encouraged to cooperate with the West," Secretary of State John Foster Dulles wrote in February 1953; he told Nagib as much personally in May.[56]

"A Complete Lack of Trust"

Distrustful of the British, the officers resisted U.S. pressure to reopen base negotiations during the autumn of 1952.[57] Instead, they turned to the issue of Sudanese sovereignty, the second major area of Anglo-Egyptian contention. Sidestepping the British, the Egyptian government in October signed an accord with the Sudanese People's party outlining procedures for a plebiscite in which the Sudanese would choose either independence or association with Egypt. In January 1953 all leading Sudanese parties gave their assent. The officers thus presented Britain with a fait accompli. Having stood resolutely in favor of Sudanese self-determination, London could not protest the arrangement. On February 12 Egypt and Britain signed a similar accord.[58] With the Sudan accord signed by all interested parties, the CCR agreed warily to move on to the Canal issue. In late March the officers withdrew their demand that the British recognize the principle of evacuation as a precondition for talks, and toned down their anti-British rhetoric.[59]

On the eve of negotiations in late April, the CCR offered a formula that to the Americans "appear[ed] to grant the substance of what the Western powers need, i.e. preservation of the Suez base and a program for starting with Middle East defense planning which once under way might very well develop quietly into the sort of formal structure envisaged by American and British planners." The officers agreed to maintain the base in full working order as well as to grant the British a reasonable amount of time to evacuate. They agreed that technical advisors should remain behind to train the Egyptians who would replace them, and were prepared to grant Britain the right of reentry in the case of external aggression against Egypt or any other Arab

League state. Moreover, they expressed a desire to discuss means to coordinate military plans with an eye toward joining a regional collective security pact.[60]

Nonetheless, the officers approached the negotiations in April "with little enthusiasm or hope of success." They expected the British to drag their feet. The officers constantly reminded the Americans of the constraints under which they acted. The future of their revolution, they asserted, hinged on their success at the bargaining table. They would settle for nothing less than "full independence," nor would they accept any formula in which the British "evacuated by the front door and returned through the window." If they allowed this, the officers assured Caffery, "they themselves would be attacked as traitors and the agreement denounced by the Egyptian people."[61]

Negotiations commenced on April 27, then broke down within ten days. Having compromised on key issues, the officers stood adamant on two points: they refused to include Turkey as a nation whose security interests might prompt British reoccupation, and insisted that British technicians not wear military dress. Trying to broker the talks, the Americans grew increasingly frustrated. Foster Dulles, who visited Egypt shortly after talks broke down, decried "a complete lack of trust and confidence among the parties" that forestalled any progress. Echoing his ambassador, Dulles expressed greatest exasperation with the British.[62]

Immediately upon the breakdown of negotiations, the CCR let loose a propaganda barrage against the British and initiated a resurgence of the "armed struggle" in the Canal Zone. Special Egyptian units organized irregulars to carry out commando operations against British bases and base personnel. Zakariya Muhyi al-Din, director of military intelligence, oversaw the activities from Cairo. In conjunction with his field commanders, he controlled the tempo of attacks, careful never to allow the scale of violence to reach a level that would provoke major British retaliation.[63] In July incidents of sabotage, looting, sniping, and harassment of British soldiers and Egyptians employed by the base became a daily routine. When the disappearance of a British corporal nearly sparked an escalation of hostilities comparable to late 1951, cooler heads on both sides prevailed, thanks in part to timely U.S. intervention.[64]

British policymakers who recognized that the CCR kept the commandos on a short leash determined to wait out the phase. In June, when Ambassador Stevenson took medical leave, Anthony Eden sent Sir Robin Hankey, an old Foreign Office hand with only minimal experience in the Middle East, as chargé d'affaires. Hankey, who walked into a rapidly deteriorating situation, carried no new proposals. He was instructed simply to toe the line and concede nothing.[65]

Two issues, Turkey and civilian dress for British technicians, continued to block any progress. In September the Americans convinced the CCR to modify its position on three key issues: terms of Suez Canal transit, duration of the transition period for evacuation, and conditions for British reoccupation of the base. When the British failed to follow suit, U.S. policymakers shared the officers' offense.[66] The officers felt they had conceded far too much already. "If we keep retreating," Nasser told Caffery with a flourish, "we will be hung in the streets one day, while you depart for other shores."[67]

Nonetheless, having exercised its military option, the CCR took care to keep diplomatic channels open. Nasser paid Britain's ranking military negotiator, General Brian Robertson, a farewell call prior to his leaving for England in mid-November. Robertson described Nasser to Caffery as a tough negotiator, whom he respected. The general assessed that the two sides had 85 percent of an agreement in hand but noted that the few outstanding issues would be difficult to conclude. "Some people in London," Robertson complained, failed to realize the import of a settlement to both Britain and Egypt.[68]

One month later, Nasser, Salah Salim, and Zakariya Muhyi al-Din attended a farewell party for Hankey. In an encounter described as affable, the officers reiterated their willingness to discuss a regional defense arrangement promptly upon conclusion of an evacuation accord, and promised to lessen tensions in the Canal Zone. They kept their promise. Although minor incidents of sabotage persisted until formal negotiations resumed the next spring, they occurred with less regularity. Armed conflict never again threatened to retard progress toward an eventual settlement.[69]

The process lurched forward. Three days after Ambassador Stevenson returned to Egypt in mid-December, he met informally with Nasser and Salah Salim. After a second meeting with Nasser on December 28, Stevenson described his own mood as "even gloomier than before."[70] Nasser too approached the new round with trepidation. He told the Americans that talks with the British would continue only because the regime needed time to prepare for the consequences of their breakdown.[71]

From the perspective of Washington the time to finalize an agreement looked ripe. Following the crackdown on the Muslim Brothers "the regime looked "at peak strength . . . fully able to withstand any attacks by dissident groups endeavoring present false picture of agreement to people." Any delay would only weaken the officers' position.[72] After a rise in the incidence of attacks on British troops in late January, Caffery again interceded, winning from Nasser tentative compromise on Turkey.[73]

The trade-off that would break the deadlock—Egypt's acceptance of Turkey's inclusion among nations covered by a security agreement for Britain's willingness to dress technical advisors in civilian clothes—needed await only the outcome of the March crisis. The officers' handling of the crisis and their consolidation of power both gave them the confidence to make further concessions and forced London to recognize their legitimacy as negotiating partners. The steady decrease in the number of incidents of sabotage in the Canal Zone underscored pronouncements, official and unofficial, to British and U.S. diplomats of the officers' desire to reopen talks at the earliest possible date. On March 11, the day after Nasser and his CCR associates were so warmly received at the Officers Club, Nasser informed the Americans he would trade Turkey for "civilian" technical advisors.[74]

The U.S. ambassador's support for the officers reflected a shrewd understanding of Nasser's thinking, as well as conviction that he and his colleagues best safeguarded Egypt's—and the West's—future. That common future rested increasingly in Nasser's hands. Recognizing Nasser's proclivity toward compromise, Caffery had welcomed his personal consolidation of authority. Based on this assessment the Americans backed the CCR when the officers broke with Nagib.[75] When the officers considered handing authority to a constituent assembly, Caffery explained that

> elections at present time would be disastrous and may well result in putting Egypt in hands of unholy alliance of right and left wing extremists. . . . United States sympathy for idea of representative government must therefore be made known privately, in a way which will support plans to restore country to civilian government, but not in a manner which will provide ammunition for opposition elements.[76]

When the crisis was over Caffery concluded: "While I do not approve all methods Nasser used during recent weekend events"—he alluded to the legions of proregime mobs assembled to intimidate the opposition—"I point out that the results from our point of view can be called satisfactory." The bottom line was simple: "Nasser is the only man in Egypt with strength enough and guts enough to put over an agreement with the British."[77]

The British came to view the CCR victory and Nasser's displacement of Nagib with similar favor. In mid-April Ralph Stevenson urged London to open a new round of talks, in large part to help the CCR regain public confidence. Initially hesitant, the Foreign Office began to come around. By mid-May the U.S. ambassador in London reported that Nasser's apparent success in consolidating his position and maintaining order "gratified" British policymakers. Nasser's ability to stabilize the internal situation, he said, "would be of great political importance in putting over agreement here."[78]

With all parties expressing serious interest and no immediate political obstacles in sight, progress toward an agreement gained momentum. In early June, Nasser told Kermit Roosevelt he wanted an agreement by July 23; to a foreign correspondent, he indicated he would welcome a British lead. Within a week he, 'Amr, and Zakariya Muhyi al-Din dined with the British ambassador and several leading embassy officers at the home of Trefor Evans.[79] In late June Caffery cabled Washington: "I still have Egyptians lined up for agreement with British, but they are becoming more and more restive."[80] Their patience held. On July 24 Anthony Head, British secretary of state for war, flew to Cairo. Three days later Egyptian and British representatives initialed Heads of Agreement. This outline provided for British evacuation within twenty months of the accord's ratification, much better terms than the British had expected. Egypt granted the British the right of reentry if Turkey or any Arab League state was attacked within a seven-year period and the right to maintain on-base technical advisors under Egyptian command. Egypt announced the immediate lifting of all curbs on the movement of British troops within the Canal Zone.[81]

In the following three months British and Egyptian delegations hammered out the final draft. Stevenson, fearing that his own government might buckle to Tory pressure, suggested that the government send a representative to Cairo, a tactic he felt would signal to Egypt and, no less, the British public its support for the accord. Anthony Nutting, under-secretary of state for foreign affairs, who arrived in late September, established an immediate rapport with Nasser. The two signed the accord on behalf of their respective governments on October 19, 1954.[82]

"A New Blank Page"

Reflecting on the signature of the Anglo-Egyptian agreement, Jefferson Caffery noted the possibilities for the two nations to set their relations on a fresh course. "The British have before them a new blank page on which to draw up their future policy toward Egypt. If they are understanding and adroit they can do a great deal in Egypt to advance the interests of the West." Echoing a favorite theme, he continued, "The greatest mistake the British (or we) could make, would be to force the Egyptian pace towards participation in area security arrangements including the Western powers. I am convinced this will come to pass, but the Egyptians and only the Egyptians, must decide when the time is ripe." Himself preparing to retire and leave Egypt, Caffery expressed hope that he had laid the foundation for closer U.S.-Egyptian collaboration. The signing of the evacuation accord, he concluded, "has stripped off the last wraps under which we have been working. It is now up to us to show what we can do."[83]

Caffery's hopes heralded a brief honeymoon between Nasser and the American public. Nasser, Americans read, was "selfless and icily intelligent," a "dictator by default of a revolution without a doctrine," a man of "uncompromising realism." Nagib, while he remained figurehead president, was chastised as a man without vision who had lent his name to those who "ranted of jihad" against the British.[84] When the CCR dumped him in November, the *New York Times* labeled him "something of a Frankenstein monster" to the young officers, and Kennett Love penned a laudatory account of Colonel Nasser.[85] While the People's Tribunal heard of the Muslim Brothers' conspiracies to overthrow the regime, Caffery proclaimed publicly that the officers had "done more for Egypt in two years than all their predecessors put together before them."[86]

Behind the ambassador's tone of nostalgic optimism lay a dire warning, one that those who had been reading his communications for the past two years should have sensed. Caffery's cables always contained one constant: to preserve and bolster its friendship with the military regime, the United States must be prepared to answer Egyptian requests for economic and military aid.

The background to this aspect of Egyptian-U.S. relations is a familiar story. In December 1952 'Ali Sabri traveled to the United States to press

Egypt's arms requests. Caffery urged Washington not to let Sabri return empty-handed, but to no avail. When Dulles visited Cairo in May 1953 he brought Nagib only a pair of silver-plated pistols, enough to raise an outcry in London but little applause in Egypt. In a letter to Nagib that July President Eisenhower promised military assistance upon conclusion of an evacuation accord. In September Caffery warned that the Egyptians were losing faith in the Americans. A great degree of residual goodwill and respect were "the chief remaining assets we have for the attainment of United States policy objectives in Egypt," Caffery wrote. "If they are to have any currency at all we shall have to 'pay off' on them soon, to the extent of some concrete military and economic assistance."[87]

Now, with the British set to exit and the CCR in place, the issue of military and economic aid came to the fore. With a draft accord signed, Washington moved to authorize foreign aid for Egypt under the Mutual Security Act. Caffery, urging his government to be as generous as possible, warned Washington that "although we have in no way encouraged Egyptians to expect huge aid, either economic or military, they very definitely do expect considerable aid."[88]

The gap between Egyptian expectations and U.S. capabilities soon became apparent. In late August Egypt informed the United States that it would not seek military aid, and sought instead $100 million in economic aid. That, the Egyptian foreign minister explained, would allow Egypt to purchase arms on the free market.[89] The State Department informed Caffery it would consider $40 million, half of which would be authorized pending further demonstration of need. This is where matters stood when Caffery wrote his reflections on the Anglo-Egyptian accord. Shortly thereafter Washington offered a $40 million economic aid package.

Anticipating the souring of the relationship, most accounts of U.S.-Egyptian ties focus on areas of tension and mistrust. Egypt's unfulfilled expectations for economic and military aid proved to be a fundamental barrier to the kind of friendship that Caffery, for one, envisioned. Related issues follow: the arms race in the region, the onset of Egyptian-Israeli military confrontation, Egypt's growing proclivity toward neutralism, and the commencement of discussions with the Soviet Union of economic and military aid, a development U.S. officials watched with increasing anxiety.[90] Usually overlooked is the extent to which the U.S.-Egyptian relationship flourished so long as other issues, more pressing and of mutual benefit, dominated political agendas in Cairo and Washington. And in London, for also overshadowed as the "new blank page" became inscribed with the Suez crisis, was the moment of goodwill felt by at least some Egyptians and some British who had bargained hard toward a compromise that satisfied realists in both countries.

This is not to say, as did regime critics, that the Free Officers were in any way subservient to foreign interests, or molded by outside forces, American in particular. There is no conclusive or convincing evidence, and much to cast doubt, on assertions advanced by Miles Copeland and others that the United States shaped the Free Officers' movement or came to any prior agreement with the officers that they would seize and exercise power. Prior to July 23 the United States watched the collapse of Egypt's old order from the sidelines, more observer than participant, much to the displeasure of many in Cairo and London. Faced with a fait accompli of a coup d'état, the United States acted swiftly to forge ties with a junta that appeared to offer more than palace or pashas.

What the United States did do, and the British as well, the latter to the extent possible given the underlying tensions between Britain and Egypt, was lend the officers technical expertise and more than a modicum of moral support in a period when they faced the future with loosely defined goals and uncertain ambitions. This bolstered their confidence and influenced their willingness to assert greater control over the political process, and at the same time move toward the middle ground on Suez base talks. U.S. and British diplomats pressed the officers to pursue domestic and foreign policies amicable to Western interests, specifically to enact social reform, suppress communist movements, and to commit to a regional defense pact.

Compared to other policy aims, for both Free Officers and U.S. and British friends, the speedy restoration of democratic institutions became less urgent, and ultimately an obstacle to be avoided. The revolution's consolidation, couched in democratic rhetoric but underlined by growing state authority still fostered fond hopes. A retiring Jefferson Caffery proclaimed in January 1955 that Egypt's future looked "brighter than ever." "It's an out and out dictatorship," he told a New York audience in March, "but a constructive, efficacious, well-meaning one."[91]

10

"Each of You Shall Be Gamal"

In the third year of their rule the Free Officers' revolution finally began to take form. Prior to March 1954 the officers defined their revolution primarily in terms of internal political struggles. Out of those struggles was born the will to rule Egypt, reinforced by the belief that only the CCR could prevent the country from reverting to the "party politics" of the old regime. Following the March crisis the officers conclusively abandoned plans to restore democratic life in the near future. An indefatigable opposition, communist and Muslim Brother led, conditioned their consolidation of power.

The regime did not hesitate to use the police to preserve order and, on occasion, create disorder. The attempt on Nasser's life in October by a Muslim Brother provoked the CCR to suppress ruthlessly its most serious adversaries. Circumstances of the attempt remain controversial. Muslim Brother assertions that the attack was staged by the CCR warrant little attention. Rather, a look into the dynamics of ongoing conflict within the Brotherhood reveals that antiregime hard-liners seized the initiative from those endeavoring once again to patch up relations between the Brothers and the CCR. The effort backfired; with the suppression of the Brotherhood in late 1954, the regime cleared the path for long-term dictatorial rule.

The attempt on Nasser's life, known in Egyptian historiography as the "Manshiya incident" after the site in Alexandria, also marks the beginning of Nasser's romance with his people, and, conversely, the acceleration of his own evolution as strongman within the CCR. In the period after March, while the CCR tightened its grip on the instruments of state rule, Nasser began to distance himself from his original comrades. His moves did not pass unnoticed, or uncriticized, by his colleagues, but common struggles— Anglo-Egyptian negotiations and opposition propaganda—held the CCR together. When the officers struck out brutally at the opposition after the assassination attempt, they also paved the way for their own diminution in the ruling procedure. Nasser emerged unscathed from the assault on his life, and determined to convert newfound popularity into personal political power.

"The Destructive Opposition"

Until the Muslim Brotherhood ended its truce with the regime in July, communists constituted the most vocal opposition to CCR rule. After March all communist movements focused their critique on the regime's efforts to gain financial and military aid from the West. In leaflets and clandestine newspapers they assailed Egypt's "shift of loyalty to the American camp and new subjugation to American imperialism." As Britain prepared to take down the Union Jack, Jefferson Caffery and Uncle Sam replaced Churchill and John Bull in antiregime pamphlet art, and the dollar sign became the new symbol of imperial domination. A DMNL leaflet printed in August denounced the Heads of Agreement as a "treaty of ignominy and shame, of treachery, imperialism, and war." The DMNL implored the peasantry to withhold taxes, the workers to take to the streets in strikes and demonstrations, and all citizens to "take up arms and join the struggle."[1]

The call for a unified opposition proved more compelling in the wake of the March crisis. Countering CCR efforts to portray the entire liberal establishment as a force of reaction, the DMNL and Workers Vanguard continued to advocate a national unity government under Wafdist leadership.[2] More noteworthy was the turnabout made by the ECP, until then committed to a policy of isolation from all other forces, communist or otherwise. Because of its rigid discipline and policy of noncollaboration, the ECP had not seen its ranks depleted by arrests, as had the DMNL. As a consequence, in 1954 it was the largest communist movement in the country. According to party secretary Fu'ad Mursi, the movement had grown from about fifteen hundred members in 1952 to three thousand by 1954. During the last days of March ECP leaders decided to enter the fray against the CCR. As a result, Mursi asserts, the movement lost its best cadres in subsequent police roundups. He remained at large and set about recruiting anew from his base in Alexandria. Due in part to the attrition of arrests, in part to the changed circumstances after March, in early April the party revised its thinking, promoting now a national unity government comprising Wafdists, Socialists, communists, and Muslim Brothers.[3]

Cooperation between communists and Muslim Brothers, although limited and not officially sanctioned by Brotherhood leaders, indicates the degree to which perceptions had changed by the end of the March crisis. Even after they had agreed to sit out the battle for political authority, Brotherhood leaders apparently turned a blind eye to a degree of unofficial cooperation between Brotherhood and leftist students, not enough to change the outcome but enough to inspire some talk of unified antiregime activism. In a manifesto dated July 8, the ECP celebrated the March alliance; this from the movement that had rejected overtures from fellow communists a year before:

> In fact the patriotic Ikhwanis [Brothers] shouldered with their Communist colleagues the national battles that took place last March. The Ikhwanis in the three universities stood shoulder to shoulder with the Communists against

'Abd al-Nasir and his gang. Indeed they fought the battle together in a United Front.[4]

Although Brotherhood leaders rejected communist overtures, even after they rejoined the opposition in the summer, a degree of low-level contact continued to take place on an unofficial basis. Communists and Brothers collaborated in distributing each other's leaflets and planned coordinated demonstrations. As a result, several Brothers were tried before a military court hearing communist cases.[5]

If Brotherhood leaders scorned cooperation with the communists, they did not do so from lack of resolve to challenge the regime. In late March mutual antipathy for the old liberal establishment, along with Nasser's promise to legalize their movement, had led them to adopt a stance of passive loyalty toward the regime. After the CCR emerged triumphant, Hasan al-Hudaybi, the general guide, reasserted the Brothers' desire for a "clean" parliamentary system, not a return of the old political parties, and a free but responsible press.[6]

But the Brothers harbored no illusions about the regime. Hudaybi responded to reporters' questions about the Brothers' future plans with circumspection, but his nonanswers hinted at a spirit not broken. Prison was agreeable, he indicated. It had allowed him the opportunity to study the Koran and Hadith. The officers' revolution might be ending, but the Brothers' revolution would proceed. 'Abd al-Qadir 'Awdah, his deputy and sometime rival, underlined the Brothers' sense of purpose: "The time for talk has passed; now is the time for work. . . . We have emerged from this simple test more unyielding in our trust in God."[7]

Within a month the heralded "new era of cooperation" gave way to deceit and mistrust. In meetings with Brotherhood representatives, Nasser, not they, now proposed formation of a joint committee to repair the rift between the two sides. Hudaybi and his allies rebuffed what they perceived as Nasser's efforts to elevate proregime members within the movement.[8] In April, without publicity, the regime brought to trial a number of Brotherhood officers whose release had been promised. First before the court was Free Officers founding member 'Abd al-Mun'im 'Abd al-Ra'uf.

In response, Hudaybi drafted an open letter to Nasser in which he chastised the CCR for reneging on its promise to exonerate the Brothers of charges leveled against them in January. He also renewed his call for the restoration of civil liberties and parliamentary life. Barred from the press, the letter soon found its way into the streets as a leaflet. Before the court passed sentence on 'Abd al-Ra'uf, he escaped custody. Hudaybi gambled, revealing the agreement in an attempt to hold Nasser to his word. Failing, he decided to go abroad, ostensibly to visit Muslim communities in neighboring Arab countries. Before his departure in late May he rebuffed a summons to meet with Nasser but informed the CCR of his hope that in his absence the opportunity would be seized to improve regime-Brotherhood relations.[9]

The Brotherhood's vocal opposition to the Heads of Agreement signaled the end of its truce with the government. In a statement published in a Lebanese newspaper Hudaybi denounced the accord. The Brothers reminded the regime that the abrogated 1936 treaty would have expired in another twenty months. By granting the British the right for a seven-year period to reoccupy the Canal base in case of aggression against the Arab world or Turkey, the Brothers charged, the government had in effect extended Egypt's treaty commitment another five years. Furthermore, Egypt had linked itself indirectly to the very alliances it had long refused to enter. The haste with which the Brothers jumped to condemn the agreement— Hudaybi's letter appeared July 31; a pamphlet by his deputy, Khamis Humaydah, was dated August 2—betrays their conviction that they had nothing further to discuss with the CCR. Two additional pamphlets, one signed by Muhammad Nagib, the other by a "former minister," later learned to be Sulayman Hafiz, both printed in similar format and on identical paper, underlined for the CCR the extent to which relations had soured.[10]

In late August the CCR mounted a counteroffensive. In a speech before Liberation Rally members on August 21, Nasser for the first time lumped the Brothers together with communists and Zionists in what he called the "destructive opposition."[11] On August 22 the government began a media offensive that continued daily for six weeks. The press repeated themes raised prior to the Brotherhood's abolition the previous January, accusing the Brothers of "trafficking in religion" in a deceitful bid for power, and focusing on Hudaybi as the prime culprit.

The press dutifully printed what the regime fed it. Even *Ruz al-Yusuf,* which had always opened its pages to the Brotherhood, joined the assault. In late September its cover cartoon portrayed Nasser's beating back a two-headed dog, the heads identified as communism and the Brotherhood. In October the communist dog disappeared and the villain, labeled "reaction," sported a tarbush and beard, a thinly veiled caricature of Hasan al-Banna.[12] The regime resurrected old charges of collaboration with Farouk and more recent charges of collusion with the British. The Brothers' general guide felt compelled to respond. In another open letter, in which he outlined his conversation with Trefor Evans in early 1953 and subsequent report to Nasser, Hudaybi denied the existence of any secret deal.[13]

Tensions quickly escalated, creating a crisis atmosphere. During the Friday noon prayer on August 27 police surrounded a mosque in Roda, a center of Brotherhood activity in Cairo. After the sermon they moved to arrest the speaker, Hasan Duh, precipitating a scuffle and necessitating a call for reinforcements. The government reported the incident as a deliberate provocation by the Brothers. Hasan Duh declares that his sermon, although critical of the government, was not inflammatory. Richard Mitchell's eyewitness account supports him.[14] A similar incident occurred in Tanta on September 10, after which the government announced that it would thenceforth supervise the content of all sermons. In a more inflammatory action, on September 23 the government stripped five Brothers, all on a mission to Syria, of their citizenship.[15]

As the date for signing the evacuation accord approached, both sides braced for trouble. In the interval between the Roda and Tanta incidents, Hudaybi, back from his travels, went into hiding in Alexandria. The Guidance Council declared him "on vacation" for an indefinite period. Nasser, too, stopped appearing in public, until the general guide assured him in another open letter, "You may walk without guard day or night in any place without fearing that the Muslim Brothers will raise one hand against you."[16] Unable to ignore the public challenge, Nasser resumed a normal schedule, but the authorities posted extra guards around public buildings and mosques. In October the CCR initiatied a reorganization of high administrative and police officials, and issued a new martial law statute, the first revision since 1923. The new order placed more direct power in the hands of the military governor-general of Egypt, the post held by Nasser since April.[17]

The regime approached the conclusion of the evacuation accord with no small amount of trepidation. British sources described public reaction to the signing on October 24 as apathetic; American sources, as relieved.[18] But the opposition remained feisty. As crowds gathered for celebratory speeches in downtown Alexandria on the evening of October 26, unruly groups pushed forward, chanting anti-CCR slogans. Police removed them and cleared a path for truckloads of workers brought in to shout approval. One man with a different aim managed to wind his way to the front: Nasser had scarcely begun his speech when Mahmud 'Abd al-Latif, a Muslim Brother from Cairo, fired eight shots at him from point blank range.[19]

Unharmed, Nasser proceeded to deliver an impromptu address, one so compelling that his opponents later asserted it had to have been orchestrated: "My countrymen, my blood spills for you and for Egypt. I will live for your sake, die for the sake of your freedom and honor. Let them kill me; it does not concern me so long as I have instilled pride, honor, and freedom in you. If Gamal Abdel Nasser should die, each of you shall be Gamal Abdel Nasser. . . ." The following day throngs of well-wishers greeted Nasser upon his arrival at the train station in Cairo; across town organized mobs set fire to the Muslim Brothers' headquarters. With the assailant positively identified as a Brother, the regime established a People's Tribunal (Mahkamat al-Sha'b) to try him and Brotherhood leaders charged as accomplices.

Who Called the Shot?

Responsibility for the attempt on Nasser's life has sparked controversy ever since. The Muslim Brotherhood said immediately, and has insisted consistently, that the CCR staged the incident as a pretext to crack down on their movement. Their arguments rest solely on circumstantial evidence, primarily the speed with which the regime responded. In 1978 Hasan al-Tuhami, a close confidant of Nasser and then Sadat, threw fuel on the fire when he revealed that Nasser had been provided a bulletproof vest by the CIA. Conspiracy theorists imputed from his revelation a foreknowledge of the attempt, contradicting earlier charges that the assailant had been instructed to miss his target, or that his gun carried blanks. The essential fact remains that the assailant was a Brother. That Nasser took precautions, that the CCR stood ready to strike, in no way mean that the regime needed to orchestrate the incident.[20]

The real question is, who in the Brotherhood ordered 'Abd al-Latif to kill Nasser, and why? This raises vital questions about not only CCR-Brotherhood relations since the coup but internal troubles within the Brotherhood since the ascension of Hasan al-Hudaybi to the post of general guide in 1951 and, more directly, since his consolidation of authority in late 1953. To answer these questions, the internal dynamics of the movement must be examined on two levels: the Brotherhood's official governing body, the Guidance Council—in which an ongoing battle for supremacy raged—and the secret organization, reconstituted in January 1954 by men loyal to Hudaybi after he ousted its erstwhile maverick leader, 'Abd al-Rahman al-Sanadi.

Hours of testimony before the People's Tribunal by nearly every leading figure in the Brotherhood provide invaluable insight into troubles within that movement. The tribunal, which convened on November 2, passed through several stages. The trial of the assailant began on November 9. Issues raised in this case surpassed immediate questions of guilt and motive to encompass a full-scale indictment of Brotherhood leaders. Next the court began the systematic and much quicker trials of Hudaybi, Guidance Council members, and secret organization officers. By the year's end two subsidiary tribunals began hearing cases of lower-level secret organization cadres.

Relying on the trial record, however, is problematic. Unlike previous show trials staged by the military regime, the People's Tribunal pursued its charge without hesitation or pretense of equity. As Mitchell noted wryly, the trials displayed "a memorable exhibition of the rights revolutionary governments have and take as regards the due process of law." Ramadan, who is not sympathetic to the Brotherhood, contends that the presideing judge, Gamal Salim, "dragged the court down to a level never before seen in Egyptian history." Salim assumed the role of inquisitor, harassing and threatening defendants and witnesses, many of whom bore marks of more-physical interrogation prior to their appearance. Among other breaches of judicial process, the court attributed false testimony and confessions to comrades not present to refute them.[21]

Nonetheless, taking care to weigh the testimony itself, and taking into consideration the conditions under which it was delivered, much may be inferred about the Brotherhood's inner workings. The speed with which the tribunal was convened and witnesses brought forth—some within a day of their arrest—precluded the construction of an elaborate orchestrated show trial. If the court improvised freely as the hearings proceeded, it could do so because of the CCR's intimate knowledge of the Brotherhood.

As striking as the brutality of the court was the ease with which it extracted confessions and induced those who stood before it to betray their comrades.[22] The trial record demonstrates amply that internal power struggles that had plagued the movement since the murder of Hasan al-Banna played into the hands of the CCR. The rapprochement between warring factions instigated by the government's dissolution order in January 1954 had lasted only until CCR-Brotherhood hostility began anew in July. Upon his return from abroad, Hudaybi faced a relentless challenge from opponents in the Guidance Council who demanded he answer charges leveled by the regime. Throughout the fall of 1954 *Al-Da'wah*, traditional mouthpiece of the anti-Hudaybi faction but silent while Hudaybi remained in prison, again echoed the regime's attack on the general guide.[23] Hudaybi's flight to Alexandria, in part a response to this internal quarrel, produced a leadership vacuum that encouraged rivals who sought to gain control of the Consultative Assembly.[24] At the assembly's annual convocation in early September, Hudaybi foes again tried to limit the general guide's term. Hudaybi's absence prompted a three-week adjournment that allowed his loyalists to plot a counterattack. In a secret session in which they held the majority, Hudaybi allies again swore fealty to him and confirmed his position for life.[25]

A period of near anarchy followed. Hoping to strike a modus vivendi with the regime, anti-Hudaybi forces issued a statement in support of the CCR and dispatched a series of delegations to the officers. In turn, the CCR stopped its media campaign. Although it appeared that Hudaybi had again asserted his dominance over the Guidance Council, Khamis Humaydah, who had represented a faction urging conciliation between Hudaybi and his rivals, now leaned toward the latter camp. On October 20 Humaydah, in collaboration with 'Abd al-Rahman al-Banna, engineered a mutiny within the Guidance Council. The two formed a new body that promptly placed Hudaybi on indefinite leave and revoked the expulsions of those members he had ousted in late 1953. As had occurred a year before, Brotherhood headquarters was the scene of flying curses and fisticuffs. A parade of Hudaybi foes, hopeful peacemakers between the Brothers and the regime, visited CCR members up to and including October 26, when the attempt on Nasser's life rendered all such efforts irrelevant.[26]

Throughout the subsequent trials the court, intent upon implicating Hudaybi, pressed the issue of ultimate responsibility for the secret organization. Guidance Council members roundly denied any knowledge beyond the existence of the organization and the name of its leader. Except for one member, Muhammad Farghali, this appears to be true. Most pointed to Hudaybi as ultimately responsible. Hudaybi acknowledged this responsibility for the special section but denied indignantly any knowledge of its organization or operation. He insisted that he ordered its ranks purged from the top down, and that the force remained armed in order to battle the British. All of this had in fact been true at one time. Yet Hudaybi also stated that he had appointed the section's new leader, Yusuf Til'at, on the recommendation of others, and insisted he had not previously known him, both patent falsehoods.[27]

Hudaybi's reticence before the court reflected his recognition of the dominant role the secret organization had come to play within the Brotherhood. When he ousted Sanadi in late 1953, Hudaybi reconstituted the secret apparatus under men committed to his leaderhsip. The three branch leaders, Til'at (civilian), Salah Shadi (police), and Abu al-Makarim 'Abd al-Hayy (army), operated with relative autonomy from Hudaybi and the Guidance Council, as the secret apparatus had in the past, yet each remained loyal to the general guide. Each of the three was arrested in January. Their stint in prison engendered a resolve to battle the regime, and shortly after their release they formed an informal "higher committee" to coordiante activities between the branches.[28] The secret organization printed and distributed the antiregime leaflets that infuriated the CCR and dismayed more conciliatory members of the Guidance Council.[29]

By midsummer more zealous members of the secret organization began to turn their sights away from clandestine propaganda and consider more extreme tactics. Discussions wavered between peaceful demonstrations, an armed uprising, and assassination of CCR members. 'Abd al-Mun'im 'Abd al-Ra'uf reportedly proposed storming the cabinet with a commando group. During Hudaybi's trial, Yusuf Til'at admitted that he had given a belt of dynamite to Ibrahim al-Tayyib, the Cairo section chief, some twelve days prior to October 26. Til'at told the court he had considered the murder of Nasser and others, including the tribunal's president, Gamal Salim. Several days later, still under oath, he denied that he plotted the actual attempt on Nasser, explaining that he had given no final order for such an act. He put the onus on 'Abd al-Ra'uf and Tayyib. The latter testified that his orders came from Til'at. Hindawi Duwayr, chief of the Imbaba district, who gave the pistol to the assailant, claimed Tayyib told him that Hudaybi had authorized the killing.[30]

The government case asserted that the general guide had personally ordered the assassination. This he vigorously denied.[31] Both Mitchell and Ramadan conclude that the assassination attempt originated among leaders of the secret organization independent of Hudaybi and the Guidance Council. Hudaybi, however, should bear more responsibility for the ultimate recourse to violence than either historian has accorded him.

In late October 1954 the Brotherhood suffered from an absence of centralized leadership and a lack of consensus on either internal affairs or relations to the government. While Hudaybi's opponents endeavored to attain greater control over the Guidance Council, he retreated into the arms of his loyalists, who ran the secret organization. When Hudaybi went into hiding in September 1954 he surrounded himself with men more willing to countenance violence than he. By this time one cannot declare, as Mitchell does for an earlier period, the previous March, that "Hudaybi appears to have remained unaware of the reversion to character of the unit which had caused so much dissention within the Society. . . ."[32] His coterie counseled assassination and armed uprising in his presence. Even those, like Shadi, who preached patience, did not rule out the use of force at a later date. If

Hudaybi is to be taken at his word, he rejected all such notions. But he did give his blessing, he and others testified, to popular demonstrations against the regime.[33] Facing the mutiny of late October and the pressures of living underground, one cannot ignore the possibility that in the end, pushed to despair, Hudaybi bowed to more zealous colleagues and condoned the use of violence. Most likely, the decision to unleash an assassin was made by them without his knowledge. Yet by his presence among them, Hudaybi acquiesced passively to the dangerous path they trod. By resignation more than will, Hudaybi lent legitimacy to the wing of the Brotherhood he had once set out to abolish, and allied himself with those dedicated to making war on the CCR against those desperately seeking peace.

"The First Time We Were Hard with Them"

Following the "Manshiya incident" the CCR moved swiftly to destroy the Brotherhood. The day after the attempt mobs organized by the Liberation Rally sacked the Brothers' Cairo headquarters. In following days offices and shops owned by Brotherhood sympathizers were attacked in the Canal cities. The police turned a blind eye; in several cases uniformed members of the National Guard led the crowds.[34] On October 29 Nasser spoke to thousands in Republic Square. He said he felt no rancor toward his would-be assassin, whom he described as a victim. Hudaybi and the Brotherhood he denounced in harsh terms, swearing that he would embark upon a bloody revolution before he would accept defeat.[35]

The regime unleashed a new propaganda barrage against the Brotherhood. It focused now not on Hudaybi but on the strength of the secret organization, and "revealed" the Brothers' plans to topple the government and impose a rigid Islamic order upon Egypt. Rekindling the nation's memories of 1947–1948, the government depicted the Brothers as zealots devoted to terror and violence.[36] Sessions of the first wave of trials were broadcast daily and transcripts printed in the press until late November, when the impetuousness of two defendants, Yusuf Til'at and 'Abd al-Qadir 'Awdah, forced the government to heavily censor press accounts of the hearings and discontinue radio broadcasts.[37]

On December 4 the People's Tribunal handed down death sentences for Hudaybi, 'Abd al-Latif, 'Awdah, Til'at, Ibrahim al-Tayyib, Hindawi Duwayr, and Muhammad Farghali. Seven Brothers received life sentences, and two were sentenced to fifteen years. 'Abd al-Rahman al-Banna and two others, friends of the regime and opponents of Hudaybi, were judged innocent.[38] The court immediately commuted Hudaybi's sentence to life imprisonment on the grounds that he had fallen under the influence of his advisors. Salah Salim admitted to a U.S. embassy officer that the CCR spared Hudaybi to avoid making him a martyr. The officers reportedly debated the wisdom of capital punishment for some eight hours before making a final decision. They also seriously considered sparing the life of the assailant but let his sentence stand. The end came on December 9, when the six on death row were hung.[39]

With swift efficiency the regime succeeded in destroying the armed power of the Muslim Brotherhood. "This was the first time we were hard with them," recalls Zakariya Muhyi al-Din.[40] Within three weeks of the assassination attempt over one thousand Brothers were rounded up. Unlike the previous January, this time the sweep extended beyond Cairo and Alexandria into provincial centers, strongholds of Brotherhood influence.[41] Then, having flexed their muscles, Nasser and the CCR decided to stem the flow of blood. Mass executions were in the long run more dangerous than clemency. On December 13 the regime commuted the death sentences of five secret organization leaders condemned the previous day. In early January the government overturned all capital sentences meted out in the third round of trials.[42]

While dismantling the Brothers' armed threat, the regime also moved to undermine their grass-roots support. On December 10, the day after the six Brothers hanged, the Social Affairs Ministry assumed adminsitrative control of Brotherhood welfare centers on the pretext that they were a front for clandestine terrorist activity. The U.S. ambassador pointed out the real motive:

> An eventual attack on the Brotherhood's welfare program was almost a certainty and the only surprising thing about the December 10 announcement was that it has been so long in coming. The welfare activities of the Brotherhood dated from the early 1940s and are the basis for the organization's strength in certain rural areas. A complete discontinuation of these activities would have caused rural elements who have benefitted from them to view the regime's move against the Brotherhood adversely; therefore the regime had little choice but to take over and continue the Brotherhood's projects if it desired to maintain its popularity in the rural areas where the Brothers have been active.[43]

The regime did not destroy the Brotherhood. Some managed to elude the dragnet; pockets of resistance remained, and Brotherhood cells reportedly operated covertly under the averted gaze of sympathetic prison officials.[44] But the Brotherhood had been dealt a staggering blow. The regime totally disrupted the organizational structure of the secret organization, and co-opted many of those who had favored cordial relations with the regime and won the loyalty or passive submission of many to whom it had granted clemency.

"Kerensky with a Fez"

The assassination attempt also provided the occasion for the revolutionary command finally to sever its bond to Muhammad Nagib. He was still president but after March 1954 became a virtual nonperson. Still hesitant to dismiss him, the officers muzzled Nagib. In early May a British embassy officer reported that "to all appearances the General has so far contented himself" with the role of figurehead.[45] But Nagib's patience soon wore thin. The officers allowed him a press conference on June 18, 1954, the first anniverary of the republic, on the condition that no photographs be taken. When Nagib tried to dissociate himself from the lack of movement toward seating a constituent assembly, Salah Salim reasserted the president's ultimate responsibility for all decision making. The incident received no coverage in the Egyptian press.[46]

In following months the opposition encouraged Nagib to assert himself against the CCR. Buoyed by what an American observer called "exaggerated applause and demonstration of support . . . whenever he appears in public," Nagib grew bolder. He rebuffed CCR pressure to speak out in favor of the Heads of Agreement, and prepared a speech for July 23 celebrations that the others deemed inflammatory. On the latter occasion Nasser reportedly "read Nagib the riot act," offering him the option of reading a prepared speech or not speaking. Nagib chose the former; still, the *New York Times* reported that his appearance highlighted the celebrations.[47] According to a U.S. embassy officer, a growing number of army officers lobbied the CCR on Nagib's behalf. Nagib reportedly had a list of demands that included formation of a national advisory council to replace the CCR, definite target dates for ratification of a new constitution and elections, the release of all political prisoners, and abolition of a new cabinet post for presidential affairs, created in April 1954 and delegated to Hasan Ibrahim.[48]

Mutual opposition drew Nagib and the Muslim Brothers, tentative allies earlier that year, together. In a pamphlet printed and distributed by the Brotherhood in late July, Nagib echoed the Brothers' critique of the draft accord as compromising Egyptian independence. In his memoirs Nagib wrote that he never intended the Brothers to distribute the statement. How he intended to keep it private he never said. In any case, Brotherhood leaders, including those in the secret organization who printed and circulated the pamphlet, testified before the People's Tribunal that he had indeed sought its publication.[49] As far as his former CCR colleagues were concerned, he had implicitly declared war on them.

Only the precarious position of the regime, preparing to sign an accord with the British, prolonged Nagib's tenure in office. In late October, 1954 with the document awaiting only the signatures, Nasser told British officials that if Nagib refused to sign he would be sacked. After the signing he told Anthony Nutting that a showdown was inevitable.[50]

On November 15, the CCR announced that it had relieved Nagib of all duties. The announcement had been predicated on testimony before the People's Tribunal linking him to the Brothers. In addition to joint pamphleteering, key figures in the secret organization confessed that they envisioned handing power to Nagib after ousting the CCR.[51] A week after his dismissal, in deference to Sudanese representatives who had expressed formal protest, the regime announced that Nagib would not stand trial.[52]

In Egypt the final rupture caused little apparent reaction. Events had overtaken Nagib. C. L. Sulzberger put it most succinctly when he described Nagib as "Kerensky with a fez."[53] Nagib was taken to a deserted villa once owned by Madam Nahhas on the outskirts of Cairo. There he would remain under house arrest for nearly twenty years.[54] Still wary of public reaction, the CCR offered the presidency to Lutfi al-Sayyid, but the aged philosopher and intellectual father of Egyptian nationalism declined, citing ill health. Leaving the office vacant, the CCR conferred executive powers on Nasser.[55]

Emboldened by its swift roundup of Brotherhood cadres, the CCR broadened the scope of its assault to encompass other opponents, old and new. A new wave of leftist journalists and intellectuals was arrested, many of which had written against the CCR in March, and some, like Mahmud 'Abd al-Mun'im Murad and Yusuf Idris, who knew the officers personally and had once been considered friends. In November the security police scored their first successful raid against the Workers Vanguard since 1950. In December the Egyptian Broadcasting Service began using scripts prepared by the Voice of America that emphasized the threat of an "international communist conspiracy."[56]

In mid-1954 the regime began denouncing the "Zionist enemy" with increasing regularity. In part this represented an effort to rally a population displeased with the proposed evacuation accord. But Israeli agents working to destabilize the regime gave the CCR the opportunity, and thus share responsibility for the intensifying war of words between Cairo and Jerusalem. In July 1954 three separate incidents of sabotage resulted in the arrests of three Egyptian Jews identified as Israeli agents. On July 2 two letter bombs exploded in the Alexandria post office; on July 14 several bombs hidden in packages of books were discovered at the U.S. embassy and Alexandria consulate. Then on July 23 police apprehended a man running from an Alexandria cinema, an incendiary device having exploded in his pocket. A search of his apartment uncovered a cache of explosives and two associates. In October thirteen Jews were arraigned on charges of espionage and sabotage.[57]

The trial of the saboteurs, which began on December 11, became a cause célèbre among supporters of Israel throughout the world. Israeli government officials exploited the case in order to portray Nasser as a dangerous threat to Egyptian Jews and Israeli security.[58] Those who knew the true circumstances of the case rendered a far different judgment. The guilt of most defendants was never an issue. U.S. and British embassy observers concluded that the trial was run fairly. The defendants cooperated with the court, and a U.S. official noted that the accused demonstrated an "unusual willingness to incriminate themselves voluntarily."[59] Two openly confessed; a third committed suicide in prison. Nasser met several times during the trial with a Jewish member of the British House of Commons who engaged in a bit of private diplomacy, and who came away impressed that the Egyptian leader was sympathetic to international concerns.[60] On January 27, 1955, the court sentenced two of the accused to death, the others, save two found innocent, to prison terms ranging from seven to fifteen years.

The discovery of an Israeli-sponsored spy ring provided the regime a convenient excuse to link widespread internal opposition to an external threat at a time of heightened sensitivity to criticism of the evacuation accord. The decision to carry out the death sentences on January 31 may have been taken, as Lacouture suggested, primarily to appease Muslim Brotherhood supporters whom the regime feared might make great capital out of a clemency decree so soon after their own martyrs hanged from the gallows.[61]

"Abdel Nasser and His Comrades"

In the months after their suppression of the Muslim Brotherhood the officers arrested nearly every major opponent of their rule. The aggressive posture of the People's Tribunal reflected their resolution to impose themselves as Egypt's sole rulers. By asserting direct authority over the media, professional associations, organized labor, education, and, most important, the military, the CCR insured that there would be no cause for further retreat, forced or tactical. With an Anglo-Egyptian agreement signed, prospects for increased British and U.S. aid seemed bright. What form their rule would assume had remained an unanswered question. Few looked with optimism to the return of parliamentary life. In July 1954 the officers had sent mixed messages. They announced that parliamentary elections would be held in January 1956, while at the same time admitting that it would not be easy for them to return to the barracks.[62] In mid-October the CCR informed the U.S. embassy that it would hold these elections after settling its score with the Muslim Brotherhood. The officers would support a handpicked slate under the banner of a Republican party and permit other parties to run. In December 1954 Nasser promised a constitution by January 1956 but said nothing of elections.[63]

The attempt on his life marked a watershed in the career of Gamal Abdel Nasser. Confident of his abilities and increasingly frustrated by the burden of group decision making, Nasser had begun to isolate himself from his CCR colleagues during the trying days of March. The moment of collective victory carried with it the seeds of division. The crisis had been a trying experience for all, and disquieting memories would linger.[64] After he escaped a potentially violent brush with a mob in Cairo's Gamaliyah district on February 27, Salah Salim did not venture near his office for seven days. Husayn al-Shafi'i recalls with great sadness the anguish he felt at his inability to persuade rebellious armor comrades to accept Nagib's ouster. As a group, the CCR had proved more of a burden than an asset in helping Nasser make the crucial decisions that saved the regime. The small coterie that worked closest with him during the latter phase of the crisis—'Amr, Zakariya Muhyi al-Din, Sadat, key Liberation Rally and military police officers—felt less alienated. For those who had been left in the dark, like Baghdadi, who argued heatedly with Nasser over tactics, a bitter aftertaste tainted the victory.[65]

After assuming the prime ministry in mid-April, Nasser appointed all but two CCR members ('Amr and Sadat) to his cabinet, presaging the transformation of the CCR from military junta to civilian cabinet. Dissatisfied with his role as CCR chief, Nasser sought a more formal arrangement. In late April he queried Trefor Evans on the workings of the British cabinet.[66] The CCR still met in special sessions, but as the officers became increasingly specialized in matters more technical than political, Nasser relied on them less. He began to cultivate a new group of political commissars, second-rank Free Officer, men like 'Ali Sabri and Lutfi Wakid, whom he brought into his office to handle political and foreign affairs respectively.

Nasser's personal consolidation of power for the first time caused serious strains within the CCR. Baghdadi's response to his cabinet postings, rural affairs, then public works, is revealing. In the latter post he initiated many of the projects that gave Cairo its modern face, the Nile "corniche" and Tahrir (Liberation) Square most notably, earning a reputation as an able administrator. Yet he viewed the posts as punishment, banishment from the center of political decision making.[67] Salah Salim's independent streak, often a source of tension, now created serious problems between him and Nasser. In August 1954, protesting Nasser's interference in his ministry (national guidance), Salim threatened to resign. During talks with Iraqi leaders in Baghdad in early September, he exceeded his brief, committing Egypt to reconsider its opposition to Western participation in an Arab collective security pact. Upon his return the CCR placed him on leave; Salim resumed his duties the following day only after a four-hour conference with Nasser. Then in late December, in off-the-cuff remarks to Syrian journalists, Salim insisted Egypt would never make peace with Israel. The Foreign Ministry quickly disavowed the statement; Nasser aides told U.S. embassy officials their boss was "furious."[68]

In public and private Nasser cultivated an image that set him apart from his colleagues. In September he published his manifesto, *Philosophy of the Revolution*, in which he outlined his vision of Egypt as a country in search of a hero, a role he now clearly saw himself fulfilling. The work revealed a man of seeming contradictions, still ill at ease with newfound fame. Jean Lacouture, a shrewd observer of the Egyptian revolution, queried, "Could it have been the same man who, so terribly adult in poltiics, had just published this adolescent document?"[69] To British Ambassador Ralph Stevenson, the tract revealed "a man of action who has trouble articulating the philosophical basis of action." The British ambassador's own ambivalence about Nasser is reflected in his assessment. Nasser's "shortcomings and prejudices are those of his class, his age, and his country," he cabled. At the same time, Nasser reflected a "certain breadth of vision, humanity, and idealism" that Sir Ralph found encouraging.[70]

In a series of *Al-Jumhuriyah* columns run in January 1955, Sadat referred routinely to the CCR as "Abdel Nasser and his comrades." This public depersonalization of the companions soon manifested itself in Nasser's personal relations with fellow CCR members. Salah Salim, who accompanied him to the nonaligned nations conference in Bandung in April 1955, resented Nasser's reliance on 'Ali Sabri and Foregin Minister Mahmud Fawzi. In May Salim ceded to Nasser responsibility for Egyptian broadcasting to foreign countries. Gamal Salim, whom Nasser named acting prime minister in his absence, took offense when he failed to receive a proper briefing.[71] In the collective memory of Nasser's colleagues the Bandung trip remains pivotal. After he returned he was no longer Gamal, even to his closest associates; they now called him "Boss," or "Chief" (ra'is). Soon after, he would be referred to as "Mister President." Seemingly trivial occurrences underlined the gap between Nasser and his comrades. When the band played the national anthem as he mounted the rostrum during celebrations for the third anniversary of the coup, Nasser refrained from asking his comrades to stand for the crowd's approbation.[72]

By this time Nasser clearly looked ahead not only to cementing his position as sole leader of the country but also to redefining the role of the revolutionary council. Shortly after Bandung he initiated discussions within the CCR on the council's future. Nasser fixed upon June 1956 as the target date for bringing the transition period to an end. A rift developed between those who sought to maintain the CCR's integrity and those who followed Nasser's lead in calling for its abolition. The former group, a majority, sought to perpetuate the council's supraadvisory status even if Nasser held ultimate decision-making power. This faction proffered the model of early 1954 when Nasser had polled each CCR member individually, establishing a consensus before acting.[73]

Nasser, who still valued the counsel of his oldest colleagues, indicated his desire that they stay on as advisors and ministers. Discussions within the CCR went nowhere, a situation reminiscent of March 1954, which only furthered Nasser's resolve to unburden himself of the council. In the autumn of 1955 foreign affairs pushed all talk of the council's future into the background. In January 1956 Nasser unilaterally created a constitutional committee. The draft charter, approved by popular vote on June 25, abolished the CCR. The same day another referendum proclaiming Nasser president won overwhelming approval. By posing as the restorer of democracy, Nasser achieved a propaganda tour de force against his comrades who, while they sought a more democratic junta, knew they could easily be depicted to the public as proponents of continued dictatorship. With the exception of Salah Salim, who had left the government the previous August, the others accepted Nasser's invitation to join his government. As required by law, they resigned from the military.

On the eve of the Suez crisis Nasser governed Egypt as he had the Free Officers executive, by force of personality more than coercion. Those who knew the young Nasser describe him as a man of few words, an intent listener who drew others out, prodding them to talk. Nasser rarely bludgeoned his colleagues; by soliciting their views, he made them feel that they had participated in the decision-making process. In late 1953 they allowed him to make executive decisions because they trusted him to solicit and weigh their opinions. Nasser always valued the counsel of others; however he grew less willing to put matters to a general vote.

Nasser's transformation from conspirator to public statesman occurred over a three-year period during which he grew more comfortable with power and saw his skills tested by a series of crises. Those crises caused him to reevaluate his perspectives on power. He had been attracted to passionate nationalists and often, although never one himself, to ideologues. As the pragmatist in Nasser emerged after the coup, he turned away from many of his closest comrades, men of charisma and passion, and turned increasingly to those more inclined to steel nerves than to dreams, and ultimately to those who would accept his authority without argument. By the time he delivered the second great speech of his career, the nationalization of the Suez Canal on July 26, 1956, Nasser had become a consummate politician, well on his way to demagoguery.

"A Pragmatic March toward Democracy"?

In late October 1954 Jefferson Caffery noted that the Free Officers' revolution could no longer be described as transitory. The officers looked ahead to the future in an "optimistic but serious manner." The U.S. ambassador deemed it unlikely that the members of the CCR "will ever voluntarily step into the background to permit others to guide the destinies of the Revolution which will now undertake long range development of Egypt."[1]

In the months after suppressing the Muslim Brothers the officers exulted in their victory. The week after Brotherhood leaders hanged, the cover of *Ruz al-Yusuf* depicted the death of "terrorism." Standing over the corpse, drawn in the familiar guise of a Brother—tarbush and short-cropped beard, the likeness of Hasan al-Banna—stood the diminutive bespectacled character, Misri Effendi, who had come to symbolize the nation during the parliamentary era. Now dressed in military uniform, a sword dangling from his belt, citizen Misri announced that the way was now safe. A month later the specter of violence began to dissipate. When Nasser confronted "terrorism" on the magazine's cover in late January, he was drawn as a football player kicking a ball ("stability") past the outstretched arms of a Muslim Brother into a goal ("domestic politics").[2]

The conjunction of the two caricatures, Nasser and Misri Effendi, is reminiscent of the photograph taken a year earlier at Hifni Mahmud's funeral, the photograph described in the introduction to this work. A transition is under way in the Egyptian mind-set, one that has yet to run its course. Old symbols retain their power; even the portrayals of Nasser, champion of the "new age," seem strikingly old-fashioned: Nasser as team captain, benevolent strongman, Nasser as the new Nagib? Somehow the revolution, proclaimed so forcefully in official pronouncements, remained unclear and undefined.

This was in part the consequence of the regime's ambivalence toward the term itself. The 1919 revolution that led to Egypt's conditional independence and the onset of the parliamentary era also set a precedent for politics in the street. In November 1924 angry crowds, protesting palace interference in parliamentary affairs, shouted "Sa'd [Zaghlul] or revolution." By the late 1940s revolution had become for many, reform-minded progressives as well as steadfast conservatives, a specter of disorder and massive social upheaval associated increasingly, rightly or wrongly, with communism.

Largely for this reason the Free Officers avoided the term *revolution* before and after July 23. For six months in power they called themselves the general command and spoke of their "army movement" or, with uncharacteristic flourish, "blessed movement." In its rhetoric the junta emphasized "purification," "reform," "reorganization," and "restoration." Still, the term could not be repressed. A leading jurist justified the extralegal appointment of a regency council as "revolutionary jurisprudence." Communist allies of the regime, despite reservations about the junta's ultimate goals, and in the face of police crackdowns and the officers' open campaigns on behalf of Muslim Brothers in university elections, nonetheless promoted the army movement as a revolution. Ahmad Hamrush used the term seven times in the first editorial he wrote for *Al-Tahrir*. But the account of the takeover published in the same journal and attributed to Nasser described "How we organized the coup d'état." When Rashad al-Barawi published his book-length account of the Free Officers' movement in late 1952, he called it *The Military Coup in Egypt*.

When the officers did declare their movement a revolution in early 1953, the term implied little more than a transitional phase of military rule. Abolition of the political parties, given the experiences of Arab neighbors, was seen as neither revolutionary nor final. The junta styled itself the Command Council of the Revolution, but its rhetoric emphasized "liberation" and stressed progress toward restoration of constitutional rule. By the year's end *revolution* defined a growing gulf between new and former rulers and the willingness of the officers to assert martial authority. The second round of corruption trials that year were held before the Revolutionary Tribunal, presided over by three CCR members and empowered to mete out capital sentences. No pashas hanged. The officers' seeming lack of will and the mixed messages emitted undercut the initial terror spawned by the trials. But the showcase of parliamentary factiousness underscored the folly of handing power back to the pashas. In March 1954, when the CCR proffered revolution as the alternative to "reaction," proregime mobs renounced parliament and democracy.

In the aftermath of the March crisis, the officers endeavored to move beyond the defensive, backward-looking rhetoric that had dominated their propaganda, a rhetoric that had placed primary emphasis on the crimes of the old regime. They still decried the forces of "reaction" but now spoke with greater certainty about grand projects, a high dam at Aswan, land reclamation in a "Liberation Province," a modern infrastructure for Cairo, and, at long last, a new constitution. Yet, as Egypt marched onward, its rulers still glanced nervously over their shoulders, compelled to answer lingering charges of critics and opponents.

The officers spoke of a peaceful, white revolution, while warning their adversaries of the bloody, red revolution they might unleash. In his *Philosophy of the Revolution*, published in the autumn of 1954, Nasser admitted at the outset he offered neither a philosophy nor a set program. He wrote of two concurrent Egyptian revolutions, "a political revolution that helps them recover their right to self-government from the hands of a despot who had imposed himself upon them, or free themselves from the domination of foreign armed forces . . . and a social revolution—a class conflict that ultimately ends in the realization of social justices for all the inhabitants of the country."[3] Toward the end of his treatise he spelled out a vision of Egypt's role in three spheres of influence, the African, Arab, and Islamic circles. But no details or programs were outlined. Nasser described Egypt in search of a hero; at the same time he and his colleagues remained heroes—and it took great temerity to consider themselves so in late 1954—in search of a clearly defined revolution.

In early 1955, in a series of *Al-Jumhuriyah* articles, Anwar al-Sadat reminded Egyptians that the revolution had been relatively bloodless and emphasized that it was not rooted in ideology. Rather, Sadat described the revolution as a "pragmatic march toward democracy." "Democracy will be determined when the people rule themselves, no longer ruled by Hudaybi, Badrawi [a large landowner], Nahhas, or Sirag al-Din—not any individual or group from the past, from before July 23." Critics of the regime had presumed the officers should "retain the 1923 Constitution and the political parties, handing power back to representatives of the feudal upper class." To what end, "so Sirag al-Din can keep smoking his cigar?!" Sadat wondered how the officers could be labeled dictators, and their opponents, the "merchants of opinion, religion, and nationalism," heralded as champions of democracy? If we erect a dictatorship, he rejoined, "we do so to watch over the succorers of imperialism and feudalism."[4] With the CCR firmly in control, Sadat went on to publish accounts of the Free Officers' formation, takeover, and subsequent confrontation with selected adversaries: the Wafd, the Brotherhood, Nagib, and Rashad Mahanna.

These accounts, along with Nasser's manifesto, formed the foundation of the regime's official history. Tight control of the media, the suppression of rival political movements, including subversive groups within the military, and the acquiescence of the public at large—subdued and fearful, yet yearning for stability—ensured that, in Egypt at least, no counterversion would be widely disseminated. To a great degree that official history persisted throughout Nasser's lifetime and was reflected in both Egyptian and foreign scholarship. Two major shifts in the Nasserist agenda, the pan-Arab, pan-African, nonaligned foreign policy orientation of the 1950s, and the state-directed "Arab socialism" of the 1960s thrust the period of political consolidation into the realm of the past. Only with the ascension of Sadat, who turned Nasserism on its head, if not discarding it altogether, did the question of the system's origins again arise.

Official history ultimately begets revisionism and where, as in Egypt, competing revisionist accounts arise simultaneously, a particularly rich composite may be constructed. Revisionist accounts tell a far different but often equally stilted story. Their greatest value lies in the wealth of detail they provide. Communists, Muslim Brothers, and left Wafdists may portray themselves as victims, the officers as deceitful, but by reintroducing themselves as major participants in a power struggle, and by challenging the official version of their demise, they construct new bounds of discussion and analysis. Ultimately, a more nuanced view of how political fortunes turn and how power comes to rest with one of many competing political forces results.

After evaluation of competing analyses of the period, it seems clear that one primary tenet of the official history remains credible. All factions, with the exception of the Muslim Brotherhood, agree that the officers seized power with no clear program and, more important, limited ambitions. Reexamination of the strategies adopted by the various political factions reveals that even the Brothers—although they deny it—recognized this. The officers' official description of the efforts made by these forces to obstruct their reform agenda or assert "tutelage" over their junta may reflect their own mind-set as accurately, if not more accurately, as it does that of the others. If their history of the breakdown in relations with former allies is too simplistic, to a certain extent that reflects their consternation with the burden of rule they assumed.

The end result, domination of the political order by the military, in alliance with civilian allies unaffiliated to any other political movement, was by no means inevitable. Where the army had seized political initiative in neighboring countries—Iraq in the mid-1930s and Syria in the late 1940s—the military had cooperated either with established political parties or with new, more radical forces such as the Ba'th. Had they been so inclined, Egypt's Free Officers might very well have struck a more lasting strategic alliance with a leftist front comprising the DMNL and Wafdist Vanguard, or with the Muslim Brothers. Sympathetic intellectuals and younger party members urged the Free Officers to follow another course—which they very well might have taken—to proceed with reforming election laws, then form a political party and run for office themselves.

This study suggests a variety of reasons for how Free Officer leaders were able to seize and consolidate power, topple the parliamentary regime, and establish themselves as the core of a new political order. Most basic, the decay of liberalism in Egypt created a situation in which a country in turmoil cried for drastic social and political reform, even if that entailed short-term support for a "just tyrant." The lack of a strong revolutionary opposition left the reform-minded officers as the sole force capable of seizing power when they found themselves compelled to take their units into the streets. The public at large, weary of the corruption and political violence of the late 1940s and early 1950s, threw its passive support behind a military movement correctly perceived as reformist. The active support of a young intelligentsia, representative of both the parliamentary establishment and antiestablishment, encouraged the officers to secure their hold over government and state. These individuals cannot be simply dismissed, as they have been, as "antidemocratic."

The distinction drawn among the intelligentsia in this work between maximalists and minimalists is especially important as a tool for analysis. Maximalists, generally individuals loyal to minority parties, saw in the officers the means to break the power of the Wafd and reorient the political order in such a way that parity could be achieved. As it became apparent to them that the leveling process would be prolonged, many shifted loyalty to the CCR. Minimalists, generally communists and young Wafdists, championed the officers' early reforms but resisted their consolidation of power. When the regime's hostility to the Left could no longer be rationalized, minimalist communists withdrew their support. When the abolition of the political order became a clear threat, young Wafdists rallied to support their party's battle for survival, putting to the side differences that had alienated them from their elders.

Divisions that rent the Wafd, as well as minority parties, communist movements, and the Muslim Brotherhood, ultimately played into the officers' hands. Each of the major forces contesting for power (including, ultimately, the CCR) suffered from internecine struggles. Generational strife plagued all the political parties. Within the Wafd, as well as minority parties, a young guard, more attuned to the political discourse of the post-Second World War era, sought to wrest leadership from the hands of the founding fathers. In the Brotherhood a power struggle among those competing to succeed Hasan al-Banna, played out against a broader background of disunity, divisions over political identity and agenda, and the autonomy of the paramilitary secret organization that often operated at cross-purposes from the movement's central leadership. For a young and growing communist movement, the divisions were within and between a variety of ideologically disparate factions, competing for members and always one step ahead of the political police. The military junta was not free of internal strife but managed to contain discord among its members, in part because the officers recognized the debilitating effects of the internecine strife that so obviously weakened its adversaries.

Help came as well from the two dominant foreign powers in Egypt, Britain and the United States. Egyptians and students of Egypt will not be surprised to learn of U.S. support for the Free Officers' endeavors. They will have difficulty producing any conclusive proof that the Free Officers were linked to the CIA prior to their coup. But what emerges clearly from State Department records, and what is ultimately of greater interest, is evidence of the extent to which the U.S. embassy adopted the officers, nurtured their rule, and promoted their cause to the British. More surprising to many will be the degree to which British embassy officials echoed policies promoted by their American counterparts. Despite constant pressure from Washington and their own diplomats in Cairo, policymakers in London accepted the compromises necessary to attain an evacuation accord—an accord the officers saw as their prime objective and so many others considered a foregone conclusion—only after the CCR's decisive domestic victory in March 1954.

If the officers did not seize power with any definite agenda, they nonetheless did so with a sense of mission. Their confrontation with competing forces strengthened their conviction that the political order needed purging, that six months of military-directed rule would not suffice, and that they best could direct the transition back to democracy. Their rejection of the ideological dogma of any particular faction allowed their own political orientation to develop as they confronted challenges to their rule. That their orientation developed toward military domination of the state did not arise from a belief that the army belonged in politics. The hasty shunning, then dismantling of the Free Officers' movement attests to that. Rather, the junta's encounter with popular discontent and organized opposition, and its brushes with defeat (and in Nasser's case, death) in 1954, led the officers to take the steps necessary to preserve public order and their own authority.

After 1954 that authority would increasingly rest with those in charge of internal security. Throughout the period of consolidation the officers did refrain from turning their revolution red. The regime executed fourteen Egyptian citizens between July 23, 1952, and January 31, 1955: two workers at Kafr al-Dawwar, four convicted of aiding the British in the Canal Zone, six Muslim Brothers, and two Zionist agents. The CCR commuted capital sentences handed old-regime politicians by the Revolutionary Tribunal and Muslim Brothers by the People's Tribunal. Nonetheless, Egypt's prisons remained full of opponents of the regime. A total of 867 Muslim Brothers appeared before three branches of the People's Tribunal in the first months of 1955, and another 254 were brought to trial before military courts. By October 1955, according to a source friendly to the regime, Egyptian jails held 2,943 political prisoners.[5]

The army became the training ground for a new elite, but the corps remained isolated from politics. Military intelligence foiled plans for purported coups in the autumn of 1957 and spring of 1958, both involving old-regime politicians.[6] However, in general, the close ties between military intelligence and the centers of state power insured a tight watch over potential troublemakers. The rehabilitation of rebellious artillery officers set the pattern for appeasing discontentment in the corps; malcontents were posted abroad or in the bureaucracy.

By the time of the Suez crisis a new political order had been born. Shrewd observers of Egyptian politics like Ihsan 'Abd al-Quddus recognized as early as 1955 that the revolution—he used the phrase—had entered a new phase, in which foreign affairs dominated.[7] In 1956 Egyptians ratified a new constitution and Nasser retained the presidency by overwhelming popular vote, the first of his famous 99.9 percent victories.

The regime had its enemies, but many had already or were soon to make their peace with the revolution. Former friends and colleagues 'Abd al-Quddus, Khalid Muhyi al-Din, Tharwat 'Ukashah, and Ahmad Hamrush again became leading figures within the regime. Two troublesome former colleagues, 'Abd al-Mun'im Amin and Yusuf Siddiq, retired from public life.[8] Communists in prison reappraised their position and threw support to the regime after Suez; many won their release. Throughout the next decade leftists chose to collaborate in hope of influencing a social transformation in Egypt. Relations remained stormy, but close enough so that communists can claim at least part of the Nasserist legacy.

For the Muslim Brothers, no such reconciliation was conceivable. Several former Brothers supported and served the regime, the most notable being Sheikh Baquri who, as minister of pious endowments, oversaw the transformation of Al-Azhar into a secular university in the 1960s. Leading Brothers convicted by the People's Tribunal remained in prison until shortly after Nasser's death.

Most old-guard politicians arrested in late 1953 remained in prison until late 1955. Those with health problems, such as Ibrahim Farag, Hafiz 'Afifi, and Fu'ad Sirag al-Din, the CCR released much earlier. During the Suez crisis and following the Syrian secession from the United Arab Republic, the regime rounded up many of the old guard as a precautionary measure, releasing them shortly thereafter. Nahhas, whom the regime never dared imprison, remained under surveillance until his death in 1965.

Two former friends, Rashad Mahanna and Muhammad Nagib remained exceptions to the general rule of rehabilitation or co-optation. The CCR released Rashad Mahanna prior to the Suez War, only to reintern him during that conflict. He remained confined until 1967. Nagib, whom the officers removed to Upper Egypt during the Suez War, presumably a precaution against his restoration, languished under house arrest until the early 1970s. As the years passed, Nagib posed less a threat than a source of shame to those who ruled Egypt.[9]

Legacies

Few Egyptians today contend that Nasser ruled with anything but dictatorial powers. As a political system, Nasserism denoted rule by a centralized party, a revolutionary vanguard theoretically free of the constraints of a multiparty system. Nasser created three successive mass parties, the Liberation Rally (1953), the National Union (1957), and the Arab Socialist Union (1962). With each he further refined a system that maintained rigid control of the polity behind a facade of popular participation. But at the same time few will dispute the claim that Nasserism significantly changed Egyptian society. By uprooting the old landed class and the foreign community, affecting a modest redistribution of their property, and extending educational opportunity to all Egyptians, Nasserism destroyed the rigid class structure that separated pasha from peasant, hastened a transition to industrialism, and gave Egypt sovereignty over its resources. The regime's repression of the Muslim Brotherhood in 1954 signaled its unwillingness to tolerate religious political activism; the secularization of Al-Azhar University further underlined the Nasserist ideal of separating mosque from state. Pan-Arabism, nonalignment, and anti-imperialism changed the way Egyptians looked at themselves and their neighbors. Egypt under Nasser became the leader of the Arab world, torchbearer for liberation from colonialism, monarchical rule, and Zionism.

In the wake of Sadatism, Nasser's reputation has undergone a substantial popular revival. Those who do consider themselves Nasserists by no means represent a unified front. Rather, many who today assert loyalty to a vision they call Nasserist are careful to set forth their criteria and to express their reservations about those aspects of Nasserism that they repudiate. Leftists, Marxists, and veterans of Young Egypt hark back to an era of statist control and regional leadership. Both Khalid Muhyi al-Din's Progressive People's Front and Ibrahim Shukri's Socialist Labor party hold separate celebrations for Nasser's birthday. Leading members of the circle known by Egyptians as the "centers of power," those whom Sadat purged in 1971 to great popular acclaim, formed a Nasserist party in 1985. Most are veterans of the intelligence service, and as such represent the face of Nasserism least favored by the population at large.

In late 1987 the Mubarak government indicted Nasser's son, Khalid, for his purported links to a secret military organization blamed for carrying out armed attacks against U.S. and Israeli diplomats in Cairo. Not inconsequentially, the movement is called Egypt's Revolution (Al-Thawrah al-Misriyah.) Khalid's cousin, Gamal Shawqi Abdel Nasser, and a son of Husayn al-Shafi'i have also been implicated. Khalid left Egypt, perhaps at the government's invitation. He threatened to return home to stand trial, but the matter has been suspended. It now appears unlikely that Gamal Abdel Nasser, in the guise of his son, will have his day in court.

Approbation for Nasser's memory is, however, by no means universal. Wafdists and others look back even further to an earlier era, the period of liberal parliamentary rule. In recent years Wafdists again celebrated the birthdays of Sa'd Zaghlul and Mustafa al-Nahhas—with a revived Wafdist Vanguard staging alternative celebrations—and the gallant stand of the auxiliary police against British forces in Ismailia in January 1952. Muslim Brothers, unsparing in their condemnation of the Nasser period, work toward the promulgation of legislation more consistent with their interpretation of Sharia law. Sadat coexisted uneasily with a reconstituted, semilegal Brotherhood; Mubarak has allowed the Brothers to sit in parliament, extending the carrot while striking out at more radical Muslim activists. These latter, primarily a younger generation of Islamic activists radicalized in Nasser's prison camps, consider the state apostate, its leadership illegitimate. Many pursue strategies of direct, often violent, confrontation with state authorities.

Those who describe Egypt have often used the metaphor of a nation in search of a hero (Nasser); of identity (Sadat); of political community (Safran); of political order (Smith); of dignity (Wynn).[10] In the early 1990s the search continues, the seekers embarked on a variety of paths, some looking backward and forward at once. In 1977, when the Wafd exhibited renewed signs of life, few might have imagined that the Sirag al-Din villa in Garden City would again become a political nerve center, that Sirag al-Din, Khalid Muhyi al-Din, Ibrahim Shukri, and a son of Hasan al-Hudaybi would constitute the leadership of the opposition, that a book purportedly by Muhammad Nagib, proclaiming, "I was the president of Egypt," would be sold at bookstalls throughout Cairo, that handbills with Nahhas's picture would be pasted on building walls and remain untouched, or that rudimentary portraits of Hasan al-Banna would be sold openly on downtown street corners. Or that the Wafdist faithful gathered outside party headquarters at a rally I attended in mid-1985 would openly chant in unison, "The Pasha speaks the truth" (*lil-basha al-haqq*), to a beaming Sirag al-Din, cigar still in hand, and that at least a few aged heads in an otherwise middle-aged audience would be wearing the tarbush.

Atop the system sits a president who is more technocrat than visionary, who expresses a dedication to progressing toward a more open political system but argues that stability requires the continued suspension of certain political and civil rights. In the eyes of most Egyptians, Hosni Mubarak may come closer than either Nasser or Sadat to fulfilling the role of benevolent strongman, the man who can maintain order and guide the nation toward "sound" democracy. At the same time he has often surrounded himself with close aides from military intelligence who strike many Egyptians as little different from those to whom Nasser turned after 1954. The opposition, however diverse its social orientation, stands united on issues of civil liberties and democratic rule. At the same time, frustration at the pace of political reform has at times produced a troublesome ambivalence toward the use of political violence, even among many who hope to constitute a new liberal establishment.[11] If the July revolution meant a "pragmatic march toward democracy," as Sadat defined it in 1955, it remains unfinished. The reexamination of the birth of Nasserism, the reassessment of both official and revisionist histories, and the debate over modern Egypt's competing political legacies speak as much to the future as to the past.

Notes

Prologue

1. See the obituary in *Akhbar al-Yawm,* 5 December 1953.

2. *Al-Misri,* 5 December 1953.

3. Clifford Geertz, "The Integrative Revolution—Primordial Sentiments and Civil Politics in the New States," in *Old Societies and New States,* ed. Clifford Geertz (Glencoe, Ill., 1963), pp. 105–57; Leonard Binder, "Egypt: The Integrative Revolution," In *Political Culture and Political Development,* ed. Lucien W. Pye and Sidney Verba (Princeton, 1965), pp. 396–449; Amos Perlmutter, *Egypt: The Praetorian State* (New Brunswick, N.J., 1974); Hamied Ansari, *Egypt: The Stalled Society* (Albany, 1986).

4. P. J. Vatikiotis, *The Egyptian Army in Politics* (Bloomington, Ind., 1961), p. 75. Vatikiotis remains committed to this view; see *Nasser and His Generation* (London, 1978).

5. British records are in the Public Records Office, London. United States records are in the National Archives, Washington, D.C. Selected State Department records are published in *The Foreign Relations of the United States (FRUS)* (Washington, D.C., Government Printing Office), cited hereafter by year and volume number.

6. Tawfiq al-Hakim, *The Return of Consciousness,* trans. R. Bayley Winder (New York, 1985). Among the most well known of the prison memoirs were those of Mustafa Amin, *Awwal Sanat al-Sijin* and *Thani Sanat al-Sijin* (Cairo, 1974 and 1975). For charges of Nasser's personal corruption, see Jalal al-Din al-Hamamsi, *Hiwar wara'a al-Aswar* (Cairo, 1972); for Nasserist response, Muhammad Hasanayn Haykal, *Li-Misr, la li-'Abd al-Nasir* (Beirut, 1976), and Fu'ad Matar, *Bi-Sirahah 'an 'Abd al-Nasir* (Beirut, 1975). For a general overview of "de-Nasserization," see John Waterbury, *Egypt: Burdens of the Past/Options for the Future* (Bloomington, Ind., 1978), pp. 235–56.

7. For the speech before the bar, see Fu'ad Siraj al-Din, *Limadha al-Hizb al-Jadid* (Cairo, 1977). Also see Donald M. Reid, "The Return of the Egyptian Wafd, 1978," *International Journal of African Historical Studies* 12 (1979): 389–415.

8. Rashed Barawy, *The Military Coup in Egypt* (Cairo, 1952); Gamal Abdel Nasser, *Egypt's Liberation* (Washington, D.C., 1955); Anwar al-Sadat, *Asrar al-Thawrah al-Misriyah* and *Qissat al-Thawrah al-Kamilah* (Cairo, 1965); the articles these books comprise were the basis for an English work, Anwar El Sadat, *Revolt on the Nile* (London, 1957); also widely cited by early scholars of Nasserism was Mohammed Neguib, *Egypt's Destiny* (London, 1955).

9. For mainstream Wafdist interpretation, see Ibrahim Faraj, *Dhikrayati al-Siyasiyah* (Cairo, 1984); for the young Wafdist perspective, see Ibrahim Til'at, "Ayyam al-Wafd al-Akhirah," *Ruz al-Yusuf*, serialized 23 August 1976–21 March 1977; Ahmed Abul-Fath, *L'Affaire Nasser* (Paris, 1962).

10. Hasan al-'Ashmawi, *Al-Ikhwan wa-al-Thawrah* (Cairo, 1977); Salah Shadi, *Safahat min al-Tarikh* (Kuwait, 1981); Mahmud 'Abd al-Halim, *Al-Ikhwan al-Muslimun: Ahdath San'at al-Tarikh*, 3 vols. (Alexandria, 1979, 1985).

11. Rif'at al-Sa'id, *Munazzamat al-Yasar al-Misri, 1950–1957* (Cairo, 1983); Anouar Abdel-Malek, *Egypt: Military Society* (New York, 1968); Mahmoud Hussein, *Class Conflict in Egypt: 1945–1970* (New York and London, 1973).

12. Sayyid Mar'i, *Awraq Siyasiyah*, 3 vols. (Cairo, 1978); Fathi Radwan, *Asrar Hukumat Yulyu* (Cairo, 1976), *72 Shahran ma'a 'Abd al-Nasir* (Cairo, 1985).

13. The best of these are Jean Lacouture and Simonne Lacouture, *Egypt in Transition* (New York, 1958), and Tom Little, *Egypt* (New York, 1958).

14. Richard Mitchell, *The Society of Muslim Brothers* (Oxford, 1969) is one early example; Joel Beinin and Zachary Lockman, *Workers on the Nile* (Princeton, 1987) is the best recent example of a work that traces developments through the period of military consolidation.

15. Ahmad Hamrush, *Qissat Thawrat Yulyu*, 5 vols. (Cairo, 1977–1984); 'Abd al-'Azim Ramadan, *Al-Sira' al-Siyasi wa-al-Ijtima'i fi Misr* (Cairo, 1975) and *'Abd al-Nasir wa-Azmat Mars* (Cairo, 1976).

Chapter 1

1. For popular contemporary accounts of the regime's last days, see Mustafa Amin, *Layali Faruq* (Cairo, n.d.); Ahmad Baha' al-Din, *Faruq Malikan* (Cairo, n.d.).

2. For the British occupation, see Afaf Lutfi al-Sayyid, *Egypt and Cromer* (London, 1968); Robert Tignor, *Modernization and British Colonial Rule in Egypt, 1882–1914* (Princeton, 1966).

3. For 1919, see 'Abd al-Rahman al-Rafi'i, *Thawrat 1919*, 3d ed. (Cairo, 1968); 'Abd al-'Azim Ramadan, *Tatawwur al-Harakah al-Wataniyah fi Misr min Sanat 1918 ila Sanat 1936*, 2d ed. (Cairo, 1983); Mu'assasat al-Ahram, *50 'Aman 'ala Thawrat 1919* (Cairo, 1969).

4. For politics of the parliamentary era, see Jacques Berque, *Egypt: Imperialism and Revolution* (New York, 1972); Marcel Colombe, *L'Evolution de L'Egypte, 1924–1950* (Paris, 1951); Marius Deeb, *Party Politics in Egypt: The Wafd and Its Rivals, 1914–1939* (London, 1979); Afaf Lutfi al-Sayyid-Marsot, *Egypt's Liberal Experiment, 1922–1936* (Berkeley, 1977); 'Abd al-'Azim Ramadan, *Tatawwur, 1918–1936* and *Tatawwur al-Harakah al-Wataniyah fi Misr min Sanat 1937 ila Sanat 1948*, 2 vols. (Beirut, 1968); Yunan Labib Rizq, *Tarikh al-Wizarat al-Misriyah* (Cairo, 1975).

5. Berque, *Egypt*, p. 519; also see pp. 524–27.

6. Stevenson no. 65, 23 May 1951, FO 371/90227/JE1914/16. Also see U.S. Ambassador John S. Badeau's recollections, *The Middle East Remembered* (Washington, D.C., 1983), pp. 117–21.

7. Mitchell, *Society*, pp. 306–20.

8. For February 1942, see Muhammad Anis, *4 Fibrayir fi Tarikh Misr al-Siyasi* (Cairo, 1982); Charles D. Smith, "4 February 1942: Its Causes and Its Influence on

Egyptian Politics and on the Future of Anglo-Egyptian Relations, 1937–1945," *International Journal of Middle East Studies* 10 (1979): 453–79.

9. Yunan Labib Rizq, *Al-Wafd wa-al-Kitab al-Aswad* (Cairo, 1978). Makram 'Ubayd's *Al-Kitab al-Aswad* has recently been reprinted (Cairo, 1984).

10. Robert Tignor, "Equity in Egypt's Recent Past: 1945–1952," in *The Political Economy of Income Distribution in Egypt*, ed. Gouda Abdel Khalek and Robert Tignor (New York and London, 1982), pp. 20–54; Eric Davis, *Challenging Colonialism: Bank Misr and Egyptian Industrialization, 1920–1941* (Princeton, 1983); Robert Vitalis, "Building Capitalism in Egypt: The 'Abbud Pasha Group and the Politics of Construction" (Ph.D. diss., Massachusetts Institute of Technology, 1988).

11. Doreen Warriner, *Land and Poverty in the Middle East* (London, 1948), pp. 34–35; Berque, *Egypt*, pp. 641–46.

12. Beinin and Lockman, *Workers;* Ellis Goldberg, *Tinker, Tailor, Textile Worker* (Berkeley, 1986).

13. Tariq al-Bishri, *Al-Harakah al-Siyasiyah fi Misr, 1945–1952*, 2d ed. (Beirut, 1983), pp. 185–229; Raoul Makarius, *La Jeunesse intellectuelle d'Egypte au lendemain de la Deuxième Guerre Mondiale* (Paris, 1960). For a study of one particular reform party, Ra'uf 'Abbas Hamid, "Hizb al-Fallah al-Ishtiraki, 1938–1952," *Al-Majallah al-Tarikhiya al-Misriyah* 19 (1972): pp. 169–214.

14. Rif'at al-Sa'id, *Tarikh al-Munazzamat al-Yasariyah al-Misriyah, 1940–1950* (Cairo, 1977); Selma Botman, *The Rise of Egyptian Communism, 1939–1970* (Syracuse, 1988).

15. Shadi, *Safahat*, pp. 29–33, 54–56.

16. For a more detailed discussion of the Wafd government, see Joel Gordon, "The False Hopes of 1950: The Wafd's Last Hurrah and the Demise of Egypt's Old Order," *International Journal of Middle East Studies* 21 (1989): 193–214.

17. Campbell to Strang, 14 January 1950, FO 371/80347/JE1016/17.

18. *Al-Ahram*, 17 January 1950.

19. Salah al-Din had served as a deputy in the Foreign Ministry and had played a key role in negotiations that led to formation of the Arab League. Farag, who was Nahhas's personal secretary, made a name for himself in the parliamentary organization. Muhammad al-Wakil, holding the new national economy portfolio, had been vice-president of the Senate (he was not related to Zaynab al-Wakil, Madam Nahhas).

20. Caffery no. 124, 774.00/1-3050.

21. Wardle-Smith to Clutton, 22 February 1950, FO 371/80348/JE1016/32. The amount, as Socialist deputy Ibrahim Shukri noted in parliament, nearly equaled the entire naval budget.

22. Caffery desp. 920, 774.00/4-2850.

23. Stevenson to Younger, 8 July 1950, FO 371/80349/JE1016/48.

24. Caffery desp. 1441, 774.00/6-2150.

25. Caffery no. 904, 18 December 1951, *FRUS 1951*, 5:441–42; no. 921, 774.00/12-2151.

26. Zaheer Masood Quraishi, *Liberal Nationalism in Egypt: The Rise and Fall of the Wafd Party* (Delhi, 1967), pp. 168–70; Ramadan, *'Abd al-Nasir*, pp. 59–60; Bishri, *Harakah*, pp. 358–59.

27. Ramadan describes the Wafd's internal organization as "based on a strange combination of liberalism and dictatorship ('*Abd al-Nasir*, pp. 51–53); also see Bishri, *Harakah*, pp. 306–7.

28. Deeb, *Party Politics*, pp. 68–70.

29. Sirag al-Din has been accused of falsifying his date of birth in 1936 in order to meet minimum age requirements to serve in parliament. For a short but valuable political biography see Donald M. Reid, "Fuad Siraj al-Din and the Egyptian Wafd," *Journal of Contemporary History* 15 (October 1980): 721–44.

30. Caffery desp. 1153, 641.74/11-1351.

31. Ahmad Abdallah, *The Student Movement and National Politics in Egypt, 1923–1973* (London, 1985), pp. 68–75; Bishri, *Harakah*, pp. 156–58.

32. Chapman-Andrews to Wright, 25 March 1950, FO 371/80348/JE1016/39; Caffery, who described Nahhas as "now partially senile," added, "We can get anything which we want from him if we are willing to pay for it. Whether we can afford the price depends on how badly we want a given object" (no. 1096, 9 November 1950, *FRUS 1950*, 5:323).

33. *Ruz al-Yusuf*, 8 July 1951, p. 3.

34. For internal Wafdist opposition to a restrictive 1951 press law, see Ibrahim Til'at, "Ayyam al-Wafd al-Akhirah," *Ruz al-Yusuf*, 14 February 1977, pp. 24–31.

35. Campbell to Bevin, 14 March 1950, FO 371/80348/JE1016/36.

36. Bishri (*Harakah*, p. 478) writes: "It was necessary for the government, if it wanted to regain the public trust it had lost, as party and a government, to adopt a public stance by which it could rally the masses. In this regard the only available option was the national cause, and the only tactic abrogation of the treaty."

37. Ibid., pp. 501–5. For the Muslim Brotherhood role, Hasan Duh, *Safahat min Jihad al-Shabab al-Muslim* (Cairo, 1979).

38. A document entitled "Legal and Political Implications of Establishing a Military Government in the Canal Zone" (FO 371/90117/JE10110/54) concluded: "On both legal and political grounds, it is most desirable that we should set up a military government only in the very last resort, on grounds of operational necessity, when all other means of maintaining the authority of the civil power have failed, and it is absolutely essential for the protection of our troops and their dependents." GHQ was given discretionary power to arrest any suspected commandos (Stevenson no. 419, 3 November 1951, JE10110/84). For plans to occupy Cairo and Alexandria, see WO 216/799, 27 December 1951.

39. Caffery no. 575, 26 October 1951, *FRUS 1951*, 5:410–11; no. 689, 12 November 1951, ibid., pp. 421–22; United States Army Military Attaché (USARMA) no. 567, 774.00(W)/11-1051 and no. 572, 11-1751; Stevenson to Eden, 6 December 1951, FO 371/90120/JE10110/167.

40. Stevenson to Eden, 6 December 1951, FO 371/90121/JE10110/167; Stevenson no. 1161, 8 December 1951, JE10110/177; WO 208/3956, no. 9, 16 January 1952; Bishri, *Harakah*, pp. 505–6, 509–15.

41. For the perspective of the British commander in Egypt, see Erskine Papers, WO 236/15, "Narrative of Events in the Canal Zone, October 1951–April 1952," the draft of a lecture presented at Camberly in November 1952; for Sirag al-Din's version, see his *Limadha*, pp. 56–57.

42. See "Report of the British Committee of Enquiry into the Riots in Cairo on the 26th January," FO 371/96873/JE1018/86. The concluding section, along with other relevant documents, is reprinted as appendices by Jamal al-Sharqawi, *Asrar Hariq al-Qahirah* (Cairo, 1985). Also Sharqawi's earlier *Hariq al-Qahirah* (Cairo, 1976), and Muhammad Anis, *Hariq al-Qahirah* (Cairo, 1982).

43. FO 371/96873/JE1018/86.

44. Foreign Office to Chancery, 11 March 1952, FO 371/96873/JE1018/86. Lacou-

ture and Lacouture, *Egypt,* pp. 108–9, credit 'Abd al-Fattah Hasan with trying to buy time and calm the mob.

45. Caffery desp. 355, 774.00/8-1351.

46. *Al-Sha'b al-Jadid,* 29 June 1951.

47. Ibid., 4 June 1951.

48. Caffery no. 823, 774.00/9-2951. Approximately ten thousand of twelve thousand copies of the leaflet, dated 12 September, were recovered by authorities.

49. Bishri, *Harakah,* p. 408; USARMA no. 161746Z, 774.00(W)/2-1651; Stevenson to Morrison, 8 September 1951, FO 371/90124/JE10114/7. For the communist press, see Rif'at al-Sa'id, *Al-Sihafah al-Yasariyah fi Misr, 1925–1948,* vol. 1 (Cairo, 1977) and *1950–1952,* vol. 2 (Cairo, 1982).

50. Abdel-Malek (*Egypt,* pp. 36–37) writes of "the national struggle that was on the point of turning into a genuine popular revolution with the massive support of the peasants." Hussein, *Class Conflict,* chaps. 2–3, advances a similar thesis.

51. Sir Cecil Campbell to Stevenson, 14 September 1951, FO 141/1433/JE1011/25/51. For a discussion of peasant political activity, see Nathan J. Brown, *Peasant Politics in Modern Egypt* (New Haven, 1990), especially chaps. 1, 5.

52. Mitchell (*Society,* pp. 84–88) credits Baquri and 'Ashmawi with maintaining the movement's morale and organization while it remained underground. Baquri has said that 'Ashmawi was clearly the most deserving to succeed Banna; see his "Malamih Dhikrayat, Yarawiha al-Shaykh Ahmad Hasan al-Baquri" *Al-Muslimun* (London), 1–7 June 1985. Also see Shadi, *Safahat,* pp. 80–83.

53. For lingering charges against Hudaybi, see *Al-Da'wah,* 5 January, 14, 28 September 1954.

54. Hudaybi's defenders argue that Farouk summoned him, and that he respectfully answered but struck no deals of any kind. See 'Abd al-Halim, *Ikhwan,* 2:494–96. For Elias Andraos's account (as reported to the British ambassador), FO 141/1433/JE1011/41/51.

55. Campbell to McNeil, 28 December 1949, FO 371/80347/JE1016/1.

56. Stevenson to Bowker, 26 January 1952, FO 371/96872/JE1018/55. Also see 96870/JE1018/1, dated 1 January.

57. Mahmud 'Abd al-Halim was among those who urged participation in the elections (*Ikhwan,* 2:543–44).

58. See the British report "The Rioting and Organised Fire Raising in Cairo on 26th January," dated 31 January 1952, cited in Sharqawi, *Asrar,* appendix, pp. 45–48.

59. Ibrahim Shukri, interview, 17 January 1985. For a critique of Husayn's leadership, see Bishri, *Harakah,* pp. 414–15.

60. Sa'id, *Munazzamat,* pp. 34–41.

61. Ibid., pp. 73–75.

62. Ibid., pp. 352–64; Fu'ad Mursi, interview, 4 May 1985.

63. Sa'id, *Munazzamat,* pp. 305–22.

64. Hilmi Yassin, interview, 5 December 1984.

65. For a detailed account of the "salvation ministries," see Joel Gordon, "The Myth of the Savior: Egypt's 'Just Tyrants' on the Eve of Revolution, January–July 1952," *Journal of the American Research Center in Egypt* 26 (1989): 223–37.

66. Western assessments of the threat of social revolution influenced the latter group. Bishri (*Harakah,* pp. 564–67) highlights a column by American journalist Stewart Alsop in which the author suggested the situation called for a despot. The column was reprinted in *Ruz al-Yusuf,* 27 November 1951.

67. The British recognized Mahir's talents but mistrusted him. Chapman-Andrews to Bowker, 8 April 1951, FO 371/90115/JE10110/12. For the program of Mahir's Egyptian Bloc, *Al-Ahram*, 3 February 1952.

68. Bishri, *Harakah*, pp. 558–59. A friend of Hilali's reported that Hilali had not left his home for two months and had rebuffed occasional attempts by Nahhas to contact him, refusing to answer the phone and pretending to be out (FO 143/1433/JE10110/20/51, 10 May 1951).

69. *Al-Ahram*, 1, 3, 4, 9, 19 February 1952; *New York Times*, 29 January, and 2, 4, 5, 11, 24 February; *Economist*, 9 February, pp. 324–25.

70. *Ruz al-Yusuf*, 11 February 1952, cover, p. 3, and 18 February, p. 3.

71. *New York Times*, 1, 2 February 1952; Stevenson no. 296, 3 February 1952, FO 371/96871/JE1018/47.

72. Bishri, *Harakah*, pp. 560–62; Musa Sabri, *Qissat Malik wa-Arba' Wizarat* (Cairo, 1964), pp. 77–82; *Al-Ahram*, 4, 5, 10, 24 February 1952.

73. Stevenson no. 438, 26 February 1952, FO 371/96872/JE1018/84; no. 452, 29 February 1952, 96873/89; Murtada al-Maraghi, *Ghara'ib min 'Ahd Faruq wa-Bidayat al-Thawrah al-Misriyah* (Beirut, 1976), pp. 133–35; *Al-Ahram*, 1, 2 March 1952.

74. *Economist*, 16 February 1952, p. 383; *Al-Ahram*, 2 March.

75. Bishri, *Harakah*, pp. 567–73; Musa Sabri, *Qissat*, pp. 90–115; *Al-Ahram*, 2, 3, 4, 7, 8 March 1952; *New York Times*, 3, 5 March.

76. *Ruz al-Yusuf*, 3 March 1952, p. 3.

77. Ibid., 24 March 1952, p. 3.

78. Caffery no. 26, 774.00/7-352. For Thabit and Andraos visits, desp. 2276, 5-1352 and no. 2292, 6-2752. Also Byroade to Acting Secretary of State, 3 July 1952, *FRUS 1952–1954*, 8:1828–29.

79. Caffery no. 47, 774.00/7-752.

80. *Al-Ahram*, 5, 6 July 1952; USARMA [unnumbered], 774.00(W)/7-1952. 'Abd al-Fattah Hasan had been released in late April, after he withdrew his case against the interior minister.

81. Fowler to Stabler, 21 July 1952, *FRUS 1952–1954*, 8:1837–38; weekly summary of 15–21 July, 774.00/7-2151.

82. Caffery no. 129, 774.00/7-2152.

83. Lacouture and Lacouture, *Egypt*, p. 126.

84. Caffery no. 77, 641.74/7-1452.

85. Maraghi, *Ghara'ib*, pp. 164–67.

Chapter 2

1. For the 'Urabi revolt, see Alexander Scholch, *Egypt for the Egyptians* (London, 1981); for statistics on the army, Eliezar Be'eri, *Army Officers in Arab Politics and Society* (New York, 1970), pp. 311–12, and Hamrush, *Qissat*, vol. 1, *Misr wa-al-'Askariyun*, p. 56.

2. Be'eri, *Army*, p. 313; 'Abd al-Wahab Bakr Muhammad, *Al-Wujud al-Biritani fi al-Jaysh al-Misri, 1936–1947* (Cairo, 1982), p. 99.

3. Muhammad, *Wujud*, pp. 31–42, 103–8.

4. Ibid., pp. 114–15, 128–31, 173–76.

5. Ibid., pp. 56–64.

6. 'Abd al-Wahab Bakr Muhammad, *Al-Jaysh al-Misri wa-Harb Filastin, 1948–1952* (Cairo, 1982), pp. 12–22, 172, 203–5; Muhammad, *Wujud*, pp. 290–300.

7. Muhammad, *Jaysh,* p. 22.

8. Hamrush, *Qissat,* 1:91.

9. Be'eri, *Army,* p. 496; also see pp. 316–19.

10. For Be'eri's list, see *Army,* pp. 481–98; the Hamrush list is compiled from *Qissat,* vol. 4, *Shuhud Thawrat Yulyu,* 2d ed. (Cairo, n.d.).

11. After the Palestine War, as part of its modernization program, the army encouraged officers to study nonmilitary subjects at the universities; see Muhammad, *Jaysh,* pp. 168–70.

12. Ibid., pp. 30–37.

13. WO 208/3965/14/54, 8-23 December 1954. Also see 3956/#1, App. B; 3960/42/53, 19 December 1953.

14. Be'eri, *Army,* p. 323.

15. Sadat's descriptions of nights around a campfire capture the spirit that infused the young officers; see, for example, *Revolt,* pp. 11–14.

16. Hamrush, *Qissat,* 1:99. For a British operative's account of Sadat's activities, A. W. Sansom, *I Spied Spies* (London, 1965).

17. Muhammad, *Jaysh,* pp. 295–97.

18. Ibid., pp. 296–300.

19. Ibid., pp. 302–4; Shadi, *Safahat,* p. 118.

20. Shadi, *Safahat,* pp. 116–17.

21. Ibid., pp. 118–19; Husayn al-Shafi'i, interview, 15 January 1985.

22. Kamal al-Din Husayn, "Qissat Thuwwar Yulyu," *Al-Musawwar,* 19 December 1975, pp. 22–25; Husayn Muhammad Ahmad Hamudah, *Asrar Harakat al-Dubbat al-Ahrar wa-al-Ikhwan al-Muslimun* (Cairo, 1985), pp. 32–33; Kamal al-Din Rif'at, *Harb al-Tahrir al-Wataniyah* (Cairo, 1968), pp. 35–36; Shadi, *Safahat,* pp. 128, 149.

23. Nasser, *Egypt's Liberation,* pp. 12–14.

24. See Mitchell, *Society,* pp. 98–99; Hamrush, *Qissat,* 4:36–37, 99, 145, 370; Hamudah, *Asrar,* pp. 44–48; Kamal al-Din Husayn, in Sami Jawhar, *Al-Samitun Yatakallamun* (Cairo, 1975), p. 33.

25. Rif'at, *Harb.*

26. Figures for the Brothers are uncertain; however, most of the 450 members arrested in January 1954 were from the army and police.

27. Hamrush, *Qissat,* 4:118–19, 136–38, 173–76, 179–80.

28. Khalid Muhyi al-Din, interview, 11 March 1985; Ahmad Fu'ad, in Hamrush, *Qissat,* 4:52–53; Sa'id (*Munazzamat,* p. 92) cites Hamrush's estimate of DMNL numbers.

29. Sa'id, *Munazzamat,* p. 88; Ahmad Hamrush, interview, 29 November 1984.

30. 'Abd al-Latif al-Baghdadi, *Mudhakkirat,* 2 vols. (Cairo, 1977), 1:35–36.

31. Interviews with Tharwat 'Ukashah, 25 April 1985; Husayn al-Shafi'i, 1 January 1985; Zakariya Muhyi al-Din, 11 April 1985.

32. For estimates of the numbers of Free Officers, see Be'eri, *Army,* p. 90. The figure of 70 to 90 that he cites from Nasser and Khalid Muhyi al-Din appears to be fairly accurate. Baghdadi, in an appendix to his *Mudhakkirat,* vol. 2, lists 337 officers who took part in the actual operation. Many of these were officers mobilized the night before; some are identifiable as Muslim Brothers.

33. Jamal Himmad, *23 Yulyu: Atwal Yawm fi Tarikh Misr* (Cairo, 1983), pp. 80–84. 'Abd al-Mun'im Amin, in Hamrush, *Qissat,* 4:244, corroborates Himmad's account of his joining, but Himmad's dates are correct. For the official version, see Sadat, *Qissat al-Thawrah,* pp. 79–81.

34. According to James P. Jankowski, *Egypt's Young Rebels: "Young Egypt,"* *1933–1952* (Stanford, 1975), pp. 118–19, Sadat, Kamal Husayn, Hasan Ibrahim, and Salah Salim were reportedly affiliated with the movement at one time. Vatikiotis (*Nasser*, pp. 33, 67) overstates the case for Ahmad Husayn's role in the ideological formation of the officers. Estimates for Young Egypt membership are from Jankowski, *Egypt's Young Rebels*, p. 31.

35. Hamudah (*Asrar*, p. 74) writes that Nasser told him he would try to enlist "non-religious officers on the condition they were courageous and able to keep secrets." Also see Kamal al-Din Husayn, in Jawhar, *Samitun*, pp. 33–34.

36. Rif'at, *Harb*, pp. 66, 72ff., 132.

37. Ahmad Anwar, in Hamrush, *Qissat*, 4:30–31.

38. For the Sirag al-Din transcript, see Salah 'Isa, *Muhakamat Fu'ad Siraj al-Din Basha* (Cairo, 1983), p. 52; for the official version, see Sadat, *Asrar*, pp. 268–83, or *Qissat Thawrah*, pp. 182–83; also see Baghdadi, *Mudhakkirat*, 1:40–41.

39. Himmad, *23 Yulyu*, pp. 152–56.

40. Baghdadi, *Mudhakkirat*, 1:45; Baghdadi, in Jawhar, *Samitun*, p. 21.

41. Rif'at, *Harb*, pp. 170–71.

42. Baghdadi, *Mudhakkirat*, 1:45.

43. Rif'at, *Harb*, pp. 173–75.

44. Hamrush, *Qissat*, 1:181.

45. Baghdadi, *Mudhakkirat*, 1:46–48; Himmad, *23 Yulyu*, pp. 32–41.

46. Muhammad Abu al-Fadl al-Gizawi, interview, 13 June 1985; Husayn, "Qissat," *Al-Musawwar*, 26 December 1975; Sadat, *Qissat al-Thawrah*, pp. 83–90; Himmad, *23 Yulyu*, pp. 163–70.

47. Husayn, "Qissat," *Al-Musawwar*, 26 December 1975; Baghdadi, *Mudhakkirat*, 1:49–54; Himmad, *23 Yulyu*, pp. 57–63.

48. Shadi (*Safahat*, pp. 146–48) insists there was no doubt from Nasser's words that he and the officers remained loyal to the Brotherhood. Also see Hamudah, *Asrar*, pp. 150–51.

49. Husayn, "Qissat," *Al-Musawwar*, 2 January 1976, pp. 30–32ff. 'Abd al-Ra'uf subsequently led forces against Ras al-Tin Palace in Alexandria on July 24–26.

50. Shadi, *Safahat*, pp. 150–59, 163–64; 'Ashmawi, *Ikhwan*, pp. 16, 19–20.

51. Shadi (*Safahat*, p. 169) says the meetings took place at the home of 'Abd al-Qadir Hilmi. Also see Kamal al-Din Husayn, in Jawhar, *Samitun*, pp. 34–40. The Brothers' role is absent from Baghdadi's memoirs; he says only that they were informed beforehand (*Mudhakkirat*, 1:48). Hamrush mentions their role only briefly in a short paragraph (*Qissat*, 1:196). Himmad, however, accepts Shadi's version (*23 Yulyu*, pp. 67–75).

52. Khalid Muhyi al-Din, interview, 11 March 1985; Ahmad Fu'ad, in Hamrush, *Qissat*, 4:52–53.

53. Note the similarity between the Free Officers' leaflet and the column by Ihsan 'Abd al-Quddus, *Ruz al-Yusuf*, 3 March 1952, p. 3, cited in the previous chapter.

54. Khalid Muhyi al-Din, interview, 11 March 1985; Hamrush, *Qissat*, 1:187.

55. Hamrush says that on several occasions when Nasser pressed for lists of DMNL officers, he rebuffed him; interview, 29 November 1984.

56. Khalid Muhyi al-Din, interview, 11 March 1985. Also see Hamrush, *Qissat*, 1:195–96; his personal account in 4:38–39; Ahmad Fu'ad, in 4:52–53; Sa'id, *Munazzamat*, p. 94.

57. Himmad, *23 Yulyu*, pp. 42–44.

58. Caffery desp. 864, 774.00/10-650; no. 479, 11–1250.

59. Sabri, *Qissat,* p. 189; Bishri, *Harakah,* pp. 580–81. 'Urabi's legacy provided a disturbing reminder to those who failed the public trust. In January 1952, when 'Abd al-Rahman al-Rafi'i, dean of modern Egyptian historians and vice-president of the Nationalist party, published his study of 'Urabi, *Al-Za'im al-Tha'ir Ahmad 'Urabi,* 3d ed. (Cairo, 1968), the Nahhas government saw fit to suppress it.

60. Stevenson no. 366, 13 February 1952, FO 371/96872/JE1018/66. Farouk also told Sir Ralph that one of these officers "had actually taken part in the mutinous demonstration by the auxiliary police on the morning of 26th January."

61. Minutes by William Morris, 22 July 1952, FO 371/96877/JE1018/207.

Chapter 3

1. *Al-Misri,* 24 and 25 July 1952.

2. For the initial contact to Mahir, see Sadat, *Qissat al-Thawrah,* pp. 123–24. According to Ihsan 'Abd al-Quddus (whom the officers approached to help contact Mahir), they considered two other candidates, Hilali and Baha' al-Din Barakat. Hilali they deemed too divisive, Barakat too inexperienced (*Ruz al-Yusuf,* 28 July 1952, p. 4). Mahir said he agreed with the decision to depose Farouk, and was glad the officers let him inform the king because the note they had addressed to Farouk was "very insulting" (Creswell no. 1132, 27 July 1952, FO 371/96878/JE1018/269).

3. According to Hamrush (*Qissat,* 1:225), those in favor of executing Farouk were Gamal Salim, 'Abd al-Mun'im Amin, and Zakariya Muhyi al-Din.

4. Soon after Farouk's departure the officers, fearing he made off with considerable quantities of state wealth, regretted not having searched his luggage. Mahir asserted that he dissuaded them from sending the navy in pursuit (Creswell no. 1130, 27 July 1952, FO 371/96878/JE1018/267).

5. Nahhas and Sirag al-Din arrived back in Egypt on the night of July 27 and went to visit general headquarters. The officers, suffering the fatigue of five sleepless nights were taken aback by Nahhas's abrupt entry and distrusted his motives. The meeting was perfunctory. Of the officers, only Nagib managed a show of congeniality (interviews with Ibrahim Farag, 18 February 1985; 'Abd al-Latif al-Baghdadi, 13 March 1985).

6. *Al-Ahram,* 31 July, 1 August 1952; Wahid Ra'fat, *Fusul min Thawrat Yulyu* (Cairo, 1978), pp. 36–37.

7. Stevenson no. 1166, 4 August 1952, FO 371/96879/JE1018/296.

8. Wahid Ra'fat, interview, 26 February 1985; Ra'fat, *Fusul,* p. 122; for the ruling, *Akhbar al-Yawm,* 2 August 1952.

9. Stevenson no. 1166, 4 August 1952, FO 371/96879/JE1018/296.

10. See Khalid Muhyi al-Din's contribution to a round table discussion, "Al-Yasar al-Misri Yuhawar Tawfiq al-Hakim," in *Al-Tali'ah* 11 (January 1975): 27.

11. For Barakat's account, "Safahat min Mudhakkirat Baha' al-Din Barakat," *Al-Musawwar,* 5 August 1977, pp. 30–31. Ibrahim Faraj (*Dhikrayati,* p. 84) says the Wafd also nominated 'Ali Shamsi and Husayn Sirri.

12. See the list of the "most important laws" passed in the first six months of army rule in *Al-Ahram,* 23 January 1953.

13. Barawi, in Ramadan, *'Abd al-Nasir,* pp. 325–28.

14. *Al-Zaman,* 4 August 1952.

15. Caffery no. 406, 774.00/8-2052; unnumbered, 774.00(W)/9-552.

16. Beinin and Lockman, *Workers,* pp. 421–26.

17. Minutes by Labour Attaché, 21 August 1952, FO 371/97078/JE2188/6.

18. Caffery no. 358, 774.00/8-1452; Stevenson no. 1228, 15 August 1952, FO 371/96880/JE1018/319; no. 1247, 20 August 1952, JE1018/327; *Al-Ahram,* 16 August 1952.

19. Stevenson no. 1222, 14 August 1952, FO 371/96880/JE1018/317; *New York Times,* 15 August 1952.

20. *Ruz al-Yusuf,* 11 August 1952, p. 3.

21. Ihsan 'Abd al-Quddus, ibid., 25 February 1952, p. 3.

22. Creswell no. 1090, 25 July 1952, FO 371/96878/JE1018/238; Stevenson no. 1188, 7 August 1952, 96879/JE1018/306.

23. Stevenson no. 1163, 2 August 1952, FO 371/96879/JE1018/293; no. 1235, 17 August 1952, JE1018/320.

24. Creswell no. 1131, 27 July 1952, FO 371/96878/JE1018/268; Stevenson no. 1163, 2 August 1952, 96879/JE1018/293; no. 1166, 4 August 1952, JE1018/296.

25. Murray, 12 August 1952, FO 371/96880/JE1018/328.

26. *Al-Ahram,* 11 August 1952. Two weeks later Mahir followed the junta lead, indicating that if party purges continued apace, elections might be held by January (*Al-Misri,* 24 August 1952).

27. Stevenson no. 1279, 27 August 1952, FO 371/96880/JE1018/336; Caffery no. 555, 774.00/9-552. Mahir appointed four new cabinet members: Mahmud Muhammad Mahmud (communications), Ibrahim Bayumi Madkur (reconstruction and rehabilitation, a new post), Mirrit Ghali (rural affairs), Nur al-Din Tarraf (municipal affairs, now separate from rural affairs). All but Tarraf, of the Nationalist party, were respected reformist independents.

28. Stevenson no. 1249, 20 August 1952, FO 371/96880/JE1018/326.

29. Muhammad Husni al-Damanhuri, in Hamrush, *Qissat,* 4:123–24.

30. Stevenson no. 1311, 5 September 1952, FO 371/96881/JE1018/352.

31. *Al-Ahram,* 6 September 1952; Ramadan, *Sira',* pp. 58–60.

32. The list included Fu'ad Sirag al-Din and two Sirag al-Din brothers, 'Uthman Muharram and Mahmud Ghannam (Wafd); Ibrahim 'Abd al-Hadi and Hamid Gudah (Sa'dist); Ahmad 'Abd al-Ghaffar (Liberal); Sayyid Salim (Wafdist Bloc); Nagib al-Hilali (independent); Hafiz 'Afifi, Yusuf Rashad, and Murtada al-Maraghi (palace).

33. Radwan, 72 *Shahran,* pp. 111–23.

34. Khalid Muhyi al-Din, interview 11 March 1985; Caffery no. 605, 774.00/9-852.

35. Nagib also assumed the portfolio for War. Other cabinet appointees were Sulayman Hafiz (interior), Ahmad Farag Tayi' (foreign affairs), Muhammad Sabri Mansur (commerce and industry), Fu'ad Galal (social affairs), Isma'il al-Kabbani (education), Ahmad Husni (justice), Husayn Abu Zayd (communication), Farid Antun (supply), Ahmad al-Baquri (pious endowments), 'Abd al-'Aziz 'Ali (rural and municipal affairs, the two posts again combined), Nur al-Din Tarraf (health), Murad Fahmi (public works), 'Abd al-'Aziz Salim (agriculture), 'Abd al-Galil al-'Imary (finance), Fathi Radwan (state).

36. Fathi Radwan, interview, 1 December 1984; Nur al-Din Tarraf, interview, 16 March 1985. For Radwan's story, also see Hamrush, *Qissat,* 4:274–80; Radwan, *Asrar,* pp. 103–19; for a refutation of his assertions, Ramadan, *'Abd al-Nasir,* pp. 32–40.

37. 'Abd al-Fattah Hasan, *Dhikrayat Siyasiyah* (Cairo, 1974), pp. 139–40, says that Nasser, in a meeting with the Wafd's purge committee, named Abu al-Fath as one of the new faces the junta wanted to see in a position of party leadership. Ibrahim

Til'at ("Ayyam," *Ruz al-Yusuf,* 13 September 1976, pp. 18–20) says that his and Abu al-Fath's names were proposed to Sirag al-Din, who agreed, but that they refused to accept promotion to the Wafd executive by fiat.

38. *Al-Misri,* 11 August 1952.

39. Stevenson no. 1166, 4 August 1952, FO 371/96879/JE1018/296.

40. *Al-Asas,* 5 August 1952; for Haykal, *Al-Misri,* 7 August and *Akhbar al-Yawm,* 16 August; for 'Ubayd, *Al-Ahram,* 24 August.

41. Mar'i, *Awraq,* 1:209–19. He was appointed party secretary on the new executive. Also see *Akhir Lahzah,* 3 September 1952; *Al-Ahram,* 4, 5 September; *Al-Balagh,* 6 September. Mahmud Ghalib, justice minister in the 1936 Nahhas cabinet, left the Wafd with the Sa'dist bloc in 1938. He served as a cabinet minister in six minority governments between 1938 and 1949. For Mahir's denunciation, *Akhbar al-Yawm,* 30 August; for Nagib, *New York Times,* 29 August.

42. *Al-Misri,* 9 August 1952. Also *Al-Balagh,* 3 August, for the Wafd's protestations of support. The purge committee consisted of Zaki al-'Urabi, Muhammad Salah al-Din, Mahmud Ghannam, 'Abd al-Fattah Hasan, and 'Abd al-Magid al-Ramli. The fourteen expelled included two other former ministers besides Hamid Zaki: 'Abd al-Latif Mahmud and Husayn al-Gundi.

43. The "honor" quotation is from *Al-Zaman,* 6 August 1952. For Hamid Zaki, see *Ruz al-Yusuf,* 11 August 1952, p. 6. Muhammad Salah al-Din responded the same day in *Al-Misri.* Also see the statement by Ahmad and Mahmud Himzawi, ibid., 6 August. Nahhas responded in the August 9 issue, and the Himzawis rebutted him the following day.

44. *Al-Ahram,* 11 August 1952. The following day Mahmud Ghannam, himself a target of the petition, asserted that he did not consider the perpetrators to be Wafdists.

45. Ibid., 4 September 1952. Gum'ah was representative of those party elders who could not match the energy or savvy of Sirag al-Din. As party secretary in 1947–1948, he continued to reside in provincial Tanta, traveling to Cairo only if pressing party business called. Sirag al-Din succeeded him in 1948. Their differences were not only personal; Gum'ah, the father of 'Aziz Fahmi, an intellectual leader of the Wafdist Left, tended to side with those pushing a reformist agenda.

46. *Akhir Lahzah,* 20 August 1952; *Al-Ahram,* 29, 30 August, 4 September.

47. Ahmad Abu al-Fath, interview, 1 March 1985. Ibrahim Farag (interview, 18 February 1985) stated that he, Nahhas, and others believed Nagib to be the junta's real leader through December 1952. This seems unlikely. Even if Abu al-Fath or Til'at did not reveal Nasser's role, Sirag al-Din could not have sat with the officers for six hours, as he did in mid-August to discuss land reform, and come away convinced Nagib was the real power.

48. *Al-Ahram,* 29 August, 3, 5 September 1952.

49. The most detailed description by a participant is Til'at, "Ayyam," *Ruz al-Yusuf,* 13 September 1976, pp. 16–21. Also see the Sirag al-Din interview in Hamrush, *Qissat,* 4:301. Ramadan (*'Abd al-Nasir,* p. 57) cites statements by Gum'ah and 'Abd al-Fattah Hasan in support of land reform, and contends, but without substantiation, that Nahhas and most of the parliamentary organization supported the measure.

50. *Al-Ahram,* 6 September 1952; Sirag al-Din interview in Ramadan, *'Abd al-Nasir,* pp. 354–56 for an explanation of his reservations. Also see Ramadan's interview with Rashad al-Barawi, ibid., pp. 327–28. Responding to the official history, many have argued that in fact the Wafd did support land reform in its September

1952 platform. See, for example, Ramadan, *Sira'*, pp. 56–57, and Sirag al-Din, *Limadha*, pp. 68–69. By this time, however, several important changes must be taken into consideration. For one, the measure had already been declared law. Second, by late September Sirag al-Din was in prison and had officially resigned from the executive. The political mood had changed and the parliamentary establishment was on the defensive.

51. Stevenson no 1228, 15 August 1952, FO 371/96880/JE1018/319.

52. Stevenson no. 1355, 11 September 1952, FO 371/96881/JE1018/374; *Al-Ahram*, 10 September 1952. The new prime minister also paid a courtesy visit on his predecessor; Mahir pledged continued support for the regime.

53. Hamrush, *Qissat*, 1:271, contends that "the sole merit" of the party law was the publication of these platforms.

54. *Al-Misri*, 9, 12 September 1952.

55. *Al-Ahram*, 11, 16 September 1952; *Al-Balagh*, 16 September.

56. Ibid., 23 September 1952.

57. According to a British report, the Wafd and the regime struck an eleventh-hour agreement allowing Nahhas to be listed as honorary president on the condition that he and several others not be listed as founding members (Creswell to Churchill, 14 April 1953, FO 371/102704/JE1015/61). For the Wafd statement, *Al Misri*, 28 September 1952.

58. See columns by Ihsan 'Abd al-Quddus and Ahmad Baha' al-Din in *Ruz al-Yusuf*, 29 September 1952, pp. 3, 5.

59. For Abu al-Fath, *Al-Misri*, 24–27 September 1952; for young Wafdists, *Al-Ahram*, 6 October.

60. *Al-Misri* or *Al-Ahram*, 30 September through 2 October 1952.

61. Payne no. 662, 774.00/10-752.

62. Radwan argued that the New Nationalists were a "popular" party as compared to the "royalist" old Nationalists (*Al-Ahram*, 11 November 1952). For the Socialist Peasants versus the Workers and Peasants, ibid., 10 October 1952.

63. For Democrats and Republicans, *Al-Ahram*, 6, 7, 16, 21 November 1952; for Socialists, 1 November. For the Democratic party, also see *Al-Mu'aradah*, first published in January 1952, especially issues of 16 October, 27 November.

64. *Al-Ahram*, 6, 7 November 1952. On January 1, 1953, the government presented its case against Tawil to the Wafd. He was charged with seven counts of abusing his power as a cabinet minister to promote and increase salaries and pensions (ibid., 1 January 1953).

65. *Al-Misri*, 21 November 1952.

66. Stevenson no. 100 saving, 6 October 1952, FO 371/96946/JE1108/1; Chancery to Department, 22 October 1952, JE1108/3.

67. USARMA no. 784, 774.00(W)/11–1452.

68. Interviews with 'Abd al-Muhsin Hamudah, a Wafdist Vanguard leader, 26 April 1985, and Hasan Duh, leader of the Brotherhood's student movement and unsuccessful candidate for president of the student union, 26 May 1985.

69. Enclosure in Caffery desp. 947, 774.00/11-1852.

70. *Al-Ahram*, 7, 8 December 1952; *Ruz al-Yusuf*, 15 December, p. 4.

71. The new supply minister was Sabri Mansur. Other new ministers were Mahmud Fawzi (foreign affairs), 'Abd al-Raziq Sidqi (agriculture), and 'Abbas 'Ammar (social affairs). Fathi Radwan became minister of state and Fu'ad Galal assumed the national guidance portfolio.

72. Wafdist delegates were Zaki al-'Urabi, Muhammad Salah al-Din, 'Abd al-

Salam Gum'ah, Taha Husayn, and 'Umar 'Umar; the Muslim Brothers appointed were 'Abd al-Qadir 'Awdah, Salih 'Ashmawi, and Hasan al-'Ashmawi.

73. See Hafiz's report to 'Ali Mahir, *Al-Ahram*, 29 August 1952.

74. Other former ministers charged were Muhammad al-Wakil, Husayn al-Gundi, and Hamid Zaki. The seven former deputies included Sirag al-Din's brothers, Gamil and Yassin, and his father-in-law, 'Abd al-'Aziz Badrawi.

75. Farag, *Dhikrayati*, pp. 110–11, is particularly harsh on Taha Husayn.

76. Ibrahim Farag, interview, 18 December 1985; *Al-Misri*, 14 December 1952; Creswell to Churchill, 14 April 1953, FO 371/102704/JE1015/61.

77. Caffery desp. 1140, 774.00/12-1352; Stevenson to Bowker, 16 December 1952, FO 371/96883/JE1018/465.

78. *Al-Misri*, 11 January 1953.

79. *Al-Ahram*, 10 January 1953.

80. See the editorial in *Al-Akhbar*, 14 January 1953, which notes the first official use of the word *revolution* in the decree creating the constitutional committee, "pursuant to aims of the revolution."

81. *Al-Misri*, 22 January 1953. The landowner, Yahya al-Badrawi 'Ashur, came from one of Egypt's wealthiest families and was a relative of Sirag al-Din.

82. Interviews with Ibrahim Farag, 18 February 1985, and Wahid Ra'fat, 26 February 1985.

83. *Al-Waqa'i' al-Misriyah*, no. 5a, 17 January 1953.

Chapter 4

1. 'Abd al-Muhsin Hamudah, interview, 26 April 1985; Stevenson no. 7 saving, 13 January 1953, FO 371/102703/JE1015/10.

2. *Ruz al-Yusuf*, 27 October 1952, p. 3, 17 November, p. 3.

3. Ibrahim Shukri, interview, 17 January 1985.

4. Caffery desp. 954, 774.00/11-1852.

5. *Al-Ahram*, 6 December 1952.

6. Ibid., 16 January 1953.

7. Stevenson no. 167, 28 January 1953, FO 371/102703/JE1015/32; Stevenson to Eden, 13 February 1953, 102704/JE1015/44.

8. 'Abd al-Salam Gum'ah sent a congratulatory telegram to the CCR on the occasion of Liberation Day. Musa Sabri, who interviewed Gum'ah (*Al-Akhbar*, 26 January 1953), concluded, "Thus a leader of the dissolved parties renounced party life (kafara bi-al-hizbiyah)." In late February Muhammad Salah al-Din, lecturing at the Press Club, advocated the return of party life. But "party factionalism," he said, "is perhaps not in the nation's best interest" (*Al-Misri*, 20 February 1953).

9. *Akhbar al-Yawm*, 3 January 1953.

10. *Ruz al-Yusuf*, 9 February 1953, p. 3.

11. Stevenson to Churchill, 21 May 1953, FO 371/102704/JE1015/77.

12. Consul General to Chancery, 20 April 1953, FO 371/102704/JE1015/67; Fortnightly Report, 13 May 1953, 102700/JE1013/21; 26 May 1953, JE1013/24.

13. Stevenson to Churchill, 1 June 1953, FO 371/102704/JE1015/81.

14. Beinin and Lockman, *Workers*, pp. 421–26.

15. Report of Labour Attaché, 4 August 1953, FO 371/102931/JE2183/15; 21 September 1953, JE2183/20. For other reports of labor trouble see FO 371/102931.

16. *Akhbar al-Yawm*, 18 July 1953.

17. For the text of the executive committee report in favor of a republic, see ʿAbd al-Rahman al-Rafiʿi, *Thawrat 23 Yulyu 1952–1959* (Cairo, 1959), pp. 68–73.

18. Caffery no. 2603, 774.00/6-1953.

19. *Al-Misri*, 22 May 1953; *Akhbar al-Yawm*, 20 June 1953.

20. Muhyi al-Din, who had been director of military intelligence, centralized all branches of the intelligence service under his command as interior minister. In 1955 military intelligence returned to the purview of the commander in chief of the armed forces; see Hamrush, *Qissat*, vol. 2, *Mujtamaʿ Jamal ʿAbd al-Nasir*, p. 130.

21. *Al-Ahram*, 21 September 1953.

22. Ibid., 26 November 1953, reported the purge of forty-five employees of the broadcasting administration, charged with corruption, influence peddling, and working while under the influence of hashish.

23. Mustafa Amin's obituary for *Al-Balagh*, "Great Newspapers Never Die," *Akhbar al-Yawm*, 26 December 1953; Husayn Fahmi, interview, 4 May 1985.

24. Caffery desp. 2201, 774.00/4-2053.

25. *Al-Ahram*, 9 April 1953; Wahid Raʾfat, interview, 26 February 1985. The presiding judge was a counsellor in the court of cassation. The other two civilian judges were counsellors in the Cairo appellate court.

26. For reports of charges against Sirag al-Din, *Al-Misri*, 28 May, 5 August 1953. The Egyptian press did not report his release; see *New York Times*, 4 August 1953.

27. Wahid Raʾfat, interview, 26 February 1985.

28. *Al-Misri*, 11 August 1953; also see 6 August.

29. Still, Farag claims in his memoirs (*Dhikrayati*, pp. 102–4) that he knew neither of the two men he defended, Yusuf Hilmi and ʿAbd al-Muhsin Hamudah. The latter insists (interview, 26 April 1985) that Farag knew him well.

30. Evans, 29 September 1953, FO 371/102706/JE1015/133.

31. Tilʿat, "Ayyam," *Ruz al-Yusuf*, 13 December 1976, pp. 23–25; 20 December 1976, pp. 18–23.

32. For ʿUbayd's speech, *Al-Ahram*, 24 August 1953; for a rebuttal, see the editorial by Hilmi Salam in *Al-Musawwar*, 11 September.

33. *Al-Misri*, 16 September 1953.

34. The eleven arrested were Mahmud Ghannam and Ibrahim Farag (Wafd); Ibrahim ʿAbd al-Hadi, Hamid Gudah, and Mamduh Riyad (Saʿdists); Karim Thabit, Ahmad al-Naqib, Kamal al-Qawish, and Prince ʿAbbas Halim (palace); Saʿd al-Din al-Sinbati and Ismaʿil al-Maligi (police; the latter was ʿAbd al-Hadi's brother). In addition to Nahhas and his wife, Hafiz ʿAfifi was placed under house arrest. After the trials began Ahmad ʿAbd al-Ghaffar (Liberals), Brigadier Hilmi Husayn, and Colonel ʿAbd al-Ghaffar ʿUthman (army) were arrested.

35. Hankey no. 1408, 6 October 1953, FO 371/102718/JE10118/14.

36. Kamal al-Qawish and Ahmad Naqib received the suspended sentences; ʿAbd al-Ghaffar ʿUthman, Ahmad Nasif, and Zaki Zahran received fifteen-year sentences; Hilmi Husayn lost his rank and property; Ahmad ʿAbd al-Ghaffar was fined; two defendants, Saʿd al-Din al-Sinbati and Ismaʿil al-Maligi, were found innocent.

37. Hankey no. 1473, 17 October 1953, FO 371/102718/JE10118/22; Creswell no. 278 saving, 2 November 1953, 102719/JE10118/35. Also see *Al-Ahram*, 12 October 1953, "The Man Who Set Dogs on the Partisans," and 23 November for stories of two accused collaborators, one of whom was hanged.

38. Conspiracy charges against ʿAbd al-Hadi, for example, rested on two visits paid him in Cairo by the British ambassador and several sightings of the ambassador's secretary's car on the defendant's street in Alexandria. ʿAbd al-Hadi testified that on

the occasion of the two Cairo visits the ambassador had sought him out, and both times he had been out. See Abul-Fath, *L'Affaire*, pp. 110–11.

39. Much of the trial transcript has been edited and published by Salah 'Isa, *Muhakamat*.

40. *Al-Ahram*, 3, 4 January 1954 for 'Ubayd; 7 January for Mahir, who declared "a plague on all your houses."

41. 'Isa, *Muhakamat*, p. 256.

42. *Al-Ahram*, 31 January 1954.

43. Ibid., 22 February, 8 March 1954.

Chapter 5

1. Stevenson no. 1240, 19 August 1952, FO 371/96884/JE1019/8.

2. Ahmad Sadiq Sa'd, a Workers Vanguard leader, asserted that Khamis had been a member of that movement but had drifted away prior to the strike (Sa'd, in Ramadan, *'Abd al-Nasir*, p. 299). Another Vanguard leader, Hilmi Yassin, disavows any affiliation between Khamis and the Vanguard (interview, 28 April 1985). ECP Secretary Fu'ad Mursi declares that Khamis was an ECP cadre, but denies he played any organizational role in the strike (interview, 4 May 1985).

3. Fu'ad Mursi, interview, 4 May 1985; Mursi, in Ramadan, *'Abd al-Nasir*, pp. 363–65; Sa'id, *Munazzamat*, pp. 391–98.

4. Hilmi Yassin, interview, 28 April 1985; Abu Sayf Yusuf and Ahmad Sadiq Sa'd, in Ramadan, *'Abd al-Nasir*, pp. 288–89, 297–98.

5. Rif'at al-Sa'id, in Ramadan, *'Abd al-Nasir*, pp. 329–30. A British report dated 7 August 1952, FO 371/96884/JE1019/6, notes the arrest of pamphleteers the previous week.

6. Hamrush wrote, "The revolution has crystallized and defined clearly its aims, so that it is no longer possible to differ about them" (*Al-Tahrir*, 17 September 1952, p. 4).

7. Ahmad Taha, in Ramadan, *'Abd al-Nasir*, p. 308; Caffery no. 383, 774.00/8-1852.

8. Interviews with Tharwat 'Ukashah, 25 April 1985, and Mustafa Bahgat Badawi, 19 March 1985.

9. Sa'id, *Munazzamat*, pp. 107–8.

10. USARMA no. 887, 774.00(W)/5-2953. For the decree banning the communist press, *Al-Waqa'i' al-Misriyah*, no. 7, 22 January 1953.

11. See relevant documents in the appendix of Sa'id, *Munazzamat*, pp. 403–78; for the self-criticism, dated 10 September 1953, p. 113.

12. Caffery desp. 1808, 774.001/3-953; Sa'id, *Munazzamat*, pp. 159–60.

13. *Al-Ahram*, 2, 6, 7 August 1953; *Al-Musawwar*, 14 August. Also see Caffery desp. 341, 774.001/8-653; desp. 1007, 10-2053.

14. Sa'id, *Munazzamat*, pp. 186–205.

15. Interviews with 'Abd al-Muhsin Hamudah, 26 April 1985, and Hilmi Yassin, 28 April 1985; Sa'id, *Munazzamat*, pp. 149–60; Ramadan, *'Abd al-Nasir*, pp. 86–87; Selma Botman, "Oppositional Politics in Egypt: The Communist Movement, 1936–1954" (Ph.D. diss., Harvard University, 1984), pp. 359–64.

16. Zaki Murad in Hamrush, *Qissat*, 4:170; Sa'id, *Munazzamat*, pp. 150–51; Ibrahim Farag, interview, 18 February 1985.

17. Sa'id, *Munazzamat*, pp. 152, 156.

18. *Al-Misri*, 9, 21, 28 August 1952.

19. Shadi (*Safahat*, p. 182), citing the account of ʿAbd al-Qadir Hilmi, says the meeting took place on July 30. Salih Abu Ruqayq (quoted in Jawhar, *Samitun*, p. 41) dates the meeting July 28. For the regime's first official account, see the decree dissolving the Brotherhood in *Al-Ahram*, 15 January 1954 (or any other daily).

20. See the treatment of Labib and the Brotherhood in a series of articles in *Al-Musawwar*, nos. 1464–1474, 1952, entitled "Hadhahi Hiyya Qissat Thawrat al-Jaysh min al-Mahd ila al-Majd." According to Mitchell (*Society*, p. 97 n.51), the author "is believed to be reporting Nasir's own recollections. . . . Their importance is greatly increased by the fact that they appeared early in the period of the revolution and are therefore uninhibited by the urgency of later events to minimize affiliations with the Brothers."

21. *Al-Misri*, 2 August 1952 (reprinted in Shadi, *Safahat*, pp. 347–56).

22. *Al-Misri*, 15 August 1952.

23. *Ruz al-Yusuf*, 18 September 1952, p. 8.

24. Mitchell, *Society*, pp. 108–9.

25. For various accounts of the dispute, see *Ruz al-Yusuf*, 15 September 1952, pp. 6f.; Radwan, *Asrar*, pp. 147–51, and 72 *Shahran*, pp. 117–18; Salah Shadi, in Jawhar, *Samitun*, p. 42; ʿAbd al-ʿAzim Ramadan, *Al-Ikhwan al-Muslimun wa-al-Tanzim al-Sirri* (Cairo, 1982), pp. 107–8; Mitchell, *Society*, pp. 107–8.

26. See Baquri's account, "Malamih," in *Al-Muslimun* (London), 22–28 June 1985. ʿUmar al-Tilmissani, *Dhikrayat, La Mudhakkirat* (Cairo, 1985), is highly critical of Baquri's collaboration with the Nasser regime.

27. *Al-Ahram*, 21 September 1952.

28. *Al-Misri*, 10–12, 16 October 1952; *Al-Ahram*, 3–4, 18 October; *Ruz al-Yusuf*, 29 September, p. 8.

29. It should be noted that Anwar al-Sadat was implicated in the Amin ʿUthman murder.

30. *Al-Ahram*, 16 November 1952.

31. *Al-Daʿwah*, 20 January 1953.

32. Mitchell, *Society*, pp. 110–11; Ramadan, *Ikhwan*, pp. 115, 389–94, the latter pages for a reprint of Salah Shadi, "Lamadha Yatajana al-Baʿd fi Taswir Jamaʿat al-Ikhwan al-Muslimin," originally published in *Al-Watan* (Kuwait), 17 December 1980.

33. ʿUmar al-Tilmissani (with the assistance of Salah Shadi), written response to questions submitted in May 1985.

34. Hasan Duh, interview, 26 May 1985; Jawhar, *Samitun*, pp. 44–47; Mitchell, *Society*, pp. 111–12.

35. For various accounts of the Hudaybi-Evans talks, see Mitchell, *Society*, pp. 112–14; ʿAshmawi, *Ikhwan*, p. 37; Shadi column from *Al-Watan* (Kuwait), 17 December 1980, reprinted in Ramadan, *Ikhwan*, pp. 394–98.

36. Stevenson no. 62, 15 January 1954, FO 371/108373/JE1054/1. Sir John Wilton, at the time assistant to Evans, told me it became possible to meet with the Brothers in the open only after the Free Officers' coup (conversation, 2 September 1985).

37. Mitchell, *Society*, pp. 114–15.

38. Ibid., p. 112.

39. What is meant by "elimination" is unclear; Caffery desp. 318, 774.00/8-553. For additional Hudaybi criticism of the regime, desp. 2849, 6-2353.

40. *Ruz al-Yusuf*, 16 March 1953, p. 7.

41. Mitchell, *Society*, p. 120.

42. For Salim, Evans, 28 September 1953, FO 371/102706/JE1015/132. A source close to Nasser reported that Nasser would most likely support Khamis Humaydah, assistant general guide, in a move to oust Hudaybi. (Caffery desp. 442, 774.00/8-1753)

43. Caffery desp. 1047, 774.00/10-2653. Also see Chancery to Dept., 5 November 1953, FO 371/102706/JE1015/146; Mitchell, *Society*, pp. 120–21.

44. In his testimony at Hudaybi's trial in November 1954, Khamis Humaydah declared that the general guide tried without success to oust Sanadi as early as February 1953. Humaydah accepted the court's assertion that the CCR first demanded dissolution of the secret organization in May 1953. 'Abd al-Qadir 'Awdah later testified that the demand was repeated in late June. See *Al-Jumhuriyah*, 23 November, 1 December 1954.

45. Duke to Allen, 17 September 1953, FO 371/102706/JE1015/129.

46. Nasser told Evans that after being taken to task by the Consultative Assembly, Hudaybi made personal overtures to him, 'Amr, and Salah Salim. Duke to Allen, 17 September 1953, FO 371/102706/JE1015/129.

47. *Al-Ahram*, 24 November 1953.

48. Chancery to Dept., 30 December 1953, FO 371/108319/JE1016/1. For the best account of the crisis, see Mitchell, *Society*, pp. 121–25; for personal accounts, Tilmissani, *Dhikrayat*, pp. 135–36, and Shadi in *Al-Watan* (Kuwait), 13 December 1980, reprinted in Ramadan, *Ikhwan*, pp. 399–407.

49. For example, Ramadan, *Ikhwan*, pp. 124–25.

50. Chancery to Dept., 30 December 1953, FO 371/108319/JE1016/1; Baghdadi, *Mudhakkirat*, 1:88.

51. For Riyad's account, Hamrush, *Qissat*, 4:402–3; for Hamudah, *Al-Jumhuriyah*, 23 November 1954. Also Ramadan, *Ikhwan*, pp. 128–29. Salah Shadi, who Hamudah said was present at the meeting when Hudaybi mentioned Nagib's overture, denies the meeting ever took place; see *Al-Watan* (Kuwait), 31 December 1980; reprinted in Ramadan, *Ikhwan*, p. 411.

52. Mitchell, *Society*, pp. 124–25; Shadi in *Al-Watan* (Kuwait), 31 December 1980, reprinted in Ramadan, *Ikhwan*, p. 407.

53. For accounts of the scuffle, Mitchell, *Society*, pp. 126–27; Hasan Duh, 25 *'Amman fi Jama'ah* (Cairo, 1983), pp. 62–63; Tilmissani, *Dhikrayat*, p. 131; WO 208/3/5/4, 16 January 1954.

54. For the decree and follow-up, *Al-Jumhuriyah*, 15, 16 January 1954 (the decree is reprinted in Shadi, *Safahat*, pp. 357–66); for British denials of contacts with Michael Creswell, Stevenson no. 68, 16 January 1954, FO 371/108373/JE1054/2; no. 15 saving, 19 January 1954, JE1054/7.

55. *Al-Ahram*, 26 January 1954.

56. *Al-Da'wah*, 16 February 1954.

57. Ramadan, *Ikhwan*, p. 135; Ramadan, *'Abd al-Nasir*, pp. 190–91.

58. Caffery no. 837, 774.00/1-2654; desp. 2180, 3-1354; Weekly Report, WO 208/3961/7/54.

59. Caffery desp. 1804, 774.00/1-3054.

Chapter 6

1. For military reform, *Al-Tahrir*, 17 September 1952, p. 4, 1 October, p. 5. The 10 percent estimate is based on a figure for 982 officers in the late 1930s (Muham-

mad, *Wujud,* p. 64), entering classes into the military academy of 300 through 1952, and a British estimate of 4,000 officers in late 1954 ("The Egyptian Army Corps and the Agreement," WO 208/3965, undated). For retirements, USARMA no. 788, 774.00(W)/11-2152.

2. The key figure in the August plot, a Corporal Shalabi, the regime presented as unstable. Shalabi was sentenced to fifteen years after a trial that received some media coverage. See Stevenson no. 1301, 2 September 1952, FO 371/96986/JE1203/5. For other cases, FO minutes, undated, JE1203/7; Caffery no. 1480, 774.00/12-1952; *Al-Misri,* 23 December 1952.

3. Ramadan, *'Abd al-Nasir,* p. 152.

4. In an oft-cited incident, Amin's wife told a gathering at the Auto Club that she had "the army in my right hand, the police in my left"; for Amin's defense of his wife, see 'Adil Hamudah, *Nihayat Thawrat Yulyu* (Cairo, 1983), pp. 267–68.

5. 'Abd al-Mun'im Amin, "'Abd al-Mun'im Amin, 'Udw Majlis Qiyadat al-Thawrah," *Al-Musawwar,* 16 April 1976, pp. 24–25. For the official history, Sadat, *Qissat al-Thawrah,* pp. 79–81, 135–36, 158–62. For Mahanna's account, "Sira' al-Ashhur al-Awwal min Thawrat Yulyu 1952," *Al-Musawwar,* 19, 26 March 1976, and "Ba'da Akthar min 20 Sanah Rashad Mahanna Yatakharaj 'an Samtihi," *Al-Ahrar,* 25 July 1983.

6. Ibrahim Shukri, interview, 6 March 1985.

7. See *Ruz al-Yusuf,* 20 October 1952, p. 13; full-page photo of Mahanna at Friday prayer in *Akhir Sa'ah,* 24 September; *Al-Ahram,* 14 October.

8. *Al-Misri,* 14, 15 October 1952.

9. *Al-Akhbar,* 15 October 1952 (reprinted in Hamudah, *Nihayat,* pp. 249–56).

10. Mustafa Amin, interview, 16 February 1985.

11. Hamzah Adham, in Hamudah, *Nihayat,* pp. 51–52. Much of the following discussion is based on testimony and interviews published by Hamudah.

12. Ibid., pp. 84, 86; Hasan, *Dhikrayat,* pp. 143–44.

13. *Al-Misri,* 20 January 1953.

14. Evans to Crossman, 5 February 1953, FO 371/102704/JE1015/43.

15. Amin, "Amin," *Al-Musawwar,* 16 April 1976, p. 25.

16. Hamrush is quoted in Hamudah, *Nihayat,* p. 103; on the other hand, Muhsin 'Abd al-Khaliq (pp. 106–13) protests the group's innocence.

17. Nasser initially sent Muhammad Abu al-Fadl al-Gizawi, a Free Officers comrade and artillery officer, along with the corps director to negotiate. They failed to placate striking officers, even after Gizawi drew his pistol and threatened to shoot the next man who voiced opposition. Finally, Nasser was compelled to address the strikers in person (interview with Gizawi, 13 May 1985).

18. *Al-Misri,* 22 January 1953; Damanhuri, in Hamrush, *Qissat,* 4:125–26.

19. *Al-Misri,* 31 March 1953.

20. Ahmad Hamrush, interview, 29 November 1984; Shawqi Fahmi Husayn, in Hamrush, *Qissat,* 4:180–81.

21. Siddiq, ibid., p. 481; Hamudah, *Nihayat,* pp. 60, 201, 222. In late December 'Abd al-Mun'im Amin told a U.S. embassy officer that the junta had decided to drop Siddiq because of his anti-west stand and growing signs of instability (McClintock no. 1259, 774.00/12-2952). However, by this time Amin was also on his way out.

22. 'Abd al-Mun'im Amin, in Hamrush, *Qissat,* 4:253; *Al-Musawwar,* 16 April 1976, pp. 24–25.

23. For a report on morale in the officer corps, see Evans, 29 September 1953, FO 371/102706/JE1015/133.

24. Baghdadi, *Mudhakkirat*, 1:78. Kamal Husayn seconds Baghdadi's assertion that he (Baghdadi) opposed the appointment of a CCR member as commander in chief and discusses the uncomfortable situation created within the junta by 'Amr's promotion ("Qissat," *Al-Musawwar*, 2 January 1976, pp. 30–32).

25. USARMA no. 850, 774.00(W)/3-2753.

26. USARMA no. 909, 774.00(W)/7-353; Baghdadi, *Mudhakkirat*, 1:77.

27. *Al-Misri*, 18 December 1953.

28. "Kayfa Dabbarna al-Inqilab," *Al-Tahrir*, 1 October 1952, pp. 8–11, 15 October, pp. 10–12; Mustafa Bahgat Badawi, interview, 19 March 1985.

29. *Al-Misri*, 31 December 1952, 24 February 1953; *Akhbar al-Yawm*, 7 February (for an early caricature), 21 February 1953. Haykal's coverage, ibid., beginning April 11.

30. 'Abd al-Latif al-Baghdadi, interview, 13 March 1985.

31. *Al-Musawwar*, 23 July 1953.

32. *Al-Misri*, 28 November 1953.

33. Sadat, *Qissat al-Thawrah*, pp. 221–29.

34. *Kalimati lil-Tarikh* (Cairo, 1975), originally published in Beirut, is widely held to have been written by Hamrush based on long interviews he held; see the Nagib interview in Hamrush, *Qissat*, 4:420–46. Among the claims made in the more recent book, *Kuntu Ra'isan li-Misr* (Cairo, 1984), are that Nagib named the Free Officers (p. 91), participated in the attempt on the life of General Sirri 'Amr (p. 97), and suggested the coup be delayed twenty-four hours (pp. 108–9).

35. Himmad, *23 Yulyu*, p. 33.

36. Nagib asserts that only Nasser, 'Amr, Khalid Muhyi al-Din, and Siddiq opposed the party reorganization law (*Kalimati*, p. 78; Hamrush, *Qissat*, 4:432). He declares that he initially opposed land reform (*Kunta Ra'isan*, pp. 157–60), and that he opposed the death sentences for the two Kafr al-Dawwar workers (*Kalimati*, pp. 16–17). However, Khalid Muhyi al-Din says only he (Khalid) and Siddiq opposed the sentences (Hamrush, *Qissat*, 4:149). For Nagib's antipathy for Mahanna, see *Kalimati*, pp. 82–84, and *Kuntu Ra'isan*, pp. 154–56. The latter account is more sympathetic to Mahanna. For Mahanna's account, see his interview in *Al-Ahrar*, 25 July 1983. Also, Salah al-Shahid, *Dhikrayati fi 'Ahdayn* (Cairo, 1976), p. 254.

37. Lacouture and Lacouture, *Egypt*, p. 180.

38. Stevenson no. 1569, 21 October 1952, FO 371/96882/JE1018/421.

39. See the role attributed to Nagib in the coup in *Al-Misri*, 3 October 1952.

40. FO 371/102704/JE1015/57; Caffery no. 2134, 641.74/3-2553.

41. Lord Reading, 19 August 1953, FO 371/102705/JE1015/110. For more general reports of internal CCR strife surrounding declaration of the republic, Caffery no. 2603, 774.00/6-1953; Dulles, 6-2353; Nagib, *Kalimati*, pp. 95–96; Nagib, in Hamrush, *Qissat*, 4:433–34.

42. Pelham to Marquess of Salisbury, 31 August 1953, FO 371/102729/JE10325/1; also see Lacouture and Lacouture, *Egypt*, pp. 180–81.

43. Khalid Muhyi al-Din, in Hamrush, *Qissat*, 4:152–53; Nagib, *Kalimati*, p. 99.

44. Evans, 29 September 1953, FO 371/102706/JE1015/133; Lacouture and Lacouture, *Egypt*, p. 181; Muhammad Riyad, in Hamrush, *Qissat*, 4:402; Nagib, *Kalimati*, pp. 100–101, 179.

45. The *New York Times* on 3 January 1953 described Nasser as "one of Naguib's closest advisers," on 18 January as his "right-hand man," and on 7 May as the Free Officers' movement's original leader. In late March Jefferson Caffery (desp. 1959, 774.00/3-2653) described Nasser as the number-one man in the country, and reported

that he clearly dominated the revolutionary command. The British remained a step behind: writing almost a month later, Michael Creswell (Creswell to Churchill, 21 April 1953, FO 371/102704/JE1015/64) indicated that Nasser's role as Nagib's right hand was becoming more apparent.

46. Baghdadi, *Mudhakkirat*, 1:87–88.

47. The CCR reportedly offered the post to ʿAli Mahir, who refused (Fortnightly Report, 3 December 1953, FO 371/102702/JE1013/63).

48. Baghdadi, *Mudhakkirat*, 1:92ff.

49. Ibid., pp. 91, 96–97; Khalid Muhyi al-Din, in Ramadan, *ʿAbd al-Nasir*, pp. 313–14.

50. *Al-Misri*, 28 November, 21 December 1953.

Chapter 7

1. *Al-Ahram*, 25–27 February 1954.

2. Interviews with Husayn al-Shafiʿi, 15 January 1985, and Muhammad Fayiq, 19 May 1985; Ramadan, *ʿAbd al-Nasir*, pp. 168–70.

3. Husayn ʿUrfa and Kamal Rifʿat, in Hamrush, *Qissat*, 4:123–24, 323–27; Nagib, *Kalimati*, pp. 193–96; Ramadan, *ʿAbd al-Nasir*, p. 171.

4. Gizawi had gone with Nasser a year before to confront angry artillery officers; Fayiq, who had been one of them, now accompanied Nasser to confront the armor officers.

5. Tharwat ʿUkashah, interview, 25 April 1985.

6. For Khalid's account of one occasion on which he resigned, in March 1953, see *Al-Ahali*, 24 July 1985.

7. Khalid Muhyi al-Din, in Hamrush, *Qissat*, 4:154; Nagib, *Kalimati*, p. 182, and *Kuntu Ra'isan*, pp. 214–15.

8. Caffery no. 1022, 774.00/3-254.

9. Ibid.

10. Baghdadi, *Mudhakkirat*, 1:105–10; Khalid Muhyi al-Din, in Ramadan, *ʿAbd al-Nasir*, pp. 314–16.

11. Caffery no. 996, 774.00/2-2854; no. 1001, 2-2854; Fortnightly Report, 11 March 1954, FO 371/108312/JE1013/12; Mitchell, *Society*, p. 129; Baghdadi, *Mudhakkirat*, 1:111–12.

12. Ibrahim Shukri, interview, 6 March 1985. A government spokesperson listed those arrested as forty-five Muslim Brothers, twenty Socialists, five Wafdists, four communists, fifteen workers, and twenty-seven others (*Al-Misri*, 3 March 1954).

13. Baghdadi, *Mudhakkirat*, 1:118–22, for a detailed account of CCR meetings in which the decrees were discussed.

14. Ibid., pp. 128–29; Caffery desp. 2207, 774.00/3-1654.

15. *Al-Misri*, 7 March 1954; Muhsin ʿAbd al-Khaliq, in Hamudah, *Nihayat*, p. 91.

16. *Al-Jumhuriyah*, 10 March 1954. Husayn al-Shafiʿi recalled the meeting vividly in an interview, 15 January 1985.

17. *Al-Qahirah*, 17, 18 March 1954; *Al-Misri*, 18 March, for Salim's warning.

18. *Akhbar al-Yawm*, 20 March 1954; *Al-Ahram*, same date, for news of the CCR-sponsored party.

19. For an example of regime rumor mongering, see Sadat's column "Haqa'iq" (Some truths), *Al-Jumhuriyah*, 10 March 1954.

20. Caffery desp. 2262, 774.00/3-2354; Baghdadi, *Mudhakkirat*, 1:143–44. The bombs exploded at the Muhammad 'Ali Club, Groppi's tearoom, the clock tower and amphitheater at Cairo University, the telegraph office of the Cairo Central Railroad, and the Ma'adi train station (*New York Times*, 21 March 1954).

21. For a detailed account of CCR discussion of the March 25 decree, see Baghdadi, *Mudhakkirat*, 1:145–55.

22. For the parties' activities, see the major dailies for 27 March.

23. *Al-Ahram*, 27 March 1954.

24. *Al-Jumhuriyah*, 23 March 1954.

25. Interviews with Mustafa Amin, 16 February 1985, and Ahmad Baha' al-Din, 4 December 1984.

26. Ramadan, *Ikhwan*, pp. 139–40; for Hudaybi's statement, *Al-Ahram*, 27 March 1954.

27. Ibrahim al-Tahawi, in Hamrush, *Qissat*, 4:17.

28. Ramadan, *'Abd al-Nasir*, pp. 211–17; Husayn 'Urfa, in Hamrush, *Qissat*, 4:135–36.

29. Ramadan, *'Abd al-Nasir*, pp. 196–206; Ibrahim al-Tahawi and 'Abd Allah Tu'ayma, ibid., pp. 291–93, 303–4; Tahawi, in Hamrush, *Qissat*, 4:17–18. Sawi's charges that Yusuf Siddiq asked that he bring transport workers into the streets against the CCR are treated in detail in Ramadan, "Muzaharat Mars Dabbaraha Yusuf Siddiq wa-Muhammad Najib," and Khalid Muhyi al-Din, "Lam Uqabil al-Sawi athna'a Azmat Mars," both in *Ruz al-Yusuf*, 5 January 1976, pp. 16–17, 30–36.

30. Stevenson no. 439, 29 March 1954, FO 371/108583/JE2187/5; minutes by Millard, 1 April 1954, JE2187/8; Marshall to Greenough, 15 April 1954, JE2187/10. For union activity against the regime, Beinin and Lockman, *Workers*, pp. 442–43.

31. *New York Times*, 31 March–4 April 1954.

32. Khalid Muhyi al-Din, interview, 15 July 1985. Khalid was one who advised Nagib; for Nagib contacts to politicians, see *Al-Jumhuriyah*, 26 March 1954.

33. Ramadan, *Ikhwan*, p. 129.

34. Muhammad Riyad, in Hamrush, *Qissat*, 4:404–5.

35. *Al-Akhbar*, 6, 12 April 1954; *Akhir Sa'ah*, 21 April, pp. 6–7.

36. *Al-Jumhuriyah*, 10 April 1954. Sadat borrowed his title from the editor of *Al-Jumhur al-Misri*, Abu al-Khayr Nagib, who had written several editorials that had particularly annoyed the CCR.

37. Fortnightly Report, 29 July 1954, FO 371/108313/JE1013/32.

38. *Akhbar al-Yawm*, 24 April, 22 May, 5 June 1954.

39. Khalid Muhyi al-Din, interview, 15 July 1985; Muhyi al-Din, in Ramadan, *'Abd al-Nasir*, p. 320; for conciliatory statements, *Al-Ahram* and *Al-Misri*, 7 March 1954.

40. USARMA no. 1079, 774.00(W)/4-954; *Al-Jumhuriyah*, 8 April 1954.

41. Fortnightly Report, 6 May 1954, FO 371/108313/JE1013/19. For the trials, *Al-Ahram*, 23 June 1954.

42. Fortnightly Report, 15 July 1954, FO 371/108313/JE1013/30.

43. WO 208/3965/9/54, 29 September–12 October 1954.

44. "The Egyptian Army Corps and the Agreement," WO 208/3965, undated.

45. After Nasser formed his cabinet on April 18, seven CCR officers held posts: Zakariya Muhyi al-Din (interior), Shafi'i (war), Salah Salim (national guidance), Gamal Salim (communication), Kamal Husayn (social affairs), Baghdadi (municipal affairs), Ibrahim (state for republican affairs). On September 1 'Amr became war minister, Sadat minister of state; Shafi'i shifted to social affairs, and Husayn became education

minister. Gamal Salim, appointed deputy prime minister, yielded communications to a civilian, Fathi Radwan.

46. Baghdadi, *Mudhakkirat*, 1:171–73.

47. The palace maintained this special fund to bankroll journalists in an attempt to buy loyalty. Mahmud ʿAbd al-Munʿim Murad, interview, 21 February 1985; Musa Sabri, interview, 18 July 1985.

48. *Al-Ahram*, 5, 10–20 May 1954.

49. Stevenson to Eden, 15 April 1954, FO 371/108316/JE1015/29; Stevenson no. 62, 10 May 1954, 108317/JE1015/37; Baghdadi, *Mudhakkirat*, 1:167–69.

50. Fortnightly Reports, 26 August 1954, FO 371/108314/JE1013/36; 9 September, JE1013/38; 23 September, JE1013/40.

51. *New York Times*, 26 September 1954; Fortnightly Reports, 23 September, FO 371/108314/JE1013/40; 7 October, JE1013/42; 19 November, JE1013/48.

52. Marshall, 3 April 1954, FO 371/108583/JE2187/9.

53. *Al-Jumhuriyah*, 28 March 1954; Caffery desp. 2429, 774.00/4-1054.

54. Husayn al-Shafiʿi, interview, 15 January 1985.

55. Marʿi, *Awraq*, 1:298–304.

56. *Al-Ahram*, 14, 30 April, 22 August 1954; Caffery desp. 2467, 774.00/4-1554.

57. USARMA no. 1158, 774.00(W)/7-3054; Caffery desp. 161, 774.00/7-2854; Fortnightly Report, 29 July 1954. FO 371/108313/JE1013/32.

58. Fortnightly Report, 12 August 1954, FO 371/108314/JE1013/34; Caffery no. 154, 641.74/8-354.

Chapter 8

1. *Akhbar al-Yawm*, 6 March 1954; *Al-Jumhuriyah*, 2, 6 March.

2. *Al-Misri*, 16 March 1954.

3. *Al-Ahram*, 24 March 1954; *Al-Jumhur al-Misri*, 22 March.

4. *Al-Misri*, 6, 8 March 1954; *Al-Tahrir*, 23 March, pp. 14–17.

5. *Ruz al-Yusuf*, 5 October 1953, p. 4, 21 September, p. 13.

6. *Akhbar al-Yawm*, 1 August, 21 November 1953; Ahmad Baha' al-Din, in *Ruz al-Yusuf*, 24 August, pp. 24ff., 21 December, p. 5.

7. Ibid., 14 December 1953; also see the article by Ahmad Baha' al-Din, 30 November, p. 5.

8. *Al-Jumhuriyah*, 17 March 1954.

9. *Al-Misri*, 19 March 1954.

10. *Al-Ahram*, 15, 18, 19, 22 March 1954; *Al-Misri*, 12 March.

11. Ibid., 13 March 1954.

12. Ibid., 3 August, 12, 15 December 1952.

13. See *Al-Ahram* or *Al-Misri*, 13–20 March 1954.

14. *Al-Jil al-Jadid*, 22 March 1954, pp. 4–8.

15. *Al-Misri*, 14 March 1954; *Al-Jumhuriyah*, 18 March.

16. For Husayn, *Al-Jumhuriyah*, 16, 18 March 1954; for Shafiq, *Ruz al-Yusuf*, 22 March, pp. 10ff.

17. *Al-Tahrir*, 30 March 1954, p. 3.

18. Saʿid, *Munazzamat*, p. 393.

19. Ibid., pp. 337–39.

20. Ibid., pp. 173–76.

21. Ramadan, *ʿAbd al-Nasir*, pp. 95–99, and his interviews with Ahmad Taha

(pp. 309–10), Zaki Murad (pp. 343–45), and 'Abd al-Mun'im al-Ghazzali (pp. 351–52).

22. Ahmad Taha, a signatory, insists that the acting leadership of DMNL misread the March crisis: "At the time our colleagues were calling for the return of bourgeois democracy, despite the fact that this would allow the old [regime] to return" (quoted in Ramadan, *'Abd al-Nasir*, p. 310).

23. Yusuf Siddiq, in Hamrush, *Qissat*, 4:481–82.

24. *Al-Misri*, 24 March 1954.

25. *Al-Ahram*, 26 March 1954.

26. *Al-Misri*, 26 March 1954; *Ruz al-Yusuf*, 29 March, pp. 8ff.

27. *Al-Ahram*, 20 March 1954.

28. *Ruz al-Yusuf*, 22 March 1954, pp. 3–5.

29. Ibrahim al-Tahawi, in Ramadan, *'Abd al-Nasir*, p. 294.

30. Caffery desp. 2292, 774.00/3-2554.

31. *Al-Misri*, 26–27 March 1954.

32. *Ruz al-Yusuf*, 29 March 1954, pp. 3–5.

33. *Akhbar al-Yawm*, 6, 20 March 1954.

34. Ibid., 20 March 1954.

35. *Al-Jumhuriyah*, 13, 17 March 1954.

36. *Al-Akhbar*, 1 March 1954.

37. Ibid., 15 March 1954.

38. *Al-Ahram*, 23 March 1954.

39. Ibid., 22 March 1954.

40. *Al-Musawwar*, 2 April 1954, p. 10.

41. Ahmad Baha' al-Din, interview, 4 December 1985.

42. For Mahir's statement, *New York Times*, 18 March 1954; for his denial, *Al-Ahram*, 21 March.

43. Duke to Allen, 27 January 1953, FO 371/102908/JE1461/3; Ibrahim al-Tahawi, in Ramadan, *'Abd al-Nasir*, pp. 293–94. For favorable press coverage of 'Abbud's contribution to national development, see *Al-Tahrir*, 1 November 1952, pp. 26–28, 8 April 1953, p. 44; *Ruz al-Yusuf*, 19 October 1953, pp. 32–33. For 'Abbud's role in Egyptian development prior to the coup, Vitalis, "Building Capitalism."

44. *Ruz al-Yusuf*, 5 April 1954, p. 5. For Abu Hurayra (d. A.H. 57 or 58/A.D. 676–78), see *Shorter Encyclopedia of Islam* (Leiden, 1953), pp. 10–11, or any other edition.

45. Muhammad Hasanayn Haykal, *Azmat al-Muthaqqafin* (Cairo, 1961).

Chapter 9

1. Bradford Perkins, "Unequal Partners: The Truman Administration and Great Britain," in *The Special Relationship*, ed. William Roger Louis, pp. 43–64 (Oxford, 1986); Bruce R. Kuniholm, *The Origins of the Cold War in the Near East* (Princeton, 1980).

2. William Roger Louis, *The British Empire in the Middle East, 1945–1951* (Oxford, 1984), pp. 715, 721. For background on the Canal base see pp. 9–13; for the 1936 treaty, pp. 229–31. British strategists held 100,000 men to be the optimal base force; War Office analysts in 1949 cited 25,000 as the minimum (WO 259/8, 31 August 1949).

3. See, for example, the cable from Ambassador Campbell to Foreign Secretary Bevin dated 14 March 1950 (FO 371/80348/JE1016/36).

4. Louis, *British Empire*, pp. 721, 723, 726–35. For Churchill, see the published diaries of Anthony Eden's private secretary, Evelyn Shuckburgh, *Descent to Suez, Diaries, 1951–56* (London, 1986), pp. 112, 121, 127, 150.

5. Louis, *British Empire*, pp. 721–25; Caffery no. 1521, 31 December 1950, *FRUS 1950*, 5:332–34; Shuckburgh, *Descent*, pp. 119, 148, 229–30.

6. Louis, *British Empire*, pp. 726–30; Caffery no. 860, 12 February 1951, *FRUS 1951*, 5:343–44.

7. Louis, *British Empire*, pp. 691–98, 717; Gifford no. 2856, 611.74/12-2251; Secretary of State no. 3566, 28 January 1952, *FRUS 1952–1954*, 8:1758–59.

8. Cited in Gifford no. 3259, 28 January 1952, *FRUS 1952–1954*, 8:1756–57.

9. Stevenson no. 452, 29 February 1952, FO 371/96873/JE1018/89. For British urging palace to draw Mahir away from the Wafd, no. 296, 3 February 1952, 96871/JE1018/47.

10. Stevenson to Eden, 10 March 1952, FO 371/96874/JE1018/108.

11. Bruce no. 8, 2 February 1952, *FRUS 1952–54*, 8:1826–27.

12. Louis, *British Empire*, p. 728; WO 208/3956/#4, 12 December 1951.

13. Creswell no. 1074, 23 July 1952, FO 371/96877/JE1018/219; no. 1084, 24 July 1952, 96878/JE1018/226; no. 1083, 24 July, JE1018/231; no. 1090, 25 July, JE1018/238; no. 1091, 25 July, JE1018/239.

14. Creswell no. 1077, 24 July 1952, FO 371/96877/JE1018/221; Minutes, 25 July 1952, 96878/JE1018/240. For details of "Rodeo" plans to occupy Egypt in case of civil disorder, see WO 216, files 433, 799, 867.

15. Stevenson recommended that the junta appoint a member of the royal family as regent (Stevenson no. 1145, 29 July 1952, FO 371/96879/JE1018/279.

16. Acheson to Johnson, 27 January 1951, OSD CD 92 092, Middle East 1951, RG 330.

17. Louis, *British Empire*, pp. 700–707, 714, Caffery no. 1001, 1 April 1951, *FRUS 1951*, 5:352–55; Peter L. Hahn, "Containment and Egyptian Nationalism: The Unsuccessful Effort to Establish the Middle East Command, 1950–53," *Diplomatic History* 11 (1987):23–40.

18. Caffery no. 616, 31 October 1951, *FRUS 1951*, 5:415–16.

19. See the following documents in *FRUS 1951*, vol. 5: Caffery no. 565, 24 October, p. 409; no. 575, 26 October, pp. 410–11; no. 689, 12 November, pp. 421–22; no. 861, 12 December, pp. 430–31.

20. Under-secretary of State James Webb made the suggestion (Webb no. 784, 15 November, *FRUS 1951*, 5:422–24); Caffery agreed (Caffery no. 788, 30 November, ibid., pp. 428–30.

21. Caffery no. 609, 30 October 1951, *FRUS 1951*, 5:413–14.

22. Memo of Conversation Between Secretary of State and British Ambassador, 774.00/1-2752.

23. Caffery no. 1395, 774.00/2-2152.

24. Miles Copeland, *The Game of Nations* (New York, 1969), pp. 62–64. In his memoirs, Maraghi says he met Roosevelt, who was introduced to him as a journalist, for the first time during Hilali's tenure, and that they discussed corruption in the parties (*Ghara'ib*, pp. 198–99).

25. Caffery, who predicted that no progress could be made "so long as Brit retain their present attitude," suggested acidly that the United States had two realistic options: to persuade Britain to accept Farouk as king of the Sudan or to "prepare

ourselves for the fact that we will have to get out of Egypt and the rest of the Middle East" (Caffery no. 1525, 8 March 1952, *FRUS 1952–1954*, 8:1773–77).

26. Byroade to Secretary of State, 14 July 1952, *FRUS 1952–1954*, 8:1830–33; Caffery no. 2292, 774.00/6-2752; no. 26, 7-352.

27. Bruce no. 8, 2 July 1952, *FRUS 1952–1954*, 8:1952.

28. Byroade to Secretary of State, 774.00/7-2152.

29. Caffery no. 355, 774.00/8-1351; no. 1525, 8 March 1952, *FRUS 1952–1954*, 8:1773–77.

30. Copeland, *Game*, pp. 65–66; Hamrush, *Qissat*, 1:184–87. For two accounts that rely heavily on Copeland, see Barry Rubin, *The Arab States and the Palestine Conflict* (Syracuse, 1981), pp. 216–25; Muhammad A. Wahab Sayed-Ahmed, *Nasser and American Foreign Policy, 1952–1956* (London, 1989), pp. 42–46.

31. 'Ali Sabri and 'Abd al-Mun'im al-Naggar, for example, were Free Officers but not part of the high command; 'Abd al-Mun'im Amin, the junta member most often noted as pro-American, joined the movement only days prior to the coup (see chapter 2).

32. See Wright no. 31, 774.00/7-2652; no. 42, 7-2852; Caffery no. 205, 7-2952; no. 228, 7-3152.

33. Caffery no. 163, 774.00/7-2452.

34. Caffery no. 228, 774.00/7-3152; Evans to Caffery, 9-2652.

35. Caffery desp. 954, 774.00/11-1852.

36. Caffery no. 178, 774.00/7-2552.

37. Caffery could not resist a chance to mock his British counterpart: "After the blackout that Stevenson had for so long from Egyptian officials he is now so delighted that Ali Maher will receive him he may be calling on him a little too often. However, no harm has been done yet and Stevenson is enjoying himself" (Caffery no. 292, 641.74/8-752).

38. Stevenson no. 1279, 27 August 1952, FO 371/96880/JE1018/336.

39. Stevenson no. 1345, 10 September 1952, FO 371/96896/JE10345/17.

40. Caffery no. 750, 774.00/9-1952.

41. FO 371/96892/JE1024/3, 16 September 1952. Also see Caffery no. 877, 641.74/10-752; no. 896, 10-852.

42. Minutes to "Joint Appreciation," FO 371/96892/JE1024/3.

43. Caffery desp. 282, 774.00/8-1852.

44. Churchill to Eden, 7 September 1952, FO 371/97023/JE1462/3. For U.S. and British advice and assistance on land reform, see FO 371/97023/JE1462 files; Stevenson no. 1242, 19 August, 96880/JE1018/324; no. 1246, 20 August, JE1018/325; Caffery no. 406, 774.00/8-2052. Sayed-Ahmed (*Nasser*, pp. 63–64) overstates the U.S. influence on the decision to enact land reform.

45. Caffery no. 1237, 774.00/11-1852. Also see Stevenson no. 1240, 19 August 1952, FO 371/96884/JE1019/8.

46. Caffery desp. 282, 774.00/8-1852. The officers also expressed their disquiet at Mahir's ties to the British embassy (Murray, 12 August 1952, FO 371/96880/ JE1018/328).

47. Caffery no. 491, 774.00/8-2752.

48. Caffery no. 581, 774.00/9-652; no. 557, 9-452; no. 576, 9-652.

49. Caffery no. 605, 774.00/9-852.

50. Caffery no. 622, 774.00/9-952.

51. Ibid.

52. Caffery unnumbered, 774.00/9-1952; for the junta's offer, see no. 730, 9-1852.

53. Acheson no. 678, 18 September 1952, *FRUS 1952–54*, 8:1863–65.

54. Caffery no. 619, 774.00/9-952.

55. Caffery no. 886, 611.74/10-852.

56. Dulles to Stassen, 19 February 1953, *FRUS 1952–1954*, 9:1991–92; Caffery no. 2417, 12 May 1953, ibid., p. 2067.

57. The Americans consistently reminded the officers that future economic aid depended on a negotiated settlement; see Caffery no. 1166, 611.74/11-1052.

58. Muddathir Abd al-Rahman, *Imperialism and Nationalism in the Sudan* (Oxford, 1969), pp. 212–19, 257–60; Hamrush, *Qissat*, 2:11–23; also the account by one of Egypt's negotiators, Hussein Zulfakar Sabry, *Sovereignty for Sudan* (London, 1982).

59. Caffery no. 2134, 641.74/3-2553.

60. Caffery desp. 2258, 641.74/4-2753.

61. Ibid.

62. Dulles noted with dismay that when the talks foundered, Stevenson and General Brian Robertson cabled London asking for new instructions. Churchill refused (Dulles to Acting Secretary of State, 641.74/5-1353).

63. Interviews with Zakariya Muhyi al-Din, 11 April 1985; Lutfi Wakid, 11 February 1985; Muhammad Fayiq, 19 May 1985. Muhyi al-Din says his commanders in the Canal Zone came to Cairo for weekly strategy sessions. Wakid was one of them. Fayiq, who worked in military intelligence in Cairo, says that Egyptian agents working on the Suez base routinely pilfered British files. For British intelligence reports and statistics on incidents of sabotage, see FO 371/102847.

64. When, on July 12, the British commanding officer in Ismailia threatened drastic measures if the corporal were not returned by the next morning, 'Abd al-Hakim 'Amr, reportedly agitated, warned the Americans Egypt would then be forced to retaliate. The Americans, who felt the British CO had blundered, warned the British against using force (Caffery no. 50, 641.74/7-1253). Corporal Ridgen, the focus of the crisis, turned up a month later in Paris traveling on an Armenian passport, apparently a willing deserter (desp. 702, 9-1253).

65. Conversation with Sir John Wilton (assistant to Oriental counsellor) and Sir Michael Weir (Foreign Office), 11 September 1985, in London.

66. Dulles to Aldrich, 641.74/10-653.

67. Caffery no. 588, 641.74/11-2253.

68. Caffery no. 577, 641.74/11-1953.

69. Caffery desp. 1455, 641.74/12-1653. A British Fortnightly Report (31 December 1953, FO 371/108312/JE1013/1) noted that when the regime instructed authorities in the Canal Zone to maintain order, the number of incidents decreased sharply.

70. Caffery no. 716, 641.74/12-2853.

71. Jones no. 717, 641.74/12-2853.

72. Acting Secretary of State to Embassy, 22 January 1954, *FRUS 1952–1954*, 9:2207.

73. Fortnightly Report, 12 February 1954, FO 371/108312/JE1013/7.

74. Fortnightly Report, 25 March 1954, FO 371/108312/JE1013/14.

75. Caffery no. 2162, 30 March 1953, *FRUS 1952–1954*, 9:2039–40; no. 2618, 774.00/6-2253; no. 963, 2-2654; *New York Times*, 26 February 1954.

76. Caffery no. 1045, 774.00/3-554.

77. Caffery no. 1218, 774.00/3-3154.

78. Aldrich no. 5111, 641.74/5-1354; also Stevenson to Eden, 15 April 1954, FO 371/108316/JE1015/29.

79. Fortnightly Report, 17 June 1954, FO 371/108313/JE1013/26; Caffery no. 1526, 641.74/6-854.

80. Caffery no. 1582, 641.74/6-2254.

81. For the transition in thinking among the British chiefs of staff, see Shuckburgh, *Descent*, pp. 217–32. The author, who accompanied Head to Egypt, also alludes to the undercurrent of distrust between Ambassador Stevenson and the Foreign Office; when he describes the "atmosphere of haggling" between Egyptian and British delegations, the onus of fault rests on Sir Ralph.

82. When Stevenson learned that British negotiators had been instructed by London to seek further concessions from the Egyptians, he sent a delegation to London to argue his case; London backed down (Caffery desp. 352, 641.74/8-3054; desp. 380, 9-354).

83. Caffery desp. 761, 641.74/10-2154.

84. "Closeup of Egypt's Strong Man," *New York Times Magazine*, 19 September 1954.

85. See *New York Times*, 16, 21 November 1954.

86. *New York Times*, 24 November 1954.

87. Caffery desp. 625, 611.74/9-453. For background to aid negotiations, see 774.5-MSP files.

88. Caffery no. 167, 774.5-MSP/8-554.

89. Caffery no. 268, 774.5-MSP/8-2954.

90. Caffery warned Washington in February 1954 that the Egyptians might "overcome present reluctance to get involved with USSR" and "probably try to use Russian offer as bargaining weapon vis-a-vis US and UK." He did not rule out the acceptance of Soviet aid and therefore urged prompt settlement of the Anglo-Egyptian dispute "before situation develops to point where such action on our part appears to be direct result of Soviet 'competition'" (no. 909, 13 February 1954, *FRUS 1952–1954*, 9:2216–17).

91. *New York Times*, 12 January, 3 April 1955. Press coverage in the United States remained favorable until the Egyptian-Czech arms deal in the autumn of 1955.

Chapter 10

1. Saʿid (*Munazzamat*, pp. 177–83, 422) points to several occasions on which the DMNL organized demonstrations in working-class neighborhoods in the Delta and Cairo, and several occasions when DMNL cadres denounced the CCR and the accord before crowds assembled for Friday prayer at mosques in Cairo and Alexandria, provoking police intervention.

2. Ibid., pp. 339–40.

3. Fu'ad Mursi, interview, 4 May 1985; Saʿid, *Munazzamat*, pp. 385–87.

4. Caffery desp. 184, 641.74/8-254.

5. *Al-Ahram*, 17 September 1954; Fortnightly Report, 23 September 1954, FO 371/108314/JE1013/40; Mitchell, *Society*, pp. 140–41.

6. *Al-Ahram*, 31 March 1954.

7. Ibid., 27 March 1954.

8. ʿUmar al-Tilmissani (with the assistance of Salah Shadi), written response to questions submitted in May 1985; Mitchell, *Society*, p. 131. In January 1953 Nasser had rejected a similar proposal from the Brothers.

9. For the text of the letter, dated May 4, see Shadi, *Safahat*, pp. 369–71; also see Mitchell, *Society*, pp. 134–35.

10. Mitchell, *Society*, pp. 136–37; for Humaydah's statement, Shadi, *Safahat*, pp. 372–81.

11. *Al-Ahram*, 22 August 1954.

12. *Ruz al-Yusuf*, 28 September, cover, and 18 October 1954, p. 3.

13. Denied access to the Egyptian press, Hudaybi published another denunciation of the accord in a Syrian newspaper. For the text, Shadi, *Safahat*, pp. 382–86; for government rhetoric, *Al-Jumhuriyah*, 22 August–early October 1954.

14. *Al-Jumhuriyah*, 28 August 1954, for the official report; for eyewitness accounts, Duh, 25 *'Amman*, p. 70, and Mitchell, *Society*, p. 139; also Caffery's somewhat different account, desp. 345, 774.00/8-2854.

15. For Tanta, *Al-Jumhuriyah*, 11, 12 September 1954; Mitchell, *Society*, p. 140. For sermons, *New York Times*, 14 September; *Al-Jumhuriyah*, 5 October. The Brothers who had their citizenship revoked were 'Abd al-Hakim 'Abdin, Al-Sayyid Ramadan, Muhammad Guwayfil, Kamal al-Sharif, and Sa'd al-Din al-Walayli.

16. For the text, Shadi, *Safahat*, pp. 387–88. Hudaybi testified at his trial (*Al-Jumhuriyah*, 19 November 1954) that he fled in fear for his life; for an account of his flight, see 'Ashmawi, *Ikhwan*, pp. 60–61.

17. Fortnightly Report, 7 October 1954, FO 371/108314/JE1013/42; WO 208/3965/9/54, 29 September–12 October 1954; *New York Times*, 8 October 1954; Caffery desp. 604, 774.00/10-454, and desp. 731, 10-1954.

18. Fortnightly Report, 4 November 1954, FO 371/108314/JE1013/46; USARMA no. 1205, 774.00(W)/10-2254.

19. Hamrush, *Qissat*, 1:357; Edgar unnumbered, 774.00/10-2754.

20. For a summary of the charges made by the Brotherhood, see Tilmissani, *Dhikrayat*, pp. 168–70. For Tuhami, *Ruz al-Yusuf*, 1 May 1978, pp. 6–7. For a critical response challenging Tuhami, 'Abd Allah Imam, ibid., 15 May 1978, pp. 24–26. The U.S. embassy immediately discounted the notion; see USARMA no. 1209, 774.00(W)/10-2954.

21. Mitchell, *Society*, pp. 145, 156 n. 134; Ramadan, *Ikhwan*, p. 15; Caffery desp. 1156, 774.00/12-1354.

22. Mitchell (*Society*, p. 156) noted, "The remarkable ease with which loyalties were broken and members pointed accusing fingers at each other showed how far mutual trust had been shaken."

23. See *Al-Da'wah*, 14 September 1954.

24. Khamis Humaydah and Muhammad Farghali both testified that they tried to persuade Hudaybi to return to Cairo (*Al-Jumhuriyah*, 23 November 1954).

25. Mitchell, *Society*, pp. 145–46; *Al-Da'wah*, 21, 28 September 1954. Hudaybi did forward a long letter in which he again recounted the breakdown of relations with the regime; for the text, Shadi, *Safahat*, pp. 389–94.

26. *Al-Jumhuriyah*, 21, 22 October 1954; *Al-Da'wah*, 5 November; Mitchell, *Society*, pp. 146–47, 150–51; 'Ashmawi, *Ikhwan*, pp. 72–76.

27. See Hudaybi's testimony, *Al-Jumhuriyah*, 18 November 1954.

28. In addition to the three branch leaders, this body included Farghali from the Guidance Council and Mahmud 'Abduh of the Cairo office (Salah Shadi, interview, 4 July 1985; testimony of Yusuf Til'at, *Al-Jumhuriyah*, 24, 28 November 1954). Farghali dissembled when he denied any knowledge of the secret organization (ibid., 17 November).

29. Yusuf Til'at and 'Abd al-Rahman al-Banna testified that members of the

Guidance Council asked that the pamphlets cease, but the secret organization continued to print them (*Al-Jumhuriyah*, 24 November, 3 December 1954).

30. Ibid., 15, 23, 24 November 1954.

31. Ibid., 19 November 1954.

32. Mitchell, *Society*, p. 148.

33. *Al-Jumhuriyah*, 15, 19, 20, 24 November 1954.

34. WO 208/3965/11/54, 28 October–10 November 1954.

35. *Al-Jumhuriyah*, 30 October 1954.

36. See *Al-Tahrir*, 3 November–7 December 1954; *Akhir Sa'ah*, 3 November–8
December.

37. Caffery desp. 1072, 774.00/12-354.

38. Brothers who received life sentences were Khamis Humaydah, Husayn
Kamal al-Din, Kamal Khalifah, Munir al-Dillah, Salih Abu Ruqayq, Hamid Abu al-
Nasr, and 'Abd al-'Aziz 'Atiyah. Sentenced to fifteen years were 'Umar al-Tilmissani
and Ahmad Shurayt. In addition to Banna, Al-Bahi al-Khuli and 'Abd al-Mu'izz al-
Sattar were found innocent.

39. Caffery desp. 1099, 774.00/12-654. For an account of the execution, see
Mitchell, *Society*, pp. 161–62.

40. Zakariya Muhyi al-Din, interview, 11 April 1985.

41. Caffery desp. 973, 774.00/11-2054; *New York Times*, 23 November 1954.

42. Among those affected was Salah Shadi. *Al-Jumhuriyah*, 14 December 1954, 3
January 1955.

43. Caffery desp. 1129, 774.00/12-1054.

44. The two outstanding fugitives were 'Abd al-Mun'im 'Abd al-Ra'uf and Hasan
al-'Ashmawi. The former's picture appeared frequently in the press; he reportedly had
fled to paris (*Al-Jumhuriyah*, 1 January 1955). He was sentenced to death in absentia on
January 19. 'Ashmawi recounted his escape in *Ikhwan*, pp. 92ff. For reports of resistance, Caffery desp. 1156, 774.00/12-1354; WO 208/3965/14/54, 8-23 December 1954.

45. Fortnightly Report, 20 May 1954, FO 371/108313/JE1013/22.

46. Fortnightly Report, 1 July 1954, FO 371/108313/JE1013/28; *New York Times*,
20 June 1954.

47. Caffery desp. 147, 774.00/7-2654; *New York Times*, 23 July 1954.

48. Caffery desp. 278, 774.00/8-1854.

49. Nagib, *Kalimati*, p. 228. Muhammad Farghali testified that Nagib wanted the
Brothers to distribute his statement (*Al-Jumhuriyah*, 17 November 1954). In addition, Hindawi Duwayr testified that Nagib phoned Hudaybi after the latter returned
to Egypt (12 November); Ibrahim al-Tayyib, that Nagib and the Brothers had been in
agreement since April (15 November); Khamis Humaydah, that Nagib visited leading
Brothers at their homes (17 November); and Husayn Hamudah recounted the role of
Muhammad Riyad as a go-between (23 November).

50. Minutes by Bromley, 25 October 1954, FO 371/108380/JE10510/16; Anthony
Nutting, *Nasser* (London, 1972), p. 62.

51. The most damning testimony came from Ibrahim al-Tayyib (*Al-Jumhuriyah*,
15 November 1954) and Sayyid Qutb (20, 23 November).

52. Ibid., 22 November 1954.

53. *New York Times*, 17 November 1954.

54. The previous April 7 *Akhir Sa'ah* (pp. 15–16) had featured a two-page photo
spread on the villa as part of a continuing campaign to vilify Nahhas and his wife.

55. Caffery desp. 923, 774.00/11-1654; Lutfi Wakid, interview, 11 February
1985.

56. USARMA, no. 1229, 774.00(W)/12-1054; Sa'id, *Munazzamat*, p. 341.

57. *Al-Ahram*, 27 July, 6, 7, 13 October 1954; Caffery desp. 1195, 774.00/12-1854.

58. The "Lavon Affair," named after the Israeli defense minister who took official blame, led to Prime Minister David Ben-Gurion's resignation in 1961. See Michael Bar-Zohar, *Ben-Gurion: A Biography* (New York, 1977), pp. 210–16; Dan Kurzman, *Ben-Gurion, Prophet of Fire* (New York, 1983), pp. 372–76.

59. Caffery desp. 1216, 774.00/12-2154; Murray no. 1835, 20 December 1954, FO 371/108548/JE1571/13. In October, when the thirteen were arraigned, Anthony Nutting's personal secretary noted that "acts of incendiarism did, however, occur during the month of July and as far as can be judged the persons now facing trial were in some way connected with them" (Rae to Nutting, 12 October 1954, JE1571/1).

60. Maurice Orbach had several meetings with Nasser; see Murray no. 1835, 20 December 1954, FO 371/108548/JE1571/13, and no. 1855, 23 December, JE1571/18.

61. Jean Lacouture, *Nasser* (New York, 1973), pp. 274–75.

62. *Al-Ahram*, 25 July 1954.

63. Caffery no. 523, 774.00/10-1954; *New York Times*, 22 December 1954.

64. Ibrahim Shukri recalls Nasser's disappointment when, at an early March meeting between the two, Shukri refused to give the regime unequivocal support (interview, 6 March 1985); Nutting relates that Nasser told him he would never forget that the universities had stood against the CCR (*Nasser*, p. 72).

65. Husayn al-Shafi'i, interview, 15 January 1985; Baghdadi, *Mudhakkirat*, 1: 174–86.

66. Chancery to Dept., 5 May 1954, FO 371/108317/JE1015/39.

67. Baghdadi, *Mudhakkirat*, 1:188; John Waterbury first pointed this out to me in a private conversation.

68. Baghdadi, *Mudhakkirat*, 1:219–20; Caffery no. 837, 774.5-MSP/12-2854; no. 848, 12-2954; no. 864, 12-3154.

69. Lacouture, *Nasser*, p. 145.

70. Stevenson to Eden, 14 September 1953, FO 371/108317/JE1015/54.

71. During Nasser's absence Salim clashed with Liberation Rally leaders who planned a major demonstration upon Nasser's return (Baghdadi, *Mudhakkirat*, 1:220–24).

72. Ibid., p. 252. Khalid Muhyi al-Din recalls that at his first meeting with former colleagues after his return to Egypt in 1955, he remained seated while they, to his surprise, stood when Nasser entered the room (Lacouture, *Nasser*, pp. 373–74).

73. Baghdadi, *Mudhakkirat*, 1:225–67.

Conclusion

1. Caffery desp. 771, 774.00/10-2354.

2. *Ruz al-Yusuf*, 13 December 1954, 17 January 1955.

3. Nasser, *Egypt's Liberation*, pp. 26–27.

4. *Al-Jumhuriyah*, 6–8, 10 January 1955.

5. According to Rafi'i (*Thawrat 23*, p. 133), the number of imprisoned Brothers dropped to 571 by 1956, and most of these were released by the anniversary of the coup in July.

6. Hamrush, *Qissat*, 2:126.

7. *Ruz al-Yusuf*, 7 February 1955, p. 3.

8. 'Abd al-Quddus resumed editorship of *Ruz al-Yusuf* in June 1954, after spend-

ing two months in prison. Khalid Muhyi al-Din returned to Egypt in 1956 and became editor of *Al-Misa'*, a new afternoon daily. Nasser appointed Tharwat 'Ukashah ambassador to France, where he remained through the Suez crisis, then Italy; in the 1960s he returned to Egypt and served two terms as minister of culture. Amin remained abroad as ambassador in Bonn until May 1956, when he returned and retired from public life. Yusuf Siddiq, imprisoned since March 1954, was freed in 1955.

9. Nahhas's funeral cortege turned into a political demonstration, provoking another wave of arrests. Mahanna, who had been freed prior to Suez, was rearrested during the war and remained in prison until 1967. Sadat freed Nagib from house arrest in the early 1970s; he died in 1984.

10. Nasser, *Egypt's Liberation;* Anwar el-Sadat, *In Search of Identity* (New York, 1977); Nadav Safran, *Egypt in Search of Political Community* (Cambridge, 1961); Charles D. Smith, *Islam and the Search for Political Order in Modern Egypt* (Albany, 1983); Wilton Wynn, *Nasser of Egypt: The Search for Dignity* (Cambridge, 1959).

11. For Mubarak's rule see Robert Springborg, *The Political Economy of Mubarak's Egypt* (Boulder, Colo., 1988); Joel Gordon, "Political Opposition in Egypt," *Current History* (February 1990): 65–68ff. In October 1990, Rif'at al-Mahgub, the speaker of parliament was assassinated in downtown Cairo, weeks before new elections to the People's Assembly were to be held.

Bibliography

Government Publications

U.S. Department of State. *Foreign Relations of the United States, 1948*, vol. 4; *1949*, vol. 6; *1950*, vol. 5; *1951*, vol. 5; *1952–1954*, vols. 8, 9. Washington, D.C.: Government Printing Office, 1974, 1977, 1978, 1982, 1986.

Egypt. Ministry of Foreign Affairs. *Records of Conversations, Notes and Papers Exchanged Between the Royal Egyptian Government and the United Kingdom Government, March 1950–November 1951.* Cairo, 1951.

Al-Waqa'i' al-Misriyah, 1952–1954.

Government Archives, 1950–1954

British Public Records Office (PRO): Foreign Office (FO) 371 (Egypt); FO 141 (Confidential Prints); War Office (WO) 208 (weekly intelligence reports); WO 216 (Operation Rodeo); WO 236 (Erskine Papers); WO 259 (Office of Secretary of State, War).

United States National Archives: 611.74 (U.S.-Egyptian Relations); 641.74 (U.K.-Egyptian Relations); 774.00 (Egypt, internal); 774.00(W) (U.S. Military Attaché, weekly reports); 774.001 (Egypt, extremist movements); 774.5-MSP (U.S. Mutual Security Program, Egypt)

Interviews, in Cairo, 1984–1985
(parentheses note positions held between 1950 and 1955)

Ihsan 'Abd al-Quddus (editor in chief, *Ruz al-Yusuf*)
Ahmad Abu al-Fath (editor in chief, *Al-Misri*)
Muhammad Sayyid Ahmad (Iskra)
Mahmud Amin al-'Alam (Nawat al-Hizb al-Shuyu'i al-Misri)
Mustafa Amin (co-owner, Al-Akhbar chain)
Louis Awad (University of Cairo)
Mustafa Bahgat Badawi (general manager, *Al-Tahrir*)
'Abd al-Latif al-Baghdadi (CCR)
Ahmad Baha' al-Din (*Ruz al-Yusuf*)
Rashad al-Barawi (University of Alexandria)

233

Hasan Duh (leader of Muslim Brotherhood student movement)
Husayn Fahmi (editor in chief, *Al-Jumhuriyah*)
Isma'il Fahmi (foreign service)
Ibrahim Farag (Wafdist parliamentary organization)
Muhammad Fayiq (military intelligence)
Mirrit Ghali (minister of rural affairs)
Murad Ghalib (University of Alexandria; assistant ambassador to USSR)
Muhammad Abu al-Fadl al-Gizawi (Free Officer)
Ahmad Hamrush (leader of DMNL military branch; editor in chief, *Al-Tahrir*)
'Abd al-Muhsin Hamudah (Wafdist Vanguard)
Kamal al-Din Husayn (CCR)
Lutfi al-Khuli (ECP)
Sayyid Mar'i (Sa'dist party; director land reform)
Khalid Muhyi al-Din (CCR)
Zakariya Muhyi al-din (CCR)
Mahmud 'Abd al-Mun'im Murad (*Al-Misri*)
Fu'ad Mursi (secretary general, ECP)
Fathi Radwan (Nationalist party; cabinet minister)
Wahid Ra'fat (State Council)
Musa Sabri (editor in chief, *Al-Jil al-Jadid*)
Rif'at al-Sa'id (DMNL)
Salah Shadi (leader of Muslim Brotherhood police cells)
Husayn al-Shafi'i (CCR)
Ibrahim Shukri (vice-president, Egyptian Socialist party)
Nur al-Din Tarraf (Nationalist party; cabinet minister)
'Umar al-Tilmissani (Guidance Council, Muslim Brotherhood)
Tharwat 'Ukashah (Free Officer; editor in chief, *Al-Tahrir*)
Hilmi Yassin (central committee, Workers Vanguard)
Lutfi Wakid (Free Officer, director of Nasser's office)

Contemporary Newspapers and Journals
(1952–1954 inclusive unless otherwise noted)

Al-Ahram (1950–1955)
Al-Ahrar (through 14 November 1952)
Akhir Lahzah
Akhir Sa'ah
Al-Akhbar
Akhbar al-Yawm
Al-Asas (ceased publication 31 August 1952)
Al-Balagh (ceased publication December 1953)
Al-Da'wah
Al-Jil al-Jadid (1954)
Al-Jumhur al-Misri (ceased publication April 1954)
Al-Jumhuriyah (began publication 7 December 1953)
Al-Hizb al-Watani (5 December 1952–11 January 1953)
Al-Ikhwan al-Muslimun (20 May–5 August 1954)
Majallat al-Azhar
Al-Misri (1950–ceased publication April 1954)

Al-Mu'aradah (4 January 1952–17 January 1953)
Al-Musawwar
Al-Qahirah (founded autumn 1953, closed March 1954)
Ruz al-Yusuf (1950–1955)
Al-Sha'b al-Jadid (20 April 1951–3 January 1952)
Al-Tahrir (began publication 17 September 1952)
Al-Zaman (ceased publication December 1953)
Economist (1950–1952)
New York Times (1950–1955)

Articles and Published Interviews in Arabic

Abu al-Fath, Ahmad. "Wa- al-Misri." In *Al-Wafd*, 6 June 1985.
Amin, 'Abd al-Mun'im. "'Abd al-Mun'im Amin, 'Udw Majlis Qiyadat al-Thawrah." In *Al-Musawwar*, 16 April 1976.
Al-Baghdadi, 'Abd al-Latif. "'Abd al-Latif al-Baghdadi Yarudd 'ala Mudhakkirat Hasan al-'Ashmawi." In *Ruz al-Yusuf*, 24 October 1977.
Al-Baquri, Ahmad Hasan. "Malamih Dhikrayat Yarawiha al-Shaykh Ahmad Hasan al-Baquri." In *Al-Muslimun* (London), 6–12 April 1985 through 13–19 July 1985.
Barakat, Baha' al-Din. "Safahat min Mudhakkirat Baha' al-Din Barakat." In *Al-Musawwar*, 29 July 1977 through 19 August 1977.
Damanhuri, Muhammad Husni. "Qissat al-Dabit al-Ladhi Atlaqu 'alayhi al-Mayyit al-Hayy." In *Al-Musawwar*, 9 July 1976.
Hafiz, Hasan. "Awwal Fatwa bil-I'tida' 'ala al-Qanun Qaddammaha al-Sanhuri Nafsahu." In *Ruz al-Yusuf*, 8 September 1975.
Hamid, Ra'uf 'Abbas, "Hizb al-Fallah al-Ishtiraki, 1938–1952." In *Al-Majallah al-Tarikhiyah al-Misriyah* 19(1972): 169–214.
Hamrush, Ahmad. "Akhir Ma'arik al-Nahhas ma'a al-Jaysh wa-Diddahu." In *Ruz al-Yusuf*, 1 September 1975.
———. "Safahat min Yulyu 'ala Firash al-Mard." In *Ruz al-Yusuf*, 17 March 1975.
Himmad, Jamal. "Kayfa Bada'a al-Sidam bayna Majlis Qiyadat al-Thawrah wa-al-Wasiy 'ala al-'Arsh?" In *Uktubar*, 4 August 1985.
Husayn, Kamal al-Din. "Hadith Ghayr 'Adi bayna Kamal al-Din Husayn wa-Fathi Khalil." In *Ruz al-Yusuf*, 4 August 1975.
———. "Qissat Thuwwar Yulyu." In *Al-Musawwar*, 19 December 1975 through 19 January 1976.
Imam, 'Abd Allah. "Al-Shuhud Yatakallamun 'an Hadith al-Manshiyah." In *Ruz al-Yusuf*, 15 May 1978.
Mahanna, Rashad. "Ba'da Akthar min 30 Sanah Rashad Mahanna Yakhruj 'an Samtihi wa-Yatahaddath lil-Ahrar." In *Al-Ahrar*, 25 July 1983.
———. "Sira' al-Ashhur al-Awwal min Thawrat Yulyu 1952." In *Al-Musawwar*, 19 March 1976–4 April 1976.
Muhyi al-Din, Khalid. "Azmah fi Majlis Qiyadat al-Thawrah ba'da 7 Shuhur min Yulyu." In *Al-Ahali*, 24 July 1985.
———. "Hiwar ma'a Khalid Muhyi al-Din." In *Al-Musawwar*, 25 July 1975.
———. "Lam Uqabil al-Sawi athna'a Azmat Mars." In *Ruz al-Yusuf*, 3 May 1976.
Murad, Mahmud 'Abd al-Mun'im. "Al-Hariq wa-al-Dimuqratiyah, Mars '54-Mars '83." In *Uktubar*, 27 March 1983.

————. "Al-Hariq wa-al-Dimuqratiyah wa-al-Thawrah al-Mudaddah." In *Uktubar*, 3 April 1983.

————. "'Aud 'ala Bad' min al-Thawrah ila al-Nasiriyah." In *Uktubar*, 10 April 1983.

Najib, Muhammad. "Muhammad Najib Yarudd 'ala 'Abd al-Latif al-Baghdadi." In *Ruz al-Yusuf*, 29 August 1977.

Nasr, Salah. "Salah Nasr Yatakallam li-Awwal Marrah." In *Al-Musawwar*, 26 September 1975.

Ra'fat, Wahid. "Al-Duktur Wahid Ra'fat Yaqul: al-'Ibrah bi-al-Rijal wa-Laysat bi-al-Qawanin." In *Al-Musawwar*, 23 May 1975.

Ramadan, 'Abd al-'Azim. "Muzaharat Mars Dabbaraha Yusuf Siddiq wa-Muhammad Najib." In *Ruz al-Yusuf*, 26 April 1976.

————. "Hizb al-Wafd bayna al-Yamin wa-al-Yasar." In *Al-Katib*, 13 (June 1973).

————. "Al-Qissah al-Kamilah li-Tazyifina al-Intikhabat." In *Ruz al-Yusuf*, 5 January 1976.

Sabri, Yusuf. "Mudhakkirat lam Tunshar li-Yusuf Siddiq." In *Ruz al-Yusuf*, 5 May 1975.

Al-Shafi'i, Husayn. "'Abd al-Nasir Kana Mukhtafiyan Tamaman qabl Qiyam al-Thawrah." In *Al-Masa'*, 30 May 1985.

Al-Sharqawi, Jamal. "Daw' Qadim 'ala Hawadith al-Shaghab al-Jadidah." In *Ruz al-Yusuf*, 3 February 1975.

Siddiq, Yusuf. "Qissat al-Khata' al-Tarikhi al-Saghir fi Thawrat 23 Yulyu." In *Al-Musawwar*, 25 July 1975.

Siraj al-Din, Fu'ad. "Asrar Hariq al-Qahirah." In *Ruz al-Yusuf*, 23 June 1975.

Til'at, Ibrahim. "Ayyam al-Wafd al-Akhirah." In *Ruz al-Yusuf*, 23 August 1976–21 March 1977.

Al-Tuhami, Hasan. "Hasan al-Tuhami Yukhrij min Samtihi li-Awwal Marrah wa-Yakshif Kull Asrar ma Jara fi Fibrayir '54." In *Al-Ahram*, 21, 22 July 1977.

————. "Khabir Amriki Iqtarah Ikhtilaq Muhawalah li-Atlaq al-Rasas 'ala 'Abd al-Nasir." In *Ruz al-Yusuf*, 1 May 1978.

'Usfur, Sa'd. "Fasaluni bi-Sabab Maqali." In *Ruz al-Yusuf*, 17 February 1975.

Wakid, Lutfi. "Bidayat al-Sira' bayna 'Abd al-Nasir wa-al-Isti'mar." In *Al-Katib*, 14 (September 1974).

"Al-Yasar al-Misri Yuhawar Tawfiq al-Hakim." In *Al-Tali'ah* 11 (January 1975): 14–38.

Books in Arabic

'Abd al-Halim, Mahmud. *Al-Ikhwan al-Muslimun: Ahdath San'at al-Tarikh*. 3 vols. Alexandria: Dar al-Da'wah, 1979, 1985.

Abu al-Nur, Sami. *Dawr al-Qasr fi al-Hayah al-Siyasiyah fi Misr, 1922–1936*. Cairo: Al-Hai'ah al-Misriyah al-'Ammah, 1985.

Amin, Mustafa. *Awwal Sanat al-Sijin*. Cairo: Al-Maktab al-Misri al-Hadith, 1974.

————. *Layali Faruq*. Cairo: Al-Akhbar, n.d.

————. *Thani Sanat al-Sijin*. Cairo: Al-Maktab al-Misri al-Hadith, 1975.

Anis, Muhammad. *4 Fibrayir fi Tarikh Misr al-Siyasi*. Cairo: Madbuli, 1982.

————. *Hariq al-Qahirah*. Cairo: Madbuli, 1982.

Al-'Ashmawi, Hasan. *Al-Ikhwan wa-al-Thawrah*. Cairo: Al-Maktab al-Misri al-Hadith, 1977.

'Atiyat Allah, Ahmad. *Qamus al-Thawrah al-Misriyah, 1954*. Cairo: Maktabat al-Anglu al-Misriyah, 1954.

'Awad, Louis. *Li-Misr wa-al-Huriyah.* Beirut: Dar al-Qadaya, 1977.

Al-'Azm, Yusuf. *Al-Shahid Sayyid Qutb.* Damascus: Dar al-Qalam, 1980.

Al-Baghdadi, 'Abd al-Latif. *Mudhakkirat.* 2 vols. Cairo: Al-Maktab al-Misri al-Hadith, 1977.

Baha' al-Din, Ahmad. *Faruq Malikan.* Cairo: Ruz al-Yusuf [?], n.d.

Al-Bishri, Tariq. *Al-Harakah al-Siyasiyah fi Misr, 1945–1952.* 2d ed. Beirut: Dar al-Shuruq, 1983.

———. *Al-Nasiriyah wa-al-Dimuqratiyah.* Cairo: Dar al-Thaqafah al-Jadidah, 1976.

Duh, Hasan. *25 'Aman fi Jama'ah.* Cairo: Dar al-I'tisam, 1983.

———. *Safahat min Jihad al-Shabab al-Muslim.* Cairo: Dar al-I'tisam, 1979.

Fadl Allah, Mahdi. *Ma'a Sayyid Qutb fi Fikrihi al-Siyasi wa-al-Dini.* 2d ed. Beirut: Mu'assasat al-Risalah, 1979.

Faraj, Ibrahim. *Dhikrayati al-Siyasiyah.* Cairo: Dar al-Ma'mun, 1984.

Al-Hamamsi, Jalal al-Din. *Hiwar wara'a al-Aswar.* Cairo: Al-Maktab al-Misri al-Hadith, 1972.

Hamrush, Ahmad. *Qissat Thawrat Yulyu.* 5 vols. Cairo: Madbuli, 1977–1984.

———. *Thawrat Yulyu fi 'Aql Misr.* Cairo: Madbuli, 1985.

Hamudah, 'Adil. *Azmat al-Muthaqqafin wa-Thawrat Yulyu.* Cairo: Madbuli, 1985.

———. *Nihayat Thawrat Yulyu.* Cairo: Madbuli, 1983.

Hamudah, Husayn Muhammad Ahmad. *Asrar Harakat al-Dubbat al-Ahrar wa-al-Ikhwan al-Muslimun.* Cairo: Al-Zahra' al-A'lam al-'Arabi, 1985.

Hasan, 'Abd al-Fattah. *Dhikrayat Siyasiyah.* Cairo: Dar al-Sha'b, 1974.

Haykal, Muhammad Hasanayn. *'Abd al-Nasir wa-al-'Alam.* Beirut: Dar al-Nahar, 1972.

———. *Azmat al-Muthaqqafin.* Cairo: Dar al-Udaba', 1961.

———. *Li-Misr, la li-'Abd al-Nasir.* Beirut: Dar al-Siyasah, 1976.

Haykal, Muhammad Husayn. *Mudhakkirat fi al-Siyasiyah al-Misriyah.* 3 vols. Cairo: Dar al-Ma'arif, 1978.

Himmad, Jamal. *23 Yulyu: Atwal Yawm fi Tarikh Misr.* Cairo: Dar al-Hilal, 1983.

Imam, 'Abd Allah. *'Abd al-Nasir wa-al-Ikhwan al-Muslimun.* Cairo: Dar al-Mawqif al-'Arabi, 1981.

'Isa, Salah. *Muhakamat Fu'ad Siraj al-Din Basha.* Cairo: Madbuli, 1983.

Jawhar, Sami. *Al-Samitun Yatakallamun.* Cairo: Al-Maktab al-Misri al-Hadith, 1975.

Al-Maraghi, Murtada. *Ghara'ib min 'Ahd Faruq wa-Bidayat al-Thawrah al-Misriyah.* Beirut: Dar al-Nahhar lil-Nashr, 1976.

Mar'i, Sayyid. *Awraq Siyasiyah.* 3 vols. Cairo: Al-Maktab al-Misri al-Hadith, 1978.

Matar, Fu'ad. *Bi-Sirahah 'an 'Abd al-Nasir.* Beirut: Dar al-Qadaya, 1975.

Mu'assasat al-Ahram. *50 'Aman 'ala Thawrat 1919.* Cairo: Mu'assasat al-Ahram, 1969.

Muhammad, 'Abd al-Wahab Bakr. *Al-Jaysh al-Misri wa-Harb Filastin, 1948–1952.* Cairo: Dar al-Ma'arif, 1982.

———. *Al-Wujud al-Biritani fi al-Jaysh al-Misri, 1936–1947.* Cairo: Dar al-Ma'arif, 1982.

Najib, Muhammad. *Kalimati lil-Tarikh.* Cairo: Dar al-Kitab al-Namudhaji, 1975.

———. *Kuntu Ra'isan li-Misr.* Cairo: Al-Maktab al-Misri al-Hadith, 1984.

Radwan, Fathi. *Asrar Hukumat Yulyu.* Cairo: Matba'at al-Misriyah, 1976.

———. *72 Shahran ma'a 'Abd al-Nasir.* Cairo: Dar al-Huriyah, 1985.

Ra'fat, Wahid. *Fusul min Thawrat Yulyu.* Cairo: Dar al-Shuruq, 1978.

Al-Rafi'i, 'Abd al-Rahman. *Fi A'qab al-Thawrah al-Misriyah.* Vol. 3, *1936–1951.* Cairo: Maktabat al-Nahdah al-Misriyah, 1951.

———. *Thawrat 1919.* 3d. ed. Cairo: Dar al-Sha'b, 1968.

————. *Thawrat 23 Yulyu, 1952–1959.* Cairo: Maktabat al Nahdah al-'Arabiyah, 1959.

————. *Al-Za'im al-Tha'ir Ahmad 'Urabi.* 3d ed. Cairo: Dar al-Sha'b, 1968.

Ramadan, 'Abd al-'Azim. *'Abd al-Nasir wa-Azmat Mars.* Cairo: Ruz al-Yusuf, 1976.

————. *Al-Fikr al-Thawri fi Misr.* Cairo: Madbuli, 1981.

————. *Al-Ikhwan al-Muslimun wa-al-Tanzim al-Sirri.* Cairo: Ruz al-Yusuf, 1982.

————. *Al-Sira' al-Siyasi wa-al-Ijtima'i fi Misr.* Cairo: Ruz al-Yusuf, 1975.

————. *Tatawwur al-Harakah al-Wataniyah fi Misr, min Sanat 1918, ila Sanat 1936.* 2d ed. Cairo: Madbuli, 1983.

————. *Tatawwur al-Harakah al-Wataniyah fi Misr min Sanat 1937 ila Sanat 1948.* 2 vols. Beirut: Al-Watan al-'Arabi, 1968.

Rif'at, Kamal al-Din. *Harb al-Tahrir al-Wataniyah.* Cairo: Dar al-Kitab al-'Arabi, 1968.

Rizq, Yunan Labib. *Tarikh al-Wizarat al-Misriyah.* Cairo: Al-Ahram, 1975.

————. *Al-Wafd wa-al-Kitab al-Aswad.* Cairo: Mu'assasat al-Ahram, 1978.

Sabri, Musa. *Qissat Malik wa-Arba' Wizarat.* Cairo: Dar al-Qalam, 1964.

Al-Sadat, Anwar. *Asrar al-Thawrah al-Misriyah.* Cairo: al-Dar al-Qawmiyah, 1965.

————. *Qissat al-Thawrah al-Kamilah.* Cairo: Al-Dar al-Qawmiyah, 1965.

Sa'id, Amin. *Tarikh Misr al-Siyasi.* Cairo: Dar Ihya' al-Kutub al-'Arabiyah, 1959.

Al-Sa'id, Rif'at. *Munazzamat al-Yasar al-Misri, 1950–1957.* Cairo: Dar al-Thaqafah al-Jadidah, 1983.

————. *Al-Sihafah al-Yasariyah fi Misr, 1925–1948.* Cairo: Madbuli, 1977.

————. *Al-Sihafah al-Yasariyah fi Misr, 1950–1952.* Cairo: Dar al-Thaqafah al-Jadidah, 1982.

————. *Tarikh al-Munazzamat al-Yasariyah al-Misriyah, 1940–1950.* Cairo: Dar al-Thaqafah al-Jadidah, 1977.

Shadi, Salah. *Safahat min al-Tarikh.* Kuwait: Sharikat al-Shu'a', 1981.

Al-Shahid, Salah. *Dhikrayati fi 'Ahdayn.* Cairo: Dar al-Ma'arif, 1976.

Shalabi, Karam. *'Ishrun Yawman Hazzat Misr.* Cairo: Dar al-Usamah, 1976.

Al-Sharqawi, Jamal. *Asrar Hariq al-Qahirah.* Cairo: Dar al-Shahid, 1985.

————. *Hariq al-Qahirah.* Cairo: Dar al-Thaqafah al-Jadidah, 1976.

Siraj al-Din, Fu'ad. *Limadha al-Hizb al-Jadid.* Cairo: Dar al-Shuruq, 1977.

Til'at, Hasan. *Fi Khidmat al-Amn al-Siyasi, Mayu 1939-Mayu 1971.* Beirut: al-Watan al-'Arabi, 1983.

Al-Tilmissani, 'Umar. *Dhikrayat, La Mudhakkirat.* Cairo: Dar al-I'tisam, 1985.

'Ubayd, Makram. *Al-Kitab al-Aswad.* Cairo: Al-Markaz al-'Arabi lil-Bahth wa-al-Nashr, 1984.

Yusuf, Hasan. *Al-Qasr wa-Dawruh fi al-Siyasah al-Misriyah, 1922–1952.* Cairo: Al-Ahram, 1982.

Works in English and French

Abd al-Rahman, Muddathir. *Imperialism and Nationalism in the Sudan.* Oxford: Clarendon Press, 1969.

Abdallah, Ahmad. *The Student Movement and National Politics in Egypt, 1923–1973.* London: Al Saqi, 1985.

Abdel-Malek, Anouar. *Egypt: Military Society.* New York: Vintage, 1968.

Abul-Fath, Ahmed. *L'Affaire Nasser.* Paris: Plon, 1962.

Ansari, Hamied. *Egypt: The Stalled Society.* Albany: State University of New York Press, 1986.

Aronson, Geoffrey. *From Sideshow to Center Stage: United States Policy Towards Egypt, 1946–1956.* Boulder, Colo.: Lynne Rienner, 1986.

Badeau, John. *The Middle East Remembered.* Washington, D.C.: Middle East Institute, 1983.

Baer, Gabriel. "Waqf Reform in Egypt." In *St. Anthony's Papers, No. 4.* London: Chatto & Windus, 1958.

Baker, Raymond William. *Egypt's Uncertain Revolution under Nasser and Sadat.* Cambridge: Harvard University Press, 1978.

Bar Zohar, Michael. *Ben-Gurion: A Biography.* New York: Delacorte, 1977.

Barawy, Rashed. *The Military Coup in Egypt.* Cairo: Maktabat al-Nahdah, 1952.

Be'eri, Eliezar. *Army Officers in Arab Politics and Society.* New York: Praeger, 1970.

Beinin, Joel. "Class Conflict and National Struggle: Labor and Politics in Egypt, 1936–1954." Ph.D. diss., University of Michigan, 1982.

Beinin, Joel, and Zackary Lockman. *Workers on the Nile.* Princeton: Princeton University Press, 1987.

Berger, Morroe. *Military Elite and Social Change: Egypt since Napoleon.* Princeton: Center for International Studies, 1960.

Berque, Jacques. *Egypt: Imperialism and Revolution.* New York: Praeger, 1972.

Binder, Leonard. "Egypt: The Integrative Revolution." In *Political Culture and Political Development,* edited by Lucien W. Pye and Sidney Verba. Princeton: Princeton University Press, 1965.

———. *The Ideological Revolution in the Middle East.* Huntington, N.Y.: Robert E. Krieger, 1964.

Botman, Selma. "Oppositional Politics in Egypt: The Communist Movement, 1936–1954." Ph.D. diss., Harvard University, 1984.

———. *The Rise of Egyptian Communism, 1939–1970.* Syracuse: Syracuse University Press, 1988.

Brown, Nathan J. *Peasant Politics in Modern Egypt.* New Haven: Yale University Press, 1990.

Burns, William J. *Economic Aid and American Policy toward Egypt, 1955–1981.* Albany: State University of New York Press, 1985.

Carre, Olivier. "Pouvoir et Ideologie dans l'Egypte de Nasser et de Sadat (1952–1975)." In *L'Egypte D'aujourdh'ui: Permanence et Changements, 1805–1976,* ed. Groupe de Recherches et d'Etudes sur le Proche-Orient. Paris: Centre Nationale de la Recherche Scientifique, 1977.

Colombe, Marcel. *L'Evolution de L'Egypte, 1924–1950.* Paris: G. P. Maisonneuve, 1951.

Copeland, Miles. *The Game of Nations.* New York: Simon & Schuster, 1969.

Davis, Eric. *Challenging Colonialism: Bank Misr and Egyptian Industrialization, 1920–1941.* Princeton: Princeton University Press, 1983.

Deeb, Marius. *Party Politics in Egypt: The Wafd and Its Rivals, 1914–1939.* London: Ithaca, 1979.

Dekmejian, Hrair R. *Egypt under Nasir.* Albany: State University of New York Press, 1971.

Eden, Anthony. *Full Circle.* Boston: Houghton Mifflin, 1960.

Eveland, Wilbur Crane. *Ropes of Sand.* New York: Norton, 1980.

Geertz, Clifford. "The Integrative Revolution—Primordial Sentiments and Civil Politics in the New States." In *Old Societies and New States*, edited by Clifford Geertz. Glencoe, Ill.: Free Press, 1963.

Ghali, Mirrit Boutros. *The Policy of Tomorrow*. Washington, D.C.: American Council of Learned Societies, 1953.

Goldberg, Ellis. *Tinker, Tailor, Textile Worker*. Berkeley: University of California Press, 1986.

Gordon, Joel. "The False Hopes of 1950: The Wafd's Last Hurrah and the Demise of Egypt's Old Order." *International Journal of Middle East Studies* 21 (1989): 193–214.

———. "The Myth of the Savior: Egypt's Just Tyrants on the Eve of Revolution, January–July 1952. *Journal of the American Research Center in Egypt* 26 (1989): 223–37.

———. "Political Opposition in Egypt." *Current History* (February 1990): 65–68, 79–80.

Hahn, Peter L. "Containment and Egyptian Nationalism: The Unsuccessful Effort to Establish the Middle East Command, 1950–53." *Diplomatic History* 11 (1987): 23–40.

Al-Hakim, Tawfiq. *The Return of Consciousness*. Translated by R. Bayley Winder. New York: New York University Press, 1985.

Harris, Christina Phelps. *Nationalism and Revolution in Egypt*. The Hague: Mouton, 1964.

Haykal, Muhammad Hasanayn. *Autumn of Fury*. New York: Random House, 1983.

———. *The Cairo Documents*. Garden City, N.Y.: Doubleday, 1973.

Hinnebusch, Raymond. *Egyptian Politics under Sadat*. Cambridge: Cambridge University Press, 1985.

———. "The National Progressive Unionist Party: The Nationalist Left Opposition in Post Populist Egypt." *Arab Studies Quarterly* 3 (1981): 325–51.

———. "The Reemergence of the Wafd Party: Glimpses of the Liberal Opposition in Egypt." *International Journal of Middle East Studies* 16 (1984): 99–121.

Holt, P. M. *Political and Social Change in Modern Egypt*. London: Oxford University Press, 1968.

Hussein, Mahmoud. *Class Conflict in Egypt, 1945–1970*. New York and London: Monthly Review Press, 1973.

Ismael, Tareq Y., and Rifa'at El-Sa'id. *The Communist Movement in Egypt, 1920–1988*. Syracuse: Syracuse University Press, 1990.

Issawi, Charles. *Egypt at Mid-Century*. London: Oxford University Press, 1954.

James, Robert Rhodes. *Anthony Eden*. London: Wiedenfeld & Nicolson, 1986.

Jankowski, James P. *Egypt's Young Rebels: "Young Egypt," 1933–1952*. Stanford: Hoover Institution Press, 1975.

Johnson, John J. *The Role of the Military in Underdeveloped Countries*. Princeton: Princeton University Press, 1962.

Kuniholm, Bruce R. *The Origins of the Cold War in Near East*. Princeton: Princeton University Press, 1980.

Kurzman, Dan. *Ben-Gurion, Prophet of Fire*. New York: Simon & Schuster, 1983.

Lacouture, Jean, and Simonne Lacouture. *Egypt in Transition*. New York: Criterion, 1958.

Lacouture, Jean. *Nasser*. New York: Knopf, 1973.

Landau, Jacob. *Parties and Parliaments in Egypt*. New York: Praeger, 1954.

Laqueur, Walter Z. *Communism and Nationalism in the Middle East*. 2d ed. New York: Praeger, 1957.

Little, Tom. *Egypt.* New York: Praeger, 1958.

Louis, William Roger. *The British Empire in the Middle East, 1945–1951.* Oxford: Clarendon Press, 1984.

Makarius, Raoul, *La Jeunesse intellectuelle d'Egypte au lendemain de la Deuxieme Guerre Mondiale.* Paris: Mouton, 1960.

Mansfield, Peter. *Nasser.* London: Methuen, 1969.

Mitchell, Richard P. *The Society of Muslim Brothers.* London: Oxford University Press, 1969.

Nasser, Gamal Abdel. *Egypt's Liberation.* Washington, D.C.: Public Affairs Press, 1955.

Neguib, Mohammed. *Egypt's Destiny.* London: Victor Gollancz, 1955.

Nutting, Anthony. *Nasser.* London: Constable, 1972.

Perlmutter, Amos. *Egypt: The Praetorian State.* New Brunswick, N.J.: Transaction Books, 1974.

Perkins, Bradford. "Unequal Partners: The Truman Administration and Great Britain." In *The Special Relationship,* edited by William Roger Louis. Oxford: Clarendon Press, 1986.

Perrault, Gilles. *Une Homme a Part.* Paris: Barrault, 1984.

Quraishi, Zaheer Masood. *Liberal Nationalism in Egypt: The Rise and Fall of the Wafd Party.* Delhi: Jamal Press, 1967.

Reid, Donald M. "Fu'ad Siraj al-Din and the Egyptian Wafd." *Journal of Contemporary History* 15 (1980): 721–44.

———. "The Return of the Egyptian Wafd, 1978." *International Journal of African Historical Studies* 12 (1979): 389–415.

Rejwan, Nissim. *Nasserist Ideology.* New York: Wiley, 1974.

Rodinson, Maxime. *Marxism and the Muslim World.* Translated by Jean Matthews. New York and London: Monthly Review Press, 1981.

Rubin, Barry. *The Arab States and the Palestine Conflict.* Syracuse: Syracuse University Press, 1981.

Saab, Gabriel. *The Egyptian Agrarian Reform, 1952–1967.* London: Oxford University Press, 1967.

Sabry, Hussein Zulfakar. *Sovereignty for Sudan.* London: Ithaca, 1982.

El-Sadat, Anwar. *In Search of Identity.* New York: Harper & Row, 1977.

———. *Revolt on the Nile.* London: Alan Wingate, 1957.

Safran, Nadav. *Egypt in Search of Political Community.* Cambridge: Harvard University Press, 1961.

St. John, Robert. *The Boss.* New York: McGraw-Hill, 1960.

Sansom, A.W. *I Spied Spies.* London: George W. Harrap, 1965.

Sayed-Ahmed, Muhammad A. Wahab. *Nasser and American Foreign Policy, 1952–1956.* London: Laam, 1989.

Al-Sayyid, Afaf Lutfi. *Egypt and Cromer.* London: John Murray, 1968.

Al-Sayyid-Marsot, Afaf Lutfi. *Egypt's Liberal Experiment, 1922–1936.* Berkeley: University of California Press, 1977.

Seale, Patrick. *The Struggle for Syria.* New Haven: Yale University Press, 1986.

Scholch, Alexander. *Egypt for the Egyptians.* London: Ithaca, 1981.

Shuckburgh, Evelyn. *Descent to Suez, Diaries 1951–56.* London: Wiedenfeld & Nicolson, 1986.

Smith, Charles D. "4 February 1942: Its Causes and Its Influences on Egyptian Politics and on the Future of Anglo-Egyptian Relations, 1937–1945." *International Journal of Middle East Studies* 10 (1979): 453–79.

————. *Islam and the Search for Social Order in Modern Egypt.* Albany: State University of New York Press, 1983.

Springborg, Robert. *Family Power and Politics in Egypt.* Philadelphia: University of Pennsylvania Press, 1982.

————. *The Political Economy of Mubarak's Egypt.* Boulder, Colo.: Westview Press, 1988.

Stephens, Robert. *Nasser: A Political Biography.* London: Allen Lane, 1971.

Tignor, Robert. "Equity in Egypt's Recent Past: 1945–1952." In *The Political Economy of Income Distribution in Egypt,* edited by Gouda Abdel-Khalek and Robert Tignor, pp. 20–54. New York and London: Holmes & Meier, 1982.

————. *Modernization and British Colonial Rule in Egypt, 1882–1914.* Princeton: Princeton University Press, 1966.

————. *State, Private Enterprise, and Economic Change in Egypt, 1918–1952.* Princeton: Princeton University Press, 1984.

Vatikiotis, P. J. *The Egyptian Army in Politics.* Bloomington: Indiana University Press, 1961.

————. *Nasser and His Generation.* London: Croom Helm, 1978.

Vitalis, Robert. "Building Capitalism in Egypt: The 'Abbud Pasha Group and the Politics of Construction." Ph.D. diss., Massachusetts Institute of Technology, 1988.

Warriner, Doreen. *Land and Poverty in the Middle East.* London: Royal Institute of International Affairs, 1948.

Waterbury, John. *Egypt: Burdens of the Past/Options for the Future.* Bloomington: Indiana University Press, 1978.

————. *The Egypt of Nasser and Sadat.* Princeton: Princeton University Press, 1983.

Wheelock, Keith. *Nasser's New Egypt.* New York: Praeger, 1960.

Wynn, Wilton. *Nasser of Egypt: The Search for Dignity.* Cambridge: Arlington, 1959.

Index

Abaza, Fikri, 139, 154, 156
Abaza, Wagih, 129
'Abbas Halim (Prince), 88, 214n.34
'Abbud, Ahmad, 35, 155
'Abd al-'Aziz, Ahmad, 45
'Abd al-Ghaffar, Ahmad, 3, 88, 91, 210n.32, 214nn.34,36
'Abd al-Hadi, Ibrahim, 20, 29, 69, 88–89, 123, 135, 210n.32
'Abd al-Haqq, 'Abd al-Magid, 146
'Abd al-Hayy, Abu al-Makarim, 182
'Abd al-Khaliq, Muhsin, 114
'Abd al-Latif, Mahmud, 179–80, 183
'Abd al-Mun'im (Prince), 61
'Abd al-Mut'al, Zaki, 21, 25, 34, 89, 162
'Abd al-Quddus, Ihsan, 25, 33, 35, 64, 66, 82, 113, 118, 139–40, 146, 152–55, 196
'Abd al-Ra'uf, 'Abd al-Mun'im, 44–45, 47, 49, 53, 106, 177, 182, 229n.44
'Abdin, 'Abd al-Hakim, 29
Abu al-Fath, Ahmad, 24, 52, 63, 69, 71–73, 78, 84, 94–95, 140, 153, 155
Abu al-Fath, Husayn, 140
Abu al-Fath, Mahmud, 140
Abu Hurayra, 155
Abu Ruqayq, Salih, 105, 229n.38
Acheson, Dean, 161–62
Adham, Hamzah, 114
'Afifi, Hafiz, 18, 34, 154, 197, 210n.32, 214n.34
Al-Ahram, 140
Al-Akhbar, 64, 113, 140, 155
Akhbar al-Yawm, 83, 135, 155
Alexandria University, 82, 140
'Allubah, Muhammad 'Ali, 146
American University in Cairo, 148
Amin, 'Abd al-Mun'im, 48, 59, 62, 110–13, 115–17, 197

Amin, 'Ali, 64, 81
Amin brothers ('Ali and Mustafa), 148, 153–56
Amin, Mustafa, 64, 84, 113, 119, 153
'Amr, 'Abd al-Hakim, 3, 42–43, 45, 47, 51–52, 114, 116, 118, 123, 129–30, 138–39, 171, 187
'Amr, Husayn Sirri, 50, 52, 55–56
Andraos, Elias, 18, 35
Anti-democratic forces, 9–11, 18, 58, 61, 194–95. *See also* Intelligentsia
Anti-establishment, 5, 8–9, 14, 18, 20, 25–26, 27–32, 49, 92–93, 109, 160, 166, 194
Al-'Aqqad, 'Abbas Mahmud, 146
Arab League, 81, 171
Arab Socialist Union, 7, 197
Al-'Arish, 51–52, 112
Army, Egyptian
  air force, 46–47, 51, 111, 118, 129
  armor corp, 41, 47–48, 51–52, 110, 114, 116, 126, 128–30, 138
  army engineers, 41
  artillery corps, 41, 46–48, 51–52
  artillery movement, 112–17, 121, 126, 129, 132, 151, 196
  and Black Saturday, 26
  British control of, 16, 40–41
  and CCR/Junta, 62, 110, 118, 123, 129, 138–39
  concerns of soldiers, 39, 56–57, 94–95
  frontier corps, 50
  high command, 4, 41, 44, 49–50, 52, 56–57, 59, 110–11, 113, 115, 117–18
  infantry corps, 47, 51, 129
  junior officers, 9, 39–40, 43–44, 56, 66, 111, 113, 117–18, 121, 160
  military academy, 39, 41–43, 110
  military intelligence, 84, 111, 118, 129, 196, 199

Army, Egyptian (*continued*)
  military missions, 41, 44
  military police, 135, 187
  morale of, 43, 160
  national guard, 183
  navy, 48
  noncommissioned officers, 46, 111
  officer corps, 7, 36, 39, 40–41, 43–46, 56,
    66, 93, 109–10, 113, 118, 126, 138,
    160
  and Palestine War, 39, 45, 57
  and "Popular Struggle," 26
  plots against CCR, 111, 196 (*see also*
    artillery movement)
  politics in, 4, 64, 72, 109–18
  presidential guard, 123
  quality of, 118, 138–39, 159
  and Second World War, 39, 43–45
  signal corps, 47, 51
  staff college, 41, 43, 47
  supply corps, 51
  and treaty of 1936, 41
Al-Asas, 69
Al-ʿAshmawi, Hasan, 53–54, 99–101, 105,
  212*n*.72, 229*n*.44
ʿAshmawi, Salih, 29, 101, 103–4, 106,
  212*n*.72
Aswan, 117, 150, 192
ʿAtif, Ibrahim, 50
Awad, Louis, 85
ʿAwdah, ʿAbd al-Qadir, 106, 131, 134–35,
  177, 183
Axis Powers, 18, 41, 48
ʿAyn Shams University, 140
Al-Azhar, 148, 197
ʿAzzam, ʿAbd al-Rahman, 41

Badawi, Mustafa Bahgat, 119
Al-Baghdadi, ʿAbd al-Latif, 3, 42, 45, 47, 50–
  51, 81, 84, 87, 114–15, 119–20, 124,
  133, 187–88
Baha' al-Din, Ahmad, 154–55
Al-Balagh, 84
Bandung Conference, 188–89
Al-Banna, ʿAbd al-Rahman, 29, 103, 106,
  181, 183
Al-Banna, Hasan, 18, 20, 29–30, 45, 88, 100–
  101, 103, 105–6, 124, 178, 181, 191,
  195
Al-Baquri, Ahmad Hasan, 29, 68, 100, 146,
  197
Bar Association (Egyptian), 134, 136, 146
Barakat, Baha' al-Din, 61, 209*n*.2
Al-Barawi, Rashad, 62, 71, 84, 94–95, 167,
  192

Al-Barudi, Mahmud Sami, 40
Baʿth (Party), 194
Be'eri, Eliezer, 42
Berque, Jacques, 17
Bevin, Ernest, 159
Black Saturday, 32–33, 50, 53, 57, 68, 94,
  121, 152, 159, 162–63
Bureaucratic reform, 19, 33–34, 65
Business interests, 42, 155. *See also*
  Industrialists
Byroade, Henry, 163

Caffery, Jefferson, 22, 27, 32, 35–37, 67, 85,
  142, 160–74, 176, 191
Cairo Chamber of Commerce, 141
Cairo University, 61, 75, 105, 131, 140, 146,
  221*n*.20
Capitulations, abolition of, 17
Central Intelligence Agency (CIA), 162–63,
  168, 180, 195
Churchill, Winston, 158, 166, 176
Command Council of the Revolution (CCR)/
  Junta
  aims and promises, 58–59, 79–80, 85, 93,
    125, 137, 144–45, 157, 165, 187, 192,
    196
  army: opposition from, 4, 91, 111, 113–16,
    125–33, 138, 196; policing of, 79,
    109–11, 117–18, 123, 138–39, 187
  British: contacts with, 76–77, 123, 160–61,
    165, 185; influence of, 13, 157–58,
    166, 174, 195–96; negotiations with,
    157, 168–72
  civilian allies of, 10, 12, 63–65, 67–68, 71–
    72, 75, 78, 113, 125, 139, 153–56,
    194–95
  communists, relations with, 9, 92–98, 106–
    9, 127, 142–43, 149–51, 175–78, 186,
    195
  consolidation of power, 13, 79–80, 83–85,
    90–91, 109–10, 125, 127–28, 137–43,
    144–45, 175, 187, 194–96
  constitutional reform, 76, 83, 132, 134,
    145–46
  divisions within, 91, 129–30: rumors of,
    75, 79, 83, 120, 125, 128
  economic troubles, 75, 82–84
  foreign policy, 13, 122, 157–74, 193, 196,
    198
  Free Officers, relations with, 111–17, 196
  king, abdication of, 60–61
  labor, relations with, 62–63, 82, 93, 95,
    108, 135–36, 141–42, 187
  Liberation Rally, formation of, 80–83, 85–
    86, 91, 101–2

and Mahanna, Rashad, 112–14, 117, 193, 197
and Mahir, 'Ali, 65–67, 75, 225n.46
and March crisis, 91, 125, 127–37, 144–56
and maximalists/minimalists, 75, 116, 145, 194–95
media, control of. *See* Press
members: as cabinet ministers, 84, 139, 187–88; resignations, 116–17, 138; rumors of impropriety, 112, 142
Muslim Brothers, relations with, 4, 53, 91–93, 98–109, 124–25, 127, 135–37, 142–43, 155, 170, 175–84, 187, 191, 193–95, 197
and Nagib, 67–68, 110, 118–26, 128–38, 167, 184–86, 193, 197
Nasser's leadership of, 123–24, 133, 187–90
parliament, decision not to recall, 60–61
political parties, policies towards, 4–5, 58, 65, 68–75, 77–78, 80, 85, 100, 114–15, 134, 139, 147, 152
and political prisoners, 75, 101, 196–97
public image, 59–61, 63–67, 82–83, 90–91, 113, 118–20, 125, 141–42, 191
reforms: early, 61–62; land, 4, 5, 12, 62, 72, 84, 109
republic, declaration of, 4, 5, 58, 114, 83–84, 95, 122
revolution: declaration of, 58, 114; definition of, 12–13, 79–80, 83, 91–93, 125, 175, 191–93, 196
and Revolutionary Tribunal, 87–90, 93, 97, 104, 125, 139, 192
and Treason Court, 76, 86, 87, 89
Wafd, struggle with, 65, 70–78, 85–91, 97, 115, 125, 134–35, 139, 193, 195
and women's suffrage, 148–49
United States: contacts with, 76–77, 108, 123, 132; influence of, 13, 67, 157–58, 166–74, 195
Zionism, attacks against, 142, 178, 186, 198
Communist movements/Communists
arrests of, 20, 26, 95, 97, 149, 186, 220n.12
anti-imperialism, 10, 95, 164, 176
claim to Nasserist legacy, 9, 197
divisions amongst, 20, 30, 93–94, 96–97, 149, 195
historiography. *See* Left, Egyptian
hostility toward, British and American, 93, 166, 174
and Kafr al-Dawwar, 63, 93, 107
in military, 39, 44, 46, 93, 109

Muslim Brotherhood, collaboration with, 176–77
opposition to regime. *See* Command Council of the Revolution: communists, relations with
origins, 19–20, 46
parliamentary order, attitude toward, 28, 30–32, 94
regime propaganda against, 178, 186
students, 75, 82, 95, 97
trials of, 87, 96–97, 149
Wafd, cooperation with, 24, 31, 75, 82, 96–98, 176
and working class, 19, 82, 95–96
Constituent Assembly, 132, 134, 145–46
Constitution, Egyptian, 4, 16, 43, 51, 58, 60–61, 65, 76–77, 97, 102, 145–46, 148, 168, 187, 193, 196
Constitutional committees, 65, 76, 80, 82–83, 85, 115, 145–46, 148, 154, 189
Copeland, Miles, 162–64, 173
Creswell, Michael, 160–61
Curiel, Henri, 30, 142
Cyprus, 161
Cyrenaica, 161

Al-Damanhuri, Husni, 116, 121
Daughter of the Nile Party, 20, 74, 148
Al-Da'wah, 28, 106, 181
Democratic Movement for National Liberation (DMNL)
arrests and trials of cadres, 94–97, 108, 150
CCR/Junta, relations with, 92, 94–95, 116, 149–51, 176
Free Officers, collaboration with, 46, 48, 53–55, 92–94, 107
and Kafr al-Dawwar, 95
leadership and schisms, 31, 44, 46, 97, 149–50
members on junta, 94, 116–17, 130, 150–51
military organization, 46–47, 109, 116, 118
military prison manifesto, 149–50
Wafd, relations with, 30–31, 96–97, 107
Democratic Nile Party, 74
Democratic Party, 74
Al-Dilla, Munir, 99–101, 105, 229n.38
Duh, Hasan, 101, 178
Dulles, John Foster, 95–96, 168–69, 173
Duwayr, Hindawi, 182–83

Economic reform, 19, 99
Eden, Anthony, 159–60, 166

Egyptian Bloc, 33
Egyptian Communist Party (ECP), 31, 46, 94, 96, 149, 151, 176
Egyptian Federation of Labor, 141
Egyptian Movement for National Liberation (EMNL), 46, 130. *See also* Democratic Movement for National Liberation
Egyptian Republican Party, 74
Egyptian Socialist Party, 26–28, 30, 32, 67, 74, 80, 112, 132, 134. *See also* Young Egypt
Eisenhower, Dwight D., 119, 173
Electoral reform, 33, 65, 194
Evans, David, 164
Evans, Trefor, 87, 102–3, 115, 171, 178, 188

Factories, 28, 81–83, 93. *See also* Workers/Working Class
Fahmi, 'Aziz, 24
Fahmi, Husayn, 84–85
Fa'iz, Sayyid, 103
Faiza (Princess), 112
Farag, Ibrahim, 21, 23, 75, 77, 86–87, 90, 97, 197
Farghali, Muhammad, 181, 183
Farouk (King)
  abdication, 4, 60, 63, 94, 98, 112
  advisers, 18, 22, 35, 86, 88, 160, 163
  and Black Saturday, 27
  and British, 159–61
  character of, 17–19, 22
  and Free Officers coup, 52
  and officer corps, 36–37, 51, 56, 117
  rumors about return, 133
  and "salvation ministries," 33–37
  and United States, 159, 162–64
  and Wafd government, 21–22
Fawzi, Mahmud, 140, 188
Fayiq, Muhammad, 129
Free Officers
  allies of, 8, 10–12, 53–55, 71, 78, 92–93, 166, 186, 194
  and Black Saturday, 50–51
  and communists, 12, 40, 53–55, 92–93, 96
  coup d'etat: aims, 4, 6, 39, 57, 59, 109; anniversary, 83; decision to call, 51–52
  dismantling of military cells by junta, 111–16
  executive committee, 47–48, 50–51, 53, 55, 59, 109–11, 123, 189
  grievances of, 47, 51, 56–57, 60
  and Hilali government, 51, 209*n*.2

and Mahir government (January 1952), 51
  Muslim Brothers, ties to, 12, 40, 44–49, 53–55
  and Nagib, 50, 121, 128
  Nasser's leadership of, 13, 55
  officers club election, 36, 48, 50–51, 56
  operational command, 47–48, 51
  organizational structure, 47–48, 51, 111–12
  origins and ideology, 10–13, 39–48, 55, 59, 84
  political independence, 12, 40, 47
  and "Popular Struggle," 46, 49–50
  second rank officers, 42, 48, 81, 111–12, 117, 126, 188
  United States, ties to, 54, 163–64
  and Wafd, 23, 48–50
  and Young Egypt, 48–49
Fu'ad, Ahmad (King), 16, 22
Fu'ad, Ahmad II (Crown Prince), 60
Fu'ad, Ahmad, 44, 46, 54–55, 94–95, 130

Gallad, Edgar, 84, 139
Garanah, Zuhayr, 152
Al-Ghad, 95
Ghalib, Mahmud, 70, 211*n*.41
Ghannam, Fathi, 95
Ghannam, Mahmud, 87–88, 90, 97, 210*n*.32, 211*nn*.42,44, 214*n*.34
Al-Gizawi, Muhammad Abu al-Fadl, 52, 96, 129, 218*n*.17
Government of Egypt
  broadcasting administration, 84, 186
  bureaucracy/civil service, 7, 17, 21, 33–34, 59, 63, 68, 90, 99, 110, 137, 196
  censor, 84–85, 132–33
  Education, Ministry of, 140
  Foreign Affairs, Ministry of, 188
  Interior, Ministry of, 30, 34, 72–74, 84, 100, 118, 142
  Rural Affairs, Ministry of, 33
  Social Affairs, Ministry of, 82, 88, 117, 184
  War, Ministry of, 36, 56
Great Britain
  ambassador: in Cairo (*see* Lampson, Miles; Stevenson, Ralph); in Riyad, 123; in Washington, D.C., 162
  Anglo-American relations, 157–58, 165–66
  Anglo-Egyptian accord (1954), 4, 172, 179, 187, 195–96
  Anglo-Egyptian negotiations: pre-July 1952, 17, 26, 30, 34, 36, 89, 159–61; with CCR, 66, 102, 122, 157, 168–72, 175

anti-communism of, 93, 166
army, British, 16, 26, 158–59, 162, 169
army, Egyptian, control of, 16, 40–41
CCR/Junta, support for, 13, 157, 165–66, 171, 174, 195–96, 225n.44
chiefs of staff, military, 159
Conservative Party, 159
Egyptian nationalism, attitude towards, 158
embassy in Egypt (residency to 1936), 13, 16, 26, 29, 37, 93, 165–66: officials in, 63, 66, 76–77, 82, 142, 165, 171, 195
and "extremists," 166
foreign aid, 166, 187
Foreign Office, 158, 160–61, 165–66, 169, 171
four "reserved points," 16, 18
and Free Officers coup, 157–58, 160–61
Heads of Agreement, 142, 171, 176, 178, 185
and Hilali government, 160, 163
House of Commons, 186
Intelligence, 138, 160–61
Labor Party, 159
and Mahir, 'Ali, 18, 33–34, 41, 159–60, 162, 165
military attaché, 71
military mission, 41, 44
Muslim Brotherhood: assessment of, 27, 29; contacts with, 102–3, 178
occupation of Egypt (1882–1952), 15–19, 22, 26, 41, 44, 161
and palace, 16–19, 160–61, 163
and political parties, 147, 159
Royal Air Force, 88
Sudan accord, 168
Suez base, 158–59, 168–70
and Wafd, 15–17, 26, 159–161
War Office, 26, 158, 160
Greece, 161
Gudah, Hamid, 69, 210n.32, 214n.34
Gum'ah, 'Abd al-Salam, 70, 73, 85, 139, 212n.72, 213n.8

Hafiz, Sulayman, 61, 64, 67–68, 73, 75–77, 100, 132, 135, 139, 148, 178
Al-Hakim, Tawfiq, 7
Al-Hamamsi, Galal al-Din, 154
Hamrush, Ahmad, 11, 26, 42, 46, 54–55, 94–95, 115–17, 130, 163–64, 296
Hamudah, 'Adil, 115–16
Hamudah, Husayn, 53, 105

Hankey, Robin, 169–70
Harb, Salih, 41, 147
Hart, Parker, 133
Hasan, 'Abd al-Fattah, 27, 34, 114, 206n.80, 211n.42
Hasanayn, Ahmad, 18
Hasanayn, Magdi, 51
Haydar, Muhammad, 56
Haykal, Muhammad Hasanayn, 119, 156
Haykal, Muhammad Husayn, 69–71, 89
Head, Anthony, 171
Al-Hilali, Ahmad Nagib, 30, 32–37, 56, 60, 65, 68, 89–90, 139, 154, 160, 162–63, 209n.2, 210n.32
Himmad, Gamal, 50
Al-Hudaybi, Hasan
  appointed general guide, 29, 100
  and artillery movement, 114
  attacked by CCR, 105–6, 193
  and British, 102–3
  and CCR/Junta, 88, 98–106, 135, 137, 155, 177–79
  and Farouk, 29, 178
  and Free Officers, 54
  internal opposition to, 29, 100, 103–6, 181–82
  and Nagib, 98, 104–5
  and Nasser, 98, 104
  politics, view of, 30, 32, 100, 103
  and secret organization, 103–5, 180–83
  trial of, 182–83
  and United States, 102–3
Humaydah, Khamis, 178, 181, 217n.42, 229n.38
Husayn, Ahmad (Independent/Wafd), 21, 25, 27
Husayn, Ahmad (Young Egypt), 18, 26–27, 30, 49, 132, 134
Husayn, Kamal al-Din, 45, 47, 53, 107, 113–15, 117, 130, 140, 208n.34
Husayn, Shawqi Fahmi, 46
Husayn, Taha, 21, 25, 149, 212n.72
Husni, Ahmad, 68, 100

Ibrahim University, 148
Ibrahim, Hasan, 45, 47, 50, 87, 185, 208n.34
Idris, Yusuf, 95, 186
Al-'Imari, 'Abd al-Galil, 67, 132, 135, 139
Independent Wafdist Bloc, 17, 19, 61, 69, 74
Independents, political, 8, 10–11, 20, 29, 32–33, 73, 81, 154
Industrialists, 19, 42. *See also* Business interests

Intelligentsia
  and CCR/Junta, 3, 12, 57, 63–65, 79–82,
    85, 87, 90, 125, 194–95
  disillusion with liberalism, 32–33, 38, 58
  during/after March crisis, 127, 133–34,
    144–56, 186
  maximalists/minimalists, 64–65, 67–68, 73,
    78, 92, 94, 107, 116, 145, 195
  nationalist struggle, pre-July 1952, 16, 40,
    43
Iran, 161
Iraq, 194
Isma'il (Khedive), 40
Ismailia massacre (1952), 26, 30, 81, 162, 198
Israel, 161, 173, 188, 198
  agents of, 186–87, 196

Al-Jil al-Jadid, 148
Journalists, 139–40, 142–43, 149, 186, 193.
    See also Press
Al-Jumhur al-Misri, 140, 221n.36
Al-Jumhuriyah, 84–85, 105, 133, 135, 140,
    147, 155, 188, 197
"Just Tyrant," 35–36, 38, 65, 194

Kafr al-Dawwar, 62–63, 93–95, 99, 108, 121,
    196
Khalid, Khalid Muhammad, 85
Al-Khamis, Mustafa, 63, 93
Al-Khattab, Muhammad, 71
Al-Khuli, al-Bahi, 102, 229n.38
Al-Khuli, Lutfi, 95

Labib, Mahmud, 45–46, 49, 53, 98
Labor disturbances/strikes, 28, 82–83, 136,
    141, 149, 153. *See also* Workers/
    Working class
Labor reform, 82, 141
Lacouture, Jean, 187–88
  and Simonne, 121
Lampson, Miles, 133
Land reform
  opposition to junta reform, 66–67, 71, 77–
    78, 99, 109, 113
  pre-July 1952 proposals, 19, 33, 84
  program of junta, 4–5, 12, 62, 72, 142, 167
  rumors of alteration or retraction, 125, 133
  support for junta reform, 96, 121, 153,
    165–66
Landowners, 19, 62, 67, 77–78, 99, 197
Left, Egyptian. *See also* Communist
    Movements; Wafd, left-wing

CCR/Junta, relation to, 3, 5, 12, 92–96,
    107–8, 127, 129, 149–50, 186, 194–95
  critique of Nasserism, 28
  divisions within, 30, 96, 149–50
  and labor unions, 19
  and Nasserist legacy, 197
  revisionist historiography, 9–11, 13, 157,
    194
Liberal Constitutionalist Party, 3, 17, 69, 71,
    74, 88, 139
Liberal order/Liberalism. *See* Parliamentary
    order
Liberation Battalions, 26. *See also* "Popular
    Struggle"
Liberation Rally, 80–83, 85–86, 91, 101–2,
    105, 119, 132, 135, 141, 149, 152,
    168, 178, 183
Libya, 18, 41
Louis, William Roger, 158–59
Love, Kennett, 172

Mahallah al-Kubra, 105
Mahanna, Rashad, 42, 44, 48, 50, 61, 112–
    15, 117, 119, 121, 132, 193, 197
Mahdi, 'Uthman, 56
Mahir, Ahmad, 20
Mahir, 'Ali
  and British, 18, 33–34, 41, 66, 159–60,
    162, 165
  and CCR/Junta, 65–66, 84, 139, 154–55,
    165
  and constitutional reform, 65, 83, 145–46,
    148
  early career, 18, 33, 41, 65
  Free Officers praise, 51
  maximalist, 64–65
  prime minister (July–September 1952),
    60–61, 65–71, 98–99, 113, 167
  and Revolutionary Tribunal, 89
  "salvation" ministry, 32–34, 36, 159–60,
    162–63
  and United States, 67, 167
Mahmud, Hifni, 3, 91, 191
Mandur, Muhammad, 24, 85, 147, 153–54
Manshiya incident, 175, 179, 183
Al-Mansurah, 94
Al-Maraghi, Murtada, 34, 37, 52, 160–61,
    210n.32
March crisis, 4, 8, 91, 125–57, 170–71, 175–
    76, 187, 189
Mar'i, Sayyid, 69, 122
Martial law
  pre-July 1952, 18, 20–21, 26–27, 34–36
  post-July 1952, 4, 65, 102, 114, 116, 153, 192

Maximalists/Minimalists. *See* Intelligentsia

Middle East Command, 161, 165

Military tribunals, 87, 96, 108, 116, 132, 138, 140, 150, 177, 186–87, 196. *See also* People's Tribunal; Revolutionary Tribunal; Treason Court

Minority governments, 19–20, 22

Minority parties, 3, 10, 12, 16–17, 22, 34, 36, 40, 64, 80, 134, 195

Al-Misri, 3, 24, 62–64, 72–73, 77, 85, 95, 119, 125, 135, 140, 147, 151, 153, 155

Al-Misri, 'Aziz, 41, 44

Misri Effendi, 81, 191

Mitchell, Richard, 178, 180, 182

Morrison, Herbert, 159

Mosques, 85, 87, 119, 178–79, 198

Mossadegh, Muhammad, 119, 160

Mubarak, Hosni, 6, 8, 128, 198–99

Mufti of Egypt, 96, 108

Muharram, 'Uthman, 21, 64, 70–72, 75–76, 86, 210n.32

Muhyi al-Din, Khalid, 42, 45–47, 51, 54–55, 62, 107, 115–17, 129–31, 138, 151, 156, 164, 196, 198–99

Muhyi al-Din, Zakariya, 42–43, 48, 50–52, 59, 71, 84, 110, 115, 118, 123, 129, 131, 133, 138, 169–71, 184, 187

Murad, Mahmud 'Abd al-Mun'im, 147, 152, 186

Murad, Zaki, 97

Mursi, Fu'ad, 31, 94, 176

Al-Musawwar, 139, 154

Muslim Brotherhood
army, organization in, 12, 44–46, 53, 93, 105, 107, 109
and artillery movement, 114
assassination of Hasan al-Banna, 20, 88, 101
and Black Saturday, 27
and British, 27, 29, 102–3, 178
and CCR/Junta, 5, 91, 98–108, 127, 131–32, 134–36, 142, 151, 155, 175–78
constitutional committee members, 76, 101
divisions within, 10, 29, 98, 100, 103–4, 180–82, 195
executions of leaders, 4, 183–84
foundation and early activities, 18–19, 43
and Free Officers, 5, 12, 48, 53–55, 92, 98
and guerrilla warfare, 26, 102–3
Guidance Council, 29, 45, 53–54, 99–100, 102–3, 106, 114, 135, 180–82
Hudaybi appointed general guide, 99–100
and Kafr al-Dawwar, 99
and land reform, 99
Left, collaboration with, 176–77
and Liberation Rally, 81, 101–2, 105
and Mahanna, Rashad, 44, 112
and Nagib, 98, 104–6, 123–24, 130, 136–37, 178, 185
Nasser, assassination attempt on, 4, 175, 179–83
Nasserism: legacy and, 8–9; official history and, 9, 193; revisionist history of, 10–11, 53, 94
outlawed: in 1948, 20, 25, 45; in 1954, 53, 98, 104–5
parliamentary order, opinion of, 28–30, 32, 100
and party reform, 100–101
and People's Tribunal, 179–85, 187, 196–97
police cells, 18, 45, 93, 105, 107, 182
press, 28–29, 181
and Revolutionary Tribunal, 88
secret organization, 10, 20, 44–46, 49, 93, 103–5, 107, 180–84
students, 75, 82, 101, 119, 176–77
under Mubarak government, 8, 198

Al-Naggar, 'Abd al-Mun'im, 164

Nagib, Abu al-Khayr, 140, 221n.36

Nagib, 'Ali, 51

Nagib, Muhammad
character and public image, 59, 109–16, 121–23, 125, 141, 191
and communist propaganda, 94–96
democracy, attitude towards, 110, 120–21
Free Officers coup, role in, 52, 121, 161
and Kafr al-Dawwar, 62–63, 93, 121
junta leader, 59, 61, 68, 70–71, 121
"Leader of the Revolution," 77
Liberation Rally president, 81
and Mahanna, Rashad, 121
March crisis and after, 127–39, 142, 152, 154, 156, 184–85
memoirs, 120–21, 185, 199
and Muhyi al-Din, Khalid, 130, 138, 221n.32
and Muslim Brotherhood, 98, 104–6, 123–24, 130, 136–37, 178, 185
Nasser, rivalry with, 110, 120–26, 149, 185
and Nasserist official history, 9, 120–21, 193
ousted from power, 172, 177, 184–86, 197
political advisors, 67, 124, 132, 136, 139
president, 83–84, 118
prime minister, 4, 65, 67, 69, 71–77, 79, 113, 165–66

Nagib, Muhammad (*continued*)
  prior to coup, 36, 50–52, 110, 121
  and Siddiq, Yusuf, 151
  support in army for, 114, 123, 125–31,
    137–38
  and United States, 164–68, 172–73
  and Wafd, 61, 72, 75–77, 130
Nahhas, Madam. *See* Al-Wakil, Zaynab
Al-Nahhas, Mustafa
  and CCR/Junta, 60–61, 70–77, 88, 193
  death and legacy, 197–98
  health as issue, 24–25, 85
  leader of Wafd old guard, 17, 23
  leaves Egypt, 35–37
  and party abolition, 85, 87–88, 123
  prime minister (1950–1952), 21–22, 25–27
  Revolutionary Tribunal, attacked before, 89
  Sirag al-Din, relationship with, 24, 85, 87
Al-Naqib, Ahmad, 86, 214*nn*.34,36
Nasser, Gamal Abdel
  and 'Amr, 118
  authoritarian tendencies, 55–56, 187, 197
  background and army career, 42–43, 45
  biographers of, 11, 127
  CCR/Junta leader, 59, 61, 120, 123–24
  character, 7, 12, 55, 119–20, 171, 188–90
  consolidation, personal, 13, 84, 122–24,
    128, 130, 139, 175, 179, 187–90, 196
  and DMNL, 54–55, 96, 150
  and dissident officers, 112, 114–16, 129–
    30, 138
  foreign policy, 119, 170–72, 186, 188–90
  and Free Officers coup, 51–52, 113, 119
  Free Officers leader, 47–48, 55–56
  heckled, 82
  legacy, 6–7, 197–99
  and Liberation Rally, 81, 135
  and March crisis, 129, 131–36, 138, 150–
    52, 156, 171, 230*n*.64
  minimalist, 61, 116
  Muslim Brotherhood: collaboration with
    and member of, 10, 45, 53, 55; guides
    regime policy toward, 98, 101–8, 119,
    123, 135, 150, 177–79; survives
    assassination attempt by, 4, 175, 179–
    80, 182–83, 187, 196
  and Nagib, 119, 122–25, 149
  Philosophy of the Revolution, author of, 9,
    188, 193
  public image, 3, 7, 113, 119–20, 137–38,
    141–42, 172, 175, 191–92, 227*n*.91
  and United States, 123, 170–72
Nasserism/Nasserist state
  foreign scholars of, 11, 127
  leftist critique of, 28, 157
  legacies, 6, 197–99
  model of development, 4, 13
  Nasserist party, 198
  official history, 5, 9, 48, 98, 101, 110, 115,
    120, 127, 156, 193–94
  revisionist histories, 7–11, 58, 110, 115–
    16, 120–21, 127–28, 193–94
  Sadat reforms of, 6–7, 193, 198
National Democratic Party (NDP), 7–8
National Union, 197
Nationalist Party, 20, 30, 64, 67–68, 74, 147,
    154
Nationalist Workers Party, 74
New Nationalist Party. *See* Nationalist Party
Nida', Galal, 50
Al-Nuqrashi, Mahmud, 20, 41, 101
Nutting, Anthony, 172, 185

Officers Club, 36–37, 50–51, 56, 110, 112,
    114, 121, 132, 163, 170
Old order/regime. *See* Parliamentary order

Palace (Egyptian)
  and army, 36–37, 39, 56–57, 117, 163
  and British, 16–19, 160–61, 163
  constitutional powers, 16
  and Free Officers coup, 12, 56
  king's men, 18, 34, 36–37, 60, 67, 86–88
  politics and intrigue of, 16–19, 27, 34–37,
    133, 160, 162–63
  Royal Cabinet, 21, 34
  Royal Treasury, 18
  and "salvation ministries," 32–37
  slush fund for journalists, 139
  and United States, 162–64
  and 1950 Wafd government, 21–22, 25
Palestine War, 39, 47, 56, 111
  arms profiteering during, 22, 50, 88–90
  influence on Free Officers, 45, 47, 49, 57
Parliament, Egyptian
  Chamber of Deputies, 83
  constituent assembly, 132, 146
  constitutional provisions for, 16
  decision not to recall by junta, 60–61, 94,
    99, 121
  dissolved, 16–17, 34, 51, 60, 151
  elections: announced by Hilali, 30, 34–35;
    communist participation in, 31–32;
    Junta/CCR promises of, 65–66, 77,
    187; Muslim Brother participation in,
    29, 32, 100; rigged, 17, 29; U.S.
    resistance to, 171; Wafd victories, 16–
    17, 20–21, 29, 31
  Senate, 22

Parliamentary order
anti-establishment attitude towards, 27–32, 107
failure of: produces tolerance for tyranny, 32–33, 63–65, 194; reasons for, 14–15, 36–38
fears for return of, 74, 127, 135, 144, 153
hopes for reform of, 3, 85, 93
officers critical of, 78, 80, 192
overthrow, responses to, 80
popular images of, 14–15, 37–38, 91
revolution defined in contrast to, 75–80, 91, 135, 142, 153–56, 192
Revolutionary Tribunal discredits, 90–91
Wafd: as defender of, 58, 77–78; role in failure of, 9–10, 25, 63
Party Reorganization Law, 72, 74, 77–78, 80, 100, 115, 148
Pashas, 3, 14, 23, 37, 59–60, 112, 158–59, 166, 174, 192, 197
Peace movement, 67, 167
Peasants, 15, 19, 28, 42, 62, 66, 75, 81, 108, 142, 166, 176, 197
Peasants League, 20
People's Tribunal, 105, 172, 179–85, 187, 196–97
Police, Egyptian, 15, 26, 106, 134–35, 175, 179, 183, 198
political/secret police, 31, 48, 53, 135, 195. *See also* Army, Egyptian: military police; Muslim Brotherhood: police cells
Political parties
journals of, 82
leaders stripped of rights, 139
March crisis and after, 127, 133–36, 142, 144–47, 152–56
in Nasserist official history, 9
new parties considered, 66, 82, 133, 145–47
outlawed, 4, 77–78, 80, 82, 86, 95, 101, 114, 192
purges of, 65–66, 68–69, 71, 99
reform blocs in, 19–20, 49
reorganization mandated, 72–75, 77–78
Sadat reforms, 7
Political prisoners, 94, 98–101, 105–6, 132, 135, 150, 166, 196, 198
Political prisons, 7, 9, 94, 196, 198
Political reform, 5, 12, 32–33, 36, 79, 92, 148, 194. *See also* Political parties
"Popular Struggle," 26–28, 32, 90, 159–62
Press
American, 74, 82, 172, 185–86
anti-Wafdist, 27–28, 84

censorship of, 63, 82, 84–85, 87, 95–96, 102, 122, 133–34, 144, 183
communist, 95, 97
coverage: of Nagib, 59, 122, 137; of Nasser, 119; of officers, 59, 83, 113, 119–20; of politicians, 135; of trials, 96, 108, 183
denounced by regime, 63, 84, 187
foreign, 154
government organs, 85, 94–95
and March crisis, 133, 135, 144–45
maximalist and minimalist, 64
and Mubarak government, 8
Muslim Brotherhood, 28–29, 181
opposition: to old regime, 27–28; to Junta/CCR rule, 95, 97, 176
party journals, 82
regime propaganda in, 87, 105, 178, 181
Sadat reforms, 7
and Wafd Vanguard, 24
Press syndicate (Egyptian), 134, 136, 139, 148, 154
Professors, 12, 21, 25, 140–41
Professional associations, 4, 134, 142, 187
Public opinion, 13–14, 21–23, 25, 56, 59, 75, 79, 81–83, 86, 88–91, 110, 122, 141–42, 179, 186, 194
Pulli, Antoun, 18
"Purification," 30, 34, 68–70, 72, 93, 103, 137, 142, 192

Al-Qahirah, 133
"Quo Vadis," 14
Qutb, Sayyid, 99

Radwan, Fathi, 18, 30, 64, 68, 74, 100, 146, 165
Ra'fat, Wahid, 61, 86, 146–47, 151
Al-Rafi'i, 'Abd al-Rahman, 147
Ramadan, 'Abd al-'Azim, 11, 115, 180, 182
Ramadan, Hafiz, 154
Rashad, Nahad, 112
"Revolution" of 1919, 7, 15–16, 43, 82
Reformers, 15, 19, 24–25, 32–33, 36, 86
Republican Party, 74
"Revolutionary Jurisprudence," 61, 65
Revolutionary Tribunal, 3, 80, 86–91, 97, 104, 123, 125, 134, 139, 192, 196
Rifa'i, Sayyid, 55
Rif'at, Fath Allah, 114
Rif'at, Kamal al-Din, 50, 129
Riyad, Muhammad, 104–5, 123, 129
Robertson, Brian, 170

Roosevelt, Kermit, 162–64, 171
Ruz al-Yusuf, 25, 33, 50, 64, 139, 151, 154–55, 178, 191

Sabri, 'Ali, 77, 129, 164, 172–73, 188
Sabri, Sayyid, 61, 65, 146–47
Al-Sadat, Anwar, 6–9, 42, 44, 47, 52, 81, 87, 105, 112, 128, 133, 137, 139, 149, 164, 187–88, 193, 216n.29
Sadiq, Fu'ad, 111
Sa'dist Party, 17, 19, 20–21, 29, 69–71, 74, 88, 101, 139
Sa'id (Viceroy), 40
Al-Sa'id, Rif'at, 31
Salah al-Din, Muhammad, 21, 23, 85, 114, 139, 147–48, 162, 211n.42, 212n.72, 213n.8
Salim, Gamal, 47, 50–51, 84, 124, 180, 182, 189
Salim, Salah, 3, 43, 47, 51, 83–84, 87–88, 103, 112–14, 117, 119, 123–24, 131, 133, 135, 137, 142, 170, 183, 187–89
"Salvation Ministries," 32–38
Al-Sanadi, 'Abd al-Rahman, 103–6, 180, 182
Al-Sanhuri, 'Abd al-Razzaq, 21, 61, 64, 67, 132, 135, 146–47, 167
Al-Sawi, Al-Sawi Ahmad, 136
Al-Sayyid, Ahmad Lutfi, 84, 122, 186
Secondary schools, 140
Shadi, Salah, 45, 53, 99, 105–6, 182
Al-Shafi'i, Husayn, 42, 48, 51, 59, 105, 107, 110, 115, 128–29, 138, 141, 187, 198
Shafiq, Dorya, 148–49
Shakir, Amin, 50–51
Shawqi, Ahmad, 52, 123, 129, 138
Shirrin, Isma'il, 56
Shubra al-Khaymah, 125
Shukri, Ibrahim, 26, 30, 80, 198–99
Al-Shurbagi, Mustafa, 154
Siddiq, Yusuf, 42, 51–52, 59, 94, 107, 110–11, 116–17, 129–30, 150–51
Sidqi, Isma'il, 18, 20, 89
Sidqi, Mustafa Kamal, 44–46, 111, 161
Sirag al-Din, Fu'ad
  anti-communist, 24, 71
  arrested, 34–35, 71–72, 75, 197, 210n.32
  and Black Saturday, 27, 37
  and Free Officers, 50
  government minister (1950–1952), 21, 23–24, 26, 30
  in hospital, 134
  and land reform, 71, 113
  leaves Egypt, 35–37
  and Nahhas, 24, 85, 87

and opposition press, 27–28
and Revolutionary Tribunal, 89–91, 104, 123, 125, 139
and Treason Court, 76, 86
Wafd: enemies in, 23–25; and New Wafd, 7, 198–99; and purge order, 70–73; rise to power in, 23–24, 89
and United States, 162
Sirri, Husayn, 21–22, 32, 35–37, 52, 56, 89, 138, 154, 163
Social reform, 5–6, 10, 12, 19, 20, 32–33, 36, 49, 79, 92, 157, 194. *See also* Land reform
Socialist Labor Party, 198
Socialist Peasant Party, 20, 74, 146
Socialist Workers Party, 146
Soviet Union, 173
State Council, 61, 72, 74–75, 77, 115, 135
Stevenson, Ralph, 17, 29–30, 34, 56, 61, 66, 71, 77, 82, 159–61, 165–66, 169–72, 188
Students, 18, 24, 26, 75, 79, 82, 87, 96–97, 101, 105, 119, 140, 148, 176–77. *See also* Universities
Sudan, 16, 21, 26, 40, 81, 119, 158–59, 162–63, 166, 168
Sudanese People's Party, 168
Suez Canal Zone
  Anglo-Egyptian negotiations on, 166, 168–72
  British rights in, 16–17, 19, 41, 157–59, 163
  CCR tour of, 82
  collaborations with British in, 88
  guerilla war: in 1951, 26–28, 32, 50, 90, 160–62; in 1953, 102, 169–71
  labor disturbances in, 136
Suez crisis, 5, 7, 173, 189, 196–97
Sulaymani, Muhammad, 86
Sulzberger, C. L., 186
Syria, 179, 194

Al-Tahawi, Ibrahim, 81, 135–36
Al-Tahrir, 94–95, 119, 129, 192
Tanta, 42, 178–79
Tarraf, Nur al-Din, 30, 68, 146, 165
Tawfiq (Khedive), 40
Al-Tawil, 'Abd al-Fattah, 74–75, 77
Al-Tayyib, Ibrahim, 182–83, 229nn.49,51
Thabit, Karim, 18, 35, 86, 88, 139, 208n.78, 214n.34
Til'at, Ibrahim, 69, 71, 87
Til'at, Yusuf, 105, 181–83
Al-Tilmissani, 'Umar, 101, 134, 229n.38

Treason Court, 76, 86–87, 89, 134
Treaty of 1936, Anglo-Egyptian, 17, 22, 26, 41, 95, 97, 101, 158–59
Tripartite Agreement, 161
Truman Doctrine, 161
Tu'aymah, 'Abd Allah, 81, 135
Al-Tuhami, Hasan, 50, 179
Turkey, 161, 169–71, 178

'Ubayd, Hamdi, 50
'Ubayd, Makram, 19, 33, 61, 69, 87, 89, 139
'Ukashah, Tharwat, 42–43, 48, 52, 95, 129, 196
'Umar, 'Umar, 146
Unions, labor, 4, 95, 136, 141, 153
United States
    ambassador: in Cairo (*see* Caffery, Jefferson); in London, 171
    Anglo-Egyptian diplomacy, 83, 157–58, 161–63, 168–72
    anti-communism, 93, 96, 160, 166–67
    and British, 158, 161–63, 168–70, 195
    CCR/Junta: contacts with, 12, 117, 158, 164–66, 168–69; informed of actions by, 67, 77, 96, 167; support for consolidation of, 13, 77, 157, 165, 167–68, 171, 174, 195; worsening relations with, 173
    communist perceptions of and rhetoric, 10, 13, 54, 93–94, 150, 157, 176
    embassy in Cairo, 13, 26, 37, 93–94, 131, 158, 164–65, 168, 195: officials of, 24, 28, 62–63, 74, 76–77, 102, 106, 130, 152, 165, 185–86, 188, 198
    and "extremists," 67, 166
    and Free Officers, 162–65, 173–74, 195
    foreign aid, 161, 166–67, 172–74, 187
    and Mahir dismissal, 67, 167
    Middle East policy, 158, 161
    and military dictatorship, 166, 174
    military mission, 41, 164
    and Nagib, 164, 167–68, 172–73
    and Nasser, 164–65, 171–72
    and palace, 35, 162–64
    political system as model, 147
    and "salvation ministries," 162–63
    State Department, 133, 162–64, 173, 195
    and Sudan, 162–63
    and Wafd, 26, 161–62
Universities
    government control over, 4, 85, 140–41
    and Liberation Rally, 81
    student union elections, 75, 101
    student unrest, 79, 82, 97, 105, 131, 134, 136, 140, 148, 176–77

'Urabi, Ahmad, 40, 56
Al-'Urabi, Zaki, 21, 211*n*.42, 212*n*.72
'Uthman, Amin, 101
'Uthman, 'Uthman Khalil, 146, 148

Voice of America, 186

Wafd
    arrest of members, 34, 71, 88, 210*n*.32
    blue shirts, 43
    and British, 15–17, 26, 159–61
    and CCR/Junta, 60–61, 70–76, 78, 86–91, 139, 142, 193
    communist support for and cooperation with, 24, 31–32, 75, 94, 96–98, 149
    and constitutional committee, 76, 80, 85
    corruption, 17, 19, 25, 30, 35, 70, 74, 76, 86, 89–90, 97
    current status, 8, 198–99
    divisions within, 9, 17, 19–20, 22–25, 58, 70–75, 93, 195
    executive committee, 23–24, 69, 72
    founding, 15, 23
    and Free Officers, 10, 50, 58, 63
    governments: (1924–1944), 16–22, 29; (1950–1952), 9, 20–28, 30–31, 34, 41, 49–50, 159, 161–62
    and Hilali, 33–36
    and Kafr al-Dawwar, 63, 93
    and land reform, 71, 142
    leadership crisis, 24–25
    left-wing, 10–11, 23, 26, 70, 94, 97
    and Liberation Rally, 81–82, 85–86
    and Mahir, 'Ali, 34, 66
    and March crisis, 134, 139, 142, 146, 151–52, 220*n*.12
    and minority parties, 17, 21–22, 34, 61, 64–65, 78, 89, 195
    and Muslim Brothers, 29
    and Nagib, 76, 125
    Nahhas, defense of, 73–75, 77–78, 87
    and Nasserism, 198
    New Wafd (1977), 7–8
    old guard, 23–25, 69–70, 73, 97
    organizational structure, 21, 23–24
    outlawed, 78, 85–87, 115
    and palace, 22, 24–25, 27
    parliamentary order: defender of, 58, 77–78; role in failure of, 9–10, 25, 63
    parliamentary organization, 23, 70, 72
    party purge, 70–75
    and "popular struggle," 26–28, 90, 97, 159
    press, 24, 27–28, 72–73, 84–85, 87, 135
    and regency, 60–61

Wafd (*continued*)
  revisionist historiography, 8–11, 58, 194
  right-wing, 23–24
  second generation, 23, 70–71
  and Sirri, 35–36
  and State Council, 61, 74–75, 77–78
  students, 31, 75, 87, 97
  Treaty of 1936, abrogation, 26, 97, 159
  trials of, 76, 86–87, 89–90
  and United States, 161–62
  young Wafdists/youth wing, 20, 24–25, 69–
      70, 73–74, 78, 87, 90, 147, 195
Wafdist Vanguard, 24, 64, 70, 75, 87, 97,
      198. *See also* Wafd: left-wing; Wafd:
      young Wafdsts/youth wing
Wakid, Ahmad Lutfi, 188
Al-Wakil, Zaynab, 24, 86, 88–90, 186
Women, Egyptian, 16, 148–49
Workers/Working class, 15, 18–19, 24, 42,
      69, 81–83, 96, 108, 122, 137, 176,
      196. *See also* Unions, labor

Workers Party, 74, 146
Workers and Peasants Party, 74, 146
Workers Vanguard, 31, 94, 97, 149, 176, 186
World War, First. *See* "Revolution" of 1919
World War, Second, 17–19, 24, 39, 41, 43–
      44, 195

Yassin, Hilmi, 94
Young Egypt, 18, 20, 30, 43 *See also*
      Egyptian Socialist Party
Young Men's Muslim Association, 147

Zaghlul, Sa'd, 16, 23, 25, 43, 61, 87, 192,
      198
Zaki, Ahmad, 146
Zaki, Hamid, 21, 25, 70
Al-Zaman, 62, 84
Zionism/Zionists, 142, 178, 186, 198: Zionist
      agents, 196. *See also* Israel: agents of